SCRIPTURAL TRACES:
CRITICAL PERSPECTIVES ON THE RECEPTION
AND INFLUENCE OF THE BIBLE

2

Published under

LIBRARY OF NEW TESTAMENT STUDIES
506

Formerly Journal for the Study of the New Testament Supplement Series

HARNESSING CHAOS

The Bible in English Political Discourse since 1968

Revised Edition

James G. Crossley

Bloomsbury T&T Clark
An imprint of Bloomsbury Publishing Plc

B L O O M S B U R Y
LONDON · OXFORD · NEW YORK · NEW DELHI · SYDNEY

Bloomsbury T&T Clark

An imprint of Bloomsbury Publishing Plc

Imprint previously known as T&T Clark

50 Bedford Square	1385 Broadway
London	New York
WC1B 3DP	NY 10018
UK	USA

www.bloomsbury.com

BLOOMSBURY, T&T CLARK and the Diana logo are trademarks of Bloomsbury Publishing Plc

First published 2014

© James G. Crossley, 2016

James G. Crossley has asserted his right under the Copyright, Designs and Patents Act, 1988, to be identified as Author of this work.

British Library Cataloguing-in-Publication Data
A catalogue record for this book is available from the British Library.

ISBN: PB: 978-0-5676-6959-9

Library of Congress Cataloging-in-Publication Data
A catalog record for this book is available from the Library of Congress.

Series: Library of New Testament Studies, volume 506

Cover design: Catherine Wood
Cover image © Kaya Mar

Typeset by Deanta Global Publishing Services, Chennai, India
Printed and bound in Great Britain

In memory of Callum Millard (1974–2014)

CONTENTS

PREFACE TO THE 2016 EDITION

Since the publication of the hardback edition of this book in 2014 and the submission of the manuscript in 2013, there have been some significant developments relating to the Bible and religion in English political discourse. In terms of publications, for instance, Andrew Crines and Kevin Theakston published on religion and British Prime Ministers, while Eliza Filby's revised PhD thesis on Margaret Thatcher and religion has since become a major book.[1] These publications have their own particular emphases and interests but broadly complement the presentations of the respective political figures analysed in *Harnessing Chaos*. While her interests concerned American politics and the use of 'Babylon', Erin Runions' conclusions on the Bible functioning as a transcendent authority likewise complement my concluding arguments, both in this book and in more detail elsewhere.[2] There are, of course, differences in nuance and interests but Runions' argument that the Bible functions as an authority for theodemocracy, interventions in modern-day Babylon, free-market economics, and debates on gender and sexuality could also be said of contemporary English political discourse.[3] What prompted the idea of a revised version of *Harnessing Chaos* were political events. David Cameron intensified Thatcher's Bible throughout 2013, 2014 and 2015, particularly to defend his position relating to 'Big Society' and in relation to a typical construction of what Islam is and is not following the emergence of ISIS and the Woolwich murder. While such developments were providing significant data for this analyst, they

1. A.S. Crines and K. Theakston, '"Doing God" in Number 10: British Prime Ministers, Religion, and Political Rhetoric', *Politics and Religion* (2015) 8, pp. 155-77; E. Filby, *God and Mrs Thatcher: The Battle for Britain's Soul* (London: Biteback, 2015).

2. E. Runions, *The Babylon Complex: Theopolitical Fantasies of War, Sex, and Sovereignty* (New York: Fordham University Press, 2014); J.G. Crossley, 'God and the State: The Bible and David Cameron's Authority', (forthcoming, 2016).

3. J.G. Crossley, 'We Don't Do Babylon: Erin Runions in English Political Discourse', *Bible and Critical Theory* (2015) 11, pp. 61-76.

were relatively (and sometimes entirely) predictable uses of the Bible. Less predictable was the presence of Russell Brand, and his constant use of the Bible, in mainstream political discourse, including guest editing the *New Statesman*, a much-watched *Newsnight* interview with Jeremy Paxman, and Ed Miliband's surprise appearance on Brand's YouTube show, 'The Trews', in the run up to the 2015 General Election. This was probably the closest the Radical Bible had been to mainstream parliamentary discourse since Tony Benn, even if it did appear to fail. But the summer following the General Election saw a far more unpredictable moment: the emergence of Jeremy Corbyn as front runner in the Labour leadership election, which, of course, he would win by a landslide. With Corbyn, the still relatively popular Radical Bible, in the guise of the Good Samaritan, came in from the cold and made its return to parliamentary discourse, though for how long will no doubt depend on the success or otherwise of the Corbyn movement. To get a sense of how unexpected this return was, it might be worth quoting from *Harnessing Chaos*:

> Yet like an occasional Tony Benn, Jeremy Corbyn or Alan Simpson remaining somewhere on the Labour back benches post-1997, the Radical Bible could still be heard…In Labour Party politics, the Radical Bible lost its power once the Bennite Left lost any serious influence with its defeat ultimately confirmed by the symbolic removal of Clause 4 and the rise of Blair. The Radical Bible was effectively pushed outside Parliament and party-politics, only retaining some connections on the fringes of the Labour Party, or its language brought into the fold of the Liberal Bible…However, just as radical politics survived outside Parliament and mainstream party politics…so the Radical Bible was able to re-emerge in different, often independent and non-affiliated groups. (pp. 233).

Harnessing the chaos ('harnessing' and 'chaos' were, happily, repeated words used in the reporting of Corbyn and his supporters) of such interests groups typically outside mainstream parliamentary discourse was crucial to the return of the Radical Bible. Thatcher harnessed the post-1968 chaos and now we are in the midst of political chaos post-2008 recession. Who (if anyone) and whose Bible (if any) will come to dominate we will only know when hindsight permits.

INTRODUCTION

As Nick Spencer has shown, there should be no doubt that the Bible has deeply embedded itself in English parliamentary politics over the centuries.[1] The Bible even has a physical presence of sorts in the Houses of Parliament, including the Latin text of Psalm 127.1 on the floor of the Central Lobby and the texts of 1 Peter 2.17 and Proverbs 11.14 on the floor of the Commons Lobby.[2] Spencer noted, however, that a certain appreciation of the Bible had changed by the end of the nineteenth century. Unlike the sixteenth and seventeenth centuries, the Bible was no longer an authoritative document which could (theoretically) decide political debates. Instead, the Bible was becoming a document which informed arguments, inspired individuals and provided rhetorical force. But in addition to no longer commanding universal deference, awareness of the contents of the Bible was changing:

> Evangelicals…also recognised that the level of biblical knowledge among their peers, particularly in parliament, could not now be assumed. When the Quaker MP John Bright spoke in favour of Gladstone's Reform Bill in 1866, accusing an opponent 'into what may be called his political cave of Adullam', many members of the House did not know where or what the cave of Adullam was. That would not have happened in Cromwell's time.[3]

This loss of biblical knowledge also echoes a wider debate, and one that will be touched upon in this book, about the apparent 'decline' in biblical literacy, that is biblical literacy as defined in a quasi-Protestant sense as knowledge of the specific details of a range of biblical passages and an

---

1. N. Spencer, *Freedom and Order: History, Politics and the English Bible* (Kindle edition; London: Hodder and Stoughton, 2011). On the history of Christianity across contemporary party politics see e.g. M.H.M. Steven, *Christianity and Party Politics: Keeping the Faith* (Abingdon: Routledge, 2011), pp. 45-64.
2. Spencer, *Freedom and Order*, Introduction.
3. Spencer, *Freedom and Order*, Chapter 8.

awareness of a range of biblical characters.[4] That there is a loss of knowledge about the details of the biblical texts is clear enough yet if the emergence of reception history has taught us anything it is that the Bible undeniably remains widely present in contemporary culture. In this book, I want to change the emphasis from a quasi-Protestant notion of biblical literacy and look at what interpreters, primarily English politicians, think the Bible 'really means' or how it might be used rhetorically, and *particularly in its public presentation rather than any hidden motives*, irrespective of whether there is an awareness of obscure biblical passages and characters, irrespective of whether a given political position can actually be found in the Bible, and irrespective of whether any given political interpretation would hold up to scholarly exegetical scrutiny. In other words, I want to look at the broad public hermeneutical assumptions among roughly contemporary politicians and how they interact with wider cultural and historical change.

Chapter 1 will give an overview of ways in which we might approach the interaction between historical change and understandings of the Bible. It will provide an explanation of the choice of post-1960s English political culture with particular emphasis on the importance of the emergence of Thatcherism and neoliberalism. It will then discuss major politicised understandings of what the Bible 'really means' and rhetorical uses (the Cultural Bible, the Liberal Bible, the Neoliberal Bible, and the Radical Bible) which will form the basis for the rest of the book and how different political figures and trends interact with these understandings. Some attention will initially be given to Tony Benn and his politically radical biblical interpretation because he represented a dwindling understanding of a once popular tradition in parliamentary politics.

Taking the examples of the Communist historian Christopher Hill and the Conservative politician Enoch Powell, the section on 'Experiencing Defeat' will look at how different political traditions engaged with the upheavals of the 1960s and the end of Empire. While both result in narratives of defeat and decline, both illustrate nascent ways in which politically radical, economically liberal, and nationalistic interpretations would survive inside and outside Parliament.

---

4. On debates over the pros and cons of biblical literacy see e.g. P.R. Davies, 'Whose Bible? Anyone's?', *Bible and Interpretation* (July 2009), http://www.bibleinterp.com/opeds/whose.shtml; H. Avalos, 'In Praise of Biblical Illiteracy', *Bible and Interpretation* (April 2010), http://www.bibleinterp.com/articles/literate357930.shtml.

The following chapter will look at Margaret Thatcher's influential understanding of the Bible. Thatcher saw the Bible as important support for her agenda of individualism and economic liberalism, or what would be labelled 'neoliberalism', and as something to be seen as part of English or British nationalism and democratic heritage. She also saw the Bible as being fundamentally anti-Marxist which was, of course, part of her Cold War thinking. But this was also in subtle contrast to her views on 'religion' which, no matter how negatively she viewed a manifestation of a given religion in the present, recognised that there was always potential for 'good'. This would be taken up in more detail by Tony Blair, in addition to his tacit general acceptance of Thatcher's reading of the Bible, even if his rhetoric occasionally suggested otherwise.

The steadily developing ideas of Thatcherism and her individualistic interpretation of the Bible in wider cultural trends are shown by looking at people who would largely be expected to be hostile to Thatcher and the Conservatives: Manchester musicians and Monty Python. These seemingly eclectic examples show how Thatcherism was, consciously or unconsciously, harnessing wider cultural trends developing since the 1960s but also how key elements of Thatcherism were, consciously or unconsciously, being transmitted by arguably more credible carriers of cultural change.

The next section will look at Thatcher's ongoing influence in party-politics and political biblical interpretation with reference to two important aspects of her legacy: the sharp fall of the Conservative Party and its 'toxic' brand and the emergence of the heavily Thatcherite New Labour. The chapter on Jeffrey Archer and his somewhat obviously semi-autobiographical novel on 'rescuing' Judas will look at how problematic hyper-Thatcherism had become but simultaneously how, outside Parliament, Archer's Bible represents an arguably unintentional by-product of Thatcherism – the amorality of the extravagant wealth of the successful entrepreneur.

The chapter on Blair will look at how, despite all the concerns of some of those around him, he regularly used the Bible in a way familiar to Thatcher while trying to incorporate the more politically radical biblical language that was deeply embedded in the Labour movement. Blair attempted to use biblical language of radical social transformation to garner support for his foreign policy and interventions, particularly in Iraq where he was struggling to gain widespread support from the Labour Party. Controversial though Blair's agenda was, there is clear evidence that his exegesis is a norm within the Parliamentary Labour Party, particularly his emphasis on social liberalism. Some attention will be paid to the Tony Blair Faith Foundation and how he has developed his understanding of the Bible internationally as part of his understanding of 'religion' and other scriptural traditions, notably the Qur'an, in terms of liberal democracy.

The next chapter will assess present day understandings of the Bible in parliamentary politics in light of these political and hermeneutical changes. The hermeneutical assumptions of Thatcherism remain among the circle around David Cameron and key Liberal Democrats but are qualified by the Blairite concern for social liberalism. The nationalism of the 'heritage' angle of the Bible has been strongly emphasised as representing English democracy, tolerance, freedom, and so on, most notably in the various utterances during the 400th anniversary of the King James Bible and Michael Gove sending a copy of the King James Bible to English schools. Some consideration is then given to the views outside of this seemingly settled political tradition: the fate of politically radical interpretations of the Bible. This will involve more politically radical interpretations of, for instance, sexuality and same-sex marriage (e.g. Peter Tatchell), foreign policy (e.g. the East Timor Ploughshares), the 2008 financial crisis (e.g. Occupy London Stock Exchange), and racial politics (e.g. Linton Kwesi Johnson). It is clear that such radical interpretations certainly remain but that they largely take place on the fringes of Parliament, or outside Parliament entirely.

Finally, some speculative consideration is given to why politicians bother using the Bible at all. In virtually all cases, the interpretation of the Bible matches the political agenda of a given politician and there is no obvious reason why the Bible is even needed. Issues of political heritage, voting, and implicit notions of authority will be briefly discussed.

In short, this book is about the parliamentary and even cultural victory of (a modified) Thatcher's Bible out of the socio-economic chaos of the 1960s and why politically radical interpretations have been pushed outside Parliament.

Chapter 1

'CHAOS IS A LADDER':
RECEPTION HISTORY OF THE BIBLE IN ENGLISH POLITICS

Put bluntly, this book is an explanation of changes in dominant political-ised assumptions about what the Bible 'really means' in *public presenta-tions* in English culture since the 1960s, but with wider implications.[1] This book reflects my wider interests in the ways in which the chaos of social upheaval and economic change can bring about shifts in, and explosions of, ideas and thinking (whether revolutionary, reactionary, creative, culturally bizarre, peaceful, violent, accidental, and so on) which may have long-term impacts, be clamped down almost immedi-ately, or have potential unrealised. In this case, I want to look at how the social upheavals of the 1960s and the economic shift from the post-war dominance of Keynesianism to the post-1970s dominance of neoliberal-ism – or, alternatively, the cultural shift from high modernity to post-modernity – brought about certain emphases and nuances in the ways in which the Bible is popularly understood, particularly in relation to dominant political ideas.

Appreciating the chaos of history within a more totalising history, and its impact on changes in the history of ideas, has a long intellectual tradi-tion but remains most useful when qualified by Foucault's reading of genealogies.[2] When taken in this sense, historical analysis looks for the

---

1. In this respect, this book echoes the some of the key methodological concerns of M.H.M. Steven, *Christianity and Party Politics: Keeping the Faith* (Abingdon: Routledge, 2011), p. 14: 'No archival work has been conducted – the premise of trawling through documents in any of the party archives in London, Oxford and Manchester was ultimately considered to be pointless. It is highly unlikely that the influence of Christianity upon policy documents – or some sort of equivalent – exists or is made available for public consumption… Media sources, however, are used… in an attempt to give the study as much impact as possible.'

2. M. Foucault, 'Nietzsche, Genealogy, History', in D.F. Bouchard (ed.), *Language, Counter-Memory, Practice: Selected Essays and Interviews* (Ithaca: Cornell University Press, 1977), pp. 139-64.

somewhat chaotic redirection of ideas without recourse to implied metaphysical origins. This Foucauldian qualification is, perhaps, especially
important in this instance because it is clear that people – including some
of those studied in this book – *really do* think the Bible and categories
sometimes associated with the Bible (e.g. marriage) can be traced back to
pure biblical and civilizational origins. Rather, to reemphasise, what is
being done in this book is tracing and unravelling the assumptions held
about what the Bible 'really means' or how it is used rhetorically and
looking at the contemporary history of accidental, purposeful, discon-
tinuous, and implicit meanings in the developments of such ideas as they
appear in English politics and culture.

On one level, this book is a narrative history, self-consciously weaving
'popular' biblical interpretation in and around a retelling of English
politics since the 1960s. The narrative of this book is very definitely *not*
an all-encompassing retelling of the Bible and biblical interpretation
since the 1960s, but rather a look at the ways in which some seemingly
very different biblical interpreters are embedded in English political
discourses and popular culture, with the major thematic links being the
Bible, the country in which the interpretation was undertaken, and the
timeframe. To take an unlikely analogy, it is using themes in a not
entirely dissimilar way to Simon Schama's *Landscape and Memory* (to
take one example) and his use of 'mythic' themes such as wood, rock,
and water as loose unifying narrative features to illustrate the ways
human beings have interacted with the world around them.[3] Though this
book obviously has more emphasis on chronology (for the purposes of
organization) than Schama's great work, the eclecticism of his choice of
individuals studied to illustrate broader issues is something I have found
appealing. Similarly, I think it remains important to focus both on politicians central to mainstream political assumptions about the Bible (e.g.
Thatcher, Blair, Cameron, Gove), as well as those figures seemingly more
incidental (e.g. Hill, Archer), and those seemingly unconnected to the
mainstream political process (e.g. Monty Python, Manchester musicians)
because I want to illustrate the widespread power of (often unconscious)
ideological and historical change and presentation in the public arena,
irrespective of whether the given politician, musician, or filmmaker
personally agreed with, or were even aware they were part of, a given
dominant ideological trend.

---

3. S. Schama, *Landscape and Memory* (London: Vintage, 1996).

There are further reasons why this book, with this sort of approach, benefits from chapters on popular culture and seemingly more incidental figures. The so-called 'anomalies' of history will always tell us something about their times. We might bring this sort of logic in line with Robert Darnton's suggestions about the role of the historian and interpreter in his book on eighteenth-century French cultural history, *The Great Cat Massacre*. For Darnton, the best starting point in attempting to penetrate an alien culture is 'where it seems to be most opaque'; by 'getting' the joke, proverb, riddle, ceremony or whatever, it is possible to start grasping a 'foreign system of meaning'.[4] We might turn Darnton on cultural contexts closer to home and those parts of our own culture which might seem alien to some investigators but which in fact help us understand our own systems of meaning. The cases of potentially surprising inclusions such as Archer, Hill, Manchester, or Monty Python will likewise tell us something about ideological developments in the period covered in this book both in terms of similarities and differences from mainstream political developments.[5]

The inclusion of what might broadly be labelled 'popular culture' has another important function in terms of change in the history of ideas. As we will see below, it was counter-cultural challenges from outside the political establishment that, in part, prepared the way for, and/or were harnessed by, the political changes of the 1970s and 1980s, even if some of the participants on all sides would no doubt be horrified to hear this. Furthermore, popular culture arguably contains more effective carriers of cultural change than parliamentary politics, holding cultural or sub-cultural capital that politicians do not always have. Besides, we are living in an era where the distinction between high and low culture has apparently collapsed, and the characters in this book are no different, whether it be the creative array of visual portrayals of Thatcher, graffiti or t-shirts bearing slogans about Enoch Powell (a one-time professor of Greek,

---

4. R. Darnton, 'Workers Revolt: The Great Cat Massacre of the Rue Saint-Séverin', in *The Great Cat Massacre and Other Episodes in French Cultural History* (London: Allen Lane, 1984), pp. 75-104 (77-78).

5. We might note here that there is no significant discussion of John Major or Gordon Brown. There are a number of related reasons for this near-exclusion. Both Major and Brown were largely continuing the agendas of their predecessors, no matter how much they might have tried to distance themselves from them. To discuss either would involve repetition. However, and certainly in the case of Major, the Bible is not used to the extent it was by Thatcher and Blair who both set the hermeneutical agenda for what followed.

brigadier, and devotee of Nietzsche), Christopher Hill embracing free-love, Ian Curtis reading Camus, Monty Python engaging with technical biblical scholarship, Tony Blair entertaining pop stars at Downing Street, or the Eton-educated Cameron texting 'LOL' to Rebekah Brooks, even if he did admittedly face media ridicule for thinking it meant 'lots of love'.[6]

1. Why 'English'?

Like the tradition-history of many books, this book has developed into something different from that which was initially intended. I initially set out to write a book on the Bible and popular and political culture with a range of diverse and eclectic examples of how different people use the Bible and how the Bible survives in different and not typically confessional contexts. I was (and to some extent still am) guided towards topics by (what seemed to me to be) sheer curiosity. Then I noticed that most of the examples were *British*. Then I noticed that most of the examples were, in fact, *English*. Nationalism and patriotism are not things that appeal to me, whether from the Enoch Powell-inspired Right or the Billy Bragg-inspired Left of the political spectrum. But English cultural history is certainly something that interests me and this has come out, unintentionally to begin with, in this book. Peter Hennessy pointed out in a slightly different context what must be close to a truism: 'The history of one's own country always has a "special claim" to one's personal attention whatever its place in the spectrum of world power'.[7] The 'special claim' to my personal attention is now obvious: the subjects of the respective chapters reflect areas of interest – whether love, hate, or mere curiosity – that are roughly contemporaneous with my life so far. As someone who was born in England and has always lived in England more-or-less for the proposed period of this book, and has written

6. 'Rebekah Brooks reveals "LOL" texts from Cameron', *BBC News* (May 11, 2012), http://www.bbc.co.uk/news/uk-politics-18032027; J. Beattie and A. Shaw, 'Oh, you are ROFL: Ex-Sun boss reveals PM signed off texts with LOL', *Mirror* (May 11, 2012); L. O'Carroll, 'Rebekah Brooks: David Cameron signed off texts "LOL"', *Guardian* (May 11, 2012); E. Branagh, J. Tapsfield, and E. Pickover, 'Lots of love: Rebekah Brooks lifts lid on David Cameron friendship at Leveson', *Independent* (May 11, 2012); J. Chapman and V. Allen, 'So that's how close they were! David Cameron signed off texts to Rebekah Brooks with "lots of love" (and they DID discuss phone hacking)', *Daily Mail* (May 18, 2012).

7. P. Hennessy, *Never Again: Britain 1945–51* (London: Jonathan Cape, 1992), pp. xiv.

(largely) in England at a time when *English* nationalism – as opposed to *British* nationalism – has been reasserted since the 1990s, it is perhaps no surprise that the subjects of interest are all part of English popular and political culture, no matter how much disdain I may have for English and British nationalism. To state what perhaps should have been the obvious all along, I am as much a part of my cultural context as a reaction against it.[8]

But there are less idiosyncratic and less parochial reasons for studying this period of English history. The 'secularisation thesis' may be controversial but we can at least follow the detailed work of those who argue that the social upheavals of the 1960s brought about significant changes in perceptions and understandings of Christianity, religion, and the Church and the decline of the social and political significance of religious institutions.[9] While such debates often look at broader post-Enlightenment trends, the intensified ideas of individualism and con-sumerism emerging from the chaos of the 1960s have been seen to be pivotal in drops in church attendance (with plenty more choices for Sundays) and the declining lack of influence of the Church of England. As Callum Brown claimed more dramatically still: 'The death of Christian British culture, or the rupture in Christianity as McLeod puts

8. Compare the issues faced by Nick Spencer when writing his book on the history of the Bible in English politics: '*Freedom and Order* focuses disproportion-ately on English politics, a fact that demands a word of explanation. This book began as a study on British politics but it soon became clear that my focus was largely south of the border… [I]t was decided to maintain that focus rather than risk doing an injustice to Scottish, Welsh or Irish politics by dealing with them cursorily. For that reasons, the "history" and "politics" of the subtitle refer primarily to English history and English politics.' See N. Spencer, *Freedom and Order: History, Politics and the English Bible* (Kindle edn; London: Hodder & Stoughton, 2011), Intro-duction.

9. See e.g. C.G. Brown, 'The Secularisation Decade: What the 1960s have done to the Study of Religious History', in H. McLeod and W. Ustorf (eds.), *The Decline of Christendom in Western Europe* (Cambridge: Cambridge University Press, 2003), pp. 29-46; C.G. Brown, *Religion and Society in Twentieth-Century Britain* (Harlow: Peason, 2006), pp. 224-77; C.G. Brown, *The Death of Christian Britain Under-standing Secularisation* (2nd edn; Abingdon: Routledge, 2009), pp. 175-233; G. Parsons, 'How the Times they Were a-Changing: Exploring the Context of Religious Transformation in Britain in the 1960s', in J. Wolffe (ed.), *Religion in History: Conflict, Conversion and Coexistence* (Manchester: Manchester University Press, 2004), pp. 161-89; H. McLeod, *The Religious Crisis of the 1960s* (Oxford: Oxford University Press, 2007); D. MacCulloch, *A History of Christianity: The First Three Thousand Years* (London: Allen Lane, 2009), pp. 985-89.

it, was a real and – I would argue – a cataclysmic event of the 1960s'.[10] This has not necessarily led to widespread atheism, of course, or even the end of denominational and Christian voting.[11] Moreover, ongoing Christian or 'religious' beliefs have been seen to permeate contemporary culture implicitly and result in a more privatised understanding of religion, leading Grace Davie famously to coin 'believing without belonging'.[12]

As Eliza Filby has shown, these cultural upheavals had a significant influence on the rise of Thatcher, her understanding of religion and the role of the Church in political life, and, to a lesser extent, her reading of the Bible.[13] This period further witnessed debates which directly affected changes in Church and State. The New Right of the 1970s (theological and political) took advantage of a rethinking of 'English-ness' and 'Britishness' generated by the perception of 1960s permissive-ness, decolonisation, immigration, and concerns about secular liberalism. Despite tensions between liberty, tradition, and conservatism, New Right thinking fed into the emerging dominance of Thatcherism.[14] This New Right thinking also included a re-emphasis on 'original sin' over-against utopianism and the perfectibility of humanity, a view we will see in the chapters on Powell and Thatcher. In less abstract terms this meant a critique of socialist emphases on the importance of the State in bettering society and the post-war Keynesian consensus. While not removing the significance of State interventionism, the alternative emerging from the New Right was a stress on economic liberalism coupled with rhetoric of freedom, liberty, and personal responsibility. With the emphasis on private sector over public sector came a restating of the significance of the entrepreneur for the re-invigoration of the economy. This, it was famously argued, would create wealth and redistribution would be rethought in terms of 'trickle-down' economics.

But there was an awareness that this ideological and cultural revolu-tion would almost inevitably result in conflict and difficulties. Most prominently this would mean confronting trade unions and risking high unemployment through controlling inflation. However, it was these

10. Brown, *Death of Christian Britain*, p. 232.

11. Steven, *Christianity and Party Politics*, pp. 21-44, 139-50.

12. G. Davie, *Religion in Britain since 1945: Believing without Belonging* (Oxford: Blackwell, 1994).

13. E. Filby, 'God and Mrs Thatcher: Religion and Politics in 1980s Britain' (PhD thesis, University of Warwick, 2010). For a detailed summary of what follows see pp. 138-57.

14. For discussion of 'Thatcherism', see Chapter 4.

issues which helped the New Right into power. The narrative is now well known but is worth summarising. A number of political crises in the 1970s aided the emergence of Thatcher and eventually the phenomenon of Thatcherism (see Chapter 4). High inflation and high unemployment had widespread effects but the then powerful National Union of Mine-workers (NUM) was representing workers from a nationalised industry whose wages were not rising with inflation. 1972 and 1974 saw two major strikes and, after the turmoil of the three-day working week and blackouts, Edward Heath's Tory government called an election to decide whether it was Parliament or unions who was running the country. Labour won but had to deal with the problems of the interests of its sup-porters among trade unions and the public sector, on the one hand, and austerity courtesy of the IMF, on the other. The result was the Winter of Discontent in 1978, with strikes affecting hospitals, transport, and even burials, and, with press and public disillusionment towards the status quo and continuing high unemployment, Thatcher was able to come to power with significant middle-class support to challenge unions and the role of the public sector.[15]

But first Thatcher had to overthrow the Conservative establishment which, though hardly uncritical, was relatively settled in the post-War Keynesian consensus by the 1970s. While the Conservative Party had suffered two narrow election defeats within a year in 1974 resulting in a minority Labour government, an ideological revolution was being plotted within the Conservative Party which was to be implemented after Thatcher emerged as the only credible figure to challenge Heath for the leadership of the Party in 1975. Influenced by the ideas of Friedrich von Hayek, and building on a range of cultural changes challenging tradi-tional upper-class and bureaucratic power, these Conservative revolu-tionaries, ultimately led by Thatcher, came to represent new changes in economics and politics in the mid-1970s, building on nearly two decades of work coming from the Institute of Economic Affairs and its advocacy of economic liberalism; those ideas that would eventually come to be labelled 'neoliberalism'. Alfred Sherman and Conservative MP Keith Joseph, one of the chief pioneers of English and British neoliberalism and one of the biggest direct influences on Thatcher, established the Centre for Policy Studies in 1974, itself soon to be followed by the Adam Smith Institute in 1976, both of which marked shifts towards

---

15. For a summary in the context of the emergence of neoliberalism in Britain see D. Harvey, *A Brief History of Neoliberalism* (Oxford: Oxford University Press, 2005), pp. 56-59.

economic liberalism in English politics at least. This intellectual revolution and changes in elite power among the Conservative Party would in many ways become a dominant – but hardly unchallenged – ideological position until the present day, at least in parliamentary politics. These developments were not simply a post-1974 implementation of the agenda of a Thatcher-led New Right; they are an Anglicised manifestation of broader ideological and economic changes which were starting to take shape at the end of the 1960s and which have become the norm for leaders of the main political parties since.

2. Why 'since 1968'?

'1968' is a date that will be used throughout this book partly out of convenience and as shorthand for wider cultural changes of the time, or indeed as a key moment of historical chaos generating such shifts. 1968 is especially convenient because it was, of course, the year of widespread international political, and social uprisings – particularly the Paris uprising – and is often associated with student movements, strikes, and the emergence or re-emergence of a range of leftist and often playful political thinking (e.g. anarchism, Situationism) which focused on individualism and personal freedom as well as collectivism associated with the traditional Communist and Socialist parties. But these uprisings, changes, and disturbances were not out of the blue and we might reasonably turn to the previous year and the 1967 Summer of Love (or indeed the coming of age of a post-war youth culture in the 1960s more generally) which likewise saw a hippy-inspired culture challenging traditional understandings of gender and sexuality and pushing for civil rights, peace, social justice, liberalisation of drugs, free-love, free-speech, and so on. As we all know, the cultural changes brought about by the mythical 1960s have been profound, as has its political impact since. However, while the rhetoric of 1960s freedom may have become more closely associated with strands of the liberal Left,[16] it is increasingly clear that the New Right likewise owe a debt to the changes generated by 1968. David Harvey has argued that the tensions between, on the one hand, the rhetoric of individual freedom, identity politics, and the intrusive state, and, on the other, the organised labour movement of the traditional Left, while not irreconcilable, could lead in different directions. For instance, Harvey notes how the rhetoric of individual freedom and identity politics

---

16. J.G. Crossley, *Jesus in an Age of Neoliberalism: Quests, Scholarship, Ideology* (London: Acumen, 2012), pp. 25-26.

could be developed into 'narcissistic consumerism' and, coupled with hostility towards the state, ultimately exploited in the development of 'neoliberalism'.[17]

Neoliberalism is associated with a variety of issues noted above in relation to Thatcher and the New Right. To generalize, neoliberalism advocates a variety of issues such as individual property rights and free trade, promotes the private sector over the public sector, supports deregulation of the market, challenges traditional manifestations of state power, urges virtually every aspect of human existence to be brought into the market, encourages individual responsibility, downplays systemic problems as a cause of individual failure, and emphasizes the importance of the market for the common good, human freedom, elimination of poverty, and creation of wealth.[18] Neoliberalism has been the dominant ideological position in the West since the 1970s, replacing the previous Fordist–Keynesian consensus. Of course, in reality, 'pure' neoliberalism does not happen and state interventionism has hardly withered. But the *ideal*, with increasingly higher degrees of implementation, has been dominant and has manifested itself in forms of high profile advocates or implementers, such as Thatcher, Reagan, Blair and Cameron. David Harvey can even write about 'the neoliberalism of culture'.[19]

Harvey, Fredric Jameson, and Perry Anderson have shown the links between late capitalism, or neoliberalism, and postmodernity,[20] all with the accompanying challenges to traditional concepts of truth and meta-narratives and greater emphasis on diversity, indeterminacy, instability, kitsch, playfulness, eclecticism, derivation, and a certain de-centeredness.[21] Assisted by the rise of mass media and communications, the instant image and PR has become more prominent than ever before. Perhaps

---

17. Harvey, *Neoliberalism*, pp. 56-59.

18. Crossley, *Jesus in an Age of Neoliberalism*, pp. 21-37. For full discussions of neoliberalism see e.g. Harvey, *Neoliberalism*; D. Plehwe, B.J.A. Walpen, and G. Neunhoffer (eds.), *Neoliberal Hegemony: A Global Critique* (London: Routledge, 2007); P. Mirowski and D. Plehwe (eds.), *The Road from Mont Pelerin: The Making of the Neoliberal Thought Collective* (Cambridge, Mass.: Harvard University Press 2009).

19. Harvey, *Neoliberalism*, p. 47; cf. F. Jameson, *Postmodernism, or, The Cultural Logic of Late Capitalism* (London: Verso, 1991), pp. 261, 263, 265-66, 278.

20. D. Harvey, *The Condition of Postmodernity* (Oxford: Blackwell, 1989); Jameson, *Postmodernism*; P. Anderson, *The Origins of Postmodernity* (London: Verso, 1998).

21. T. Eagleton, *The Illusions of Postmodernism* (Oxford: Blackwell, 1996), p. vii.

paradoxically, however, we find nationalism, jingoism, imperialism, and war taken up by neoliberal states to promote or provoke, directly or indirectly, neoliberalism (think of the Falklands or the Iraq wars), or indeed as a reaction to the globalizing tendencies of neoliberalism.[22] This tension between non-intervention and state intervention partly explains why neoconservatism came to the fore in the past decade. Neoconservatism has not only provided vigorous support for neoliberal economics but has positively revelled in the possibilities of militarisation, authoritarianism, and threats to the order (whether real or otherwise).

3. Political Receptions of the Bible since 1968

Nick Spencer has suggested that the Bible and its uses in English political history contain two distinctive, and potentially contradictory or complementary, tendencies between freedom and order.[23] I want to develop this further and look at how some of the distinctive post-1968 trends (in both global and Anglicised manifestations) outlined above intersect with four related, inherited, and, mostly, deeply embedded understandings of what the Bible 'really means' or how it is used rhetorically, particularly, but not exclusively, in the context of Anglicised political discourses. Once these four broad understandings are established, we can then proceed to look at how they are negotiated and nuanced by various political figures throughout the rest of this book. These four understandings are: the Cultural Bible; the Liberal Bible; the Neoliberal Bible; and the Radical Bible.

a. *The Cultural Bible*

The one assumption that runs throughout all political persuasions is what we can call, following Jonathan Sheehan, the Cultural Bible.[24] Sheehan has shown in detail how the Enlightenment produced a Bible which was (sometimes contradictorily) a philological and pedagogical resource, a literary classic, a moral guidebook, and a historical archive. These

---

22. See e.g. Jameson, *Postmodernism*, p. 5; Harvey, *Neoliberalism*, pp. 64-86; N. Klein, *The Shock Doctrine: The Rise of Disaster Capitalism* (London: Allen Lane, 2007), pp. 136-40; W. Brown, 'American Nightmare: Neoconservatism, Neoliberalism, and De-democratization', *Political Theory* 34 (2006), pp. 690-714; R. Boer and A. Andrews, 'Thin Economics; Thick Moralising: Red Toryism and the Politics of Nostalgia', *Bulletin for the Study of Religion* 40 (2011), pp. 16-24.

23. Spencer, *Freedom and Order*.

24. J. Sheehan, *The Enlightenment Bible: Translation, Scholarship, Culture* (Princeton: Princeton University Press, 2007), pp. 93-258.

different strands were encapsulated by the Cultural Bible, and biblical readers and interpreters interacted with developing ideas of secularisation. That these developments were taking place at a time of developing nationalism and Orientalism, particularly in the nineteenth century, is of some significance. This Bible was part of 'our' Western culture and civilisation and even an English classic.[25] Examples of the Cultural Bible abound and we will see numerous examples running throughout this book.[26] One particular twentieth-century example, though, might show us some of the assumptions underpinning discussions of the role of the Bible in English culture: the publication of the *New English Bible* New Testament in 1961. T.S. Eliot was less than impressed with this new version, claiming that it lacked the 'verbal beauty of the Authorized Version' and 'it would be good if those who have authority to translate a dead language could show understanding and appreciation of their own'. Eliot went further still and emphasised the importance of biblical translation for an English heritage:

> The age covered by the reigns of Elizabeth I and James I was richer in writers of genius than is our own, and we should not expect a translation made in our time to be a masterpiece of our literature or, as was the Authorized Version of 1611, an exemplar of English prose for successive generations of writers. We are, however, entitled to expect from a panel chosen from among the most distinguished scholars of our day at least a work of dignified mediocrity. When we find that we are offered something far below that modest level, something which astonishes in its combination of the vulgar, the trivial, and the pedantic, we ask in alarm: 'What is happening to the English language?'[27]

As we will see in Chapter 9, proclamations about the importance of the King James Bible in connection with an English heritage were not difficult to find during its 400th anniversary in 2011. For Richard Dawkins,

---

25. On the on-going influence of the Enlightenment and Cultural Bible more generally see S.D. Moore and Y. Sherwood, *The Invention of the Biblical Scholar: A Critical Manifesto* (Minneapolis: Fortress Press, 2011).

26. The Cultural Bible shares common features with earlier assumptions of the Bible, what Sherwood has labelled the 'Deferential/Passive Bible' and the 'Monarchical/Patriarchal Bible', in its emphasis on order and respect. See Y. Sherwood, 'On the Genesis between the Bible and Rights', in M.J.M. Coomber (ed.), *Bible and Justice: Ancient Texts, Modern Challenges* (London: Equinox, 2011), pp. 13-42 (22-28). However, we will see that the Cultural Bible has long been utilised by radical and liberal readers of the Bible as well.

27. Available at http://www.bible-researcher.com/neb-eliot.html and originally published in the *Sunday Telegraph* (December 16, 1962).

the English Bible 'needs to be part of our education', 'is a major source-book for literary culture', and 'a treasured heritage'.[28] Similarly, Michael Gove, who sent out King James Bibles to English schools in his role as Secretary of State for Education, spoke of how the King James Bible 'has had a profound impact on our culture' and that every school child 'should have the opportunity to learn about this book and the impact it has had on our history, language, literature and democracy'.[29]

b. *The Liberal Bible*

The connection between the Bible and democracy brings us on to another dominant form of understanding of what the Bible 'really means'. Looking partly at George W. Bush's use of the Bible, Yvonne Sherwood coined the phrase the 'Liberal Bible' which she described as an interpre-tative tradition developing since the sixteenth and seventeenth centu-ries.[30] The Liberal Bible is an understanding of the Bible as supportive of freedom of conscience, rights, law, government, and consensus, and marks a shift from the Absolute Monarchist's Bible where decisions made by the monarch were to be seen as proof of divine power. The Liberal Bible has also produced the (mistaken) assumption that the Bible is the foundation, and consonant with the principles, of western democ-racies without acknowledging that such a view of the Bible has its roots in sixteenth- and seventeenth-century Europe. The Liberal Bible is able to endorse actions against its constructed opposite: the undemocratic, tyranny, and terror. Unsurprisingly, it can follow from this anachronistic perspective that the Bible and Jesus are believed to be more representa-tive of democracy than the Qur'an and Muhammad. Because of its early modern origins, the Liberal Bible is continually vague. As Sherwood put it, 'It reduces the Bible to a few benign and vague axiomatic politico-theological principles that can be liberally applied (excuse the pun) thereafter'.[31] In the case of Bush's speeches, for instance, there were just enough biblical allusions to win key electoral support from Protestant Christians, with the specifics of faith left ambiguous. Indeed, Jacques Berlinerblau has additionally argued that successful American politicians

28. R. Dawkins, *The God Delusion* (London: Bantham Press, 2006), pp. 340-41, 343, 344.

29. 'Schools get King James Bible to mark 400th anniversary', *BBC News* (May 15, 2012), http://www.bbc.co.uk/news/education-18073996.

30. Y. Sherwood, 'Bush's Bible as a Liberal Bible (Strange though that Might Seem)', *Postscripts* 2 (2006), pp. 47–58; Sherwood, 'On the Genesis between the Bible and Rights'.

31. Sherwood, 'On the Genesis between the Bible and Rights', p. 35.

over the past thirty years have always used the Bible in a vague, non-polemical manner in order to signal to the electorate that the politician is a decent God-fearing person while simultaneously trying to avoid controversial debates about the Church/state distinction and a backlash from the liberal media.[32] While there may be different emphases and nuances depending on the party-political persuasion of the interpreter, the use of the Liberal Bible, like the Cultural Bible, along with the related rhetorical moves, is a common feature of all the major British and English politicians, an assumption shared with much of the contemporary media.[33]

An example of the interpretation of the Ten Commandments – itself an important text (or texts) for the Liberal Bible tradition – highlights the point well. In one of his regular criticisms of the BBC, social liberals, and multiculturalism, *Daily Mail* columnist Richard Littlejohn used the Ten Commandments to show a vague legal underpinning of social values, in particular to argue that (male) homosexuality is not really prominent in the UK outside liberal types. In defence of this worldview, Littlejohn claimed that 'OK, so we may not all be regular churchgoers, but we are still cultural Christians, who broadly buy into the Ten Commandments – if only in the breach rather than the observation'.[34] We will turn to another overlapping emphasis on the Cultural Bible in due course but a parlour game might show the potential disjunction between the content of the Ten Commandments and their apparent application in contemporary British law and culture. We can start by establishing a checklist of commandments:

> You shall have no other gods before Me.
> You shall not make for yourself an idol, or any likeness of what is in heaven above or on the earth beneath or in the water under the earth.
> You shall not worship them or serve them; for I, the LORD your God, am a jealous God, visiting the iniquity of the fathers on the children, on the third and the fourth generations of those who hate Me, but showing loving-kindness to thousands, to those who love Me and keep My commandments.
> You shall not take the name of the LORD your God in vain.

---

32. J. Berlinerblau, *Thumpin' It: The Use and Abuse of the Bible in Today's Presidential Politics* (Louisville: WJK, 2008).

33. J. G. Crossley and J. Harrison, 'The Mediation of the Distinction of "Religion" and "Politics" by the UK Press on the Occasion of Pope Benedict XVI's State Visit to the UK', *Political Theology* 14 (2015), pp. 329–45.

34. R. Littlejohn, 'Whatever the BBC say, Britain is still mainly white, Christian and straight', *Daily Mail* (September 30, 2011).

> Remember the Sabbath day, to keep it holy. Six days you shall labour and
> do all your work, but the seventh day is a Sabbath of the LORD your God;
> in it you shall not do any work, you or your son or your daughter, your male
> or your female servant or your cattle or your sojourner who stays with you.
> Honour your father and your mother.
> You shall not commit adultery.
> You shall not steal.
> You shall not murder.
> You shall not bear false witness against your neighbour.
> You shall not covet your neighbour's house; you shall not covet your
> neighbour's wife or his male servant or his female servant or his ox or
> his donkey or anything that belongs to your neighbour. (Exod. 20.1-17;
> Deut. 5.1-21)

A reasonable case might be made that in neither the Exodus nor the
Deuteronomy versions are the people who might be expected to observe
these commandments (even in breach) 'Christians'. Moreover, Sabbath
observance might, of course, be alternatively be understood as the Jewish
Shabbat. And what relevance to the Littlejohn household is avoiding
'any likeness of what is in heaven above or on the earth beneath or in the
water under the earth'? But even if we bring a number of the more
famous commandments into the present, a number of sentiments (e.g.
honour parents, do not steal, do not murder) are general sentiments that
would no doubt unite people from a number of backgrounds, religions,
countries, moral systems, and so on, whether a BBC employee or *Daily
Mail* columnist. It might even be suggested that a male homosexual is
less likely to covet his neighbour's wife than Littlejohn's heterosexual
English male. So, if we were to follow Littlejohn this literally, his view
of Christian Britain is problematic. But this is not the point. The Ten
Commandments are simply deemed to be more-or-less part of British
democracy, laws, rights, society, and so on, irrespective of their actual
contents. The Liberal Bible understood this way is an extremely common
phenomenon in political discourse as we will see throughout this book,
and has manifestations across the mainstream political spectrum.

In a recent study of the British Press and their treatment of Benedict
XVI's papal visit in 2010, Jackie Harrison and I showed that a dominant
positive understanding of 'religion' was that it was, or indeed had to be,
compatible with liberal democracy. Correspondingly, the positive use of
the Bible (invariably the King James Bible) was largely from the Liberal
Bible tradition, typically using the KJV-isms, *love thy neighbour* or
render unto Caesar.[35] For instance, the *Daily Mail* quoted the Catholic

---

35. Crossley and Harrison, 'The Mediation of the Distinction of "Religion" and
"Politics"'.

MP, Mark Pritchard, as saying 'The Catholic Church is an imperfect institution but it is amazing the BBC has found nothing positive to say about a church whose key message is to love thy neighbour including feeding the poor and helping the homeless'.[36] Of course, transubstantiation, sin, salvation, sacraments, anti-contraception, and so on might alternatively be thought of as central to understandings of Catholic history but, as ever, that is not the point: once in the contemporary political and cultural arena, and with the need to be seen as acceptable, 2000 years of complex history is boiled down to *love thy neighbour*. More explicitly, Dominic Lawson removed any political danger away from 'religion' by claiming that Benedict was an 'un-political' Pope who had 'no interest in inserting the Catholic Church into the political process'. This is because Benedict apparently inherited his worldview from Jesus who declared 'that the temporal and spiritual worlds should be entirely separate'. To support this argument, Lawson quoted 'Render unto Caesar the things that are Caesar's and unto God the things that are God's'.[37] What we have here is the Bible being used to support the typical privatisation of 'religion' and the historic rhetoric concerning the separation or integration of the seemingly binary categories of 'Church and State', which covers up a much more complicated, interrelated reality.[38] This is, as Russell McCutcheon put it, 'firmly entrenched in the well-established liberal tradition of distinguishing the relatively apolitical freedom "to believe" from the obviously political freedom to behave, organize, and oppose. It is none other than the rhetorical distinction between private and public…that makes possible both the internalization of dissent and conformity of practice.'[39]

c. *The Neoliberal Bible*
In fear of stating the obvious, the Neoliberal Bible can simply be understood to be largely compatible with the ideals of neoliberalism. In this vein, we could fast-forward to Chapter 4 and Thatcher's Bible which, as

36. S. Doughty, 'Pope faces atheist hate campaign in UK after top German aide says: "When you land at Heathrow you think you're in a Third World country"', *Daily Mail* (September 16, 2010).

37. D. Lawson, 'Pope Benedict…an apology', *Independent* (September 21, 2010).

38. For a detailed history, deconstruction, and analysis of the rhetorical distinction between 'religion' and 'state' from early modern Europe and as a product of modernity see C. Martin, *Masking Hegemony: A Genealogy of Liberalism, Religion and the Private Sphere* (London: Equinox, 2010), pp. 33-57.

39. R.T. McCutcheon, *Religion and the Domestication of Dissent: or, How to Live in a Less than Perfect Nation* (London: Equinox, 2005), p. 62.

we will see, emphasised individualism over state, characters like the Good Samaritan for his money to enable charitable giving, patriotism, and social order. In fact, Thatcher's Bible, as will be argued throughout much of this book, could be said to be the template for political exegetes, just as Thatcherism (in some form) has become the dominant ideological position of the main political parties. There will be much more detail on this in due course but there is another aspect of the Neoliberal Bible which needs to be highlighted and which had less direct input from Thatcher but tallies with neoliberal trends more generally. Indeed, it might even be suggested with only slight exaggeration that neoliberalism provides the ideal economic and ideological conditions for the idea that the actual contents of the Bible barely matter in understanding what the Bible 'really means', particularly in the idea of the importance placed on marketing and instant imaging.

For instance, the commodity fetishism involved in (re-)packaging already existing biblical translations for a targeted audience/market neatly replicates the relentless postmodern interest in, and market of, multiple identities. And it is surely Zondervan who has cornered the market for identity marketing of effectively the same Bible, more precisely the *New International Version* repackaged in different forms, such as: *Playful Puppies Bible*; *Curious Kittens Bible*; *The Holy Bible: Stock Car Racing Edition*; *True Images: The Teen Bible for Girls*; *Revolution: The Bible for Teen Guys*; *Couples' Devotional Bible*; *Engaged Couples' Bible*; *Life Journey Bible*; and so on and so on. By way of analogies from memetics, Hugh Pyper has suggested that multiple manifestations of biblical books, versions, translations, and so on, have generated the Bible's own survival.[40] We might rethink Pyper's suggestion in more economic terms and argue that the Bible has survived by these multiple manifestations being embedded in capitalism's relentless quest for more markets.

Of course, the (re-)packaging of these Bibles conveys a range of ideological meanings. The instant imagery of military insignia, photographs of soldiers and a helicopter, and the background picture of the American flag on the cover of *The Soldiers' Bible* (2004) are all that are needed to convey a certain ideological message. This is a message – effortlessly combining the core of American neoliberalism and neoconservatism in convenient green bonded leather with slide-tab closure – that probably does not need spelling out. And nor does the significance of the quotations, prayers, and inspiration from, among others, President George W. Bush and General George S. Patton, the description that it is for those

40. H.S. Pyper, *An Unsuitable Book: The Bible as Scandalous Text* (Sheffield: Sheffield Phoenix Press, 2006).

'men and women who serve the cause of freedom around the world', or the words to America the Beautiful contained therein. Indeed, a glance at the covers and additional advice interspersed between the pages of the *New International Version* will immediately tell readers what sort of gender, cultural and political positions can be expected for the ideal buyer of the *Teen Bible for Girls* or the *Bible for Teen Guys*.[41] Likewise it is easy enough to guess what interests are at play by the mere title of the 'Queen James Bible'. We are informed that the Queen James Bible has been 'edited…to prevent homophobic interpretations', that the King James Bible (in its 1769 version) was chosen for the revision because of, among other reasons, 'The obvious gay link to King James, known amongst friends and courtiers as "Queen James" because of his many gay lovers',[42] and the title on the home webpage tells us that this is 'A Gay Bible'.[43] However, this information is, to some extent, superfluous, as the white cover with a cross in the colours of the LGBT rainbow flag conveys enough information for a market audience with interest in such identity politics.

Indeed, image is further significant for the range of meanings it can convey *instantly*. Katie Edwards has shown that the Bible in advertising only needs a split-second viewing as pages are turned or an advertising board passed to convey a range of ideological meanings. For instance, a standard glossy magazine advert with an Eve-type figure tempted by an apple can convey a set of assumptions about consumerist desire and constructions of gender, whilst an advertising board featuring England footballer Wayne Rooney in a 'Messianic' pose shows the intersection of (among other things) branding, masculinity, and nationalism.[44] There is a lot of discussion about declining standards of biblical literacy which work with a Protestant model of knowing the details of given passages and stories; does the Neoliberal Bible not suggest that biblical literacy still exists, just in a radically different way?[45] We will see in Chapter 9 how this sort of Bible has manifest itself in contemporary political debates.

41. J.G. Crossley, 'OH-MY-GOD – It's So the Teen Bible!', *SBL Forum* (January, 2007), http://sbl-site.org/Article.aspx?ArticleID=615.

42. http://queenjamesbible.com/gay-bible/.

43. http://queenjamesbible.com/.

44. K.B. Edwards, *Ad Men and Eve: The Bible and Advertising* (Sheffield: Sheffield Phoenix Press, 2012); K.B. Edwards, 'Sporting Messiah: Hypermasculinity and Nationhood in Male-targeted Sports Imagery', *Biblical Reception* 1 (2012), pp. 323-46.

45. The Neoliberal Bible, alongside the importance of the image and economics, is not, of course, an entirely new phenomenon and familiar in the history of, for instance, propaganda or any number of historical antecedents. I hope this will be

d. *The Radical Bible*

The Radical Bible is a historic tradition of understanding the Bible which, put crudely, equates the Bible with socialism in one form or other or even with revolutionary transformation. Or, as Tony Benn put it, 'the origins of socialism can be traced back as far as the time of Christ himself and even to the Old Testament'.[46] A number of themes about what the Bible 'really means' in the Radical Bible tradition include: land and wealth redistribution, confronting power and wealth, communitarianism, egalitarianism, anti-clericalism and direct access to God, the importance of conscience and/or the Spirit, prophetic critique, and even 'apocalyptic' language, particularly with reference to a radical transformation of the social, economic, and political order.[47] To rephrase Morgan Phillips, the Radical Bible owes as much to Marx as it does to Methodism. What I label the Radical Bible is perhaps best known, at least among theologians and biblical scholars, from Liberation Theology. Yet we should not forget that there is a long, wide-ranging history of radical and popular readings of the Bible or biblical texts which have challenged ecclesiastical, priestly, economic, social, or imperial authority and hierarchies, even if they are not all technically 'socialist' and some only show elements of what we might label 'political radicalism'. These might include (among many others): early Jewish bandits, at least as described by Josephus (*War* 2.228-231; 2.247-248; 2.274-276; *Ant.* 20.113-117); perhaps Jesus himself (e.g. Mark 10.17-31; Luke 16.19-31); the Cathars; Müntzer and the radical Reformation; Catholic Worker Movement; a range of Marxist

assumed by readers. A painting as famous as Thomas Jones Barker's 'The Secret of England's Greatness' (1863) illustrates the use of the Bible and its interaction between image, politics, imperialism, and economics. We might, alternatively and not unreasonably, call the Neoliberal Bible the 'Postmodern Bible', but I prefer Neoliberal Bible for a number of reasons, including the follow two. First, it maintains the more explicit economic element in the analysis, though readers of, for instance, David Harvey, Fredric Jameson, and Perry Anderson will be well aware of the economic underpinnings of postmodernity. Second, the term 'neoliberal' retains the important connections with 'liberal' and, more to the point, the tradition of the Liberal Bible.

46. T. Benn, *Arguments for Socialism* (London: Jonathan Cape, 1979), p. 23.

47. The literature on radical interpretations of the Bible is vast, wide-ranging, and diverse. Two helpful summaries of key points in the history of politically radical biblical interpretation are R. Boer, *Rescuing the Bible* (Oxford: Blackwell, 2007), pp. 105-27, and C. Rowland and J. Roberts, *The Bible for Sinners: Interpretation in the Present Time* (London: SPCK, 2008). Sherwood, 'Alliance', pp. 21-22, discusses the 'Revolutionary/Republican Bible' with particular reference to the seventeenth and eighteenth centuries.

intellectuals, including the relatively recent interest in Paul as a revolutionary thinker by philosophers such as Alain Badiou and Slavoj Žižek; and even Marx and Engels themselves.[48]

The importance of the Radical Bible in English politics and culture likewise has a long history (e.g., among many others, Peasants' Revolt, Wyclif and the Lollards, Blake, F.D. Maurice, Chartists, Socialist Sunday Schools etc.). One of the most important moments in terms of its potential influence on party politics was the English Civil Wars and Cromwell's harnessing (and ultimate rejection) of politically radical readers of the Bible, such as Gerrard Winstanley and the Diggers. But it was not until the turn of the twentieth century and the emergence of the Labour movement with its strong Nonconformist contingent that the more sustained influence of the Radical Bible was felt in party politics.[49] The Radical Bible features in the rhetoric or upbringing of a number of major Labour party figures associated with the Left and leftist causes, such as Keir Hardie, Margaret and Rachel MacMillan, Will Crooks, R.H. Tawney, George Lansbury, Ellen Wilkinson, Aneurin Bevan, Stafford Cripps, Donald Soper, and Eric Heffer,[50] as well as in radical movements and figures with some connections with the Labour Party in the twentieth century, such as the Campaign for Nuclear Disarmament (CND), and even the Marxist historian E.P. Thompson,[51] and with ongoing echoes in the contemporary think-tank Ekklesia.

48. J. Økland, 'The Spectre Revealed and Made Manifest: The Book of Revelation in the Writings of Karl Marx and Friedrich Engels', in J. Økland and W.J. Lyons (ed.), *The Way the World Ends? The Apocalypse of John in Culture and Ideology* (Sheffield: Sheffield Phoenix Press, 2009), pp. 267-88. Cf. F. Engels, 'On the History of Earliest Christianity (1894)', in K. Marx and F. Engels, *Collected Works Volume 27, Engels: 1890–95* (London: Lawrence & Wishart, 1990), pp. 447-69.

49. See e.g. Spencer, *Freedom and Order*, Chapters 7–10.

50. See e.g. G. Dale, *God's Politicians: The Christian Contribution to 100 Years of Labour* (London: HarperCollins, 2000).

51. On Thompson's little-known poetic engagement with the Bible (and in relation to CND) see E.P. Thompson, *Infant and Emperor: Poems for Christmas* (London: Merlin Press, 1983), and R. Boer, 'Apocalyptic and Apocalypticism in the Poetry of E.P. Thompson', *Spaces of Utopia* 7 (2009), pp. 34-53. On Thompson's uneasy relationship with the Labour Party see e.g. S. Hamilton, *The Crisis of Theory: E.P. Thompson, the New Left and Postwar British Politics* (Manchester: Manchester University Press, 2011), pp. 162-63, 180.

4. Tony Benn and the Decline of the Radical Bible

From the 1970s onwards, Tony Benn became the standard-bearer for the Radical Bible in party-politics and the Labour movement. Benn came from a Nonconformist and politically dissenting background but between 1964 and 1970 settled into the Labour establishment serving as Postmaster General and Minister for Technology under Harold Wilson. However, by the end of the 1960s, and after experiencing the constraints of government first-hand, he started his move to the radical (or 'hard') Left of the Labour Party where he championed a number of major leftist (and, at the time, often unpopular) issues, such as post-1968 feminism, syndicalism, the Miners' Strike of 1984–85, Irish unification, anti-war(s), unilateral disarmament, and anti-hierarchical radical democratic equality (not least in the Labour Party), as well as continuing his long-standing opposition to racism and the treatment of immigrants.

Some of this radicalism was influenced by Benn's mother, Margaret 'Didi' Holmes, who was a feminist, from a background of liberal Nonconformist (Congregationalist) dissent, a biblical scholar of some training (e.g. she read Hebrew and Greek), and contact of the American theologian Reinhold Niebuhr (whom Benn visited as a young man).[52] On meeting the Archbishop of Canterbury, Randall Davidson, Holmes said that she wanted her sons to grow up in a world where women would be given 'equal spiritual status',[53] a view which would chime with Benn's radical egalitarian democratic views and his understanding of the Bible with a radical Protestant spin. Citing texts such as Mark 12.29-31 in support,[54] Benn argued that the concept of the 'priesthood of all believers' was 'based on the belief that every person had a direct line to the Almighty and does not require a bishop to mediate concerning what to believe and what to do',[55] nor indeed the 'intervention of an exclusive priestly class claiming a monopoly right to speak on behalf of the Almighty, still less of a king claiming a divine right to rule'.[56] He labelled this religious dissent as 'a completely revolutionary doctrine

---

52. T. Benn, *Conflicts Of Interest: Diaries 1977–80* (London: Hutchinson, 1990), pp. 7-8; Dale, *God's Politicians*, p. 196. Benn parallels Niebuhr's views on democracy and sin with those of the Levellers whom Benn also admired. See e.g. T. Benn, *The Levellers and the English Democratic Tradition* (Nottingham: Russell Press, 1976), p. 14.

53. D. Powell, *Tony Benn: A Political Life* (New York: Continuum, 2001), p. 13. Cf. T. Benn, *Dare to Be a Daniel: Then and Now* (London: Arrow Books, 2004), p. 5.

54. E.g. Benn, *Arguments for Socialism*, pp. 24-25.

55. Benn, *Dare to Be a Daniel*, p. 5.

56. Benn, *Arguments for Socialism*, p. 25.

because it undermined authority, disturbed the hierarchy and was seen as intolerable by the powers that be, in exactly the same way that, today, political dissenters are projected as trouble-makers and members of the "awkward squad", whose advice would lead to chaos'.[57]

The interconnected themes of individual conscience and confronting power and hierarchy are common in Benn's understanding of the Bible. Citing Amos 5.24 and Micah 6.8, Benn looked to the 'deep conviction to be found in the Old Testament that conscience is God-given, or derives from nature or reason' and is supreme over human-made law, a conviction that is 'still passionately held today'.[58] Perhaps most famously, Benn recalled his father's fondness for the story of Daniel in the lions' den and the words from the Salvation Army hymn, 'Dare to Be a Daniel' ('Dare to be a Daniel, Dare to stand alone, Dare to have a purpose firm, Dare to make it known'). Benn claimed that that these sentiments 'greatly influenced my life' and 'taught me the importance of consistency and courage in the face of adversity – essential for anyone who is criticised for his convictions'. He even photographed a picture he saw in the YMCA in Nagasaki in 1983 of Daniel – head bowed, hands behind back, and surrounded by lions – and hanged the photograph in his office 'to remind me of those qualities that are most important in public life' before citing the hymn.[59] Not everyone had Daniel's good fortune however. Individuals, Benn argued, may always rebel against systems of power and think for themselves but such people have been 'generally excommunicated or even killed'. Yet, Benn has added, the importance of 'teachers who explained the world without wanting to control it themselves' is of great importance in the development of ideas.[60]

Benn's mother continued to have an influence in reading biblical stories to Benn's children, as well as in Benn's remembering of her continued presence in his own radical politics, notably in standing up to power. He recalled:

> I was brought up on the Bible by my mother who told me about the age-old conflict between the kings who had power and the prophets who preached righteousness. She taught me to support the prophets against the kings, meaning that each of us had the responsibility for learning to differentiate between good and evil and make that our guide for action.[61]

57. Benn, *Dare to Be a Daniel*, p. 5.
58. Benn, *Levellers*, p. 7.
59. Benn, *Dare to Be a Daniel*, pp. ix, 11.
60. Benn, *Dare to Be a Daniel*, pp. 4-5.
61. T. Benn, *Free Radical: New Century Essays* (New York: Continuum, 2003), p. 226.

The prophets-versus-kings model may sound an abstracted kind of radicalism but Benn immediately gave it contemporary application with specific reference to well-known and precise causes most readily associated with the contemporary political Left:

> She was right, we should all have the confidence to think things out for ourselves, and if we do it must be clear that Bush's plan to make war on Iraq is wrong, as is the conduct of Sharon in oppressing the Palestinians, or whipping up of hostility against asylum-seekers, or accepting the present grossly unfair division between rich and poor in a world dominated by globalization.

This application of the Radical Bible also reflects deeply rooted ideas about the nature of political power and democratic ideals which can often implicate the established church on the side of the 'kings'. A good example of this is found in Benn's diary entry for April 25, 1991, when Benn recalled a 'crowded meeting' at Hartlebury Castle, the home of the Bishop of Worcester. After giving a speech, Benn engaged in questions of democracy, which included the following incident:

> Then two Evangelicals got up and said, 'Do you accept that Jesus is our Lord?'
> I said, 'I don't like the word Lord. I don't believe in Lords'. This brought us on to the whole question of the Kingdom of God, and I did describe my Constitutional Reform Bill. What you realise is that an authoritarian Church, where power comes from the Creator mediated through the bishops to the clergy to the laity, can't really take on board democracy at all because everything is done from the top.[62]

But individual conscience did not, of course, lead to a Thatcherite reading of the Bible. Indeed, Benn contrasted Thatcher's Nonconformist roots and individualism as freedom from the State with his mother's Congregationalism which 'was interpreted quite differently. She was a very devoted and serious Christian and gave me a grounding in both the Old and New Testaments of the Bible.'[63] More specifically, the idea of individual conscience transferred into more collective justice. Indeed, in this respect Benn took the significant example of Marx whom he came to believe 'was the last of the Old Testament prophets, a wise old Jew…'[64]

---

62. T. Benn, *Free at Last! Diaries 1991–2001* (London: Hutchinson, 2002), p. 17. Cf. T. Benn, 'The Power of the Bible Today', in *Sheffield Academic Press Occasional Papers: The Twelfth Annual Sheffield Academic Press Lecture, University of Sheffield, March 17, 1995* (Sheffield: Sheffield Academic Press, 1995), pp. 1-13 (4).

63. Benn, *Dare to Be a Daniel*, p. 10.

64. Benn, *Dare to Be a Daniel*, p. 14; Benn, 'Power of the Bible Today', pp. 7-8.

Applying ideas of eschatological judgement and justice familiar to both the Radical Bible tradition and the Labour movement (see also Chapter 8), as well as elsewhere in Benn's thinking on the Bible,[65] he further argued that the idea of Heaven on Earth ('or justice in practice') is not only 'an integral part of the dissenting tradition' but also of 'the trade-union movement, which recognised that you could only improve conditions by your own collective efforts'.[66] This integration of individual dissent and collectivism can, he claimed, be found throughout history. In a House of Commons debate on 'Socialism', Benn suggested:

> The Bible has led to many revolutionary ideas – for instance, that we were and are all equal in the sight of God – which is why, in 1401, the House of Commons passed the Heresy Act, which condemned any lay person reading the Bible to be burned at the stake for heresy. The Bible has always been a controversial document. At the time of the Peasants' Revolt and the English revolution, people started thinking of common ownership, based on the life of the apostles. (House of Commons debate on Socialism, May 16, 2000)[67]

What is also notable in this respect is that Benn rejected a famous view that, as we saw, has been associated with Conservative understandings of the Bible and taken up by Thatcher but which has a long history of being questioned in radical theological thinking: Original Sin. Whereas Conservatives such as Thatcher saw the rejection of Original Sin as leading to misguided ideas of social utopianism and the perfectibility of humanity (see Chapter 4), for Benn the very idea of Original Sin 'is deeply offensive' because 'I cannot imagine that any God could possibly have created the human race and marked it at birth with evil that could only be expiated by confession, devotion and obedience'. Whereas Thatcher could associate the rejection of Original Sin with totalitarianism, Benn took the opposite view. This 'use of Christianity to keep people down was...destructive of any hope that we might succeed together in building a better world'.[68]

---

65. 'Whether you believe that you are accountable on the Day of Judgement for the way you have spent your life, or have to account to your fellow men and women for what you have done during your life, accountability is a strong and democratic idea' (Benn, *Dare to Be a Daniel*, p. 17).

66. Benn, *Dare to Be a Daniel*, p. 7. See also Benn, 'Power of the Bible Today', p. 3.

67. Cited in Benn, *Dare to Be a Daniel*, pp. 268-78 (269).

68. Benn, *Dare to Be a Daniel*, p. 13.

The idea of later corruptions of an original purer message is common to all the major traditions of reading the Bible discussed in this book but Benn, of course, followed the standard rhetorical move of the Radical Bible. He saw Jesus (notably labelled 'the Carpenter of Nazareth') as 'one of the greatest teachers, along with Moses and Mohammed' and that Christianity, Judaism, and Islam teach 'that we are brothers and sisters with a responsibility to each other'.[69] But these religions can distort the message of the great leader. While rejecting the 'implicit atheism' in Marx, Benn believed it was possible to accept the argument that religion is the opium of the people 'without in any way demeaning the importance of the teachings of Jesus'.[70] Benn's views of the Bible and faith may have changed over the years but, he claimed, such changes were not 'influenced by atheistic arguments, which were extreme and threw doubt on the value of the Bible and the historical truth of Jesus' life'. Rather, the real challenge for Benn was 'the nature of the Church and the way in which it sought to use the teachings of the Bible to justify its power structures in order to build up its own authority'.[71] Benn, typically, has provided concrete examples of 'the one characteristic of most religions when they become established…the entrenchment of authority at their heart', whether the Archbishop of Canterbury or the Pope, 'each in their time having great power over their respective churches and enforcing Christian doctrine, sometimes ruthlessly, as at the time of the Inquisition and on other occasions when heretics were burned at the stake'.[72] Benn also believed that this characteristic was part of the political arena, and perhaps not surprising given his views on Marx as Old Testament prophet, and Stalinism ('supposedly the teachings of Marx'), to the 'Labour Party itself, which was inspired by men and women of principle, [who] became corrupted by the same power structures, leading to the expulsion of different people on the grounds that they were not prepared to accept orders from the Party hierarchy'.[73]

Benn saw the Bible and biblical interpretation as part of a specifically English or British (he has used both terms) radical tradition. This English or British tradition can be seen with particular reference not only to the

---

69. Benn, *Dare to Be a Daniel*, p. 15. The title 'Jesus Christ the Carpenter of Nazareth' and the 'revolutionary' nature of monotheism turn up elsewhere in Benn's reflections on the Bible. See e.g. Benn, *Levellers*, pp. 5-6.

70. Benn, *Dare to Be a Daniel*, p. 14.

71. Benn, *Dare to Be a Daniel*, p. 13.

72. Benn, *Dare to Be a Daniel*, p. 4. Cf. Benn, *Arguments for Socialism*, p. 39.

73. Benn, *Dare to Be a Daniel*, p. 4. Cf. Benn, 'Power of the Bible Today', pp. 3-5, 7-8.

Labour movement, but also to the Levellers, a common point of refer-ence in the English Radical Bible tradition, and one to which we will return in Chapter 2. For Benn, the Levellers 'won wide public support among the people as a whole' and 'their ideas still retain a special place in the political traditions of the people of England'.[74] These 'political traditions', Benn argued, were very much socialist, though he acknow-ledged that the democratic ideals of the Levellers were also picked up by liberals, and that such ideals have a lineage stretching back further still:

> The Levellers can now be seen…as speaking for a popular liberation movement that can be traced right back to the teachings of the Bible, and which has retained its vitality over the intervening centuries to speak to us here with undiminished force… [T]o understand what the Levellers said, and why, we must delve back far into our own history. For the Levellers drew many of their ideas, and much of their inspiration, from the Bible, with its rich Jewish and Christian teaching.[75]

The Bible was the 'basic text' for Benn's Levellers and, 'as now in many parts of the world', it was seen as a 'revolutionary book', partly because it was 'not to be trusted to the common people to read and interpret for themselves'.[76]

Benn went further still in placing the Bible prominently in the origins of British or English socialism. In his 1979 book, *Arguments for Socialism*, which sold over 75,000 copies,[77] Benn attempted to counter the suggestions that the origins of the Labour party did not justify shifts to the Left by foregrounding the Bible, along with the Levellers, Marx, and the Labour Party's Constitution, as some of the most important influences.[78] Again, the Bible, and Jesus, through the Levellers, were a crucial part of 'democratic socialism', which 'is very much a home-grown British product which has been slowly fashioned over the centuries'. Benn added that its 'roots are deep in our history and have been nourished by the Bible, the teachings of Christ, the Peasants' Revolt, the Levellers, Tom Paine, the Chartists, Robert Owen, the Webbs and Bernard Shaw…'[79] The Bible also had another important aspect for Benn's socialism: to counter criticisms of atheism being integral to socialism. While socialism may be criticised for its atheistic element, Benn further added that this is 'not true as far as British Socialism is

74. Benn, *Levellers*, p. 7.
75. Benn, *Levellers*, pp. 5, 7.
76. Benn, *Levellers*, p. 9.
77. Dale, *God's Politicians*, p. 194.
78. Benn, *Arguments for Socialism*, p. 23.
79. Benn, *Arguments for Socialism*, p. 146.

concerned' because 'the Bible has always been, and remains, a major element in our national political – as well as our religious – education', which Benn contextualised in terms of his regular refrain of Kings versus Prophets.[80]

Benn would narrowly lose the Labour Party Deputy Leadership election in 1981 and this would mark the decline of the Bennite Left in the Labour Party, and such radicalism was eventually pushed to the fringes of the party. By the end of the 1980s, the centrist ideas of Neil Kinnock were dominating the Labour Party and were pushed further to the right by Tony Blair in the 1990s. As Blair was removing Clause 4 (a commitment to common/public ownership or nationalisation) from the Labour Party Constitution, Benn was claiming that 'anyone who really thinks that Clause 4 and common ownership was invented by Karl Marx, and I think there are some people quite high up in the Labour Party who think that, might go back to the Acts of the Apostles for the idea of all things in common'.[81] But any serious influence Benn had on the Labour Party had now gone and with it the Radical Bible was no longer the force it once was. Indeed, leading Labour users of the Bible slowly began embracing some of the rhetoric of Thatcherism which, as we will see in Chapter 8, was most fully developed in Blair's hermeneutics.

A significant moment came in 1993 in a Christian Socialist Movement (CSM) publication edited by Christopher Bryant (then press officer for the Christian Socialist Movement, later its chair) called *Reclaiming the Ground: Christianity and Socialism*, largely a collection of then recent Tawney Lectures.[82] The book foregrounded the role of then Labour leader John Smith and included a foreword by Blair. As might be expected, Smith's article contained anti-Thatcher polemics but the ideas of individual freedom ('our ultimate moral goal'[83]) and their relationship with collectivism is the dominant theme. Smith turned to the Christian socialism of the anti-Marxist of the lecture series, R.H. Tawney, and advocated a 'democratic socialism' which was 'ethical, individualistic, parliamentary and pragmatic' and would seek to enhance 'individual freedom in a framework of collective common purpose'.[84] Smith made a rhetorically surprising move by also turning to Adam Smith who, he pointed out,

80. Benn, *Levellers*, p. 5. Cf. Benn, *Arguments for Socialism*, pp. 23-24.

81. Benn, 'Power of the Bible Today', p. 7.

82. C. Bryant (ed.), *Reclaiming the Ground: Christianity and Socialism* (London: Hodder & Stoughton, 1993).

83. J. Smith, 'Reclaiming the Ground – Freedom and the Value of Society', in Bryant (ed.), *Reclaiming the Ground*, pp. 127-42 (130).

84. Smith, 'Reclaiming the Ground', p. 127.

balanced 'support for public investment in infrastructure, in education and the arts…the hidden gems of intervention that can be found alongside his thesis of the invisible hand'.[85] This allowed (John) Smith to place some significance on the market which, he argued, remained a 'useful means of enabling choice and distribution of myriad goods and services'.[86] Smith, via Tawney, constructed this democratic socialism between the constructed extremes of *laissez-faire* capitalism and 'Marxist collectivism', 'the *laissez-faire* Right' and the 'Marxist Left'.[87] Smith was, of course, preparing the way for the rise of New Labour under Blair and Gordon Brown.

Reclaiming the Ground still featured more radical traditions, including the Tawney Lecture by John Vincent. However, it is clear that the signs of the decline of the Radical Bible are found in other key places, as well as being notable that Vincent is a voice from outside Parliament. Bryant's editorial essay certainly picked up on themes from the Radical Bible tradition, including the abolition of poverty and collectivism, as well as discussing biblical passages in relation to radical themes. But what is also clear is that Bryant does not push the potentially radical conclusions too hard and would often leave the ramifications sufficiently general that they could be embraced by a centre-leftist politician, or in several instances, even Conservative or Liberal politicians. Moreover, whereas Tony Benn was always keen to give precise contemporary application to major leftist causes, Bryant remained general and largely non-committal. Reviewing the history of influences on Christian socialism, Bryant noted that the 'inspired prophets of the Old and New Testament recognised that there is something "unfair" in human society'.[88] William Blake may have wanted a 'New Jerusalem' and Keir Hardie may have 'asserted that a society could and should be built on the precepts of Jesus' Sermon on the Mount, with its emphasis on the poor, the hungry and those who thirst for justice' but we do not discover much more in terms of detail.[89] Indeed, Christian socialism was said to have witnessed 'the rediscovery of the Bible' and a much-neglected biblical theme which is likewise general: 'enjoining Christians to practise justice'.[90] Even when it seems more details of 'justice' are forthcoming,

---

85. Smith, 'Reclaiming the Ground', p. 133.
86. Smith, 'Reclaiming the Ground', p. 133.
87. Smith, 'Reclaiming the Ground', pp. 135, 37.
88. C. Bryant, 'Introduction', in Bryant (ed.), *Reclaiming the Ground*, pp. 13-28 (16).
89. Bryant, 'Introduction', p. 17.
90. Bryant, 'Introduction', p. 18.

conclusions are left open. For instance, 'justice' in the Sermon on the Mount was applied in 'many different directions', including collectivism. Yet while co-operative movements may have 'believed in a society far more akin to the early Church where all things were held in common' the 'extension of common ownership to State socialism…was a more contentious matter'.[91]

Bryant's handling of wealth and inequality is particularly significant because he refrained from a more fully blown rejection of wealth inequality and edged more towards lack of fairness and mistreatment of 'the poor'. Bryant even referenced Liberation Theology and the 'biblical understanding of poverty…as a sign that society has turned its back on God'. From this perspective, 'the poor' are those who 'lack food, water and a home' or are 'oppressed by the wealthy, denied their rights, their wages or their land'. God, in this tradition, has a 'preferential option for the poor'.[92] In addition to such generalisations, there are other hints of more relativised thinking. The Old Testament prophets may have 'rounded on the rich' but only the rich 'who abused their privilege and bore scant regard for the poor'.[93] A particularly notable example of the treatment of wealth and the Bible is Bryant's handling of the rich man and the eye of the needle. Bryant made the interpretative decision to read something which could be deemed, as certain disciples thought, impossible (a camel passing through the eye of a needle) as something less stark: '[Jesus] clearly asserts that it will be more difficult for the rich man to enter the kingdom of heaven than for a camel to pass through the eye of a needle'.[94] Bryant likewise recognised the importance of working-class education, which has a long history in the radical tradition, but this too was ultimately believed to be about relative fairness. The 'Old Testament Wisdom tradition' and 'Jesus' own emphasis on teaching' meant that for Christian socialists 'the wider dissemination of knowledge and education' had previously left them 'to organise against unfair pay and working conditions'.[95] Notably, their educational interests are summarised with a vague generalisation. The Socialist Sunday School (founded in 1892) with its 'Socialist Ten Commandments' tried to 'both teach and build solidarity'.[96]

91. Bryant, 'Introduction', p. 19.
92. Bryant, 'Introduction', p. 22.
93. Bryant, 'Introduction', p. 18.
94. Bryant, 'Introduction', p. 22.
95. Bryant, 'Introduction', p. 20.
96. Bryant, 'Introduction', p. 21.

Within ten years of *Reclaiming the Ground*, Bryant had become a fairly conventional New Labour MP, even if on occasion there is a hint of the old radicalism. He voted 'very strongly' in favour of the Iraq War, 'very strongly' against an investigation into the Iraq War, 'strongly' for a stricter asylum system, and 'very strongly' for introducing ID cards, while still voting 'very strongly' for the removal of hereditary peers from the House of Lords and for a wholly elected House of Lords.[97] As the example of Bryant shows, the Radical Bible has not disappeared entirely from English political discourse, but it has had its sting removed from party politics and has been largely pushed out of Parliament (see Chapter 9). In Chapter 8 we will also look in more detail at how the rhetoric of the Radical Bible became absorbed into the Liberal Bible under Blair, particularly in his interventionist policies.

5. 'The Good Man Jesus'

We should finally turn to a recurring issue relating to the Radical Bible and the Liberal Bible which involves singling out Jesus as a particularly inspirational figure, typically misunderstood by the church, and even by the New Testament writers. This singling out of 'the good man Jesus' in distinction from his ecclesiastical interpretations has proven to be a notable way for certain atheists, or those generally hostile to anything associated with 'organised religion', to embrace the Bible in some form and has been used by figures as diverse as Pierre-Joseph Proudhon, Oscar Wilde, H.G. Wells, John Lennon, and Bill Hicks. To take a typical example, in *The Hitchhiker's Guide to the Galaxy*, the openly atheist Douglas Adams wrote about a girl in a café in Rickmansworth who realised how the world could be a decent place, echoing the views of a man who was nailed to a tree nearly two-thousand years earlier for advocating people being pleasant to each other for once. This rescuing or singling out of 'the good man Jesus' also has a long history which also relates to the tradition of Enlightenment and post-Enlightenment critical biblical scholarship and the quest for the (typically heroic) historical figure of Jesus.[98] Indeed, as Diarmaid MacCulloch wrote concerning (former Lib-Dem supporter) Philip Pullman and his novel with the relatively self-explanatory title, *The Good Man Jesus and the Scoundrel Christ* (2010), 'Pullman knows his biblical scholarship. Virtually everything in

97. Details are available at http://www.theyworkforyou.com/mp/chris_bryant/rhondda.

98. On nineteenth-century quests for the historical Jesus, see H. Moxnes, *Jesus and the Rise of Nationalism: A New Quest for the Nineteenth Century Historical Jesus* (London: I.B. Tauris, 2012).

his novella, except for the storyteller's brilliant restructuring of the tale as of two brothers, is foreshadowed in what Protestant professors have been saying in Tübingen and Berlin over the last two centuries.'[99] While Pullman was emphatic in claiming that the novel really was fiction, he did claim that 'I think my version is much closer to what Jesus would have said. The version in the Gospels is so different from what he said usually.'[100] Indeed, the Afterword to *The Good Man Jesus* tries to explain precisely this, as well as laying down a challenge to Christians.

There are also plenty of examples of Jesus as a positive figure in traditions which might otherwise be potentially hostile or indifferent to the Christian Bible. Jacob Taubes noted the long Jewish tradition of reclaiming Jesus: 'There's a literary corpus about Jesus, a nice guy, about the rabbi in Galilee, and about the Sermon on the Mount; it's all in the Talmud and so on…a sort of pride in this son of Israel. But when it comes to Paul, that's a borderline that's hard to cross.'[101] However, this was written in the context of his attempted reclamation of Paul for Judaism ('the Jewish study of Paul is in a very sad state', he claimed).[102] Taubes was himself anticipating the return of the radically political Paul singled out in Marxist philosophy and where both Jesus and Paul have received supreme compliments by way of analogy:

> I am not the first to risk the comparison that makes of him [Paul] a Lenin for whom Christ will have been the equivocal Marx.[103]

> Paul goes on to his true Leninist business, that of organizing the new party called the Christian community. Paul as a Leninist: was not Paul, like Lenin, the great 'institutionalizer,' and, as such, reviled by the partisans of 'original' Marxism-Christianity? Does not the Pauline temporality 'already, but not yet' also designate Lenin's situation in between two revolutions, between February and October 1917? Revolution is already behind us, the old regime is out, freedom is here – *but* the hard work still lies ahead.[104]

99.   D. MacCulloch, 'All Too Human', *Literary Review* (April 2010), http://www. literaryreview.co.uk/macculloch_04_10.html.

100.   C. Higgins, 'Philip Pullman creates a darker Christ in new assault on the church', *Guardian* (March 26, 2010).

101.   J. Taubes, *The Political Theology of Paul* (Stanford: Stanford University Press, 2004), p. 5.

102.   On Paul and contemporary Judaism, see D.R. Langton, *The Apostle Paul in the Jewish Imagination: A Study in Modern Jewish–Christian Relations* (Cambridge: Cambridge University Press, 2010).

103.   A. Badiou, *Saint Paul: The Foundation of Universalism* (Stanford: Stanford University Press, 2003), p. 2.

104.   S. Žižek, *The Puppet and the Dwarf: The Perverse Core of Christianity* (Cambridge, Mass.: MIT Press, 2003), p. 9.

Of course, singling out Jesus (or even Paul) is hardly restricted to atheistic, Marxist, or Jewish traditions, as the centrality of Jesus in Christian theology obviously implies. Variants of this singling out of Jesus are seemingly endless. Stephen Prothero was no doubt scratching the surface in his popular book, *American Jesus*, where he looked at different appropriations of Jesus in American culture (Jesus as rabbi, Jesus as enlightened sage, oriental Christs, the superstar, the fighter, and so on).[105] The cultural context of the Jesuses collected by Prothero is, unsurprisingly, American, but an American context which, for all its religious pluralism, retains a strongly Christian overlay and influence and also a context wherein religious pluralism, Christianity, and understandings of secularism play their role in shaping the culture and portrayals of Jesus.

As the mention of Pullman, Adams, and even Lennon already implies, the Radical Bible does not have a monopoly on singling out Jesus. The familiar theme of Jesus being tolerant, inclusive, and an all-round decent person equally lends itself as much to the Liberal Bible as it does to radical democracy, and the tensions and overlaps between the Liberal Jesus and the Radical Jesus emerge in some of the studies in this book. This means that when looking at the different Jesuses and different Bibles, there will need to be some concern with broader ideological tendencies at work in an individual or group. For instance, the scathing comments by Bill Hicks – the American comedian who found greater popularity in the UK – could, theoretically, come from someone sympathetic to the Liberal Jesus/Bible or the Radical Jesus/Bible. Hicks denounced Christians such as George Bush Sr and Pat Robertson for their support for nuclear armament and sarcastically commented that their Jesus would come back with an Uzi shooting Pilate and everyone else.[106] However, we know from Hicks' generally consistent ideas that this Jesus takes his place in a more politically radical tradition which, at least in terms of American foreign policy, is broadly in line with Chomsky's critiques and, more generally, is hostile to and critical of anyone in power (whether Republican or Democrat, church or media), wealthy comedians advertising whatever products, and any possible government or corporate conspiracies. But Jesus, like Hicks, figures as part of the resistance that has to be killed (Hicks sometimes performed mock-executions of himself at the end of his act). Hicks' Jesus was

105. S. Prothero, *American Jesus: How the Son of God Became a National Icon* (New York: Farrar, Straus & Giroux, 2003).

106. B. Hicks, 'Relentless' (Centaur Theatre, Montreal, 1991), http://www.youtube.com/watch?v=JIA5dL7VJxg.

brought into such an overall system of thought. In a performance at the Oxford Playhouse in 1992, he made some of his more well-known claims about the world being 'just a ride'. Hicks' visionary figures who proclaimed that 'it's just a ride' have been murdered, in contrast with Reagan who was merely wounded and the 'demons' that run riot on the planet. Jesus takes his place among Martin Luther King, Gandhi, and Malcolm X as Hicks' 'good guys'.[107] A variant addition given at the Dominion Theatre in London only heightened the radical Jesus (and, of course, Gandhi, Malcolm X, etc.). Hicks did this by emphasising a choice between 'fear and love', between those who want weapons and insularity and those who want a better ride, that is, a world where money is not relentlessly spent on defence but on education, food, and clothing for all humanity, who could then be released to explore inner and outer space.[108] This version did not mention Jesus by name but when pieced together we can see Jesus take place in a system of radical political thought. It may be an obvious point, but it is still worth stressing that we sometimes have to do some detective work to establish the ideological position underpinning the understanding of Jesus. This point is particularly important when dealing with figures in the Labour Party where both the language of radicalism and liberalism has been historically present.[109]

6. Concluding Remarks

Given these summaries of the Cultural Bible, Liberal Bible, Neoliberal Bible, and Radical Bible, as well as the ongoing significance of a singling out of Jesus, it may be less surprising than might be thought that

---

107.   B. Hicks, 'Shock and Awe' (Oxford Playhouse, November 11, 1992), http://www.youtube.com/watch?v=UTwgooaYC3U.

108.   B. Hicks, 'Revelations' (Dominion Theatre, London, September 14, 1993), http://www.youtube.com/watch?v=w7bcxBf2vK4.

109.   To confuse matters further, Labour MP Stephen Pound advocated an early day motion to the House of Commons on the ten-year anniversary of Bill Hicks' death. It read: 'That this House notes with sadness the 10th anniversary of the death of Bill Hicks, on 26th February 1994, at the age of 33; recalls his assertion that his words would be a bullet in the heart of consumerism, capitalism and the American Dream; and mourns the passing of one of the few people who may be mentioned as being worth of inclusion with Lenny Bruce in any list of unflinching and painfully honest political philosophers' ('Early day motion 678 [2003–4]: Anniversary of the Death of Bill Hicks', http://www.parliament.uk/edm/2003-04/678). This did not stop Pound voting in favour of the Iraq war which the Chomsky-inspired Hicks would have bitterly opposed, as he did the first Gulf War. See http://www.theyworkforyou.com/mp/10484/stephen_pound/ealing_north.

the Bible has been used in contemporary English politics during a period of 'believing without belonging' and apparent 'secularisation'. Of course, using the above labels for understanding what the Bible 'really means' does not mean that a range of readers with a range of different interests are not in existence. Some might like rediscovering the Otherness of the ancient world, some might rely on biblical texts for converting non-believers to an opening of the heart, and some may know the whole lot off by heart. Some readers may laugh at or even hate the Bible, believing that using the Bible for politics is entirely anachronistic, though such readings might complement the assumptions outlined above (e.g. if the Bible is not compatible with liberalism then it should ideally be removed from any political debate working with liberal assumptions).[110] Some readers may enthusiastically see the Bible as profoundly anti-liberal, anti-Marxist, and supportive of theocratic political thinking, though it is difficult to see how this might influence mainstream party-politics.[111] Nor is any of the above meant to imply that the Liberal Bible, Cultural Bible, Neoliberal Bible, or Radical Bible are unchanging traditions sealed off from one another or any other ways of reading the Bible. Rather, the emphasis is on how these understandings are major trends and dictate some of the ways in which the Bible is understood, whether users know it or not or like it or not.

What we are also dealing with in this book is a localised and histori-cally situated example of what Roland Boer described as 'the tension between reaction and revolution that one so often finds with Christian-ity', which, he added, is also found in the Bible and its various uses.[112] This sort of tension, as Filby has shown, was being debated in overlap-ping contexts of Church and State, just prior to and during Thatcher's premiership.[113] The rest of this book is in many ways about the decline of the Radical Bible in parliamentary politics and the victory of (a modified form of) Thatcher's re-reading of the Liberal Bible tradition, and the normalisation of (a modified form of) Thatcherism more generally. The

110. See further Sherwood, 'On the Genesis between the Bible and Rights'.

111. John Milbank and Phillip Blond, along with the associated Radical Orthodoxy and Red Toryism, come to mind and might even challenge the idea that such theocratic thinking cannot influence party-politics. However, it is striking that whenever Milbank, Blond, and associated Red Tory and Radical Orthodox thinkers engage in party-political debate and in the mainstream media, they invariably conform to standard mainstream political rhetoric and drop much of their theologi-cal language. For discussion with bibliography see Crossley, *Jesus in an Age of Neoliberalism*, pp. 189-209.

112. Boer, 'Apocalyptic and Apocalypticism', pp. 45, 50.

113. Filby, 'God and Mrs Thatcher', pp. 29-45.

following two chapters will look at how the Bible features in political discourses which paved the way for the Thatcher revolution. After Thatcher, we will then turn to how her ideas were becoming embedded in wider culture as well as in mainstream political power. The book will then finish by looking at the place of the Radical Bible in political discourse and, briefly, at why any politician is using the Bible at all. But first we turn to events at the beginning of the period which help explain the fall of the Radical Bible as well as the seeds of its survival outside Parliament and against the backdrop of emerging Thatcherism and neoliberalism.

Part I

EXPERIENCING DEFEAT

Chapter 2

CHRISTOPHER HILL'S WORLD TURNED UPSIDE DOWN

1. The Problem of 1968

We have seen why 1968 is regarded as a watershed year in the more contemporary history of western radical thought. However, one of the seemingly curious features of the student-led radicalism of the late 1960s is the problem it posed for some western Marxists, particularly those of an ageing Marxist intellectual establishment. It might be thought that such figures would have been among the most enthusiastic supporters of the uprisings (as plenty of Marxists indeed were), particularly given that the American involvement in Vietnam was the most high profile point of unity across the Left, though even here there were notable exceptions such as Max Horkheimer. On the one hand, 1968 did overtly challenge dominant notions of power but, on the other, might not this radicalism be merely romantic and hopelessly ineffective? Or worse still, was it complicit or even potentially repressive?

Arguably the most famous example of Marxist establishment ambivalence was Theodor Adorno.[1] The final years and months of Adorno's life – at this point he was now denounced as a 'classicist' – involved some very personal tensions with the West German student movement. Infamous moments included the police being called in when the Institute for Social Research was occupied or when three women, with naked breasts on full show, theatrically confronted him with flower petals during one of his lectures. Some even blamed the student conflict for causing Adorno's fatal heart attack in 1969. This conflict was in part a debate over theory and practice but also the return of an old challenge from the radical Left. In 'Resignation' – an essay of defiance against his

---

1. For overviews and discussion see e.g. L. Jäger, *Adorno: A Political Biography* (New Haven: Yale University Press, 2004), pp. 192-208; S. Müller-Doohm, *Adorno: An Intellectual Biography* (Cambridge: Polity Press, 2005); D. Claussen, *Theodor W. Adorno: One Last Genius* (Cambridge, Mass.: Belknap Press of Harvard University Press, 2008), e.g. pp. 1-2, 10, 201, 332-39.

perception of practice-dominated radicalism – Adorno laid some blame at the feet of a resurgent anarchism: 'Its return is that of a ghost. The impatience with theory that manifests itself in its return does not advance thought beyond itself.'[2]

The British Marxist establishment was no exception to this ambivalence or even hostility. Eric Hobsbawm (1917–2012), a younger contemporary of Adorno, reacted in a number of ways to 1968, which included a fierce denunciation of anarchism that he saw as playing a prominent role in the upheavals. Hobsbawm claimed the main appeal of anarchism

> was emotional and not intellectual... Admirable but hopeless... [T]he monumental ineffectiveness of anarchism...for most people of my generation...determined our rejection of it... Spanish anarchism [was] a tragic farce... [A]narchism as a revolutionary movement has failed... [T]he revival of interest in anarchism today seems so unexpected, surprising and – if I am to speak frankly – unjustified... [A]narchism has no significant contribution to socialist theory to make.[3]

That the prominence of anarchism in 1968, alongside the emergence of a range of playful (as well as serious) radicalisms, had the potential to cause problems for the generation of Marxists radicalised in the 1930s should not be that surprising. Furthermore, anarchism has, of course, had a long history of an uncomfortable relationship with Marxism, particularly over issues concerning the dictatorship of the proletariat and the role of the state, and highlighted most famously in the spats between Bakunin and Marx. To make matters worse for Hobsbawm, his politics and historical method were coming under attack from an emerging public intellectual with anarcho-syndicalist sympathies who also published in an influential book for the radical Left. In 1969, Noam Chomsky – who was until this moment better known for his study of linguistics – published his first major book on international politics, *American Power and the New Mandarins*. Among Chomsky's criticisms of intellectuals was a sustained attack on establishment historians but which now included the Marxist Hobsbawm and his handling of Spanish anarchism three years prior in *New Left Review*:

2. T.W. Adorno, 'Resignation (1969)', in *Critical Models: Interventions and Catchwords* (New York: Columbia University Press, 2005), pp. 289-93 (292).

3. E. Hobsbawm, 'Reflections on Anarchism (1969)', in *Revolutionaries* (New York: New Press, 2001), pp. 97-108 (98-100, 105). For Hobsbawm's ambivalent attitudes towards the political impact of the 1960s and 1968, see e.g. Hobsbawm, 'Revolution and Sex' (1969) and 'May 1968' (1968), in *Revolutionaries*, pp. 256-60, 279-91; E. Hobsbawm, *Interesting Times: A Twentieth Century Life* (London: Abacus, 2002), pp. 246-62.

the Spanish Civil War is not only one of the critical events of modern history but one of the most intensively studied as well. Yet there are surprising gaps. During the months following the Franco insurrection in July 1936, a social revolution of unprecedented scope took place throughout much of Spain. It had no 'revolutionary vanguard' and appears to have been largely spontaneous, involving masses of urban and rural laborers in a radical transformation of social and economic conditions that persisted, with remarkable success, until it was crushed by force. This predominantly anarchist revolution and the massive social transformation to which it gave rise are treated, in recent historical studies, as a kind of aberration, a nuisance that stood in the way of successful prosecution of the war to save the bourgeois regime from the Franco rebellion. Many historians would probably agree with Eric Hobsbawm that the failure of social revolution in Spain 'was due to the anarchists', that anarchism was 'a disaster', a kind of 'moral gymnastics' with no 'concrete results', at best 'a profoundly moving spectacle for the student of popular religion.'[4]

Around this time, the pair would also clash on this issue at the informal 'Problems of Contemporary Socialism' seminar at LSE where the challenges raised by student radicalism in the late 1960s were being hammered out in what is remembered as an electrifying environment.[5]

Questions relating to the re-emergence of anarchism more generally were also a serious issue for the Marxist establishment in the 1960s, and one full of ambivalence and ambiguity when such questions about the role of the state and the dictatorship of the proletariat inevitably meant (whether implicitly or explicitly) questions about the role of the Soviet Union. By 1968, the image of revolutionary Russia had long been tarnished, particularly due to Khrushchev's revelations about Stalin and the Soviet invasion of Hungary in 1956, after which the Communist Party of Great Britain – previously the overwhelmingly dominant group on the radical British Left – had been haemorrhaging members.[6] But now a range of post-1956 alternatives were becoming available in the more fragmented British radical Left, such as various Trotskyite movements and the emergence of CND in 1958, in which E.P. Thompson would find a new political home after he left the Communist Party in 1956. There were also various publishing endeavours (albeit with a shared family

4. N. Chomsky, *American Power and the New Mandarins* (New York: Pantheon Books, 1969), pp. 76-77, referring to E. Hobsbawm, 'The Spanish Background', *New Left Review* 40 (1966), pp. 85-90.

5. J. Derbyshire, 'The NS Profile: Ralph Miliband', *New Statesman* (30 August, 2010).

6. On the story of the post-1956 decline of the CPGB see e.g. F. Beckett, *Enemy Within: The Rise and Fall of the British Communist Party* (London: John Murray, 1995), pp. 124-228.

tree), such as *The Reasoner*, *The New Reasoner*, the *Universities and Left Review*, and the *New Left Review*, reflecting in different ways a new range of Marxist and leftist perspectives, including the more theoretically inclined strands of the New Left and the rise of British cultural studies, both of which would gain greater momentum post-1968.[7]

Of course, with hindsight it is easy enough to be a critic of the Soviet Union, but in the nineteenth century Bakunin had actually managed to make a famous and unnerving prediction about Marxism. He claimed that 'the revolutionary State' will be 'very powerful and highly centralized', that this State will 'establish a single state bank which will finance all labour and national commerce', that 'regimented workingmen and women will sleep, wake, work, and live to the beat of a drum' where 'the shrewd and educated will be granted government privileges', and that the State 'will be even more despotic than the former State, although it calls itself a Peoples' State'.[8] And, after *Animal Farm* and 1956, Bakunin was proven right, was he not? And was he not proven *uncomfortably* right if you were a supporter of the Soviet Union who had lived through 1956? Was 1968 not a further warning to the old Marxist guard that their influence was waning?

This historic questioning of Marxism would pose a particular problem for a Marxist like Hobsbawm because of his personal investment in the Communist Party. Hobsbawm joined the Communist Party in 1936 after being converted as a teenager in Berlin in 1932 and, like many others radicalised in the 1930s, Communism seemed the only obvious choice in the face of the international ascendancy of fascism in Germany, Spain, and Italy, as well as the crisis of American capitalism and unemployment in Britain. Moreover, for this generation, the October Revolution was still a relatively fresh memory and the hope for world revolution was still very real. For the Jewish Hobsbawm, these concerns were more personal still as he came to England from central Europe after witnessing the fall of the Weimar Republic and the rise of German fascism. As he would later defend his post-1956 affiliation with the Communist Party, 'For someone who joined the movement where I came from and when I did, it was quite simply more difficult to break with the Party than for those who came later and from elsewhere'.[9] Moreover, Hobsbawm, like other

---

7. See further D. Dworkin, *Cultural Marxism in Postwar Britain: History, the New Left and the Origins of Cultural Studies* (Durham: Duke University Press, 1997).

8. M. Bakunin, *Selected Works* (New York: Alfred A. Knopf, 1972), pp. 283-84.

9. Hobsbawm, *Interesting Times*, p. 218. See further E. Hobsbawm with A. Polito, *The New Century* (London: Abacus, 2000), pp. 158-62.

Communist Party members and sympathisers, justified his ongoing membership by pointing out that there was a genuine fear that America would wipe out the USSR and that the USSR was the only serious hope for socialism and related movements in the decolonising world.[10] Siding with and using power for the perceived good of the cause, as well as a Popular Frontist mentality, would never leave Hobsbawm.[11]

Hobsbawm's politics are not to be removed from his historical writing: he was a committed Marxist in both areas, even if being a historian was most crucial for his self-identity (a recurring theme in his autobiography, *Interesting Times*).[12] This is well illustrated by his active participation in the Communist Party Historians' Group (1946–56), which also broke up after the drama of 1956.[13] The Communist Party Historians' Group would prove to be one of the most significant influences on British history writing. Its members (with lesser or greater commitment)

10. Hobsbawm, *Interesting Times*, p. 195.

11. Popular Frontism would mark Hobsbawm's political interests post-1968, including his involvement in Eurocommunism and the Kinnock-led Labour Party, where he was again highly critical of the Bennites as 'left sectarians' who would have left Labour as a 'marginalized socialist chapel' (Hobsbawm, *Interesting Times*, p. 272).While this was effectively the party line of the centre-left Labour Party of the 1980s (and Hobsbawm was famously known as Kinnock's favourite Marxist), it is an argument still framed more generally within a Marxist and Eurocommunist framework (pp. 263-81).

12. E.g. 'Fortunately, moving out of London had put me out of the range of London local branch work…for which I had no natural taste or temperament. From then on, in effect, I operated entirely in academic or intellectual groups… Why did we…find ourselves in the front line of opposition from the start? Essentially, because we had to confront the situation not only as private individuals and communist militants but in our professional capacity. The issue of what had been done under Stalin, and why it had been concealed, was literally a question about history' (*Interesting Times*, pp. 190, 207).

13. On the Communist Party Historians Group see e.g. E. Hobsbawm, 'Communist Party Historians' Group 1946–56', in M. Cornforth (ed.), *Rebels and their Causes: Essays in Honour of A.L. Morton* (London: Lawrence & Wishart, 1978), pp. 21-48; B. Schwarz, '"The People" in History: The Communist Party Historians Group 1946–56', in R. Johnson (ed.), *Making Histories: Studies in History Writing and Politics* (London: Hutchinson, 1982), pp. 44-95; H.J. Kaye, *British Marxist Historians* (Cambridge: Polity Press, 1984), pp. 10-18; D. Parker, 'The Communist Party Historians' Group', *Socialist History* 12 (1997), pp. 33-58; S. Ashman, 'Communist Party Historians' Group', in J. Rees (ed.), *Essays on Historical Materialism* (London: Bookmarks, 1998), pp. 145-59; M. Perry, *Marxism and History* (London: Palgrave Macmillan, 2002), pp. 88-94; D. Renton, 'Studying their Own Nation without Insularity? The British Marxist Historians Reconsidered', *Science and Society* 69 (2005), pp. 559-79.

included Hobsbawm, Dona Torr, Christopher Hill, E.P. Thompson, and Rodney Hilton, all of whom were or would become pioneering figures in 'history from below', and would be central in the founding of the now leading social history journal, *Past and Present*, in 1952. But there were certainly restrictions on discussions of the more ideologically sensitive areas of recent history, such as the British labour movement, the Soviet Union, and the Hitler–Stalin pact,[14] and consciously or unconsciously Stalinism left its mark on the work of the Group.[15] For instance, E.P. Thompson, who would become scathingly anti-Stalinist, had to remove 'a few Stalinist pieties' found in his 1955 book on William Morris for the second edition published in 1977, as well as explain that he previously held 'a somewhat reverent notion of Marxism as a received orthodoxy'.[16] Yet, for Hobsbawm, who was cynical in some respects about the USSR, a 'reverent notion of Marxism as received orthodoxy' never really left his historical work. Readers only need look at Hobsbawm's treatment of the Spanish Civil War and political radicalism in his more recent magnum opus, *Age of Extremes* (1994), to realise that not only does Chomsky's earlier assessment of Hobsbawm remain relevant (and more broadly applicable than to the Spanish Civil War alone) but that its ideological perspective, while not entirely uncritical, was still heavily influenced by Popular Frontism and would have resonated with that of an official Communist Party line in the 1930s, at least in the sense that it largely takes the side of a perceived pragmatism of the Communists prepared to seize power.[17]

14. Hobsbawm, 'Communist Party Historians' Group', pp. 30-31; Ashman, 'Communist Party Historians' Group', pp. 148-49; Perry, *Marxism and History*, pp. 91-93.

15. Kaye, *British Marxist Historians*, pp. 17-18; Dworkin, *Cultural Marxism in Postwar Britain*, pp. 24-25; Perry, *Marxism and History*, p. 92; Ashman, 'Communist Party Historians' Group', p. 148 ('They were all, whether they liked it or not, apologists for Stalinism').

16. E.P. Thompson, *William Morris: Romantic to Revolutionary* (2nd edn; London: Merlin Press, 1977), p. 769. See further Ashman, 'Communist Party Historians' Group', p. 148.

17. E. Hobsbawm, *The Age of Extremes: The Short Twentieth Century 1914–1991* (London: Abacus, 1994), e.g. pp. 74, 142-77, 188, where the non-official Communist Party radicals (anarchists, Trotskyites, POUM, etc.) are typically 'insignificant', 'eccentric', 'ultra-Left' etc. See D. Evans, 'Spain and the World: Aspects of the Spanish Revolution and Civil War (7)', *Radical History Network* (August 31, 2011), http://radicalhistorynetwork.blogspot.co.uk/2011/08/spain-and-world-aspects-of-spanish.html.

The background of those radicalised in the 1930s gives us some indication of why a figure like Hobsbawm would have been so troubled by the perception of anarchism emerging as a potential alternative to Marxism–Leninism. From the perspective of such committed Communists, anarchism might at best be seen as an irrelevance and at worst a crypto-liberal alternative with no serious understanding of, or taste for, power and which needed to be combated. But whether Hobsbawm liked it or not (not), it also raised some uncomfortable questions about the nature of Soviet power which could only have been made more uncomfortable still after the experience of 1956. We might add that the more playful attitudes spawned in 1960s radicalism (which, as we saw in the previous chapter, was to be a significant trend in the shift towards postmodernity) would have raised further questions for a Marxism where a tradition of seriousness and austerity played a significant role.

Such an intellectual tradition of a kind of conservative or traditionalist Marxism, combined with his damning diagnosis of popular culture, can certainly help us account for Adorno's reaction, and this is not unrelated to issues which emerge in the cultural history of British Communism. Stephen Woodhams could likewise write about how being a (pre-1956) Communist was 'a serious calling', that the Communist Party 'would support a self-nurtured respectability', that the image of the Communist was as a 'serious citizen', and of 'the 'necessity to maintain civility' whether in the home or in the street. The Communist Party was not, Woodhams argued, about 'being subversive and undermining values of decency'; on the contrary, it was 're-enforcing them all the stronger'. There are a range of complex reasons for the emphasis on seriousness and austerity but one was the need to maintain self-respect during long periods of unemployment and provide discipline and cohesion 'in a world where all around were apparently lost to the lure of transient pleasures'.[18] The semi-autobiographical recollections of Raphael Samuel give some insight into this 'lost world of British Communism':

> Hollywood films were rubbish, popular reading 'trash'... Dance halls, despite a certain Party recruitment, during the 1930s and 1940s, in the Musicians Union, were viewed with suspicion, as apeing the manners (and the costume) of the bourgeoisie. (At YCL socials we sang American union songs but never, in my experience, danced... For one thing – at least in the 1940s and 1950s – they would have been suspicious of 'trashy American music'... So far as its working-class membership was con-

18. S. Woodhams, *History in the Making: Raymond Williams, Edward Thompson and Radical Intellectuals 1936–1956* (London: Merlin Press, 2001), pp. 103-104, 106.

cerned, the Communist Party made its recruits among the respectable. The appeal was to the studious 'serious-minded young workers' and, subliminally at least, to the clean… Whereas the Labour Party attracted a sprinkling of working-class rogues, Communists were noted for their strictness – or what was sometimes referred to as 'clean living'. They eschewed 'foul' language – the 'effing' and 'blinding' of the 'politically illiterate'. Members who ran up debts – 'borrowing' from Party funds – were expelled as a matter of course. So were those who got into trouble with the police, unless it was for political reasons… The Communist Party functioned as a kind of workers' university, and not the least of the satisfactions which it offered was that of opening up a vast field for those with a thirst for knowledge – the 'serious-minded young workers' to whom it directed its recruiting appeals… The Party also provided an elementary schooling in public life, teaching its worker-recruits how to be methodical and organized… It diffused, if unevenly, a reverence for culture—'good' books, 'serious' music, 'logical' argument.[19]

Raphael's recollections are reflective of a more working class Communist Party experience but the emphasis on discipline, dedication, efficiency, seriousness, and even purposeful tedium comes through strongly in Hobsbawm's own recollections; as he concluded: 'Communist Parties were not for romantics'.[20] While some of this tradition would not be wholly incompatible, we should not underestimate the extent to which 1960s radicalism was as potentially shocking to those who grew up in, or were associated with, the social world of British Communism as it was to the conservative mainstream political establishment and to non-Marxist conservative social mores.

19. R. Samuel, *The Lost World of British Communism* (London: Verso, 2006), pp. 185-200. Marion Maddox drew my attention to this more derogatory perception of communism and socialism from Dorothy L. Sayers, *Clouds of Witness* (1925): 'You know, Peter, if you will haunt low places full of Russians and sucking Socialists taking themselves seriously, you ought to know better than to encourage them by running after them, however futile, and given to drinking coffee and writing poems with no shape to them, and generally ruining their nerves'.

20. Hobsbawm, *Interesting Times*, p. 133. See, e.g., pp. 132-32 for Hobsbawm's account of life in the Communist Party. Compare also Hobsbawm's attitude towards Raphael Samuel's rethinking of Marxism in the face of Stalinism (Hobsbawm, *Interesting Times*, pp. 212-13): 'With two generations of Jewish revolutionary Marxists from Eastern Europe behind him, he dreamed of replacing the Stalinist authoritarianism of the Party with a free-wheeling creative mobilization of political minds, and what better centre for doing so than a café?… [A] real Soho café, in which people could discuss theoretical issues, play chess, consume *strudel* and hold political meetings in a back room, as on the continent before innocence was lost… It was a scheme designed for disaster.'

Having said that, it is not as if a tradition of challenging the Communist Party line was entirely absent from those associated with the Communist Party Historians' Group. There was a degree of openness in the discussions. There were, for instance, disagreements between the Party leadership and the Historians' Group over the writing of the history of the Communist Party of Great Britain, with the leadership edging towards a glorious history of past victories, if indeed it should be written at all, whereas the Communist Party Historians' Group were drawn to the idea of a more critical history.[21] But it was the post-1956 generations of historians influenced by or involved with members of the Communist Party Historians' Group that would steer radical historians away from the Communist Party's dominance. Such younger figures would also embrace more libertarian aspects of the Left, most notably E.P. Thompson who effectively became the anti-Stalinist torchbearer for the post-1956 intellectual radical Left, as well as injecting a notable degree of agency, empathy, and humanism into Marxist history in his 1963 classic, *The Making of the English Working Class*. Indeed, Hobsbawm reflected on Thompson's landmark book, labelling it 'an erupting volcano of 848 pages...which captured young radical readers on both sides of the Atlantic overnight... Escaping from the cage of the old Party orthodoxy, it allowed him as well to join a collective debate with other hitherto isolated thinkers of the left old and new.'[22] Certainly influenced by the older generation of Marxist historians (particularly Dorothy and E.P. Thompson), Sheila Rowbotham would push radical history in different directions untainted by the Stalinist politics of her older contemporaries. Rowbotham's formative years of radicalism were the 1960s. In particular, it would be the 1960s' take on feminism, radical thought, counter-culture, and – tellingly – embrace of the re-emergence of anarchism that would leave their mark on her work. Additionally, Rowbotham had a much more internationalist approach to, and understanding of, history and culture than most of her older British radical contemporaries. But Rowbotham hardly represents a complete break with the past; her first book, *Women, Resistance and Revolution* (1972), shows an interest not only in revolutionary women but also the Bible, particularly in seventeenth-century England,[23] a familiar haunt of the older generation of radical historians.

---

21. Hobsbawm, *Interesting Times*, pp. 207-209.

22. Hobsbawm, *Interesting Times*, pp. 214-15.

23. S. Rowbotham, *Women, Resistance and Revolution* (London: Penguin Books, 1972), pp. 15-34.

Some of the older generation of Marxist historians would come to regret not paying sufficient attention to gender and the role of women in history and historical change, even though they were writing prolifically as Rowbotham was starting to publish.[24] And one such figure who found himself in the midst of all the controversies and contradictions of post-war Marxist history – and who was also writing extensively about the importance of the Bible in seventeenth-century radical thought at the same time as Rowbotham – was one of the most prominent of all the historians radicalised in the 1930s: Christopher Hill.

2. Christopher Hill

Christopher Hill (1912–2003) is arguably still the most famous name in the study of seventeenth-century English history and was one of the more high profile figures among the British and English Marxists. In many ways, Hill embodied the tensions surrounding 1968 for those radicalised in the 1930s. On the one hand, Hill and Bridget Sutton (his second wife) were said to have 'embraced the counter-culture of the sixties and celebrated the 1650s as a sister decade of free love and free thought'.[25] On the other hand, the radicalism of 1968 posed intellectual problems for Hill. As Penelope Corfield put it:

> Hill was by no means an uncritical advocate of 'let-it-all-hang-out' alternative culture, which differed diametrically from his own reserve. Nor was he ever anything other than sceptical when faced with euphoric claims in 1968–9 that either 'flower power' and/or student unrest were about to topple international capitalism. He knew much too much about the resilience of established power-structures to believe that.[26]

These tensions were deeply entrenched in Hill's upbringing and major life choices. Hill's background was certainly one of dissent. In addition to becoming a Marxist and Communist Party member in the 1930s, Hill was, like others in the Communist Party Historians' Group and the Communist Party Group at Oxford and Balliol, from a Nonconformist

---

24. See Dworkin, *Cultural Marxism in Postwar Britain*, pp. 198-202, for the criticisms levelled at Hobsbawm's reaction to, and engagement with, feminism and gender and the reception of Thompson's *Making of the English Working Class* in socialist feminist historiography.

25. T. Hunt, 'Back when it mattered', *Guardian* (March 5, 2003).

26. P.J. Corfield, '"We are All One in the Eyes of the Lord": Christopher Hill and the Historical Meanings of Radical Religion', *History Workshop Journal* 58 (2004), pp. 111-27 (122).

background, even if some members were 'culturally' rather than 'religiously' so. As Rodney Hilton recalled, 'I think that many had a strong Nonconformist upbringing, or (as in my case) deliberately irreligious, though with all the cultural attributes of Nonconformity. In fact it was not difficult for people with this sort of background to become Communists.'[27] Although Hill would become a sceptic, his family had deep Methodist roots and he would never fully lose his attachment to this background: 'he was not militantly anti-religious... Hill never shed his nonconformist conscience, which, in a liberalized and secularized form, governed his personal moral code.'[28] Yet this same politically dissenting background could be culturally conservative. While not quite the working class Communist households and workers' groups described by Raphael Samuel, Samuel Beer still recalled Hill's father in the following manner: 'our rating of Mr. Hill was high: I would call him a strict, but genial Puritan. The strictness was fairly severe, even for those days: no drinking and no smoking – and no evidence, e.g. on the breath, of having indulged in either.'[29] Tensions or compromises between liberal, bohemian, and conservative morality would play out throughout Christopher Hill's life; Hill and Bridget Sutton may have embraced the aspects of 1960s counter-culture but 'he was no fan of the drugs culture'.[30]

Like Hobsbawm, Hill's Marxism was firmly rooted in the political and economic situation of the 1930s ('slump, dreadful unemployment, danger of World War II, apparent successes of the USSR – the usual things'). Hill recalled that the dramatic events and horrors may have since become too familiar but that they had previously come as 'a terrible shock to middle-class English children brought up to assume that even if England was just not still top nation, still it was stable and secure' and that 'the bottom fell out of our universe in 1931, the year I went to Balliol'. Marxism for Hill and others appeared to make 'better

---

27. R. Hilton, 'Christopher Hill: Some Reminiscences', in D. Pennington and K. Thomas (eds.), *Puritans and Revolutionaries: Essays in Seventeenth-Century History Presented to Christopher Hill* (Oxford: Oxford University Press, 1978), pp. 6-10 (7).

28. Corfield, 'Christopher Hill', p. 114.

29. S.H. Beer, 'Christopher Hill: Some Reminiscences', in Pennington and Thomas (eds.), *Puritans and Revolutionaries*, pp. 1-4 (4). Compare also the comments (pp. 1-2) on the student Hill: 'I remember V.H. Galbraith, a tremendous admirer, reciting Hill's exploits of the previous day on the rugger field... The Spring of 1934 was glorious... For in spite of his gaiety there was no frivolity in Hill. He spent most of his time not in politics or womanizing or chit-chat, but working.'

30. Corfield, 'Christopher Hill', p. 114. On the general tensions, see further pp. 113-15.

sense of the world situation than anything else just as it seemed to make better sense of seventeenth-century English history'.[31] And so it happened that he joined the Communist Party in 1934. The importance of the USSR in the development of Hill's Marxism cannot be underestimated (he visited in the 1930s), and there have even been suggestions that Hill was a Soviet spy in the 1940s, though he did a poor job in hiding his sympathies if this were the case.[32] By the time of Stalin's death in 1953, he was, as a loyal Communist Party member, a Stalinist and orthodox Leninist. In 1947 Hill even published *Lenin and the Russian Revolution* for the popular Teach Yourself History series which effectively repeated the official Party line, much to the bemusement of the series editor A.L. Rowse. In this book, the treatment of Lenin was hagiographical, the continuity and collaboration between Lenin and Stalin emphasised,[33] and virtually all references to Trotsky were (therefore) implicitly or explicitly negative.[34] One example may give something of the flavour of the book: 'Generalissimo Stalin likes to be called Lenin's disciple. Even Trotsky... found it expedient to claim Lenin's authority for his views.'[35] More striking still, in 1953 Hill would write that Stalin was 'a very great and penetrating thinker... [A]ll countries will always be deeply in his debt.'[36] Little surprise, perhaps, that Hill and Hobsbawm, along with Robert Browning and A.L. Morton, would be the distinguished guests of the Soviet Academy of Sciences, with whom they

31. Hill interviewed and quoted in Kaye, *British Marxist Historians*, p. 102.

32. I. Cobain, 'Was Oxford's most famous Marxist a Soviet mole?', *Times* (March 5, 2003); O. Bowcott, 'Outcry as historian labelled a Soviet spy', *Guardian* (March 6, 2003); F. Mount, 'Stalin's ghost sits too easily among us', *Sunday Times* (March 9, 2003). Letters by John Saville and David Renton were published in the *Guardian* (March 10, 2003) defending Hill as an 'out' Communist at the time. The letters are available at http://www.guardian.co.uk/theguardian/2003/mar/10/ guardianletters2. Hill's alleged spying even gets an entry in R.C.S. Trahair (ed.), *Encyclopedia of Cold War Espionage, Spies, and Secret Operations* (Westport, Ct.: Greenwood Press, 2004), pp. 116-18.

33. Hill, *Lenin and the Russian Revolution*, e.g. pp. 90, 136.

34. For instance, we read typical phrases such as: Lenin, 'unlike Trotsky' was 'always realistic' about world revolution; 'such a view exaggerates, I think, the importance of Trotsky in the party'; 'morally, the oratorical spell-binder Trotsky "was incapable standing against Lenin as a flea would be against an elephant", observed Bruce Lockhart'; and '...the romantic supporters of Trotsky' (C. Hill, *Lenin and the Russian Revolution* [London: Hodder & Stoughton, 1947], pp. 157, 196, 220-21, 226).

35. Hill, *Lenin and the Russian Revolution*, p. 216.

36. C. Hill, 'Stalin and the Science of History', *Modern Quarterly* 8 (1953), pp. 198-212 (209).

would collaborate in the USSR during the Christmas break of 1954–55.[37] To this general background, 1968 would pose more of those tricky questions.

Unlike Hobsbawm, however, Hill would leave the Communist Party in 1957 after battling for greater Party democracy against the backdrop of Khrushchev and Hungary in 1956. While he would certainly come to regret his 'Stalinist pieties' (to use E.P. Thompson's phrase), he did not move towards the right, he would not give up his Marxism, and he continued to defend Marxist history against charges of decline and irrelevancy in his later career.[38] Furthermore, he regarded the discussions during the Communist Party Historians' Group years (1946–56) as 'much the greatest stimulus I have ever known'.[39] Nostalgia for a lost Communist past is found among other close associates who did not follow Hobsbawm and remain within the Communist Party fold. For example, his former associate in the Communist Party Historians' Group who left the Communist Party in 1956, Raphael Samuel, would claim: 'there was the "unity of theory and practice" which completely identified Marxism with the progress of Communism (even now, thirty years after leaving the Party, I still find it difficult to take the idea of non-Party Marxism seriously).'[40]

37. Hobsbawm, *Interesting Times*, pp. 197-200.

38. Corfield, 'Christopher Hill', pp. 118, 123. On Hill's embarrassment at his Stalinism see Dworkin, *Cultural Marxism in Postwar Britain*, p. 266, who interviewed Hill in 1984: 'When interviewing Hill, I remarked that I was embarrassed to bring up this essay. Hill responded that he should be embarrassed, not me.' Compare the language towards the end of Hill's career: 'Russian revolutionaries worried about Bonapartism, military dictatorship, and did not notice Stalin creeping up from within' (C. Hill, *The English Bible and the Seventeenth Century Revolution* [London: Penguin Books, 1993], p. 8). This is why contextualising Hill's post-1956 work in the context of a dedicated Stalinism is not correct. With not untypical certainty of his own rightness, Ferdinand Mount wrongly implied that Hill was a lifetime devotee of Stalin: 'Here in Britain it is a pity that Stalin's most devoted admirer, Christopher Hill, the Marxist historian and former master of Balliol college, Oxford, should have died' (Mount, 'Stalin's ghost'). As this chapter hopefully shows, while there was certainly continuity in Hill's work pre-and post-1956, works such as *The World Turned Upside Down* are better contextualised in terms of Hill (and other Marxists) coming to terms with Stalinism and engaging with 1960s radicalism.

39. Kaye, *British Marxist Historians*, p. 102. Cf. Dworkin, *Cultural Marxism in Postwar Britain*, p. 25.

40. Samuel, *Lost World of British Communism*, p. 94. Cf. Hobsbawm, *Interesting Times*, p. 206: 'Wherever our political future was to take us – and even those who left or were expelled from the Party overwhelmingly remained on the left – all of us lived through the crisis of 1956 as convinced communists'.

But there is another twist to Hill's story. We should not forget that Hill was the only one of his generation of Communist historians to gain an Oxbridge position, and he was even Master of Balliol College, Oxford University, from 1965 until his retirement in 1978. While the general consistency of Hill's ideas over his career supports the argument that we should not make a stark distinction between the Hill before and the Hill after he became Master of Balliol, the importance of this position in relation to 1960s radicalism should not be underestimated. As a former pupil and Fellow of Balliol, Maurice Keen recalled, a decade after 1968:

> Very few of those who elected Christopher to Master in February 1965 can have foreseen 1968, the year of student revolution. That year and what has happened since then have made sure that the headship of an Oxbridge College must carry with it strain, difficulty, and immersion in controversy. For Christopher Hill the problems must have been much harder than for almost anyone else. On the one hand his deep-seated views, feelings, and loyalties must have drawn him strongly toward the radical side, graduate and undergraduate; on the other the office of Master in itself has put him in the 'establishment' that radicals would wish to undo; and he has had a college and governing body to preside over in which every shade of opinion, to right or left, has had passionate and engaged partisans. His part has been one that could not be played without becoming involved in uncomfortable debate or without incurring harsh criticism from one quarter or another.[41]

Hill would face criticisms for being part of a leftist establishment[42] which were not wholly unjustified, irrespective of whether Hill intended such a thing. We see, for instance, the tensions between radicalism and establishment Oxford at play in the reception of Hill (though stemming from Hill's own sentiments), notably in the obituaries after his death in 2003. While hardly downplaying the Marxist Hill, some of the more establishment writers could still claim him as one of their own. Tristram Hunt (a Cambridge-trained historian and now Labour Party MP for

---

41. M. Keen, 'Christopher Hill: Some Reminiscences', in Pennington and Thomas (eds.), *Puritans and Revolutionaries*, pp. 17-21 (19-20). Similar comments are found elsewhere in Keen's recollections (p. 18): 'One thing about those parties [at Balliol] puzzled me, though. If one took a pint glass before one's third year one would be chided. I have never understood why so committed an egalitarian as Christopher should have given the impression of caring about such a curious status symbol. As Hugh Stretton, 'Christopher Hill: Some Reminiscences', in Pennington and Thomas (eds.), *Puritans and Revolutionaries*, pp. 10-17 (15), put it: 'Some issues were intrinsically difficult for the Left. They were against privilege – but they were employed in Oxford.'

42. Corfield, 'Christopher Hill', p. 116.

Stoke-on-Trent Central) pointed out that Hill scored an apparently 'famous' winning try in an intercollegiate rugby tournament nicknamed 'Cuppers', a sure sign that Hill was also 'a college man' according to an anonymous obituary in the *Telegraph* no less.[43] This intra-Oxbridge language shows how enshrined Hill's memory had become in the sort of event unlikely to resonate much with those outside, much less in the world of political radicalism, at least as we might conceive of it today.

So how does a figure such as Hill deal with something like 1968 and events which he should both endorse and oppose at the same time? The most obvious way this might have been done (consciously or unconsciously) was through his history writing. Hill was not only a prolific writer, he was a prolific writer of *revolutionary* English history. For all the nuances and qualifications, throughout his career Hill would argue that seventeenth-century England saw a revolution which should be deemed as significant as those in France and Russia. In fact, Hill claimed that there were two revolutions. The successful revolution was bourgeois in its consequences in that, with the power of the Crown and Church tamed by Parliament, it created a state ready for capitalist development and an international empire. The unsuccessful revolution was more radically democratic in its nature and, Hill suggested, generated ideas from proto-Communism and free love to questioning ideas about a creator God and the existence of Hell. While the support of the radical revolution was important for the bourgeois revolution, and, Hill argued, for regicide, once power was consolidated it then had to be suppressed.

The radical revolution was dealt with in detail in Hill's most famous and popular book, *The World Turned Upside Down*.[44] Published in 1972 (the same year as Rowbotham's *Women, Resistance and Revolution*), *The World Turned Upside Down* was a book clearly influenced by 1968 and 1960's iconoclastic youth culture.[45] This book looked at those typically pushed by scholars to the 'lunatic fringe',[46] from various radical individuals such as Gerrard Winstanley, Abiezer Coppe, James Nayler,

43. Hunt, 'Back when it mattered'; Anonymous, 'Obituary: Christopher Hill', *Telegraph* (27 February 2003).

44. C. Hill, *The World Turned Upside Down: Radical Ideas during the English Revolution* (London: Penguin, 1972).

45. J.C. Davis, *Fear, Myth and History: The Ranters and the Historians* (Cambridge: Cambridge University Press, 1986), pp. 132-34 (which ties these historic influences with the intellectual influence of Marcuse and Gramsci in the 1960s); Corfield, 'Christopher Hill', p. 122.

46. Cf. C. Hill, *A Nation of Change and Novelty: Radical Politics, Religion and Literature in Seventeenth-Century England* (London: Routledge, 1990), p. 212.

and the anonymous author of *Tyranipocrit Discovered* to various radical groups such as the Quakers, Diggers, Ranters, and, to a lesser extent,
Levellers. Page after page discusses antinomianism, hostility to wealth,
anticlericalism, antiroyalism, extension of democratic rights, land redistribution, class consciousness, idealism, utopianism, collectives, sexual
freedom, and so on. Radical sentiments, which could be as much about
the student-led radicalism of 1960s as the 1640s, penetrate almost every
page of *The World Turned Upside Down*. To take a random example
among many: 'The radicals, not unexpectedly, came from the younger
generation of those who had no aspirations to an official career... Part of
the ebullience I have been discussing springs from the youth of the
actors. Young men of ability have far more chance of coming top in a
revolution... It was a young man's world while it lasted.'[47]

But it is arguably the most famous chapter – 'Base Impudent Kisses' –
that is the most striking example for reading *The World Upside Down* in
relation to 1960s radicalism.[48] This chapter gives us stories such as that
of a woman who, in 1652, stripped naked during a church service and
shouted out, 'Welcome the resurrection!' However, for at least some of
the twenty-first-century readers of my book, there are less alien examples. In 'Base Impudent Kisses', Hill repeated phrases which would
hardly be out of place when discussing 1960s radicalism, such as 'sexual
revolution', 'sexual freedom', and 'free love'. It might be one thing to
discuss sexually liberated Ranters or naked Adamites but this sort of
language even gets used in the chapter's two subheadings with reference
to a certain group not conventionally associated with sexual frivolity:
'The Puritan Sexual Revolution' and 'Beyond the Puritan Sexual
Revolution'. Sometimes Hill would make the connection between the
past and the present perfectly clear: 'Unfortunately Ranter theology leapt
ahead of the technical possibilities of their society: equal sexual freedom
for both sexes had to wait for cheap and effective methods of birth
control'.[49] As Hill later reflected:

> As I was doing the research which culminated in *The World Turned
> Upside Down*, analogies between the cultural circumstances of the period I
> was describing and of the period in which I was writing forced themselves
> upon me. I found some Ranter ideas interesting in that connection – not
> least their detestation of holy conservative humbug, not extinct today. I
> admitted recently to having perhaps over-stressed Ranter libertinism...[50]

47. Hill, *World Turned Upside Down*, pp. 188, 366.
48. Hill, *World Turned Upside Down*, pp. 306-23.
49. Hill, *World Turned Upside Down*, p. 321.
50. Hill, *Nation of Change and Novelty*, p. 210.

3. Christopher Hill's Bible

Hill's Nonconformist background was never far from his writings and the importance of Puritanism in developing bourgeois thought (and the significance of religion more generally) is integral to his thinking on the seventeenth century. But it was *The World Turned Upside Down* that marked the intensification of Hill's interest in the role of the Bible in the seventeenth century, an unfortunately overlooked area in the reception and discussion of Hill which, for all the detailed and important work done on Hill, betrays the kind of intellectual 'Bible-blindness' that is hardly untypical in research across the humanities and social-sciences.[51] Not only does *The World Turned Upside Down* stand firmly in the tradition of the Radical Bible, it is arguably the pivotal book in both appreciating the modern developments of the Radical Bible and one of the most famous works *perpetuating* the contemporary Radical Bible.[52] David Renton's comments from a different context equally apply to the case of Hill's use of the Bible in *The World Turned Upside Down*: 'Hill's essay was so sympathetic to its sources that a reader might lose track of where Hill was speaking, and where the 17th century began'. Nor would this be an unusual reading of Hill's work.[53] The Bible would become even more significant in Hill's work and he also went on to write *The English Bible and the Seventeenth-Century Revolution* (1993), as well as starting to emphasise more and more the importance of Numbers 35.33 (cf. Judg. 9.24) in the regicide ('So ye shall not pollute the land wherein ye *are*: for blood it defileth the land: and the land cannot be cleansed of the blood that is shed therein, but by the blood of him that shed it').[54]

A striking feature of Hill's discussion of Bible-use for our purposes is his constant focus on the Radical Bible, *despite* being perfectly aware of other uses of the Bible. *The English Bible and the Seventeenth-Century Revolution* opens with a general statement of intent. 'My object in this book', Hill claimed, 'is to try to assess the part played by the Bible in

---

51. A notable exception is the biographical work of Penelope Corfield ('Christopher Hill') who knew Hill well and traced the importance of the Bible in Hill's early years and in his work, including *The World Turned Upside Down*. I owe the phrase 'Bible-blindness' to my colleague Hugh Pyper.

52. In academic biblical studies and theology in the UK, Hill's book had clearly had a profound influence on arguably the two leading socialist biblical scholars and theologians, Christopher Rowland and Timothy Gorringe.

53. Renton, 'British Marxist Historians', p. 564.

54. On the significance of Num. 35.33, Hill was influenced by P. Crawford, '"Charles Stuart, That Man of Blood"', *Journal of British Studies* (1977), pp. 41-61. See Hill, *English Bible*, pp. 324-31.

the lives of Englishmen and women during England's revolutionary seventeenth century'. He even notes that the ideas which divided the two parties in the civil war 'were all found in the Bible', before commenting, 'For my purposes the more traditional views of Catholics and high Anglicans seemed less relevant'.[55] The book also has two appendices, both overtly geared towards the Radical Bible: 'God the Highwayman' and 'A Note on Liberation Theology'.[56] To give some indication of Hill's overriding concern, we might turn towards the end of the book (page 397, to be precise), where he tellingly wrote: 'So far I have been discussing mainly radical uses of the Bible during the revolutionary decades. But there had always been more conservative readings.'[57] Aside from a comparatively minor discussion of conservative readings, and a few throwaway lines, we get little in the way of interpretation from 'the other side' in this 400-plus page book![58] In other words, Hill's political interests in the Bible are clear.

In *The World Turned Upside Down*, there are the expected themes from the tradition of the Radical Bible. We even see this emphasis on the Radical Bible in the framing of the book and in the structure of his arguments. From the outset there is a clear indication of just how significant a role the Bible will play in the book because the epigraph contains three biblical quotations (King James Version) concerning the world turned upside down:

> The Lord preserveth the strangers; he relieveth the fatherless and widow: but the way of the wicked he turneth upside down. (Ps. 146.9)

> The Lord maketh the earth…waste, and turneth it upside down… And it shall be, as with the people, so with the priest; as with the servant, so with his master; as with the maid, so with her mistress… The earth shall reel to and fro like a drunkard, and shall be removed like a cottage…the Lord shall punish the host of the high ones…and the kings of the earth upon the earth. (Isa. 24.1-2, 20-21)

---

55. Hill, *English Bible*, p. vii.
56. Hill, *English Bible*, pp. 443-51.
57. Hill, *English Bible*, p. 397.
58. A point picked up by, for instance, W. Lamont, 'Review: *The English Bible and the Seventeenth Century Revolution* by Christopher Hill', *English Historical Review* 108 (1993), pp. 979-81. In an interview on BBC Radio 4, Hill claimed that the Bible includes a 'great deal of anti-monarchical stuff' and 'a lot of democratic stuff', before adding with telling language, 'as well as stuff you can use on the other side'. The interview is with John Miller, 'Conversations with Historians', and available on http://www.youtube.com/watch?v=qkf_oYvJVXM. The interview took place in the 1990s as it mentions John Major's government.

> They came to Thessalonica…and Paul…reasoned with them out of the Scriptures… And some of them believed…of the chief women not a few. But the Jews which believed not, moved with envy, took unto them certain lewd fellows of the baser sort, and gathered a company, and set all the city on an uproar…crying, These that have turned the world upside down are come hither also. (Acts 17.1-6)

Corfield explains that Hill liked, and was inspired by, Acts 17.6 and the sentiment of the world turned upside down because of the subversive nature of truth and an egalitarianism available to the most lowly.[59] Such thinking ran throughout Hill's regular treatment of the Bible in *The World Turned Upside Down*. Typically we are introduced to a not-inherently radical general issue relating to the use of the Bible before a conclusion (often at the end of a paragraph) concerning something politically radical to such seventeenth-century uses.[60] The following sentence (concluding a paragraph) illustrates this well: 'The Bible should be used to illustrate truths of which one was already convinced: Winstanley was prepared to use Acts 4.32 to justify community of property'.[61] In another paragraph on relative cheapness and accessibility of the Bible, Hill soon shifted the emphasis. We are given the example of the Welshman Arise Evans, who came to London in 1629, and shown how his attitude towards the Bible 'changed in the decade before the Revolution'. The paragraph finishes first with a quotation from Evans ('I am as Paul of this time…he was a mechanic, a tent maker, Acts 18.3. I am a tailor') before finally concluding with a quotation from William Dell: 'Poor, illiterate, mechanic men turned the world upside down'.[62]

Conversely, note the following example where the final sentence is almost a throwaway line as more space is covered explaining the radical and progressive ideas that *really* underpinned strange acts such as prophecy:

> The idea that there was a secret traditional wisdom, Egyptian or Hermetic, to be wrung from nature, died very hard… Ordinary Bible-readers in the sixteenth and seventeenth centuries wanted to democratize these mysteries;

59. Corfield, 'Christopher Hill', p. 112.

60. There are, of course, the now expected references to prophets versus monarchs. E.g. 'The Reformation, for all its hostility to magic, had stimulated the spirit of prophecy… The abolition of mediators, the stress on the individual conscience, left God speaking direct to his elect… And God was no respecter of persons: he spoke to John Knox rather than Mary Queen of Scots… The common man, Luther, Calvin and Knox showed, could remake history if kings and princes did not' (Hill, *World Turned Upside Down*, p. 91, end of paragraph).

61. Hill, *World Turned Upside Down*, p. 144.

62. Hill, *World Turned Upside Down*, p. 94.

to abolish mumbo-jumbo men, whether priests, lawyers or scholars. They believed, on good protestant authority, that *anyone* could understand God's Word if he studied carefully enough, and if God's grace was in him. And then the Bible could be made to reveal the key to events in his own time.[63]

The idea of the popularist, millenarian Bible versus the elites and intellectuals is another common theme and again it was given a radical spin. For instance, in a discussion of millenarianism and predictions of the end, Hill made the following point: 'English translations and popular summaries of the works of Napier, Brightman, Mede and Alsted were published, all seeming to underpin the utopian hopes of less scholarly readers of the Bible'.[64] Of course the spirit-led and democratising enthusiasm described throughout *The World Turned Upside Down* was seen as providing a challenge to the traditional authority of the Bible. Hill certainly did not shy away from the ways in which the inner light can overrule the Bible but a theme emerges of the ongoing importance of Jesus who does not get so downplayed, a theme we saw was a significant part of the Radical Bible tradition. To take one example, when paraphrasing William Dell, Hill wrote, 'we can hear what Jesus Christ will say to our spirits and stick to it'.[65]

One of Hill's more sustained themes concerning the Bible and radicalism is his treatment of Antichrist (Hill drops the definite article), a theme developed elsewhere at book length.[66] While Hill traced the Antichrist myth through medieval Europe and the Reformation, it takes on anti-Anglican and anti-Royalist meaning in the English Civil War. By the 1650s, Hill argued that there was something of a millenarian consensus, namely the fall of Antichrist, possibly marking the beginning of the Second Coming. Note in the following example the implicit distinction between limited bourgeois-Puritan use and the ongoing radicalism of Hill's radical democratic revolution in words that – of course – end a paragraph: 'This underlay the confident energy, the utopian enthusiasm, of the Puritan preachers in the early 1640s. With what subsequently seemed to them naïve optimism, they called the common man to fight the Lord's battles against Antichrist.'[67] This was taken in

63. Hill, *World Turned Upside Down*, p. 93.
64. Hill, *World Turned Upside Down*, p. 96.
65. Hill, *World Turned Upside Down*, p. 370.
66. C. Hill, *Antichrist in Seventeenth-Century England* (London: Oxford University Press, 1971).
67. Hill, *World Turned Upside Down*, pp. 92-93.

a more radical direction in Hill's reading of Winstanley. Whereas the more radical Puritans may have seen bishops or the Church of England as antichristian, and the Civil War as a crusade against Antichrist, Winstanley, so Hill argued, 'again pushed this farther still, seeing property itself as antichristian, embodied in covetousness or self-love'.[68]

But one issue Hill the Marxist had to face is that of the logic of the democratization of the Bible and the guidance of the inner light leading to individualism, reflecting, of course, the tensions in Hill's reading of the English Revolution being both radical and bourgeois. Hill is aware of the importance of the role English translations of the Bible were playing. Of the Geneva Bible (which, thanks to its notes, could be used to justify the end of the divine right of monarchs) Hill points out that it

> was published in pocketable editions, so that men could study it in the privacy of their own homes, or could produce it in a church or an ale-house to knock down an argument with a text… [T]he reading of books is even less possible to control than the reading of manuscripts. The pocketable Geneva Bible could be privately digested and privately interpreted. Once the masses of the population were called into political activity, whether in sixteenth-century Germany or seventeenth-century England, some were bound to demand salvation for themselves.[69]

However, when discussing the radicals in *The World Turned Upside Down*, it is notable that Hill reined in any individualist-capitalist readings of radical interpretations, at least in their mid-seventeenth-century manifestations. For example, in his discussion of the Quakers and the ideal of the spirit of God within a believer being the only way to understand the Bible seriously, Hill acknowledged that 'we get an intense sense of the immediate personal relevance of the Bible's message' but qualifies this as a 'radical reply' to 'priests and scholars' who 'would have liked to keep interpretation of the Bible the monopoly of an educated elite…for seventeenth-century English radicals the religion of the heart was the answer to the pretensions of the academic divinity of ruling-class universities.'[70]

Hill was aware that private readers of the Bible could lead to 'mere absolute individualism' but as a good Marxist he rejected this by stressing the importance of the congregation as a place for interpretations to be 'tested and approved', thereby guaranteeing 'the validity of the interpretation for the given social unit' as a check on what he tellingly labels

68. Hill, *World Turned Upside Down*, pp. 148-49.
69. Hill, *World Turned Upside Down*, pp. 93, 162.
70. Hill, *World Turned Upside Down*, p. 95.

'individualist absurdities'.[71] Given the context of 1968, Hill also has his eye on another potential problem for a Marxist confronted by radical individualism in the source material – anarchism. While the language of anarchism was not developed to confront explicitly the anarchism re-emerging in the 1960s, there are certainly jarring similarities (and caricatures). Hill dealt with this particular problem in the same way as his treatment of other 'individualist absurdities'. So, for instance, 'acceptance of interpretations of the Bible by a congregation guarantees their relevance for the given group, [and] is a check against mere anarchist individualism'.[72] What is striking about Hill's phrase 'mere anarchist individualism' is that Hill also used the pejorative phrase 'mere absolute individualism', as we saw above and as we can see elsewhere.[73] It might be easy to dismiss this use of 'anarchist' as unrelated to more modern political uses (e.g. in the sense of 'chaotic') but Hill immediately follows this up with a contemporary comparison: 'Today, in our atomized society, the appeal to the individual conscience, to the integrity of the isolated artists, is ultimately anarchistic, the extreme of illusory withdrawal from society'.[74] The ghost of anarchism was also lurking closely behind the back of the Balliol Marxist.

There should be little doubt that the Radical Bible was central to Hill's understanding of his popular-democratic reading of one aspect of the English Revolution. But what is also striking is a sub-theme running throughout and which makes some sense in light of certain Marxist ambivalence towards 1968, that is, biblical interpretation as a *serious* work of scholarship and the Bible as a book of cultural importance, what was labelled in the previous chapter as the Cultural Bible. The importance of the Bible as a work of serious culture is clear enough in Hill's reading of the radicals and we should not forget that Hill was also a pioneer in bringing literary figures like Milton – whose work is one of the most famous examples of biblical interpretation in the western literary canon – into the arena of historical research. In some ways the Cultural Bible protects Hill's radicals against contemporary scholarly accusations of being on the 'lunatic fringe'.

There are several examples of this tradition of the Cultural Bible in *The World Turned Upside Down*. The importance of the symbolism of the garden for Winstanley can, for instance, be compared to that of

71. Hill, *World Turned Upside Down*, p. 95.
72. Hill, *World Turned Upside Down*, p. 372.
73. Hill, *World Turned Upside Down*, p. 371.
74. Hill, *World Turned Upside Down*, p. 372.

Milton or Marvel.[75] Hill also argued that one of the two dominant approaches to the Bible by the radicals was to hark back to the classical tradition, 'to use its stories as myths, to which each could give his own sense, a sense that need not consider the original meaning of the text – rather as Bacon used classical myths in The Wisdom of the Ancients'.[76] But more than anything, it is the other dominant approach of the radicals identified by Hill upon which he placed greatest emphasis: the radical as *scholarly and rational* biblical interpreter. Hand-in-hand with a denial of the infallibility of the Bible was the idea of close textual analysis which, Hill argued, anticipated later developments in academic biblical scholarship.[77] While Winstanley was deemed to hold this sort of position, Hill gives a whole chapter (Chapter 11) dedicated to the (ultimately) Quaker interpreter Samuel Fisher. Hill has seemingly throwaway lines such as 'The scholarly underpinning of this position' and, of Fisher's *The Rustics Alarm to the Rabbies* (1660), he comments that it 'is a remarkable work of popular Biblical criticism, based on real scholarship'.[78] Such comments on the intellectual integrity of Fisher's interpretation can be found alongside more dramatic judgments ('no more and no less than renaissance scholarly standards of textual criticism applied to the Bible').[79]

This emphasis on the scholarly nature of radical interpretations is perhaps an unsurprising judgment given Hill's lifelong career and interests. On the other hand, it might be surprising to a reader of *The World Turned Upside Down* given just how much stress Hill places on hostility towards scholars among the English radicals. Hill was aware of this tension and we have various arguments made about how shocking the exegesis of figures like Fisher must have been to 'University divines', effectively 'committing treason to the clerical caste, by using the apparatus of scholarship to expose the scholarly mysteries to public obloquy…'[80] In fact, we could make the argument that Hill's reading of radical scholarly biblical interpretation in the seventeenth century was akin to their political contribution to historical development: bourgeois biblical interpretation may have won in the long run but not without the mark of popular radical interpretation. Not only did Hill claim that the Bible 'would never be the same again' after the 'revolutionary decades',

---

75. Hill, *World Turned Upside Down*, p. 145. Hill would develop the importance of the Bible in English literature in *English Bible* (see below).
76. Hill, *World Turned Upside Down*, p. 261.
77. Hill, *World Turned Upside Down*, pp. 261-62
78. Hill, *World Turned Upside Down*, pp. 266-67.
79. Hill, *World Turned Upside Down*, p. 268.
80. Hill, *World Turned Upside Down*, p. 268.

but that a figure such as Fisher, like others, 'deserves greater recognition as a precursor of the English enlightenment'.[81] But what we may also see happening here in this understanding of biblical interpretation is Hill's own re-reading of 1968 either with protection from anything *too* anarchistic or *too* playful, or as it really should have been: radical, fairly serious, and scholarly.

4. Experiencing Defeat: 1640s–1660s, 1960s–1980s

But this is not the end of the story of Hill's use of the Bible in relation to 1960s radicalism. He again turned to the Bible in works ostensibly about revolutionary failure in the seventeenth century – such as *The Experience of Defeat* (1984) and *Milton and the English Revolution* (1978) – which have at least one eye on the post-1968 failures of the radical Left, as neoliberalism and Thatcherism were in the ascendancy and redefining the centre ground of political discourse. As discussed in Chapter 1, by the 1980s a significant strand of 1960s radicalism was morphing into the new political and economic establishment, or at least certain radicals were following that time-honoured pattern and becoming a more 'moderate' form of their former radical selves. The Radical Bible of Tony Benn and the Labour tradition was in decline as Kinnock's Labour Party was shortly to pass the baton to the media savvy and Thatcher-inspired New Labour. At the same time, Marxism – certainly intellectual Marxism in the West – was losing its influence and postmodernity, in part, channelled the playful radicalism away from the politically revolutionary to the culturally subversive, as popular culture was less about a radical revolution within a revolution and more about collapsing high and low culture into market forces or provocative art. From the perspective of radical (leftist) political transformation, 1968 had seemingly failed as a revolutionary force. In what follows, it should be clear that I am implicitly reading Hill as an indication of differences in radical attitudes (or at least Hill's) between the 1960s and the mid-1980s, as much as the differences in radical attitudes between the 1640s and 1660s (or 1668).

The Experience of Defeat (as with *Milton and the English Revolution* shortly before it) looked at ways in which people coped with the failure of the Revolution and how God might let this happen after such spectacular revolutionary successes against the backdrop of the Restoration and the rise of capitalism and the bourgeois Protestant work ethic.

---

81. Hill, *World Turned Upside Down*, p. 268. Cf. 'Modern Biblical scholarship has caught up with and justified them' (p. 375).

Or, as Hill ended his introductory chapter with a reference back to his most famous book, 'knowing that many good and intelligent people believed this may help us to understand the elation of the fight and the desolation of defeat when they realized that the world was not after all to be turned upside down... A climax of elation was reached in 1649, only to be followed by the slow betrayal of the 1650s. How could the God who willed 1649 also will 1660?'[82] If that did not set the tone, then the titles of the first two major chapters that follow (Chapters 2 and 3) should: 'The First Losers, 1649–1651' and 'The Second Losers, 1653–1660' (Chapter 9 has a telling subsection: 'Other Losers'). A comparison of endings illustrates both the theme of defeat and the idea that Hill's treatment of this theme tells us something about his present. *The World Turned Upside Down* ends in a positive fashion, even if qualified, with even the long-term future something worth celebrating: 'Our story ends by pointing towards the Age of Reason rather than the upside-down world. But the English Revolution's "teeming freedom" did liberate the imagination as Christ rose, however briefly, in sons and daughters'.[83] In contrast, *The Experience of Defeat* ends more ominously: 'In 1644 Milton saw England as "a nation of prophets". Where are they now?'[84]

Topic-wise, *The Experience of Defeat* tackles a number of issues related to the experience of revolutionary defeat. For instance, it looks at the origins of apostasy and the establishment of the state or official church with its lord bishops, sometimes traced back to Constantine or even to the time of the Apostles, and which may even last until the Second Coming. In *The Experience of Defeat*, the importance of focusing on long-term apostasy of the illegitimate church for those experiencing the failed revolution is part of the necessity of patiently waiting while the true, sometimes persecuted, church remains in exile, as it had been for centuries. For Hill's defeated radicals and rebels, the present post-Revolutionary setting was a time when thinkers had to come to terms with the wicked flourishing and even put God's justice on trial. *The Experience of Defeat* is certainly not blindly pessimistic and hope always remains a theme, even if this hope now looks to sometime in the more

82. C. Hill, *The Experience of Defeat: Milton and Some Contemporaries* (London: Faber & Faber, 1984), pp. 28, 307.

83. Hill, *World Turned Upside Down*, p. 414. Compare also Hill's *The English Revolution 1640* (London: Lawrence & Wishart, 1940), which stresses the importance of revolutionary struggles and the kinds of long-term influence such victories have even on those in power. This was published 300 years after the events described as the Second World War was under way.

84. Hill, *Experience of Defeat*, p. 328.

distant future, or rests on assurances of the idea of an Everlasting Gospel to always outlast the established church. And the ramifications for the present are not simply a message of vague promises but action too. Milton's experience of defeat, for instance, meant that he took his role as poet and prophet even more seriously. Yet Hill was aware that defeat really was defeat. He could argue that the universalistic tendencies in the revolutionary impulses and millenarianism of the 1640s and 1650s could be turned into English imperialism and that the combinations of revolution and restoration paved the way for eighteenth-century Whiggery, again with 'a sense of England's destiny to rule the world'.[85]

As this already shows, Hill again paid a great deal of attention to the centrality of the Radical Bible in this line of post-revolutionary disappointment and now with a subtly different spin to correspond to the new context. While there are discussions of Antichrist and ongoing rule of the wicked in the post-revolutionary era,[86] there are other discussions of figures now using biblical stories for understanding the Revolution as part of divine necessity, purification, and reform, and of how tolerance (sometimes on both sides) was now needed.[87] There were also discussions of the Radical Bible becoming the Bible for more elite or bourgeois use. Hill, for instance, looked at how sects could now place a 'heavy emphasis' on Bible reading and biblical literacy and exclude the illiterate, confirming 'that they had little appeal for the very poorest classes in the community'.[88]

The despair of failure in *The Experience of Defeat* can be compared with the same theme of defeat (and the accompanying use of the Bible) in *The World Turned Upside Down*, which is much more optimistic and written before Thatcherism and neoliberalism had so obviously started to take hold. For a start, the relevant section in *The World Turned Upside Down* carries a more positive subtitle – 'Defeat *and Survival*' (my italics) – than anything offered in *The Experience of Defeat*.[89] As this would suggest, defeat of the radical revolution could hardly be ignored even in Hill's most positive reading of the seventeenth century in *The World Turned Upside Down*. On this he is explicit:

85. Hill, *Experience of Defeat*, p. 325.
86. Hill, *Experience of Defeat*, e.g. pp. 91-95, 97.
87. Hill, *Experience of Defeat*, pp. 110-14, 262.
88. Hill, *Experience of Defeat*, pp. 291-92.
89. The chapter, 'Survivors', in *Experience of Defeat* (pp. 220-77) tends to focus, significantly, on those who were able to adapt and conform to the developing capitalist world and the restoration of state church power.

Property triumphed. Bishops returned to a state church, the universities and tithes survived. Women were put back into their place. The island of Great Bedlam became the island of Great Britain, God's confusion yielding place to man's order. Great Britain was the largest free-trade area in Europe, but one in which the commerce of ideas was again restricted. Milton's nation of prophets became a nation of shopkeepers.[90]

But Hill immediately added a qualification important for understanding defeat: 'Yet nothing ever wholly dies'. For Hill, just as the Lollard tradition survived and fed into the English Reformation, and the radical Reformation fed into the English Revolution, so the radical ideas – including those about God within, no heaven or hell, and antinomianism – would survive in the underground and influence more radical thinking in the following centuries. Hill suggested that echoes of revolutionary ideas from the mid-seventeenth century may be heard in a range of contexts from the American Revolution and English 'plebeian radicalism' of the 1790s through to Blake and the rise of biblical criticism (see above). But Hill tellingly added an even more relevant example for our purposes where developments in biblical interpretation are part of similar developments in 1960s love-making:

> Even more important, perhaps, for our generation, were their glimpses of a possible society which would transcend the property system, of a counter-culture which would reject the protestant ethic altogether... Again and again in this book we have noticed the seventeenth-century radicals shooting ahead of the technical possibilities of their age. Later Biblical scholarship and anthropology make better sense than they could of the mythological approach to the Bible; cheap and easily available contraceptive devices make better sense of free love.[91]

The radicals and the Radical Bible do not really leave the stage in the section on defeat in *The World Turned Upside Down*, whereas in *The Experience of Defeat* what we saw was adaptation to a post-revolutionary capitalist world, coping mechanisms, disappearance of the radical, and a future hope sometime in the not-so-imminent future. It is difficult not to see these different emphases telling us as much about differences in revolutionary experience between the 1960s and 1980s.

However, it is noticeable that in *The Experience of Defeat*, the Radical Bible does continue in the post-Revolutionary era and is combined, implicitly, with the Cultural Bible, in particular in its focus on Milton. As Hill was aware elsewhere, Milton could equally be labelled as part of

---

90. Hill, *World Turned Upside Down*, p. 379.
91. Hill, *World Turned Upside Down*, p. 383.

bourgeois elitism,[92] though in the instance of his discussion of Milton's Bible we find a more sustained optimism beginning to break through. Hill's Milton, like other *dramatis personae* in *The Experience of Defeat*, was certainly confident in the victory of good over evil, even if the reign of Christ was pushed into the distant future, and the events of the 1640s remained a 'necessary phase in which tyranny and superstition would be overcome...'[93] More specifically, Hill read Milton's use of Samson as a type of Christ in *Samson Agonistes*, initially with all the connotations of heroic failure but ultimately with the hope of a future divine intervention. Through Milton's favourite – Martin Bucer – Samson and Christ are but the *beginning* of the liberation of the people of God and God's purposes will finally come to pass when history reveals them.[94] Hill pointed out that the history revealed to Adam in *Paradise Lost* (Books XI and XII) may appear to be a series of defeats but, like *Samson Agonistes*, there is 'hope' and the poem provides a challenge 'in the present. Some time we must break out of the cycle of failure and defeat.'[95] Indeed, Hill argued that from *Comus* to *Samson Agonistes*, 'Milton depicted characters capable of standing alone in discouraging circumstances against the power of evil'.[96] As with *The World Turned Upside Down*, the Cultural Bible provides protection for the survival of, and hope for, the Radical Bible.

5. A Radical, *English* Bible

The events of 1968, and the experience of defeat that followed, were not the only contemporary echoes in Hill's work. In fact, Hill played his role in the development of *the* defining myth of contemporary English and British identity: the Second World War. In 1940, Hill published a blunt, popularising account of events 300 years earlier in *The English Revolution 1640*. Here there is a thoroughgoing interest in the reclaiming of a radical English tradition running throughout but several arguments have obvious contemporary implications and with only a few changes of words could be as much about the battle against fascism:

---

92. Cf. Hill, *World Turned Upside Down*, p. 400: 'Milton was a leisure-class intellectual, who never knew what it was to labour under a small taskmaster's eye. His contempt for the common people is explicit, at least from 1645 onwards. What I do suggest is that some of Milton's religious and political convictions...derive from the radical traditions of the Familiarist underground...'

93. Hill, *Experience of Defeat*, p. 319.

94. Hill, *Experience of Defeat*, pp. 312-13.

95. Hill, *Experience of Defeat*, p. 313.

96. Hill, *Experience of Defeat*, p. 327.

In time of war men must choose one side or the other... They were fighting a system... Nor was it a war of the rich only... Many of those who fought for Parliament were afterwards disappointed with the achievements of the revolution, felt they had been betrayed. But they were right to fight... The fact that the revolution might have gone further should never allow us to forget the heroism and faith and disciplined energy with which ordinary decent people responded when the Parliament's leaders freely and frankly appealed to them to support its cause... The important thing is that the social order was new and would not have been won without revolution... It is struggle that wins reforms, just as it is struggle that will retain the liberties which our ancestors won for us... That is the lesson of the seventeenth century for to-day.[97]

Indeed, Hill came close to admitting this dual frame of reference when he claimed that he wrote *The English Revolution 1640* as 'a very angry young man, believing he was going to be killed in a world war... [It] was written very fast and in a good deal of anger, [and] was intended to be my last will and testament.'[98]

While *The English Revolution 1640* was as much a rallying call for the English in 1940 as it was a popular work of history, we should not forget that it was partly a product of the Popular Front mentality against fascism. Conversely, while Hill's later use of the Bible may reflect a feeling of defeat on a global scale, we should not underestimate the importance of an experience of defeat, as well as the reclamation of a radical *English* tradition, in a specifically *English* context. Like E.P. Thompson's *The Making of the English Working Class* before him, Hill's focus is, of course, relentlessly *English*. After the war, Hill reflected in a programmatic element about the national element in Marxist history:

the Marxist conception of a bourgeois revolution restores the English revolution to its proper central place in the history of England; and that in itself helps to illuminate the whole course of English history down to the present. A correct appreciation of the seventeenth century revolution helps us to understand many otherwise unaccountable features of English life today – the survival of the monarchy and the House of Lords, English parliamentarism and 'the English genius for compromise', English nonconformity and the pacifist tradition in English radical movements. All these are due to specific characteristics like English bourgeois revolution... [T]he Marxist approach, and it alone, can restore to the English people part of their heritage of which they have been robbed. For every Frenchman 1789 has a deep significance; but for most Englishmen 1640 means nothing... [T]he absurd theory of the Puritan Revolution emphasizes the differences between our seventeenth century forefathers and present-day

97. Hill, *English Revolution 1640*, pp. 56-58, 80-82.
98. M. Kettle, 'Obituary: Christopher Hill', *Guardian* (February 26, 2003).

Englishmen, between their struggles and ours…all these and many more are figures of whom the progressive movement today, in England and elsewhere, may well be proud. In 1949 it was the Communist Party which recalled the revolutionary achievements of the English people 300 years earlier.[99]

It is not without reason that the place of Hill, Hilton, Hobsbawm, Morton, and Thompson in the Marxist canon is due not only to their role as historians but also to the perception that this is *Anglicized* Marxism and a rescuing of an English radical and popular tradition. Though, again, it should be stressed, this cannot be removed from internationalism nor from the Popular Frontism, or possibly even from a form of left-wing/Communist Party nationalism, none of which ever left these British Marxist historians radicalised in the 1930s.[100] Indeed, *The World Turned Upside Down* opens with the following words: 'Popular revolt was for many centuries an essential feature of the English tradition'.[101] We find similar important emphases when Hill, hardly for the first time, lets the dispassionate historian's guard down. It is of no minor significance that at the heart of this tradition for Hill was his great hero, Winstanley, who is effectively shown to be the dominant figure working innovatively with, but firmly within, a particularly English radical tradition.[102]

This stress on the 'Englishness' of the radical tradition comes through by way of contrast and uniqueness claimed by Hill's subjects, but also through Hill's analysis of them. On the one hand we get Hill looking at

99. C. Hill, 'Historians and the Rise of British Capitalism', *Science and Society* 14 (1950), pp. 307-21 (321).

100.   For further discussion see e.g. Kaye, *British Marxist Historians*, p. 120; Schwarz, '"The People" in History'; Dworkin, *Cultural Marxism in Postwar Britain*, p. 41; Ashman, 'Communist Party Historians' Group'; Renton, 'British Marxist Historians'; D. Renton, 'English Experiences: Was There a Problem of Nationalism in the Work of the British Marxist Historians' Group?', http://dkrenton.co.uk/research/cphg.html.

101.   Hill, *World Turned Upside Down*, p. 13.

102.   Such an emphasis runs throughout C. Hill, 'The Religion of Gerrard Winstanley (1978–1980)', in C. Hill, *Religion and Politics in 17th Century England* (Brighton: Harvester Press, 1986), pp. 185-252, e.g., 'He has been classed with Richard Coppin as one of the first English universalists… They may have been the first to make the positive point in print; but the heresy was attributed to Elizabethan Familiarists, and John Penry said in 1587 that such beliefs were popular… Anti-Trinitarianism has a long history in England, going back to the Lollards, the Marian martyrs, Familiarists and the last two heretics to be burned in England, in 1612… Winstanley's equation of the rights of Englishmen with the creation of liberties of all men, including the descendents of the free Anglo-Saxons, drew on the same traditions [of the Norman Yoke]' (pp. 194, 197, 219-20).

the acceptance of the idea of England as 'the chosen model to the world' from Winstanley to Milton.[103] On the other, Hill might analyse the genealogy of the English radical tradition, aware that historians may find sources or antecedents in 'Italian Neo-Platonists' and 'German Anabaptists' but stressing that 'what gives life and vigour to these ideas is the relevance which men felt that they had to the affairs of England in the revolutionary decades... [T]he form and shape [of their ideas] were their own, drawn from experience of their daily life in England.'[104] A notable point of comparison here might again be Hill's younger contemporary, Sheila Rowbotham, who as we saw above published *Women, Resistance and Revolution* in the same year (1972) as *The World Turned Upside Down*. Rowbotham was part of the general intellectual movement of radical British historians, influenced by figures such as Thompson and Hill, and likewise looked at seventeenth-century revolutionary thought (including reference to the role of the Bible) in a chapter called 'Impudent Lasses' (compare Hill's 'Base Impudent Kisses'). But Rowbotham does not focus attention on England alone and has a much more overtly internationalist perspective as she looks at women and revolutionary struggles from France to China, from America to Vietnam. By contrast, Hill's voluminous output looks positively provincial.

As might be expected, the Bible was integral to Hill's recovery of a radical English tradition. The 'revolution' of the English Bible is developed most thoroughly in Hill's later work, *The English Bible and the Seventeenth-Century Revolution*. By the seventeenth century, the vernacular Bible had become popularly available and in the hands of Hill this of course meant that it had become popular for lower class resistance. When 'Englishmen had to face totally unexpected revolutionary situations in the 1640s and 1650s', they could not turn to a Rousseau or a Marx but had to improvise with the only guidance they really knew: the Bible. By the time of the Revolution, Hill argued, the survival of the English Bible was a part of a deep-rooted tradition of lowly illegal gatherings in the time of Wyclif where participants could find the 'profoundly subversive messages' in the Bible which had ultimately been placed in the hands of the revolutionary English because of the martyrdoms of the subsequent English Reformation.[105] However, this Bible in English, he argued, was part of the development of the Protestant English *nation*.[106] And again, tied in with this radical and quasi-nationalistic

103. Hill, *Experience of Defeat*, p. 39.
104. Hill, *World Turned Upside Down*, pp. 363-64.
105. Hill, *English Bible*, pp. 8, 10.
106. Hill, *English Bible*, p. 8.

Bible, we again get the idea of a Cultural Bible. The availability of the English Bible was not only 'a great stimulus to learning to read' but was also 'a cultural revolution of unprecedented proportions, whose conse-quences are difficult to underestimate'.[107] Moreover, in *The English Bible and the Seventeenth-Century Revolution*, a book, as we saw, dedicated to the Bible and radical politics, there is a major section on 'The Bible and English Literature'. The radical edge was not lost but what Hill did additionally stress was that the 'century from the 1580s to the 1680s is the greatest age in English literature' and the importance of 'the Eng-lish Bible…in the transformation of English literature in this crucial period'.[108]

One distinctive area of historical research running throughout much of Hill's career, and one which brings all these strands of biblical interpretation together, is Hill's work on the 'Norman Yoke', that is, the idea that despotism is a foreign (Norman) import alien to the more benign Anglo-Saxon mentality.[109] Hill studied the history of this myth in radical English tradition and it can be understood, he argued, as a variant of the peasant myth of a golden age. In *The World Turned Upside Down* and elsewhere, one of the revolutionary seventeenth-century arguments, Hill would argue, was to blend the myths of the Norman Yoke and The Fall through a non-historical, 'poetic' reading of the Bible. In other words, radicals (notably Winstanley) could go beyond a call for the restoration of Anglo-Saxon laws and look to a pure state of humanity before the Fall where Adam and Eve, and therefore humanity, should have rights to the products of nature, whether on waste or common lands (see Gen. 1.28).[110] Further seventeenth-century biblical topics intertwined with the myth of the Norman Yoke and picked up by Hill were ideas that lawyers and priests represent the Norman army of Antichrist's laity and clergy respectively and that the Norman Yoke could be coded as 'Philistine'.[111] More broadly, the very development of a Bible *in English* was, for Hill, part of this resistance to the Norman Yoke. In line with a

107.   Hill, *English Bible*, p. 11.

108.   Hill, *English Bible*, p. 335, in the section on 'The Bible and English Literature', pp. 335-93.

109.   The classic essay is C. Hill, 'The Norman Yoke', in J. Saville (ed.), *Democracy and the Labour Movement* (London: Lawrence & Wishart, 1954), pp. 11-66.

110.   Hill, *World Turned Upside Down*, pp. 134, 145; C. Hill, *Liberty against the Law: Some Seventeenth Century Controversies* (London: Penguin Books, 1996), pp. 87-88.

111.   Hill, *World Turned Upside Down*, p. 271; Hill, *English Bible*, p. 32.

key emphasis in *The English Bible and the Seventeenth-Century Revolution*, the Bible is said to have played 'a large part moulding English nationalism' by 'asserting the supremacy of the English language in a society which from the eleventh to the fourteenth century had been dominated by French-speaking Normans'.[112]

However, in the grand scheme of English history, not to mention Hill's career, the English Bible is both a recovery of a radical English tradition and also its decline as the ramifications of the bourgeois revolution became embedded. We saw above how we might read Hill's use of the Radical Bible as part of Hill's bourgeois revolution: bourgeois biblical interpretation may have won out but the Radical Bible left its mark, especially in the rise of Enlightenment biblical criticism. For Hill, particularly as he experiences defeat, there is another angle to the dominance of the bourgeois Bible: *which* Bible would win the day. The radical revolution was about the recovery of a more radical *Geneva Bible* but, due in part to 'market forces', the state-authorised *King James Version* (Hill uses 'AV', the abbreviation for Authorized Version) would go on to be the dominant Bible. Hill argued that the AV was 'far cheaper to produce than the Geneva Bible with its copious notes, illustrations and other accessories' and, with the 'decline of theological politics, consequent on Parliament's victory in the civil war, failure to reach agreed solutions and the fading of the millenarian hope', the Geneva Bible's notes lost their revolutionary relevance and led to the conservative (and bourgeois) victory of the Authorized Version.[113]

As we will see further in Chapter 9, similar things could equally be said of the fate of the Radical Bible post-1968.

112. Hill, *English Bible*, p. 7.
113. Hill, *English Bible*, p. 435.

Chapter 3

THIS WAS ENGLAND:
THE SIMILITUDES OF ENOCH POWELL

1. Rivers of Blood

> If you want a nigger for a neighbour, vote Liberal or Labour ('unofficial'
> slogan during the 1964 General Election Campaign in Smethwick,
> Birmingham).[1]

It is easy to think about 1968 being a year of revolution and student
upheavals and the 1960s being a decade of dramatic cultural change. But
while there were hippies, flower-power, Vietnam protests, free-love,
recreational drugs, and Christopher Hill, capitalism was not the only
thing not overthrown. Even though the student upheavals would point to
a future of increasingly liberal attitudes and the advent of cultural
postmodernity, things were not-so-obvious on the ground, where reactions to change also manifested themselves in a number of cultural
forms. The 1960s may have brought the world the music of The Beatles,
The Rolling Stones, and Kinks but it also brought spectacular success
for Cliff Richard, *The Sound of Music*, Ken Dodd, and Engelbert
Humperdinck. As Dominic Sandbrook claimed in his perhaps overstated
corrective to the nostalgic recollections of the seemingly widespread
radicalism of the 1960s: 'amid the hurly-burly of the late sixties and

---

1.   The slogan (and its variants) was (rightly or wrongly) attributed to the Tory
MP Peter Griffiths. For further of the slogan see e.g. 'Looking back at race
relations', *BBC News* (October 29, 1999), http://news.bbc.co.uk/1/hi/482565.stm;
E. Lange, 'Afro-Caribbean Communities', in P. Childs and M. Storry (eds.),
Encyclopedia of Contemporary British Culture (London: Routledge, 1999), pp. 13-
14; D. Brown, 'A new language of racism in politics', *Guardian* (April 27, 2001);
A. Geddes, *The Politics of Migration and Immigration in Europe* (London: Sage,
2003), p. 34; D. Sandbrook, *White Heat: A History of Britain in the Swinging Sixties*
(London: Abacus, 2006), pp. 668-68; Anonymous, 'Peter Griffiths: an obituary',
Telegraph (November 27, 2013); A. Bonnett, *Radicalism, Anti-racism and Repre-
sentation* (London: Routledge, 2013), p. 20.

seventies, millions of people shared the old-fashioned vision of England…'[2]

In British political circles, 1968 – April 20, 1968, to be precise – has arguably become at least as well-known for the infamous Rivers of Blood speech on immigration delivered by Enoch Powell (1912–1998) to the Conservative Political Centre, Birmingham:

> A week or two ago I fell into conversation with a constituent, a middle-aged, quite ordinary working man employed in one of our nationalised industries… [H]e suddenly said:… 'I have three children, all of them been through grammar school and two of them married now, with family. I shan't be satisfied till I have seen them all settled overseas. In this country in 15 or 20 years' time the black man will have the whip hand over the white man.'
>
> …What he is saying, thousands and hundreds of thousands are saying and thinking – not throughout Great Britain, perhaps, but in the areas that are already undergoing the total transformation to which there is no parallel in a thousand years of English history… Those whom the gods wish to destroy, they first make mad. We must be mad, literally mad, as a nation to be permitting the annual inflow of some 50,000 dependants, who are for the most part the material of the future growth of the immigrant-descended population… I am going to allow just one of those hundreds of people to speak for me: 'Eight years ago in a respectable street in Wolverhampton a house was sold to a Negro. Now only one white (a woman old-age pensioner) lives there. This is her story. She lost her husband and both her sons in the war. So she turned her seven-roomed house, her only asset, into a boarding house. She worked hard and did well, paid off her mortgage and began to put something by for her old age. Then the immigrants moved in. With growing fear, she saw one house after another taken over. The quiet street became a place of noise and confusion… She is becoming afraid to go out. Windows are broken. She finds excreta pushed through her letter box. When she goes to the shops, she is followed by children, charming, wide-grinning piccaninnies. They cannot speak English, but one word they know. "Racialist", they chant. When the new Race Relations Bill is passed, this woman is convinced she will go to prison. And is she so wrong? I begin to wonder.'
>
> …Here is the means of showing that the immigrant communities can organise to consolidate their members, to agitate and campaign against their fellow citizens… As I look ahead, I am filled with foreboding; like the Roman, I seem to see 'the River Tiber foaming with much blood'.[3]

2. Sandbrook, *White Heat*, p. 792.

3. E. Powell, 'To the Annual General Meeting of the West Midlands Area Conservative Political Centre (Birmingham, April 20, 1968)', in *Reflections: Selected Writings and Speeches of Enoch Powell* (London: Bellew, 1992), pp. 161-69. According to Tom Paulin, around the time of Powell's speech, John Robinson (Bishop of Woolwich and New Testament scholar) claimed that if Jesus returned as

This speech – which also advocated expatriation – was personally significant for Powell. His career as a successful Conservative Member of Parliament was effectively at an end. Powell was a Conservative MP between 1950 and 1974, a Minister of Health between 1960 and 1963, and then Shadow Defence Secretary. However, the Conservative leader Ted Heath had little choice but to sack him from the shadow front bench for this extraordinarily provocative speech with its far-right racial slurs and propaganda.[4] But, while the political and media establishment largely denounced him, the speech had given Powell remarkable levels of popular support (notably from traditional Labour voters too) in the form of thousands of letters, petitions for his reinstatement, overwhelming backing in opinion polls, dockers and meat porters marching in his defence, and even strikes in his favour.[5]

In some ways Powell's story is a lesson in how a politician might become a successful front-bench politician or an unsuccessful politician doomed to a life on the back-benches and high on ideals but low on power and influence. It is certainly common for a successful politician to speak generally about immigration negatively, and even to use the language of 'swamping' or claim to empathise with 'the ordinary voter' who is, so the rhetoric goes, emphatically 'not racist'. But there are more liberal restrictions (and voters) and one feature that has united the major post-War political parties: to identify themselves over against known

Blake had suggested in 'Jerusalem', he would be stopped by immigration officers! Powell was said to have claimed in response that the poem was blasphemous. See N. Spencer, 'Into the mystic', *Observer* (October 22, 2000).

4. Sandbrook, *White Heat*, p. 680: 'Powell's story about the old lady, the "excreta" and the "piccaninnies" seemed to have been borrowed directly from the stock racist fables of the far right. Although newspapers sent reporters to discover the woman in question, she was never found, and probably never existed. Very similar anecdotes were circulated in the late sixties by the National Front, the British National Party and others: it was the kind of story that most councillors and MPs regularly dismissed as extremist rabble-rousing.'

5. D. Childs, *Britain since 1945: A Political History* (London: Routledge, 2001), pp. 149-50. Tony Benn, *Office without Power: Diaries 1968–72* (London: Hutchinson, 1988), p. 60, conveys some of the unease: 'The press is still full of the repercussions of Enoch Powell's speech just before the weekend. Yesterday 200 dockers came to the House of Commons and shouted obscene things at Labour MPs and called Ian Mikardo a "bloody Chinese Jew". He recognised some of the East End Fascist leaders among these guys. The white trash have picked this speech up. It has suddenly liberated them and there are strikes all over the place in support of Enoch Powell. He really has opened Pandora's Box. I should think Enoch Powell will get an enormous vote in his constituency, but from the Government's point of view the situation could be very dangerous and difficult.'

far-right groups and individuals, a move which partly functions as a means to prove that such politicians and parties are 'not racist' when talking about immigration in particular.[6] It would be unlikely for a *successful* career-politician in the UK (with very few exceptions) to tell propagandist tales about 'wide-grinning piccaninnies' and predict that shortly 'the black man will have the whip hand over the white man'.[7]

Powell's political career was certainly not a success in the sense that he did not become a leading front-bench politician or Conservative Party leader (as some were predicting). He would eventually serve out his time as a controversial Ulster Unionist MP between 1974 and 1987, often making life uncomfortable (but little more) for the Conservative front bench. However, it is difficult to think of a failed post-War political politician who has wielded so much influence or who held such cultural currency as Powell. Already by 1968 Powell was developing the combination of neoliberal and nationalistic ideas that would later be taken up by Thatcher who, for all Powell's criticisms of her, claimed that he was one of the most important influences on her Conservative leadership.[8] From 1968 onward, Powell would become one of the most divisive figures in late twentieth-century political discourse, being eulogised by nationalist and far-right groups and being condemned by anti-racist and anti-fascist groups. 1968 would thus mark the rise of Powell as a cultural

6. Crossley, *Jesus in an Age of Neoliberalism*, pp. 10-12.

7. Boris Johnson also once used the term, along with 'watermelon smiles' in a *Telegraph* article, though more patronising than Powell-style provocation and not about immigration nor 'the white man' being under the whip hand of 'the black man': 'What a relief it must be for Blair to get out of England. It is said that the Queen has come to love the Commonwealth, partly because it supplies her with regular cheering crowds of flag-waving piccaninnies; and one can imagine that Blair, twice victor abroad but enmired at home, is similarly seduced by foreign politeness. They say he is shortly off to the Congo. No doubt the AK47s will fall silent, and the pangas will stop their hacking of human flesh, and the tribal warriors will all break out in watermelon smiles to see the big white chief touch down in his big white British taxpayer-funded bird' (B. Johnson, 'If Blair's so good at running the Congo, let him stay there', *Telegraph* [January 10, 2002]). Johnson is one of those rare politicians who appear to be able to use language that would potentially end any other politician's career. With his bumbling upper-class persona he is constantly the exception that proves the rule and is even expected to make such remarks. The *Telegraph* article re-emerged in a 2008 London mayoral debate and Johnson, typically, apologised. Clearly, this has not harmed Johnson's career but it is notable that he did apologise over offence caused when it was raised. See O. Bowcott and S. Jones, 'Johnson's "piccaninnies" apology', *Guardian* (January 23, 2008).

8. S. Heffer, *Like the Roman: The Life of Enoch Powell* (London: Weidenfeld & Nicolson, 1998), p. 958.

icon; phrases such as 'Enoch Powell was right' and 'Powell for PM' entered popular parlance while Powell was named BBC 'Man of the Year' in 1972, voted the Number 1 would-be face on beer-mats by the Society of British Beer-Mat Collectors, and as late as 2002 (and amidst the mass of celebrities and the occasional politician) he could still gain enough votes to come 55th in the BBC's 100 Greatest Britons.[9] Powell even claimed he owned an 'Enoch for Prime Minister' t-shirt.[10] And we should not forget that, throughout the period of Powell's fame, the popular working-class Conservative and similarly controversial TV character, Alf Garnett, was infused with the spirit of Powell in Johnny Speight's successful sitcoms, *Till Death Us Do Part* (1965–75) and *In Sickness and in Health* (1985–92). Indeed, in the 1972 Christmas special, Garnett even commented on the status of Jesus (who was English) and God (who was Church of England) in a monologue on the decline of the Englishness of Christmas.

But when Powell was comparing himself to 'the Roman' and foreseeing the Tiber foaming with blood, the sun had just about set on the British Empire. And yet it was, of course, a direct consequence of the Empire that saw mass immigration from former colonies in Asia and the Caribbean that so troubled Powell and has been an issue that has never left the political agenda. Post-War British and English mainstream and sub-cultural political discourse surrounding immigration has been tied with a range of emotive perceptions, including a lost British imperialism, cultural difference, class, employment, housing, and, of course, questions about what it 'means' to be English and British, particularly in relation to an immigrant Other, and even questions about the nature of the nation state itself. Indeed, the post-War period of 'imperial decline' right up to the present has spawned a number of far-right 'street' movements and minor political parties such as the National Front, British National Party, Combat 18, and the English Defence League, and generated groups and movements formed in reaction such as Rock against Racism, Anti-Nazi League, Unite against Fascism, and Love Music Hate Racism. Indeed, Rock against Racism was effectively founded after a 1976 Eric Clapton concert in Birmingham (where Powell delivered the Rivers of Blood speech) when Clapton drunkenly proclaimed: 'Vote for Enoch Powell… I think Enoch's right, I think we should send them all back. Stop Britain

---

9. H. Pedraza, *Winston Churchill, Enoch Powell and the Nation* (London: Cleveland, 1986), pp. 124, 166-67; '100 great British heroes', *BBC News* (August 21, 2002), http://news.bbc.co.uk/1/hi/entertainment/2208671.stm.

10. Pedraza, *Enoch Powell*, pp. 166-67.

from becoming a black colony. Get the foreigners out. Get the wogs out. Get the coons out. Keep Britain white.'[11] Clapton has since tried to defend his remarks against allegations of racism.[12] In a sober interview on the *South Bank Show* in 2007, he continued to defend Powell by claiming that the speech at his concert was not as important as people thought but that the government's attitude towards immigration was 'corrupt and hypocritical' and that his impression of Powell was that he was telling the truth about the situation and 'predicting that there would be trouble, and of course there was, and is'. Clapton denied that this was a 'racial thing' because he 'always identified strongly' with 'the black community'.[13]

Such sentiments reveal some of the inconsistencies, confusions, and tensions surrounding the post-War debates about immigration and race in the UK where the reception of Powell has become softened into the idea that he simply predicted tensions among the populace. Like others who continue to claim that 'Enoch was right', Clapton made no mention of the story about the 'wide-grinning piccaninnies', 'excreta' posted through the door, or the prediction that 'the black man will have the whip hand over the white man' in 15-20 years' time, and it would be interesting to know how he would otherwise classify the use of language such as 'black colony' (mentioned to Clapton in the interview), 'get the wogs out', 'get the coons out', 'keep Britain white', or how such language managed to make its way into such 'honest debates' about immigration. Or we could stop being respectful about such things and just state more bluntly that no matter how hard people try, no matter what their intentions may be, no matter how convincing the common arguments that Powell's speech was not personally racist may or may not be, race and racism has only ever been superficially removed from debates about immigration and what it apparently 'means' to be English or British. And we should not forget this whenever we read or hear any discussion of the nation state and immigration, no matter how idealised or rarefied, intellectual or liberal, the rhetoric may be.

11. R. Heddle and L. Bellingham, 'Anti-Fascism: That Was Then, This Is Now' *Socialist Review* (June 2004), http://www.socialistreview.org.uk/article.php?articlenumber=8931; L. Bainbridge, 'Ten right-wing rockers', *Guardian* (October 14, 2007); I. Goodyer, *Crisis Music: The Cultural Politics of Rock against Racism* (Manchester: Manchester University Press, 2009), pp. 10, 18.

12. E. Clapton, *Clapton: The Autobiography* (London: Century, 2007), p. 100.

13. Available at https://www.youtube.com/watch?v=4YTmEw5IqMU.

2. Rethinking the Post-Imperial Nation

As the allusion to Virgil's *Aeneid* and identification with 'the Roman' in the Rivers of Blood speech might suggest, Powell had a love of Classics.[14] Indeed, by this point Powell had already had some significant career success as a Classicist, as had so many who had taken up major public roles in the service of king, country, and Empire. In 1937, aged just 25, he became Professor of Classics at Sydney University (almost matching his hero Nietzsche who achieved professorial status at 24) and went on to publish a number of significant academic works, such as *A Lexicon to Herodotus* (1938), *The History of Herodotus* (1939), and *Herodotus: A Translation* (1949).[15] This interest in Classics was not, however, simply some disinterested hobby, as Powell himself once implied.[16] Consciously or not, it was connected to his admiration of the Roman Empire,[17] itself a reflection of his admiration of the British Empire and assumptions of civilisation, language, and culture derived from the Greeks.[18] But his love of imperial culture and civilisation was not something restricted to the ancient past or the patriotic present or recent past. As a teenager and young man, Powell developed a great admiration for, and affinity with, the achievements of Germanic culture, including an appreciation of German language and a perception of Germanic scientific rigour.[19] Coupled with the impact of his early biblical study and growing dedication to atheism, his interest in things Germanic was increasingly tied in with his particular love of Nietzsche (he read all

---

14. For earlier developments of ideas in the rest of this chapter with reference to concepts of 'homeland' and 'Holy Land', see J.G. Crossley, 'Enoch Powell and the Gospel Tradition: A Search for a Homeland', in K.W. Whitelam (ed.), *Holy Land as Homeland? Models for Constructing the Historic Landscapes of Jesus* (Sheffield: Sheffield Phoenix Press, 2012), pp. 134-50.

15. J.[E.] Powell, *A Lexicon to Herodotus* (Cambridge: Cambridge University Press, 1938); J.[E.] Powell, *The History of Herodotus* (Cambridge: Cambridge University Press, 1939); J.[E.] Powell, *Herodotus: A Translation* (Oxford: Clarendon Press, 1949). See further, R.B. Todd, 'Enoch Powell's Classical Scholarship: A Bibliography', *Quaderni di Storia* 42 (1995), pp. 89-96; R.B. Todd, 'Enoch Powell as a Classicist: Two Studies', *Quaderni di Storia* 45 (1997), pp. 81-103; M. Mountford, 'Enoch Powell as a Classicist', in Lord Howard of Rising (ed.), *Enoch at 100: A Re-evaluation of the Life, Politics and Philosophy of Enoch Powell* (London: Biteback Publishing, 2012), pp. 237-50.

16. Heffer, *Like the Roman*, p. 46.

17. See e.g. Heffer, *Like the Roman*, p. 28.

18. Mountford, 'Enoch Powell as Classicist', pp. 239-40.

19. Pedraza, *Enoch Powell*, pp. 83-84; Heffer, *Like the Roman*, pp. 10, 24.

of Nietzsche by his early twenties).[20] There was a problem, however; in the post war years Powell was becoming convinced that another Great War with Germany would follow – though the immediate rise of Hitler did not worry Powell any more than usual[21] – which would cause some tension between Powell's Germanophilia and patriotism. This tension was drastically eased – both historically and personally – in 1934 on the Night of the Long Knives. For Powell, the greatness of Germanic culture had 'all been an illusion, all fantasy, all a self-created myth'. The music, philosophy, poetry, science, and language 'was demolished, broken to bits on the cliffs of a monstrous reality'. For Powell, Germany could no longer be a 'spiritual homeland' because 'nothing can be a homeland... where there is no justice, where justice does not reign'. Powell's spiritual homeland had 'disappeared' and he now claimed he was left with only his 'geographical homeland'.[22]

Powell never lost interest in German culture but now his patriotism could dominate his thinking for the rest of his life. Fighting in World War II (he rose rapidly through the ranks to reach Brigadier) also meant defending the British Empire, another great Powell-passion doomed to failure. This concern for the preservation of the British Empire in the face of internal talk and external threats concerning its disintegration was to be found in his career ambitions (he wanted to be Viceroy of India) to the extent that, when in India in 1944, he decided the battle would be best fought as an MP.[23] But World War II would, of course, usher in the decline of the British Empire, including independence for Sudan and, most symbolically, India. Powell was less than impressed with the replacement for the Empire: the Commonwealth (a 'gigantic farce').[24] Unlike the apparent nostalgia of the Conservative party line, Powell was a realist during the Suez Crisis. He opposed the 1956 intervention and believed that Britain should stop pretending it was an Empire and accept that it had no real power in the Middle East, a view he held throughout his political career. Powell may have entered Parliament intending to save the Empire but by the 1950s he had to re-evaluate his thinking in terms of nationalism without Empire, including, at least in abstract terms, some strongly anti-Empire ideas

20.   Heffer, *Like the Roman*, pp. 22-23.

21.   Pedraza, *Enoch Powell*, pp. 83-84; Heffer, *Like the Roman*, p. 22.

22.   Quoted in Heffer, *Like the Roman*, p. 24; cf. Pedraza, *Enoch Powell*, pp. 83-84.

23.   Pedraza, *Enoch Powell*, p. 89.

24.   Pedraza, *Enoch Powell*, p. 95; Heffer, *Like the Roman*, p. 350. See also Pedraza, *Enoch Powell*, pp. 106-107; Heffer, *Like the Roman*, pp. 132, 335-40.

after the surrender of India... He now felt Britain should be unchanged by
the passage of Empire; that, as a nation, she had never depended on the
Empire for her self-awareness or identification – an idea he would be
forced publicly to contradict at the next two elections. He exorcised from
his spirit the idea of the nation he had formerly held.[25]

But even with Powell's pragmatic nationalism and disdain for the
Commonwealth, and despite the apparent influence of the seemingly
faux imperialism of certain Tories, Powell could not quite let go of his
nostalgic view of the British Empire. Counterfactually speaking from
this sort of perspective, if Britain had not given up India then might
things not have turned out differently? In 1991, when his main research
on the Gospels was being published, Powell made some revealing
remarks to the Institute of Contemporary British History's Summer
School at the London School of Economics:

> When I resigned my chair in Australia in 1939 in order to come home to
> enlist, had I been asked 'What is the State whose uniform you wish to wear
> and in whose service you expect to perish?' I would have said 'The British
> Empire'... I also know that, on my deathbed, I shall still be believing with
> one part of my brain that somewhere on every ocean of the world there is a
> great, grey ship with three funnels and sixteen-inch guns which can blow
> out of the water any other navy which is likely to face it. I know it is not so.
> Indeed, I realised at a relatively early age that it is not so. But that factor –
> that emotional factor...will not die until I, the carrier of it, am dead.[26]

Powell's post-war thinking may have included a seam of pessimism due
to his views on the British Commonwealth and immigration but there
was also a seam of optimism based on English and/or British culture and
a concept of 'Englishness' focussed on, for instance, values, culture, a
state of mind, economics, and institutions, which were in turn a product
of a distinctly English evolution and key institutions of Parliament and
Church.[27] Such thinking could at times be sentimental but contemporary
examples proved the point for Powell. For example, he thought that the
Falklands War was a prime example of how Britain as a nation could
fight a war, just as he thought that Britain as a nation had the resources to
compete economically with other nations.[28] Unlike the dominant feature
of post-war Conservative thinking, particularly in the 1980s, Powell's

---

25. Heffer, *Like the Roman*, p. 120; cf. pp. 119-21, 335, 431-32.
26. Quoted in P. Hennessy, *Never Again: Britain 1945–51* (London: Jonathan
Cape, 1992), pp. xiv-xv; see also Heffer, *Like the Roman*, pp. 172-73.
27. For useful overviews see Pedraza, *Enoch Powell, passim*; Heffer, *Like the
Roman*, pp. 334-40.
28. Pedraza, *Enoch Powell*, p. 147

nationalism developed into a strong disdain for American power from which he believed Britain should be distinct, not least because, in an extension of the pragmatic awareness that ran alongside his idealism, the United States will ultimately care about the United States and not Britain. From this logic, it followed that a hermeneutic of suspicion was cast over other dominant and ostensibly pan-national organisations such as NATO, the UN, and the EEC.[29] So strong were Powell's views of this critical distance that in 1974 he advised people to vote Labour over Conservative on the issue of the EEC. Powell certainly disliked anything faintly socialist but at least Labour promised to renegotiate terms of entry into the EEC and a referendum.[30]

For Powell, then, the nation was the ultimate political reality and one worth dying for.[31] The nation dictated virtually all of Powell's thinking and this nationalism was as much embodied in Parliament as it was manifest in Powell's support for Ulster and opposition to the European Common Market and American power.[32] But the concept of the nation was also embodied in another institution that was less obviously 'political' by the mid-twentieth century: the Church of England.

3. Church of England

Despite – or, if we take the old *Yes, Prime Minister* cliché about the Church of England, because of – his atheistic and Nietzschean thinking, Powell converted from atheism to Anglicanism in 1949. Given his nationalism, it should probably not be a surprise that Powell would answer 'Anglican' when asked about being a Christian, nor that he would be keen on understanding the social function of religion and its relationship to the state.[33] Powell's emphasis on a this-worldly English church was obviously important for his nationalism. But it was also important for Powell on an emotional level and clearly provided a degree of replacement for the failures of Germany and the Empire. All these factors were recalled in Powell's recollection of the calling of the Evensong bells of St Peter's church in Wolverhampton:

29. Pedraza, *Enoch Powell*, pp. 147-50; Heffer, *Like the Roman*, pp. 517, 579-80.

30. Cf. Pedraza, *Enoch Powell*, p. 118; Heffer, *Like the Roman*, pp. 579-80.

31. Pedraza, *Enoch Powell*, pp. 125, 167; Heffer, *Like the Roman*, pp. 5, 153, 334-40, 580, 822, 843; A. Roberts, 'Enoch Powell and the Nation State', in Rising (ed.), *Enoch at 100*, pp. 123-42.

32. Pedraza, *Enoch Powell*, pp. 92, 103; Heffer, *Like the Roman*, pp. 116, 119, 338-39.

33. Heffer, *Like the Roman*, pp. 131, 134-38.

> However, ashamed or not, I came again and again, until presently I real-
> ised that I was caught fast...by an inner logic or necessity... [O]nce got
> within the walls, physical and liturgical, of the Church of England, I was
> proud enough to see that it was a goodly inheritance from which, like a
> prodigal son, I had so long deliberately exiled myself... [L]ike someone
> who returns after a long absence to an ancestral home, I looked at the
> half-familiar scenes with new eyes... I had stepped inside the Church
> Universal...compelled to acknowledge a truth that is corporate... I
> noticed that the loyalties I had lived with in war and peace had been
> corporate too.[34]

Powell would also become identified with the High Tory Anglo-
Catholicism with emphasis placed on 'tradition' in worship. Tellingly,
Powell would distinguish himself from the 'evangelical' and 'literalist'
believers.[35]

For Powell, the intertwining of Anglicanism and nation had deep
historic roots. 'Perhaps the Celtic Church, distinctive though it was,
cannot be thus classified [as a national church]', Powell speculated, 'but
there was certainly a Gallican Church and an Anglican Church before the
Reformation was dreamt of'. Powell argued that in the twelfth century,
the king, like any modern Prime Minister, was insistent on the right to
nominate bishops and in the Middle Ages the *Ecclesia anglicana* 'was an
accepted political as well as ecclesiastical reality... [T]he Church, the
universal, catholic church, could also be a national church.' A decisive
moment in Powell's history of England is when Henry VIII as monarch
asserted spiritual authority through Parliament which would be the
beginning of the end of external influence on national affairs.[36] The
English church evolved through compromise and debate, and with its
own distinctively English character. But the authority of the Church was,
like Parliament, firmly grounded in the Crown.[37] While Powell was
hardly immune to thinking along the lines of the Cultural Bible, nationalism must always take priority – even over aesthetics. On the legislating

34. Quoted in Pedraza, *Enoch Powell*, p. 91. Compare E. Powell, 'Interview with
Anne Brown, BBC Radio, April 13, 1986', in Powell, *Reflections*, pp. 27-38 (30-31):
'One night...I passed St Peter's Church and the bells were ringing for Evensong... I
opened a prayer book and I thought to myself..."This is wonderful".'

35. J.E. Powell, *Wrestling with the Angel* (London: Sheldon Press, 1977), pp. 87-
94; J.E. Powell, 'Genesis of the Gospel', *JSNT* 42 (1991), pp. 5-16; Heffer, *Like the
Roman*, pp. 135-36.

36. E. Powell, 'A National Church (1981)', in Powell, *Reflections*, pp. 72-76
(73).

37. For a summary of Powell's context in wider debates over the place of the
Church of England, see Filby, 'God and Mrs Thatcher', pp. 138-75.

of the entrenchment of the Book of Common Prayer in 1981, Powell believed too much stress had been placed on the 'literary and linguistic excellences of the Prayer book' because the real gain is that Parliament is the guardian of the Prayer Book which 'embodies forms of worship and expressions of faith that are broad, generous and deep enough to embrace the wide spectrum which a national church must comprehend... [A] Church of all the English.'[38] It is no doubt significant that the opening essay in Powell's book of sermons, exegesis, and religious reflection is on 'Patriotism'.[39]

This prioritising of the power of nation over church would again suggest that it was partly *because of* his admiration for Nietzsche that Powell could espouse the kind of Anglicanism he did. In fact it is not even clear that the importance of Powell's atheism disappeared in his conversion to Anglicanism. Even in 1962 Powell was still recalling the influence of J.G. Frazer's *The Golden Bough* on his own thought and his boyhood atheism.[40] Powell had little interest in personal faith and belief and towards the end of his life he would claim greater interest in a more materialistic reading of religion as a significant factor in the history of human survival, an idea which had already come through by the mid-1970s in, for instance, his discussion of immortality.[41] Simon Heffer has claimed that 'one of his [Powell's] closest friends, himself deeply religious', suggested that Powell never ceased to be an atheist and that the role of the church as a social and national institution kept him within the fold. Another close friend and Powell archivist, Richard Ritchie, said that the aging Powell at least did not believe in an afterlife, while another friend, the MP and churchman Frank Field, claimed Powell had no concern for the mission of the Church.[42]

Whatever the truth of Powell's actual belief in the existence of God and life eternal, it is clear that, as a Member of Parliament, Powell's concerns for the Church consistently related to issues of the church–state relationship.[43] Powell was also not a supporter of the idea that the Bible and Christianity had serious relevance for contemporary political

38. Powell, 'National Church', pp. 73-74.

39. See also his essay, 'God Save the Queen', in Powell, *Wrestling with the Angel*, pp. 74-82.

40. Heffer, *Like the Roman*, p. 11.

41. Powell, *Wrestling with the Angel*, pp. 65-70.

42. Heffer, *Like the Roman*, pp. 134-36; cf. Pedraza, *Enoch Powell*, p. 103. For Powell's intellectualized reflections see Powell, *Wrestling with the Angel*, pp. 52-58, 65-70.

43. Heffer, *Like the Roman*, p. 136.

issues. 'Faith in action' was, at best, meaningless or, at worst, dangerous.[44] 'Christianity', Powell claimed, 'does not help me decide to vote
for or against a United Kingdom in the European Community, or for or
against the capital penalty for murder, or for a flat-rate or graduated
system of state pensions or, for that matter, for or against state pensions
at all'.[45] For Powell, such politically active thinking was a misreading
of the Bible and a naïve understanding of the nation and politics. The
modern clergy, he argued, should only be providing guidance and
preparation for kingdom come and had no authority to provide guidance
for an earthly kingdom in the here and now. As Powell emphatically
claimed, 'Christianity does not, repeat not, look forward to a gradual
betterment of human behaviour and society or to the progressive spread
of peace and justice upon earth. Still less does Christianity purport to
offer a scheme or general outline for bringing that about. Quite the
reverse...'[46] Not even the Archbishop of Canterbury was immune from
this sort of criticism: Powell accused Donald Coggan of 'bad elementary
economics... economic errors...damaging to this nation and its people'
when Coggan spoke about issues of neglecting the needs of other nations.
Of Coggan's role as Archbishop of Canterbury, Powell claimed that:

> I owe respect to Dr Coggan, as Archbishop of Canterbury, a respect
> which I gladly yield. I also owe him more than respect when he speaks
> with the voice of his Master, to tell me that the blessed are the poor, the
> hungry, the thirsty and the oppressed, and that a rich man – and presuma-
> bly a nation of rich men – cannot by any contrivance enter into his
> Kingdom. But it is not with that voice that his Grace was speaking in the
> words I have just quoted. He was speaking the language of materialism
> and bad elementary economics, and when he so speaks, it is the right and
> duty of a politician...to refute and to rebuke.[47]

4. Like the Roman? The Lost Gospel of Enoch

Powell's Anglo-Catholicism and lack of concern for the 'relevance' of
the Bible did not mean an avoidance of the Bible, however. While Powell
may have seen the present threatened by immigration and Europe, this
did not stop him creatively, and perhaps 'unconsciously', creating his

---

44. See e.g. Powell's chapters 'Christianity and the Curse of Cain', 'Action for
World Development', 'My Country, Right or Wrong', and 'Christianity and Social
Activity', in Powell, *Wrestling with the Angel*, pp. 12-13, 14-19, 20-24, 30-51.
45. Powell, *Wrestling with the Angel*, pp. 63-64.
46. Powell, *Wrestling with the Angel*, p. 61.
47. Powell, *Wrestling with the Angel*, p. 20.

own nostalgic and idealised version of an invented tradition of English nationhood and British Empire with the help of the Bible and reconstruction of what the Bible 'really says'. Powell's politics would certainly have to overrule anything smacking of the Radical Bible. But one thing that can be said about the Radical Bible is that there are at least some seemingly clear-cut passages which manifest a degree of confrontation against economic injustices. The Parable of the Rich Man and Lazarus is one of the most explicit passages in the New Testament but Powell rejected any apparently superficial reading of this passage which might condemn the rich man to Hades for being rich and put the poor man into the embrace of Abraham for being poor because such readings would inevitably put people off reading the Bible![48] Of one of the other most famous New Testament passages condemning wealth – the Rich Man and the Eye of the Needle – Powell insisted that it was instead an attack on personal merit and reliance on works, which was something Powell believed to be more typical of Judaism and/or the early Jewish church.[49]

Biblical studies appear in books in which he combined his academic, confessional, and popularist interests, such as *No Easy Answers* (1973) and the more developed *Wrestling with the Angel* (1977).[50] But Powell's academic study of the Bible – the genesis of Matthew's Gospel in particular – came to fruition towards the end of his life. *The Evolution of the Gospel* was published in 1994 but it was foreshadowed by a *Journal for the Study of the New Testament* article in 1991, a published version of a lecture he gave at the University of Sheffield.[51] His study of Matthew was heavily philological and an outworking of his career as a Classicist.[52] In *Evolution of the Gospel*, for instance, and echoing his work on Herodotus, Powell provided his own translation of Matthew's Greek and an accompanying commentary. Powell of course knew Greek and even as a schoolboy he had already memorized the entirety of Galatians in Greek.[53] In the research for the book, Powell had liaised with celebrated scholars of early Christian history. For example, in the acknowledgments in *Evolution of the Gospel*, Powell gives due credit to Henry Chadwick

48. Heffer, *Like the Roman*, p. 137.

49. Powell, 'Genesis of the Gospel', p. 12; cf. Powell, *Wrestling with the Angel*, pp. 30-34, 39-40.

50. E. Powell, *No Easy Answers* (London: Sheldon Press, 1973); Powell, *Wrestling with the Angel*.

51. Powell, 'Genesis of the Gospel'; J.E. Powell, *The Evolution of the Gospel* (New Haven: Yale University Press, 1994).

52. Cf. Mountford, 'Enoch Powell as Classicist', p. 248.

53. Heffer, *Like the Roman*, p. 12.

and William Horbury. Powell also consulted – as he did for his other work on the Gospel tradition – with Semitic and Ethiopic expert, and Fellow of the British Academy, Edward Ullendorff. On the surface, then, Powell's approach to Matthew was very much in the tradition of the Cultural Bible, particularly in the sense of Enlightenment biblical criticism. However, the more 'unconscious' political function of his work clearly relates to his version of liberal parliamentary democracy which is also in line with a more traditionalist version of the Liberal Bible. To reveal this political unconscious requires a closer look at Powell's exegetical approach to Matthew.

Powell's views on Matthew and the Gospel tradition could be deemed somewhat eccentric in scholarly terms. For instance, Powell argued that the historical Jesus was not in fact crucified by the Romans but stoned to death by Jewish authorities. While this was probably the most unlikely view to be found in New Testament scholarship,[54] Powell's major work on Matthew remained idiosyncratic. Whereas the overwhelmingly dominant view in Gospel scholarship for about a century has been that Mark's Gospel was the earliest and that Matthew and Luke used Mark, Powell argued that Matthew's Gospel (in approximately the form we now know it) was the earliest Gospel and was used by Luke and Mark, with Mark also using Luke. When Mark and Luke deviated from Matthew, this was, Powell argued, because of their own creative freedom rather than their use of alternative sources. The primacy of Matthew thus meant that Matthew demanded a dedicated analysis.[55] And when the Matthean tradition was to be studied in depth, Powell believed it was possible to find an underlying text, a text 'severely re-edited, with theological and polemical intent', and with the resulting edition then recombined with the underlying text to produce the Gospel of Matthew.[56] For Powell, the distinctive features of the final form of Matthew's Gospel (e.g. contradictions, duplications, and abrupt breaks) betray a lack of smooth editing of the sort which Powell believed were found in

54. Compare Heffer, *Like the Roman*, p. 94: 'though the oldest teachings on this question also point to stoning'. Heffer provided no indication of what these 'oldest teachings' are. Heffer is not reflecting any mainstream scholarly view on this matter. For a slightly different reaction, compare the comments of Frank Field, 'Enoch Powell as a Parliamentarian', in Rising (ed.), *Enoch at 100*, pp. 47-53 (53): ' "You're opening yourself up for a heresy trial", I replied, for this beautifully written text agued either that Jesus was stoned to death or that the key New Testament figure was John the Baptist. I cannot now remember which. Enoch laughed.'

55. Powell, *Evolution of the Gospel*, pp. xii-xvii; see also Powell, *Wrestling with the Angel*, pp. 108-21.

56. Powell, *Evolution of the Gospel*, pp. xi-xii; Powell, 'Genesis of the Gospel'.

Mark and Luke. For Powell, these Matthean 'blemishes' are revealing clues about the compositional history of a Gospel 'produced in haste and under pressure'.[57]

Duplications were among the most important 'blemishes' in helping establish the earliest history behind Matthew's Gospel, the 'underlying book', and the earliest theological developments in the Christian church. Powell focused heavily on the feeding miracles and, as part of his understanding of the historical Jesus' death, he went as far as claiming that there are 'vestiges at least of a duplicate execution'.[58] The 'most portentous' of the duplications was deemed to be the trial before the high priest and the trial before the Romans, the former being known to the latter. The apparent disputes behind such duplications concerned the identity of Jesus. For Powell's underlying narrative the identity of Jesus concerned the incarnation: 'he was divine, a victim and victor, not Jewish, but universal'. It was the theology of this text which generated a rival and alternative Jewish narrative.[59]

Unsurprisingly, then, Powell's earliest reconstructed text had concern for a Gentile mission. The narrative 'starting point' was the 'Galilee of the gentiles' (Matt. 4.14-15) which Powell argued 'was an allegory of the great sea which united the Roman world'.[60] In order for believers to inherit the kingdom of everlasting life they would become sons of God through faith in Jesus' identity. This, according to Powell, does not require fulfilment of the Law because Jesus' death brought mercy and forgiveness. The earliest level of the Matthean tradition is a historical narrative which roughly approximated to historical reality and was also designed to establish Jesus' identity as Son of God and in a way that is constructed over against Judaism. This is where we find Powell's most striking argument – Jesus was stoned to death – which meant that he was convicted by the 'Jewish establishment' and this was because of 'the blasphemy of allowing himself to be called "the son of God"'.[61]

Powell's book was not well received and, despite acknowledgment of his learning, was even ridiculed.[62] But Powell's construction of a

57. Powell, *Evolution of the Gospel*, p. xviii.

58. Powell, 'Genesis of the Gospel', p. 9. For Powell's earlier interest in the feeding miracles see Powell, *Wrestling with the Angel*, pp. 95-98.

59. Powell, 'Genesis of the Gospel', p. 9.

60. Powell, *Evolution of the Gospel*, pp. xxiii.

61. Powell, *Evolution of the Gospel*, pp. xxi, 207-208.

62. Compare, for instance, N.T. Wright's assessment: 'This is clearly a work of great erudition, which seems to have lost touch with the distinction between that which is possible and that which is plausible... There is something to be said for starting again from scratch, but the catty answer is that he has chosen to ignore

negative Jewish foil, in particular that 'the Jewish establishment' had Jesus stoned to death, led to more serious criticisms. Hyam Maccoby was reported as claiming that 'It could undoubtedly have anti-Semitic repercussions' which were already present, Maccoby claimed, in the Gospels. 'If it is now said that the Romans did not do the executions, the Jews did, this intensifies the blame against the Jews even more'.[63] Obviously, this is hardly an unfair reading of Powell's exegesis but we should not single Powell out for blame for the negative construction of Judaism and we should probably not, should we be tempted, tie such negative constructions of Judaism too closely with his views on immigration. Powell was almost certainly not motivated by a personal antisemitism. He even argued that World War II was less a battle against the Nazis and more against a development of the negative Germanic traits such as hero-worship, power hunger, a love of force, and anti-semitism, all of which were apparently out of kilter with an English mindset.[64] Irrespective of whether this is a fair reading of national 'mindsets', Powell believed that antisemitism was most 'un-English'.

Having said that it is undeniable that Judaism was constructed nega-tively in Powell's exegesis and that he does make remarks about Jews and Judaism which are hardly complimentary. We might, for instance, compare Powell's comments about Jewish and Christian eschatology published in the 1970s:

> This, like so much else that is Christian, represents a reinterpretation of the Jewish revelation so profound as to be a contradiction of it. The Jew looked forward – still does look forward – with the practical, earthbound, matter-of-factness characteristic of the Jew, to the actual establishment of his own theocracy in the world... The Christian is at once more humble and more realistic, and his hope is of a different sort...[65]

This is typical of a long tradition of downgrading Judaism found throughout the history of biblical scholarship. Christian supersessionism and nineteenth-century discussions of the 'Jewish question' have both had a significant influence on modern biblical scholarship.[66] Since

everyone else, so he can't grumble if they return the compliment.' Reported in A. Brown, 'Gospel according to Powell: Christ was stoned to death', *Independent* (August 16, 1994).

63. Reported in Brown, 'Gospel according to Powell'.

64. Heffer, *Like the Roman*, p. 60.

65. Powell, *Wrestling with the Angel*, p. 61.

66. See e.g. M. Casey, 'Some Anti-Semitic Assumptions in *The Theological Dictionary of the New Testament*', *NovT* 41 (1999), pp. 280-91; E. Schüssler Fiorenza, *Jesus and the Politics of Interpretation* (New York: Continuum, 2000);

E.P. Sanders' widely praised criticisms of anti-Jewish readings in New Testament scholarship (published in 1977),[67] New Testament scholarship has regularly patted itself on the back for praising Judaism and using Judaism as the most important context for understanding the New Testament. However, the downgrading of Judaism and the superiority of Christianity remains but now with a more liberalising and rhetorically positive gloss. For all the emphasis on Jesus the Jew, Jesus regularly comes out over against Judaism in one way or another. This 'Jewish... but not that Jewish' Jesus (and New Testament) and the stress on a stable Jewish background identity is partly a product of the limited tolerance of liberal multiculturalism, reactions to globalisation, and an intense Anglo-American interest in Israel and Judaism after the 1967 Six Day War.[68]

This tradition of using Judaism as a negative foil in Powell is likewise ideologically significant but also because the Roman Empire comes out positively.[69] Integral to Powell's reconstruction of Matthew is the importance of Rome and the Empire. Even some of Powell's description of Jesus is dressed up in imperial language: 'like the centurion ordering soldiers, Jesus designates missionaries to do his bidding, and dispatches them to work in the mission field'.[70] Powell's reading of the geography of Matthew's narrative, or at least of the underlying book, has probably more to say about the Roman Empire than the area it purports to be describing, Galilee. We should recall that, for Powell, the 'sea' in Matthew was an 'allegory of the great sea which united the Roman world', and a code word 'which often, if not always, represents the Mediterranean and signifies the gentile mission field'.[71] We might even

---

S. Kelley, *Racializing Jesus: Race, Ideology and the Formation of Modern Biblical Scholarship* (London: Routledge, 2002); P. Head, 'The Nazi Quest for an Aryan Jesus', *JSHJ* 2 (2004), pp. 55-89; W. Arnal, *The Symbolic Jesus: Historical Scholarship, Judaism and the Construction of Contemporary Identity* (London: Equinox, 2005); J.G. Crossley, *Jesus in an Age of Terror: Scholarly Quests for a New American Century* (London: Equinox, 2008); S. Heschel, *The Aryan Jesus: Christian Theologians and the Bible in Nazi Germany* (Princeton: Princeton University Press, 2008); T. Penner, '*Die Judenfrage* and the Construction of Ancient Judaism: Toward a Foregrounding of the Backgrounds Approach to Early Christianity', in P. Gray and G. O'Day (eds.), *Scripture and Traditions: Essays on Early Judaism and Christianity* (Leiden: Brill, 2008), pp. 429-55; Crossley, *Jesus in an Age of Neoliberalism.*

67. E.P. Sanders, *Paul and Palestinian Judaism: A Comparison of Patterns of Religion* (Philadelphia: Fortress Press, 1977).

68. Arnal, *Symbolic Jesus*; Crossley, *Jesus in an Age of Terror*, pp. 143-94; Crossley, *Jesus in an Age of Neoliberalism*, pp. 105-32.

69. Powell, 'Genesis of the Gospel', p. 15.

70. Powell, *Evolution of the Gospel*, p. xxiv.

71. Powell, *Evolution of the Gospel*, pp. xxiii, xxvi.

suggest that, 'like the Roman', Powell effectively conquers Galilee for
the Empire. Here another Powell idiosyncrasy becomes important. Unlike
the dominant scholarly view which locates the writing of Matthew's
Gospel somewhere in the eastern Mediterranean such as Antioch, Powell
is adamant ('there would be little hesitation about the answer') that the
provenance of the underlying book is Rome. Powell's argument for this
is telling: it is because of the apparent Roman bias and Gentile mission
which Powell believed was brought to the fore in the Matthean tradition.
While Powell gives no indication about how he would account for any
pro-Roman bias and concern for a Gentile mission elsewhere in early
Christianity, the other Gospels evolve 'presumably in other quarters of
the Mediterranean world'.[72]

Clearly Powell's idiosyncrasies betray more than mere scholarly
curiosity. And the ultimate idiosyncrasy perhaps reveals Powell's bias
best: Rome had nothing to do with the death of Jesus and Jesus was
emphatically not a threat to Roman power. But here Powell had a problem: whatever the historical reality, the Gospel of Matthew *does* have
Jesus receive the punishment of crucifixion. Powell dealt with this by
arguing that substituting crucifixion for stoning was 'made conditional'
upon Pontius Pilate being exonerated from blame.[73] Powell also
faced a similar kind of problem with the Kingdom of Heaven which
Powell realised was 'not self-evidently compatible with the *imperium
Romanum*'. However, Powell once again turned to the negative Jewish
foil and developed a reading clearly reminiscent of his views on the role
of the Anglican clergy. He argued that the Kingdom was 'painstakingly
distanced' from the Jewish uprising (Matt. 24.27) and 'allowed to remain
in an unexplored limbo between individual immortality and a new world
order'. Importantly for Powell, as Pilate did not really believe Jesus was
guilty (Matt. 27.23), 'Caesar's judgement-seat was in no imminent danger
of being replaced by God's'. Instead, Powell claimed, the blame for
Jesus' crucifixion in Matthew, as it was for the stoning in the underlying
text, gets laid upon 'the Jews themselves', who were likewise to blame
for the destruction of the Temple.[74]

No doubt this use of the negative Jewish foil to produce a 'pro-
Roman' reading of Matthew and Matthean tradition owed much to
Powell's own idealistic views of Empire. Of course, Powell believed that
Britain was no longer a serious imperial force and he was far from
impressed with contemporary American imperialism but, as we saw,

72. Powell, *Evolution of the Gospel*, p. xxvii.
73. Powell, *Evolution of the Gospel*, pp. xxiii, 207-208.
74. Powell, *Evolution of the Gospel*, p. xxiii.

Powell did find himself getting sentimental about the British Empire and he did have a profound admiration for the Roman Empire and 'classical civilisation'. Powell's reading of Matthew was clearly an idealised retelling of his own views on what an/the Empire really ought to be, but also implicit here is Powell's idea of the hierarchy of political power where the State has priority over the subservient Church. We find this made more explicit, and with reference to Rome, in Powell's reading of other New Testament texts:

> 'Fear God, honour the king' in the First Epistle General of St Peter (2.17), or St Paul's injunction (Rom. 13.1-4) to 'be subject unto the higher powers' because 'the power' 'is the minister of God', who 'beareth not the sword in vain', will get us nowhere. Those are admonitions that were addressed to a tiny religious community who 'confessed that they were strangers and pilgrims on the earth' (Heb. 11.13), advising them that it was not their duty therefore to revolt against the Roman world-empire. Good behaviour and passive obedience were to be their proper attitudes towards it.[75]

Powell may have written more truth than he thought when he claimed that 'when we read the New Testament we all do our own expurgation… [C]ertainly every age has proceeded in this way with the Gospel.'[76]

Powell might have claimed that worship is not dependent on textual history and 'derives its authority and its persuasiveness from the immemorial practice and experience of the Church itself',[77] but it remains clear that such immemorial practices are an integral part of his reading of the Gospel tradition. For instance, he claimed, in language that could easily be reapplied to his understanding of the Anglican Church, that 'the most surprising experience has been to be led to perceive from how early a period in the evolution of the gospel the forms and ideas of worship were recognizably the same as they have continued down the ages'.[78] This comes through in Powell's understanding of the duplications in Matthew's Gospel, and the feeding miracles in particular, which were given most attention. The duplication of feeding miracles, Powell argued, did not mean they were to be understood as actual historical events but rather 'symbolically' in order to understand a theological or liturgical history and the evolution of church history with its compromises and cohesion. For Powell, the language of the feedings of the Five Thousand and the Four Thousand 'unmistakably' and 'self-evident

---

75. Powell, *Wrestling with the Angel*, p. 79.
76. Powell, *Wrestling with the Angel*, p. 59.
77. Powell, *Evolution of the Gospel*, p. viii.
78. Powell, *Evolution of the Gospel*, p. viii.

to anybody not determined to avoid its implications' alluded to 'the liturgical act of the Church known as the holy communion or mass… Those who originally read or heard the narrative could not fail to understand what it was about.'[79] This obviousness was because Jesus created a large surplus – including consecrated bread – which could then be taken up after the multitude had eaten and remain 'supernaturally' equal to the food consumed by the multitude.[80] For Powell, the feeding miracle was composed in an 'already existing Church with an already recognizable liturgical practice'.[81] However, the duplication also reveals conflict and tension in Powell's argument. The feeding miracle was also part of a quarrel over the significance of the consecrated elements and the duplication is evidence of reconciliation between two opposing schools ('dare I say churches?') over disputed Eucharistic details.[82]

As with Powell's understanding of Anglicanism, tracing the history of the earliest church was important for Powell because ecclesiastical evolution should reflect the culture and interests of its people. The anachronistic ἐκκλησία/'church' of the narrative underlying Matthew was, Powell claimed, no less an authority than the Church of Peter, whose theology was unquestionably orthodox, while the less orthodox alternative version lost out, even if it was absorbed into Matthew's text.[83] The orthodoxy of the Church of Peter included an emphasis on the incarnation, 'mass', and the Gentile mission. This was a church for the whole world where works of the Law and personal merit are no longer required because of, as we saw, faith in the propitiation and the identity of Jesus. And, significantly, the Church of Peter already possessed a book. But it was a church prepared to compromise. It had been in conflict with a Jewish church centred on the role of the Law. This Jewish church had used the Gentile Gospel to create its own myth of origins where Jesus was a prophet hero and martyr for Israel. To deal with this alternative and potential schism, a 'concordat' was drawn up and compromise reached between the Gentile and Jewish churches. The new single Gospel of Matthew, with its duplication and tensions, represented a mutual agreement.

Powell's reading of the Gospel tradition was, then, replicating the idea of a church of consensus and a Gospel of societal cohesion. Powell pushed this idea close to being a historical and theological necessity

---

79. Powell, 'Genesis of the Gospel', p. 6.
80. Powell, 'Genesis of the Gospel', pp. 6-7.
81. Powell, 'Genesis of the Gospel', p. 6.
82. Powell, 'Genesis of the Gospel', pp. 8-9.
83. Powell, 'Genesis of the Gospel', p. 11.

because a narrative was required for missionaries of the sort who would have converted Gentiles such as the addressees of Paul's letters. What was needed, Powell argued, was 'a book accepted by every section of Christianity – in Jerusalem as well as in Rome. That would be a book such as might have evolved by AD 100 into the document which we possess under the title of "the gospel according to Matthew".'[84] And now we arrive at the final idiosyncrasy where Powell was at odds with dominant trends in biblical scholarship, that is, Powell's claim that Paul and Matthew represented the same orthodox Christian tradition. In fact, Powell went further still and claimed that the Pauline epistles could assume familiarity with the Matthean traditions: 'the theology of the principal Pauline epistles is quite at home in the environment where Matthew originated'.[85] This gradual evolution of Christian orthodoxy ultimately became crystallised in the Gospel of Matthew which, we should not forget, was also engaged with its own compromises with the secular world. Powell admitted he could not prove precisely why this Gospel came about but would claim that it is 'impossible to avoid the fact' that the Gentile church had been validated by the Roman victory in Jerusalem: 'the *imperium Romanum* could be seen as, however involuntarily and unconsciously, the executant of the divine purpose'.[86] And we are now back to the implicit claims for priority of imperial and secular power in Powell's idealised understanding of Church, Crown, and Empire.

Yet, as Powell was only too aware, his nostalgic dream was dead in the water long before he died. He did not need to be on his deathbed to know that those great, grey ships with three funnels and sixteen-inch guns were no longer going to be blowing out of the water any other navy which is likely to face it, as much as he wished it so. That Britain had been blown out of the water by World War II. But the idea of reading a Church into the Bible as a part of English heritage and culture, and one constructed as subservient to State power, remains buoyant and, as we will later see, would be taken up in new directions by a new generation of political leaders. And his challenge to liberal-left Anglicanism and 'faith in action' was one which became integral to the battles of his great admirer and arguably his most potent legacy: Margaret Thatcher.

---

84. Powell, *Evolution of the Gospel*, p. xxviii.
85. Powell, *Evolution of the Gospel*, pp. xxvii-xxviii.
86. Powell, 'Genesis of the Gospel', p. 15.

Part II

THATCHERISM AND THE HARNESSING OF CHAOS

Chapter 4

'YOUR ARMS ARE JUST TOO SHORT TO BOX WITH GOD':
MARGARET THATCHER'S NEOLIBERAL BIBLE

1. Margaret Thatcher: Cultural Phenomenon and Nonconformist

The chaos of the individualism, nostalgia, counter-culture, radicalism, internationalism, consumerism, patriotism, and conservatism generated or intensified by the 1960s would appear to have been harnessed and controlled, at least temporarily, by Margaret Thatcher (1925–2013) and the movement bearing her name, Thatcherism. After the Conservative defeat in 1974, she would soon re-emerge with a distinctive monetarist vision, challenging the consensual nature of post-war, old-Etonian Conservative politics and the dominance of Keynesianism. Unlike Christopher Hill, Thatcher had less inhibition about unleashing the power of the morally righteous individual and was furiously hostile to all things Communist; unlike Enoch Powell, Thatcher was less tied to a nostalgic vision of the Church and 'Englishness' grounded in the age of Empire, even if inspired by his then political eccentricities. Of course, Thatcher shared a similar nostalgic vision but it was a nostalgia partly designed to support a shift to a new form of Conservatism and a new vision for Britain. As Jonathan Raban wrote towards the end of her time in office:

> Mrs Thatcher uses two of her most cherished words, 'history' and 'roots'. Her own break with the past has been radical to the point of revolutionary, yet, like those scriptural annotators for whom every verse of the New Testament can be grounded in the foretext of the Old, she continually employs 'history' as a great licensing authority, to validate each new departure from historical practice.[1]

---

1. J. Raban, *God, Man and Mrs Thatcher: A Critique of Mrs Thatcher's Address to the General Assembly of the Church of Scotland* (London: Chatto & Windus, 1989), p. 23.

The dramatic story of Thatcher's new Britain is now well known. This was a new Britain of privatising national industries, private ownership of council houses, the Falklands War, mass unemployment, close ties with Reagan's America and NATO, increased fears of a nuclear holocaust, the end of the Cold War, a year-long Miners' Strike, the end of any serious union influence, inner-city and Poll Tax riots, entrepreneurs, celebrity entrepreneurs, new money, yuppies, identity politics, the sharp decline of Old Labour, garish colours, and all the other familiar things television documentaries play to the music of The Specials, Wham!, and Duran Duran.

When Thatcher died on April 8, 2013, there was something distinctively odd about the public re-emergence of old battles from the 1980s. On the one hand, some protesters were paying for their effectively privatised protest by downloading 'Ding Dong! The Witch is Dead' from the *Wizard of Oz*, while, on the other, hardened Thatcherite publications like the *Daily Mail* were calling for a state funeral to be paid for with public money.[2] It is perhaps the greatest victory of something as divisive as Thatcherism (and neoliberalism) broadly understood to have its negative affects attributed and diverted to one person while at the same time being so widely accepted (no doubt at times unconsciously) even by those who denounced her so strongly.[3] What Žižek wrote of the reception of Fukuyama (which applies in practice to the Left and the Right) could equally be said of Thatcher and Thatcherism in the UK: 'It is easy to make fun of Fukuyama's notion of the "End of History", but most people today are Fukuyamean, accepting liberal-democratic capitalism as the finally found formula of the best possible society, such that all one can do is try to make it more just, more tolerant, and so on'.[4] Indeed, it now appears that Thatcherite views on work, free-market, collectivism, and welfare are more prominent among the younger the generation, and effectively the norm among those born between 1980 and 2000

---

2. We might add that, unlike the *Daily Mail*, Ken Loach (albeit jokingly) called for a privatised funeral ('Put it out to competitive tender and accept the cheapest bid. It's what she would have wanted'). On such ironies surrounding Thatcher's funeral, see e.g. S. Jeffries, 'The old lefties are back – and so are all the old insults', *Guardian* (April 14, 2013).

3. We might recall the classic arguments associated with Stuart Hall and the hegemony of Thatcherism. See e.g. S. Hall, 'The Great Moving Right Show', *Marxism Today* (January, 1979), pp. 14-20; S. Hall and M. Jaques (eds.), *The Politics of Thatcherism* (London: Lawrence & Wishart, 1983); S. Hall, *The Hard Road to Renewal: Thatcherism and the Crisis of the Left* (London: Verso, 1988).

4. S. Žižek, *First as Tragedy, Then as Farce* (London: Verso, 2009), p. 88.

('Generation Y'), and perhaps this comes as no surprise with the decline of unionism and as a more atomistic culture has become more embedded, even if the evidence has been over-exaggerated at times.[5] As John Harris remarked, such Thatcherism is 'seemingly as ordinary and immovable as the weather' and that 'the up-by-the-bootstraps Conservatism of Norman Tebbit and Margaret Thatcher' is 'now built into millions of young lives as a simple matter of fact'.[6] David Cameron may have been more right than even he thought when on the occasion of Thatcher's funeral he claimed that we are all Thatcherites now.[7]

The confusions about Thatcher's legacy (and her death and funeral are only the tip of the iceberg, of course) highlight a key point in understanding Thatcher and Thatcherism: Thatcher herself remains a 'toxic' brand (especially for Conservative Party electioneering) while at the same time Thatcherism in one guise or other became the economic, political, and, arguably, though obviously to a lesser extent, even the cultural norm across the political spectrum, if we understand Thatcherism as Nigel Lawson did. 'Thatcherism', Lawson recognised in his oft-cited definition, should not be everything Margaret Thatcher said and did but rather more generally it 'involves a mixture of free markets, financial discipline, firm control over public expenditure, tax cuts, nationalism, "Victorian values" (of the Samuel Smiles self-help variety), privatisation and a dash of populism'.[8] In fact, Thatcherism still remains the idealised economic norm (arguably in an intensified form) even after the 2008 recession which was widely claimed to be a failure of the financial deregulation her government instigated in the 1980s and taken up by subsequent governments. Of course, we might make the repeated claims against a coherent phenomenon called 'Thatcherism' by pointing

5. J. Ball and T. Clark, 'Generation Self: what do young people really care about?', *Guardian* (March 11, 2013); J. Harris, 'Generation Y: why young voters are backing the Conservatives', *Guardian* (June 26, 2013); Anonymous, 'Generation Boris', *Economist* (June 1, 2013); D. Stuckler and A. Reeves, 'We are told Generation Y is hard-hearted, but it's a lie', *Guardian* (July 30, 2013). For the reports see Ipsos-MORI, 'Generations', http://ipsos-mori-generations.com/Assets/Docs/ipsos-mori-the-generation-frame.pdf?utm_source=website&utm_medium=link&utm_campaign=generationsreport; British Social Attitudes, '29th British Social Attitudes Report: Anxiety Britain', http://www.bsa-29.natcen.ac.uk/.

6. Harris, 'Generation Y'.

7. 'Margaret Thatcher funeral: Cameron speaks of personal debt to former PM', *BBC News* (April 17, 2013), http://www.bbc.co.uk/news/uk-politics-22180610.

8. N. Lawson, *The View from No. 11: Memoirs of a Tory Radical* (London: Bantam Books, 1992), p. 64.

to Thatcher's pragmatism, a range of party-political perspectives, or her hope for charitable giving and social responsibility generated by wealth and standing in contrast to amoral, deregulated casino-banking. But in many ways this would miss the bigger picture. It is sometimes helpful to think less about the person and personalities and more about Thatcherism as a phenomenon generated by her intellectual circle of the 1970s and government of the 1980s, irrespective of whether Thatcher personally intended or wanted all the results that have come with these changes. While there will no doubt be more discussion over precisely what 'Thatcherism' is or is not, in broad terms, then, it is reasonable to think of it as a general Anglicised manifestation of neoliberalism and the economic successor to Keynesianism.

As Thatcherism was beginning to gain momentum in the 1970s, Keith Joseph made the distinction from the economic past rhetorically stark and in ways which would leave their mark on Thatcher's ideas and speeches: Thatcherism was the alternative to Socialism. Indeed, Joseph even claimed that public spending in the UK meant that, in many ways, it was more socialist than any other country outside the Eastern Bloc.[9] Joseph, along with, for instance, Friedrich Hayek, Milton Friedman, Alan Walters, and Enoch Powell, were among the most profound influences on Thatcher and the development of Thatcherism and were, as we saw in Chapter 1, part of the wider developing neoliberal trend.[10]

But this does not mean, of course, that we should downplay the influence of Thatcher herself, even if some commentators have bought into the rhetoric of Thatcherism by hugely over-emphasising her individual significance. In particular we should not neglect her Methodist upbringing, or at least her memory of it. When looking at the role of the Bible and religion in the thinking of political figures, political commentators and historians have tended to provide cursory accounts at best, but this is probably less so in the case of Thatcher, if only because of the sheer volume of literature on her life and premiership. Indeed, she even

9. H. Young, *One of Us: A Biography of Margaret Thatcher* (London: Macmillan, 1989), p. 84.

10. Compare the recollections of John Ranelagh, *Thatcher's People: An Insider's Account of the Politics, the Power, and the Personalities* (London: Fontana, 1992), p. ix: 'On the occasion of Thatcher's only visit to the Research Department, in the summer of 1975, a friend and colleague, Michael Jones and I prepared a paper for her meeting with us... Another colleague also prepared a paper... Before he had finished speaking to his paper, the new Party leader reached into her briefcase and took out a book. It was Friedrich von Hayek's *The Constitution of Liberty*. Interrupting our pragmatist, she held up the book for all of us to see. "This", she said sternly, "is what we believe", and banged Hayek down on the table.'

claimed that 'I believe in what are often referred to as "Judaeo-Christian" values: indeed my whole political philosophy is based on them'.[11] Her Methodist upbringing in particular has been well documented and some of Thatcher's own Christianised rhetoric has long been noted. But this type of analysis of Thatcher's career appears to be increasing recently, with Graeme Smith and Eliza Filby particularly showing in a more thoroughgoing way how Thatcher's Nonconformism had a significant influence on her politics.[12]

Thatcher described her parents as 'staunch Methodists' and recalled that her childhood home was 'practical, serious and intensely religious… Our lives revolved around Methodism.' On Sundays she had morning Sunday school, followed by the 11am Morning Service, more Sunday school in the afternoon and, from the age of 12, piano playing for children to sing hymns.[13] Methodism made up much of her social and cultural life. Thatcher reminisced about her enjoyment of the musical side of Methodism, particularly piano playing and her love of poetry with Methodism and Wesley's hymns providing 'some really fine religious poetry' alongside Kipling and Milton.[14] Tellingly, John O'Sullivan, a Thatcher speechwriter, claimed that one of her favourite sayings of Wesley was 'Earn all you can; save all you can; give all you can'.[15]

Thatcher's father, Alfred Roberts, was a local councillor and town Alderman in Grantham, as well as being a local lay preacher. In terms of politics, seeds of Thatcherism can be found here too, as commentators typically point out. Though he stood as an independent, Thatcher described her father's politics as 'old-fashioned liberal', though she never remembered him 'as anything other than a staunch Conservative'.[16]

11. M. Thatcher, *The Downing Street Years* (London: Harper Press, 1993), p. 510.

12. G. Smith, 'Margaret Thatcher's Christian Faith: A Case Study in Political Theology', *JRE* 35 (2007), pp. 233-57; Filby, 'God and Mrs Thatcher', pp. 176-211; Eliza Filby, 'Margaret Thatcher: her unswerving faith shaped by her father', *Telegraph* (April 14, 2013). Cf. P. Riddell, *The Thatcher Era and its Legacy* (Oxford: Blackwell, 1991). Although not a conventional historical account, Raban, *God, Man and Mrs Thatcher*, is still well worth reading.

13. M. Thatcher, *The Path to Power* (London: Harper Press, 1995), pp. 5-6.

14. Thatcher, *Path to Power*, pp. 8-9, 17. Cf. C. Moore, *Margaret Thatcher: The Authorized Biography. Vol. 1, Not for Turning* (London: Allen Lane, 2013), p. 6.

15. J. Kirchick, 'A friendship without prejudice: Thatcher's kinship with Jews and Israel', *Haaretz* (April 10, 2013).

16. Thatcher, *Path to Power*, p. 21. Cf. J. Campbell, *Margaret Thatcher. Vol. 1, The Grocer's Daughter* (London: Jonathan Cape, 2000), pp. 11-14; Moore, *Margaret Thatcher*, pp. 15-16.

John Campbell similarly summed up Alfred Roberts' Methodism as
one of 'personal salvation' and his preaching as 'fundamentalist, Bible-
based, concerned with the individual's responsibility to God for his own
behaviour', with 'an uncompromisingly individualistic moral code which
underpinned an individualistic approach to politics and commerce'.[17]
We have seen in previous chapters, including that on Christopher Hill,
that Methodism and Nonconformism provided important influences and
ideas for twentieth-century leftist thought. This was not quite the case
for Thatcher's upbringing, which was a result of the split in Methodism
between the Methodist Free Churches and the Wesleyans. The Methodist Free Churches became more in line with the emerging Labour Party
and the political radicalism found in Nonconformism. The Wesleyans
claimed greater affinity with the teaching of John Wesley himself and a
social and theological conservatism, including a Conservative tendency
following the split in the Liberal vote in the 1920s.[18] The Roberts family belonged firmly to the Wesleyans. Grantham had churches of both
Methodist types and in inter-war Grantham the differences were not
reconciled as they were elsewhere in the reunifications under the Methodist Union in 1932.[19] Thatcher, of course, knew that the 'general political
tendency' among Methodists and other Nonconformists in Grantham
was 'somewhat to the left wing and even pacifist'.[20] Her memory of
Methodists in Grantham included those prominent in organising the
'Peace Ballot' of 1935: 'we had our own views about that in the Roberts
household... On this question and others, being staunchly Conservative,
we were the odd family out.'[21] If we were going to push the influence on
Thatcherism perhaps a little too far, we might further note that Thatcher
claimed that 'Religious life in Grantham was very active and, in the days
before Christian ecumenism, competitive and fuelled by a spirit of
rivalry'.[22]

But in her Methodism and the 'religious life' of Grantham we certainly can find further influences on Thatcherism, particularly in ways
which would run counter to some ideas about the role of state support.
There were networks of private charity and church events in Grantham
for 'elderly folk living alone or who were sick' and 'children who needed
help', or just 'either to keep young people happy or to raise funds for one

17. Campbell, *Grocer's Daughter*, p. 16.
18. Filby, 'Margaret Thatcher'.
19. See further Campbell, *Grocer's Daughter*, pp. 15-16.
20. Thatcher, *Path to Power*, p. 10.
21. Thatcher, *Path to Power*, p. 11.
22. Thatcher, *Path to Power*, p. 8.

purpose or another',[23] though Alfred Roberts did not, significantly, appear to stretch such charity to the Jarrow Marchers.[24] The importance of family support played a distinctive role in Thatcher's memory of her Methodist upbringing. She remembered a debate between her father and a church-goer about the 'prodigal son' of a friend who had spent his parents' savings and returned with a young family. The church-goer had insisted that the son was always going to be a problem and should be turned away. Thatcher's father gave a reply which remained 'vivid in my mind': 'A son is a son, and he must be greeted with all the love and warmth of his family when he turned to them. Whatever happens, you must always be able to come home.'[25] Among the values 'instilled in church…faithfully reflected in my home' was the 'emphasis on hard work… [W]e were never idle – partly because idleness was a sin.'[26] More generally, the social side of Methodism, such as meals with fellow church-goers, would anticipate her later career: she found herself enjoying the conversation as it moved from religion to national and international politics.[27]

Thatcher preached as a Methodist while at Oxford[28] and she married the divorcee Denis Thatcher (1951) and christened her children (1953) in John Wesley's Chapel in London but her church affiliation would change, perhaps superficially, when she shifted to Anglicanism in the 1950s. However, her retrospective reasoning tried to keep the Methodist and Wesleyan link and betrayed no particularly strong yearning for the Church of England, suggesting, perhaps, that establishment assimilation, political ambition, and convenience could have been as good reasons as any for her new home.[29] In an interview with the *Catholic Herald* in 1978 she is reported to have said:

> You know, John Wesley would of course say that he was a member of the Church of England, and the service he believed in was the Church of England service; but it was too high for the kind of evangelical work he was doing. Methodism is the most marvellous evangelical faith and there is the most marvellous love and feeling for music in the Methodist Church which I think is greater than in the Anglican Church. But you sometimes feel the need for a slightly more formal service and perhaps a

23. Thatcher, *Path to Power*, pp. 9, 13, 17.
24. Campbell, *Grocer's Daughter*, pp. 16-17.
25. Thatcher, *Path to Power*, p. 6.
26. Thatcher, *Path to Power*, p. 11.
27. Thatcher, *Path to Power*, p. 9.
28. Moore, *Margaret Thatcher*, p. 49.
29. Filby, 'God and Mrs Thatcher', pp. 182-83.

little bit more formality in the underlying theology too. So throughout my life I have felt the need for both things, to some extent for the informality, for the works you do; but always I found myself groping out for more of the actual teaching of the religious basis...but not the real High Church.[30]

As Campbell argued, despite Thatcher's own romantic spin on her childhood, there still remains evidence of a yearning for a life beyond Grantham and provincial Methodism.[31] In this respect, it is notable too that Thatcher did not wish to force her children into attending church and have the strict Christian upbringing she had.[32] Nevertheless, Thatcher continued to talk to different church groups in the 1950s and 1960s typically covering themes of patriotism, public service, Christian decency, and even the provision of welfare. Indeed, none of this particularly marks her out from standard Tory Christianity of the time.[33] However, along with her political conversion to monetarism, the 1970s saw her return to the Nonconformism of her earlier life which she believed provided answers to perceived social permissiveness and helped her answer some of the questions raised by the collapsing dominance of Keynesianism. As Filby has shown in more detail, 'Mrs Thatcher deliberately evoked Nonconformist ideas such as self reliance, hard work and moral restraint as the only true path for a nation overwhelmed by the excesses of bureaucratic welfare, union militancy and immoral conduct... Thatcher's Nonconformist religious ethos and specifically that of her father, provided the means, language and motifs through which she articulated the neo-Conservative agenda.'[34] It is from this time onwards, with her Nonconformism always in the background, that we will contextualise Thatcher's Bible. But first we need to look at another important and related contextual issue: Thatcher on Communism.

30. R. Dowden, 'The Thatcher Philosophy', *Catholic Herald* (December 22, 1978).

31. Campbell, *Grocer's Daughter*, p. 25.

32. Filby, 'God and Mrs Thatcher', p. 182.

33. Filby, 'God and Mrs Thatcher', p. 182.

34. Filby, 'God and Mrs Thatcher', p. 184. Filby provides further contextualisation of Thatcher's Christianity in strands of 1970s English Christianity concerned with individual salvation, moral conservatism, and various 'middle-class values', and wider debates on the interaction between politics and religion in the Anglican Church and the Conservative Party (pp. 138-75). Compare Thatcher's memories in e.g. M. Thatcher, 'I Believe: A Speech on Christianity and Politics (St Lawrence Jewry)', *Margaret Thatcher Foundation* (March 31, 1978), http://www.margaretthatcher.org/document/103522, and M. Thatcher, 'Speech at St Lawrence Jewry', *Margaret Thatcher Foundation* (March 4, 1981), http://www.margaretthatcher.org/document/104587.

2. Thatcherite Anthropology: Thatcherism versus Communism

From the days of her first seeking a parliamentary seat to her time as Prime Minister, Thatcher's thinking about the priority of the individual and freedom over the State was intertwined with her sharply negative attitude towards Communism and shaped by the Cold War.[35] Her fierce rhetoric of the 1980s is well known but it was already an important part of her thinking in the 1970s in the run-up to her becoming Prime Minister.[36] It was a speech she gave at Kensington Town Hall in January 1976 that would lead to the Soviet media describing her as the 'Iron Lady', a title that would not only stay with her but one she happily accepted. The speech was about the importance of defence expenditure to counter Soviet Russia which she claimed was 'bent on world domi-nance, and they are rapidly acquiring the means to become the most powerful imperial nation the world has seen... The advance of Commu-nist power threatens our whole way of life.'[37] Soviet world domination would obviously put its interests at odds with British national interests but Thatcher's profound dislike for Communism was based on a number of factors related to her thinking on human freedom and State control, as well as the influence of her father's thinking on religious affiliation and membership.[38] Not only did she attack the human rights record of the Soviet Union, but she believed that this was a direct consequence of Marxist thinking which, she argued, placed economics (and State-controlled economics at that) at the heart of human existence. For Thatcher, the boundless capabilities of the individual are what make a society or country great and from which economic growth would flour-ish. In her first party conference speech as Tory leader in 1975 she outlined her vision of the new Conservatism: 'Our capitalist system produces a far higher standard of prosperity and happiness because it believes in incentive and opportunity, and because it is founded on human dignity and freedom'. A free economy 'guarantees our liberties'

---

35. For summaries see e.g. Young, *One of Us*, pp. 31, 169-70, 389-90; Campbell, *Grocer's Daughter*, pp. 150, 338-42, 353-76; R. Vinen, *Thatcher's Britain: The Politics and Social Upheaval of the1980s* (London: Pocket Books, 2009), pp. 236-46; Moore, *Margaret Thatcher*, pp. 51-56, 306, 310-11, 320, 330-31, 552-86; R. Harris, *Not for Turning: The Life of Margaret Thatcher* (London: Bantham Press, 2013), pp. 40-41, 133-36, 252-78.

36. Thatcher, *Path to Power*, pp. 340-93.

37. M. Thatcher, 'Britain Awake: Speech at Kensington Town Hall', *Margaret Thatcher Foundation* (January 19, 1976), http://www.margaretthatcher.org/document/102939.

38. Filby, 'God and Mrs Thatcher', pp. 181-82.

and is 'the best way of creating wealth and prosperity for the whole country'. In turn, the greater the private enterprise, the more money people will have to spend as they choose, which will include more money for charitable giving, 'to help the old and the sick and the handicapped'.[39]

She further put a distinctive nationalist spin on her understanding of Socialism, claiming it is 'bad for Britain' and that 'Britain and Socialism are not the same thing'. The rights to work and spend what is earned on personal property, while having the State as servant rather than master, 'are the British inheritance'.[40] This British emphasis was expanded further and would partly underpin her international allies. She pro-claimed that the Conservative Party believe that foreign policy should involve a close relationship with America ('our traditional ally') because this is 'part of our Anglo-Saxon tradition…and it adds to our contribution to the European Community'. Similarly, this Anglo-Saxon slant would mean embracing 'the countries of the Old Commonwealth' who are 'always close to the hearts of British people': Australia, New Zealand, and Canada. Indeed, she suggested that Australians and New Zealanders had concluded, as had she, that Socialism had failed and that Austral-asian thinking is 'part of a wider reawakening' to the 'need to provide a more positive defence of the values and traditions on which Western civilisation, and prosperity, are based'.[41]

Thatcher extended this sort of nationalist and anti-Socialist thinking to her criticism of the Labour Party and post-war economic thinking more generally. In her criticism of the lack of spending on defence before she was Prime Minister, she argued that Britain was 'poorer than more of our NATO allies' which was 'part of the disastrous economic legacy of Socialism'.[42] However, she would even claim that there were 'voices', including a 'sizeable chorus' from the Labour Party, who wanted to exploit British economic problems of the 1970s and 'put a Marxist system' in place of a 'free enterprise society'.[43] This sort of language was possible because of her hostility to nationalisation and State control. Thatcher claimed that it would be more beneficial to the country if the Labour Party would act more like West German Social Democrats and 'stop trying to prove their Socialist virility by relentlessly nationalising

39. M. Thatcher, 'Speech to Conservative Party Conference, Blackpool', *Margaret Thatcher Foundation* (October 10, 1975), http://www.margaretthatcher.org/document/102777.

40. Thatcher, 'Speech to Conservative Party Conference'.

41. Thatcher, 'Britain Awake'.

42. Thatcher, 'Britain Awake'.

43. Thatcher, 'Speech to Conservative Party Conference'.

one industry after another'.[44] In her memoirs she recalled that she was never in doubt that the 'true aim' of the 'hard Left' was revolutionary in that it 'sought to impose a Marxist system on Britain' and for whom 'the institutions of democracy' were little more than 'tiresome obstacles on the long march to a Marxist Utopia'.[45]

But it was not just the Labour Party, or even the post-war British economy more generally, which faced being contaminated by the labels 'Marxist' or 'Communist'. A number of 'enemies within' were described as 'Marxist' or 'Communist', some plausibly so (e.g. Arthur Scargill), others less so, including the institution formerly known as the Tory Party at Prayer.[46] Forming another important context for Thatcher's exegesis (see below), Thatcherite economics and individualism brought her government into conflict with the Church of England, epitomised by the report, *Faith in the City*.[47] While the Church would move more towards critiquing the amorality of the market and the dangers of greed and consumerism in the late 1980s, *Faith in the City* (published in 1985) represented a response to the early years of the Thatcher government, particularly high unemployment and the inner-city riots of 1981.[48] What brought *Faith in the City*, and some high-profile Anglican clergy, in direct ideological conflict with the Thatcher government was that the report advocated the importance of State interventionism and welfare support in the prevention or alleviation of poverty and unemployment, as well as condemning the morality and negative impact of Thatcherite economics. While the dominant Anglican position (including *Faith in the City*) in relation to 1980s Thatcherism is probably best described as centre-left or social democratic, this did not stop the Thatcher government placing *Faith in the City* firmly into the camp of the enemy. Before it was even published it was infamously labelled by one unnamed member of Thatcher's government (thought to be Norman Tebbit) as 'pure Marxist theology' while another MP claimed it was proof that a 'load of Communist clerics' were running the Church of England.[49]

44. Thatcher, 'Speech to Conservative Party Conference'.

45. Thatcher, *Downing Street Years*, p. 339.

46. See e.g. H.B. Clark, *The Church under Thatcher* (London: SPCK, 1993); J. Campbell, *Margaret Thatcher. Vol. 2, The Iron Lady* (London: Jonathan Cape, 2003), pp. 389-95; Filby, 'God and Mrs Thatcher'.

47. The Archbishop of Canterbury's Commission on Urban Priority Areas, *Faith in the City: A Call for Action by Church and Nation* (London: Church House Publishing, 1985).

48. Filby, 'God and Mrs Thatcher', pp. 64-99.

49. Staff Reporters, 'Thatcher clashed with Church, despite her faith', *Church Times* (April 12, 2013); Young, *One of Us*, p. 417; Campbell, *Iron Lady*, p. 390.

3. From the Evil Empire to the Axis of Evil

After the fall of the Soviet Union, Thatcher's economic and political Manichean outlook did not disappear. Indeed, it could be similarly applied to her Orientalist (and arguably theologically unorthodox, though with echoes of an anti-Calvinist Methodism/Wesleyan Arminianism) understanding of religion East and West. She distinguished between attitudes which make a society more enterprising (e.g. curiosity, imagination, ingenuity, application, and risk taking) and those that do not, adding that these attitudes reflect different religious and philosophical traditions. These different traditions and societies are further marked by those, on the one hand, who promote creativity and individual uniqueness (i.e. the 'Judaeo-Christian tradition' of the West) and those, one the other, who limit free will and stress the importance of fate (i.e. 'the great Asian religious traditions' of the East and African religious traditions). Thatcher's Jews and Christians respect the value of work and accept that the human is master of their environment rather than an offshoot of environment, a view Thatcher attributed to pantheists. Thatcher was aware of qualifications but ultimately believed that these distinct traditions were reflected in differences in economic progress and living standards.[50]

Her binary thinking, like so much of the dominant Anglo-American high-political thinking, could, of course, be transferred to Islam or tailored accordingly; indeed her handling of binary opposites in relation to her constructions of religion and politics was already being developed in her handling of the *Satanic Verses* controversy and in her justification of western support for the Afghan Mujahidin and Zia's Pakistan over against Soviet Russia.[51] We will look at the contexts for these sorts of ideas in more detail in the chapter on Tony Blair because Thatcher's major statements on Islam were given over ten years after she had been ousted from power. And, after all, if Thatcher was to be marked by the Cold War, Blair was to be marked by the 'war on terror' and all the implications concerning 'religion' that have accompanied it. Nonetheless, it is worth discussing Thatcher's views on Islam because they are understood in very similar terms to her Cold War thinking and, as we will see in the chapter on Blair, the key Blairite positions are all implicit in the logic of Thatcher's assessment of 'religion' and Islam after the Cold War.

50. M. Thatcher, *Statecraft: Strategies for a Changing World* (London: HarperCollins, 2003), pp. 418-19.

51. Filby, 'God and Mrs Thatcher', pp. 200-201; Moore, *Margaret Thatcher*, pp. 563-64.

Indeed, Thatcher was able to make the transition from the Evil Empire to the Axis of Evil and the War on Terror with relative ease through categorising Communism as a pseudo-religion and the development of 'Marxist-Leninist ideology...as a kind of substitute for faith' and comparing them with Islam which, she claimed, is definitely a 'real' religion.[52] She made the common claim that there is a 'disturbing' connection between Islam and violence and noted that apart from the Cold War remnant that is North Korea, 'all of the states classed as "rogues" – Iraq, Syria, Libya, Iran and Sudan – are mainly, and in some cases militantly, Muslim', as are those listed by the US State Departments as state sponsors of terrorism.[53] In one sense, then, we might wonder if the more things change, the more they really do stay the same. However, there was something different in Thatcher's thinking on religion and terror. For a start, Thatcher claimed that much of 'the Muslim world' after the end of the Cold War has shown that 'secular ideology...shrivels in the face of religious belief'.[54] But also recall her distinction between 'pseudo-religion' and 'real' religion when comparing Communism and Islam. This seemingly small distinction is important because in Thatcher's thinking 'religion' almost always had some redeeming feature.

So, for instance, she would also leave the door open, or at least unlocked, to an idea that would get more emphatically taken up by Blair: the idea that there is a purer (and potentially democratic) strand in Islam which can be traced back to its origins in the Qur'an. In the same context as writing about Osama bin Laden and what 'appears to many' (and nothing more definitive than that) to be a close connection between 'Islamic extremism' and 'terrorist violence', she could also suggest that 'Islamic scholars and Western experts will continue to argue about what the Koran says and means on the subject'.[55] There are further hints that there was, for Thatcher, something inherently positive in 'religion', no matter how negative it may seem at a given time. Indeed, she followed the common rhetorical move, again pushed more vigorously by Blair, that when 'religion' has often played a role in terrorism it is 'a twisted justification', obviously implying that there is a purer or untwisted form of religion. Indeed, note the subtle rhetorical move Thatcher made when listing examples of terrorism, particularly in her treatment of 'Marxism' and 'religion':

52. Thatcher, *Statecraft*, p. 216.
53. Thatcher, *Statecraft*, p. 220.
54. Thatcher, *Statecraft*, pp. 216-17.
55. Thatcher, *Statecraft*, p. 220.

> From the Assassins of the twelfth century through to their successors, the
> suicide bombers of Hamas, Hizbollah and Islamic Jihad in the twenty-first
> century, professed Muslims have certainly been involved. But the Tamil
> extremists…claim to be Hindus. ETA…and the murderous Shining Path
> guerrillas in Peru are both Marxist. Even where religion appears to be at
> the core of violence, appearances can deceive. Most Irish Republican
> terrorists long ago stopped considering themselves – and stopped being
> treated by the Church – as Catholics.[56]

'Professed' Muslims have certainly been involved, Tamil extremists
'claim' to be Hindus, the IRA long stopped being 'considered' Catholics
but ETA and Shining Path *are* Marxists! This distinction may be subtle
but it is important: Thatcher was prepared to claim openly the philosophical incompatibility of her politics and her Christianity with Marxism
and Communism; in 'religion' there was something which could still be
salvaged. The reason for this was her intense interest in individualism
which she thought was probably present in 'religion'. 'The idea that an
individual human being has a moral value in his or her own right', is
something she suspected is present to some extent in what she saw as
the major religions. She reasoned that this was because once there is
acceptance of the concept of a unique and eternal human 'soul', there
is the beginnings of recognition of someone as a person who must therefore be given dignity and rights.[57]

This sort of elevation of the individual, she would often argue, was
alien to Marxism and Communism and it is instructive to compare
Thatcher's thinking on the previous Great Enemy: the Soviet Union. Of
the Cold War, she claimed to have 'never forgot' that it was 'a conflict
of one system against another' where 'ultimately, our two opposing systems were incompatible' and that the West would inevitably win
'because it rested on the unique, almost limitless, creativity and vitality
of individuals'.[58] Moreover, in contrast to her thinking on religion and
Islam, the idea that there was a glimmer of hope in the system of Soviet
Communism was ruled out by Thatcher. She disagreed with 'the opti-
mists' whom she claimed appeared regularly on television analysing the
Soviet Union 'in terms borrowed from liberal democracies' and were 'in
search of light at the end of even the longest tunnel, confident that
somehow, somewhere, within the Soviet totalitarian system rationality
and compromise were about to break out'. Thatcher's own thinking was
'much closer' to those 'who grasped that totalitarian systems are different

56. Thatcher, *Statecraft*, p. 221.

57. Thatcher, *Statecraft*, pp. 250-51. Cf. Smith, 'Margaret Thatcher's Christian
Faith', pp. 251-55.

58. Thatcher, *Downing Street Years*, pp. 450-52.

in kind, not just degree, from liberal democracies and that approaches relevant to the one are irrelevant to the other'. But did not Thatcher end up 'doing business' with Gorbachev? Thatcher recalled that contrary to those with whom she would normally agree, she did not accept that a totalitarian system was 'more-or-less unable to produce an individual to that system'. But this was not due to an inherent goodness of Communism; on the contrary, she argued that 'even a system like that of the Soviets, which set out to crush the individual' could not totally succeed in doing so and, by the same logic, 'at some time the right individual could challenge even the system which he had used to attain power'. This is why Thatcher could claim that she sought out a figure like Gorbachev: 'I was confident that such a person could exist, even within a totalitarian structure, because I believed that the spirit of the individual could never ultimately be crushed in the Kremlin any more than in the Gulag'.[59]

Even when editing her book *Statecraft* in the aftermath of September 11 – an attack she believed was aimed at the heart of American culture and values[60] – Thatcher could still claim to find positive values in a religion like Islam that she did not in Soviet Communism. For instance, she claimed that, as a conservative and a Christian, she could appreciate a great deal of what she saw when visiting the Middle East and claimed to appreciate the opinions of 'sophisticated' Muslim writers. She further claimed to admire strong family ties, dislike of anti-social behaviour, generally low levels of crime, and an obligation to help the poor.[61] However, Thatcher also argued that there was another side to Muslim society exemplified in corruption and hypocrisy of certain people in power, including the oppression of women, cruelty in punishments, and a certain 'seediness' and 'backwardness' seen in 'many' Middle Eastern cities.[62] As this would imply, and would be made much more explicit by Blair, the measurement for the validity of Islam was its compatibility with liberal democracy and a certain Anglo-American vision of the world. Although bin Laden's view 'is shared by few' and his actions have been widely condemned by 'devout Muslims', this condemnation was not, she pointed out, universal. Moreover, she claimed, Muslim leaders who denounce Israel regularly and promote an anti-American

59. Thatcher, *Downing Street Years*, pp. 452-53.

60. Thatcher, *Statecraft*, p. 60. *Statecraft* was published in 2002 but the first draft was completed before September 11, 2001 (Thatcher, *Statecraft*, p. xxiii). The final form of the book contains a number of references to the attacks as well as to bin Laden, al-Qaeda and the Taliban.

61. Thatcher, *Statecraft*, p. 217.

62. Thatcher, *Statecraft*, pp. 217, 220.

struggle should not be surprised when some of their audience and followers begin to act on such sentiments.[63] But there was also another, more instantly recognisable, Thatcherite problem; she would claim that, so far, it appears that predominantly Muslim states are unable to develop liberal political institutions. For Thatcher, this meant that such political problems are connected to economic underdevelopment which was only made harder because her construction of the values of Islamic society are described in terms in which she would describe Communism, in that there is less emphasis placed on the individual and greater on the community than there is outside Muslim societies. However, unlike much of her rhetoric on Communism, she could still see a glimmer of goodness, claiming it is still too early to state that Islam is compatible with democracy.[64]

4. Let My People Go! Margaret Thatcher's Bible

One of the most well-known uses of the Bible by Thatcher came in 1988 when she resolved to read the entirety of the Old Testament. She would update and quiz her staff and, no doubt partly due to her long history as an exegete and speaker, believed parts of the Old Testament should not be left in the hand of those untutored.[65] The choice of, what was to her, the Old Testament was particularly fitting because Thatcher had, as we have already seen in passing, a distinctive interest in Jews and Judaism, firmly putting the 'Judeo' back into 'Judeo-Christian'.[66] There are a number of reasons for this. Politically, she was a strong (though not uncritical) supporter of Israel and its role in the Middle East and, more locally, her Finchley constituency was around twenty percent Jewish when she was elected in 1959.[67] Unlike some of those we might euphemistically label 'traditional Tories', including those in her Finchley constituency, she felt an affinity with Jews and Judaism.[68] Not against

---

63. Thatcher, *Statecraft*, p. 221.

64. Thatcher, *Statecraft*, p. 222.

65. Young, *One of Us*, pp. 425-26; Campbell, *Iron Lady*, p. 389; Smith, 'Margaret Thatcher's Christian Faith', p. 233. Thatcher seemed to prefer quoting the Old Testament more than the New Testament (Filby, 'God and Mrs Thatcher', p. 189).

66. Young, *One of Us*, pp. 422-26; Filby, 'God and Mrs Thatcher', pp. 199-201; Moore, *Margaret Thatcher*, pp. 136-37.

67. Young, *One of Us*, p. 422; Moore, *Margaret Thatcher*, p. 137.

68. For a range of retrospectives see e.g. C.C. Johnson, 'Thatcher and the Jews', *Tablet* (December 28, 2001), http://www.tabletmag.com/jewish-news-and-politics/87027/thatcher-and-the-jews; T. Lazaroff, G.F. Cashman, and J. Pau,

working with stereotypes herself, she claimed that Jews and Judaism (as well as her Old Testament) effectively encapsulated Thatcherite ideals in terms of individualism, self-help, entrepreneurism, and community support which in part reflected her promotion of Jewish Tory politicians:

> I have enormous respect for the Jewish people, inside or outside Israel. There have always been Jewish members of my staff and indeed my Cabinet. In fact I just wanted a Cabinet of clever, energetic people – and frequently that turned out to be the same thing… In the thirty-three years I have represented it I never had a Jew come in poverty and desperation to one of my constituency surgeries. They had always been looked after by their own community… But I often wished that Christian leaders would take a leaf out of the teaching of Britain's wonderful former Chief Rabbi, Immanuel Jakobovits, and indeed that Christians themselves would take closer note of the Jewish emphasis on self-help and acceptance of personal responsibility.

Thatcher was 'wary of falling into the trap of equating in some way the Jewish and Christian faiths' and believed that the Old Testament can only be fully understood with the New Testament.[69] Nevertheless, it was indeed the former Chief Rabbi, Immanuel Jakobovits, who became the closest ally of Thatcher from the religious establishment, not only in terms of support for Thatcherite Conservatism but also in his criticisms of Anglican clergy and theologians who openly attacked the impact of Thatcherite economics in the controversies surrounding *Faith in the City*.[70]

'PM: Thatcher a true friend of Jewish People, Israel', *Jerusalem Post* (April 8, 2013); Kirchick, 'A friendship without prejudice'; J. Lipman, 'Margaret Thatcher: One of Us', *Jewish Chronicle Online* (April 11, 2013), http://www.thejc.com/news/uk-news/105333/margaret-thatcher-one-us; C. Shindler, 'In her fury, I saw values alien to us', *Jewish Chronicle Online* (April 11, 2013), http://www.thejc.com/comment-and-debate/analysis/105329/in-her-fury-i-saw-values-alien-us; A. Bermant, 'Don't believe the hype: Thatcher's "friendship" with Israel based on pragmatism not love', *Haaretz* (April 17, 2013); J. Cummings, 'How British Jews built Thatcherism', *Haaretz* (April 17, 2013).

69. Thatcher, *Downing Street Years*, pp. 509-10. Cf. Moore, *Margaret Thatcher*, p. 137.

70. Young, *One of Us*, pp. 423-25; Campbell, *Iron Lady*, pp. 394-95; Filby, 'God and Mrs Thatcher', pp. 199-200; Harris, *Not for Turning*, p. 21. See further I. Jakobovits, *From Doom to Hope: A Jewish View on 'Faith in the City', the Report of the Archbishop of Canterbury's Commission on Urban Priority Areas* (London: Office of the Chief Rabbi, 1986).

This understanding of Thatcherism through the Old Testament, Jews, and Judaism is typical of Thatcher's understanding of the Bible more generally and an, or perhaps the, ideal of what she thought Christianity should be. Yet throughout her career as a front bench politician her exegesis would be delivered to audiences who were not always as welcoming as Jakobovits. She gave exegetically grounded addresses to St Lawrence Jewry (the official Church of the Corporation of London), to the Greater London Young Conservatives (the Iain Macleod Memorial Lecture),[71] and most famously – and controversially – to the General Assembly of the Church of Scotland in 1988, the so-called 'Sermon on the Mound', which in many ways functioned as a response to criticism such as that found in *Faith in the City*.[72] It is from these speeches in particular that we can piece together the tenets of Thatcherite exegesis.

Having said that, for Thatcher, the Bible ('as well as the tradition of the Church') was more about general principles and tells us 'very little directly about political systems or social programmes'; the nearest it got was 'Christ telling his disciples to render unto Caesar that which is Caesar's, and unto God that which is God's'. While political judgments could rest on moral assumptions, they owed more to pragmatic decisions about what was right for the country in the here and now rather than to rigidly applied universal truths.[73] Thatcher further noted that 'nowhere in the Bible is the word democracy mentioned' and, ideally, when Christians meet, the purpose should not be 'to ascertain the mind of the majority' but 'the mind of the Holy Spirit'. However, this did not stop Thatcher from using the Bible as a reference point for her key ideas. Indeed, she claimed she was 'an enthusiast for democracy' because it 'most effectively safeguards the value of the individual, and, more than any other system, restrains the abuse of power by the few. And that *is* a Christian concept.'[74]

The idea of safeguarding the individual was central to Thatcher's exegesis and so it should be no surprise that the Liberal Bible is consistently present. Thatcher claimed that Britain had gradually adopted a 'system of government and a way of living together which reflected the

71. M. Thatcher, 'Dimensions of Conservatism: Iain Macleod Memorial Lecture: Speech to Greater London Young Conservatives', *Margaret Thatcher Foundation* (July 4, 1977), http://www.margaretthatcher.org/document/103411.

72. M. Thatcher, 'Speech to the General Assembly of the Church of Scotland', *Margaret Thatcher Foundation* (May 21, 1988), http://www.margaretthatcher.org/document/107246.

73. Thatcher, 'I Believe'.

74. Thatcher, 'Speech to the General Assembly of the Church of Scotland'.

values implicit in that Book [the Bible]' and that 'the teachings of Christ applied to our national as well as personal life'. Thatcher acknowledged that there were 'considerable blotches' in British history but, thanks to the patience and vision of people like Lord Shaftesbury and William Wilberforce, Parliament could be convinced that 'it was inconsistent for a nation whose life was based on Christ's teachings, to countenance slave labour, children and women working in the mines and criminals locked up in degrading conditions'.[75] Thatcher was, of course, aware that non-Christians were part of British history, particularly in more recent history, even in her own party and among her own supporters.[76] But this too could be reconciled with the idea of Britain as a country that 'most people would accept' as having a national 'way of life…founded on Biblical principles'.[77] In the Sermon on the Mound, she argued that 'one of the great principles of our Judaic-Christian heritage is tolerance'. People 'with other faiths and cultures' have 'always been welcomed' and 'assured of equality under the law, of proper respect and of open friendship… There is no place for racial or religious intolerance in our creed.'[78]

If we cut through Thatcher's rhetoric here, we find that it aligns to the developing notions of neoliberal multiculturalism discussed in the previous chapter. We can see that her Bible re-inscribed the primacy and paternalism of a white, Anglo-Saxon history, an acceptance of the Other who accepts the rules of this history and who, presumably, supports the right national cricket team, as well as, perhaps, an implicit or perceived 'Englishness'; Thatcher's government did, after all, provoke Scottish and Welsh nationalism.[79] This comes through stronger still in Thatcher's

---

75. Thatcher, 'Speech at St Lawrence Jewry'.

76. E.g. 'Today, we live in what the academics call "a pluralist society". My Party, like most others, is not only drawn from all Christian denominations and from other religions, but also contains some who would hotly deny that religion has anything at all to do with politics or even with morality' (Thatcher, 'I Believe'). Or again: 'Today we live in what is called a "plural society", one in which many different traditions of belief exist alongside each other and also alongside other more recent fashions – those of total disbelief or even nihilism' (Thatcher, 'Speech to the General Assembly of the Church of Scotland').

77. Thatcher, 'Speech at St Lawrence Jewry'.

78. Thatcher, 'Speech to the General Assembly of the Church of Scotland'.

79. Smith, 'Margaret Thatcher's Christian Faith', refers to Thatcher's theology as 'Anglo-Saxon Nonconformity'. On the contextualisation of the discussions, and contradictions, of race, ethnicity, nationalism, and 'Englishness' of Thatcher's Christianity see Filby, 'God and Mrs Thatcher', pp. 21, 56-62, 139, 174, 195-99, 219-31. For a summary of Thatcher's government on race, religion, and nationalism,

inevitable endorsement of what we have called the Cultural Bible (see Chapter 1). Thatcher believed that Britain is 'a nation whose ideals are founded on the Bible' and that this has been 'our very life blood'. This, she claimed, was a heritage which should be 'preserved and fostered'. She made the familiar claim that without such an understanding 'it is quite impossible to understand our history and literature' and that there is a 'strong practical case' for 'ensuring that children at school are given adequate instruction in the part which the Judaic-Christian tradition has played in moulding our laws, manners and institutions'. How else, she asked, can we make sense of Shakespeare or Walter Scott, or seventeenth-century history in England and Scotland, without knowledge of the Bible?[80] She would also recall the story of Mary and Martha through one of her favourite poets, Kipling, as a means of explaining the apparent practicality of her mother.[81] This Cultural Bible was, Thatcher argued, tied up with the political heritage of her own party. Thatcher explained that the Tory Party was not just a British party but *primarily* a Church party whose concerns for Church then State were then expanded to other fields such as economics.[82] In this context, Thatcher argued that the values that have driven this tradition were historically rooted in the Bible:

> For through the Old Testament our spiritual roots go back to the early days of civilisation and man's search for God. The New Testament takes us on through Greek philosophy, Roman law, the Church Fathers and the great flowering of a specifically Christian civilisation in the middle ages from which our own characteristic way of life emerged.[83]

This is not simply deference to tradition or an embrace of the importance of 'culture'. Thatcher believed that Tories have 'always believed' in the primacy of the Church 'because it was concerned with those things which matter fundamentally to the destiny of mankind'.[84]

---

see e.g. Vinen, *Thatcher's Britain*, pp. 225-29. Cf. Raban, *God, Man and Mrs Thatcher*, p. 58, on Thatcher's claim to 'tolerance' and loving your neighbour as yourself in the Sermon on the Mound: 'Immigrants must, of course, live up to our standards'.

80. Thatcher, 'Speech to the General Assembly of the Church of Scotland'.

81. M. Stoppard and M. Thatcher, 'TV Interview for Yorkshire Television, *Woman to Woman* (November 19, 1985)', *Margaret Thatcher Foundation*, http://www.margaretthatcher.org/document/105830. On the significance of using the Kipling version, see Moore, *Margaret Thatcher*, p. 9.

82. Thatcher, 'Dimensions of Conservatism'; Thatcher, 'I Believe'.

83. Thatcher, 'Dimensions of Conservatism'.

84. Thatcher, 'I Believe'.

But even with the paternalistic Tory spin, there is little so far that we have not already seen in other manifestations of the Liberal or Cultural Bible. Yet, as Graeme Smith has shown, running throughout Thatcher's speeches on religion, Christianity, and the Bible is the theological idea of renewing the spirit of the nation for the present.[85] And renewal, of course, meant a more distinctively Thatcherite vision for Britain and it is here that we get something closer to what we might identify as the Neoliberal Bible and her dismissal of post-war alternatives which she believed were too state-heavy and functioned at the expense of the individual. For Thatcher, 'men of good will must be concerned with the relief of poverty and suffering' without reliance on the State, and a renewal of 'the spirit of the nation' for the here and now was needed. Again, Thatcher looked to the past and the Bible for inspiration and those 'few' individuals 'who see visions and dream dreams'. The individuals who revived such values come from a 'predominantly Christian culture' and were 'the prophets in the Old Testament, the Apostles in the New, and the reformers in both church and state'.[86] And we can overlook (in terms of exclusive access to such illustrious leadership) the gendered language of Thatcher's time – such visionaries no doubt implicitly included Thatcher herself.[87] In a barb aimed at Jim Callaghan during the 1979 General Election, she tacitly outlined her leadership credentials in elevated and biblical terms of the prophetic outsider bringing change: 'The Old Testament prophets did not say, "Brothers, I want a consensus". They said, "This is my faith. This is what I passionately believe. If you believe it, too, then come with me."'[88] Commentators such as Filby have further noted a strong streak of charismatic, evangelical, and missionary zeal in her political rhetoric, influenced by her father the lay preacher and now part of her vision of leading Britain into the new

---

85. Smith, 'Margaret Thatcher's Christian Faith', pp. 248-51. See also Filby ('God and Mrs Thatcher', pp. 195-99) on Thatcher's broader model of a 'Christian Nation'.

86. Thatcher, 'I Believe'.

87. On Thatcher's general 'sense of destiny' see Moore, *Margaret Thatcher*, pp. 291, 302, 536.

88. Quoted in B. Särlvik and I. Crewe, *Decade of Dealignment: The Conservative Victory of 1979 and Electoral Trends in the 1970s* (Cambridge: Cambridge University Press, 1983), p. 29. It is too tempting not to make a comparison with her recollections of the religious life of Grantham: 'In a sermon just after the Battle of Britain, 'the preacher told us that it is "always the few who save the many": so it was with Christ and the apostles' (Thatcher, *Path to Power*, p. 11).

neoliberal era.[89] Here Filby was building on the work of Heather Nunn
on the construction of the Thatcher persona and the interaction between
gender, nationalism, and power, including a sustained use of the language and imagery of militarism and conflict, all functioning against the
forces of chaos.[90] As part of this public construction, Nunn showed how
Thatcher saw herself as a lay preacher whose political leadership was an
extension of her religious values, and that her speeches contain the
specific imagery of the Egyptian exile, wilderness and tablets of stone,
Babylon, and the battle with Satan.[91]

Much use of biblical language in liberal democratic tradition is, at
least in terms of domestic policy, unlike that of Thatcher's Old Testament prophets in that it is typically consensual.[92] But Thatcher-the-
visionary, in her own way, as her own speeches and rhetoric suggest, was
attacking a consensus and leading her own neo-Conservative revolution
in political thinking which marks her out from most major politicians
who have used the Bible. And such revolutionary thinking almost
inevitably needs the Devil, or a battle of Good versus Evil. This sort of
quasi-biblical, 'apocalyptic' thinking is, of course, classic Thatcher,[93] and
something we have already seen in her views of the Evil Empire and
implicit in her thinking about the enemies within. Thatcher certainly
claimed that there is 'always a temptation, not easily resisted, to identify
our opponents with the Devil' and the suggestion that politics can be
presented as 'clear and simple choices between good and evil' was
likewise tempting. But she dismissed such ideas as 'dangerous and evil
tendencies' which 'embitter politics' and 'trivialise religion and morality'.[94] However, note that she constructs even this dismissal of the language of evil in nothing less than the language of evil. She also claimed
more fundamentally that 'there is some evil in everyone and that it
cannot be banished by sound policies and institutional reforms' and in
basic terms, Thatcher believed that 'to most ordinary people, heaven and
hell, right and wrong, good and bad, matter'.[95]

---

89. Filby, 'God and Mrs Thatcher', pp. 186-88. Cf. Moore, *Margaret Thatcher*,
p. 7.

90. H. Nunn, *Thatcher, Politics and Fantasy: The Political Culture of Gender
and Nation* (London: Lawrence & Wishart, 2002).

91. Nunn, *Thatcher, Politics and Fantasy*, pp. 88-89.

92. Sherwood, 'Bush's Bible'; Berlinerblau, *Thumpin' It*. See also Chapter 1.

93. E.g. Campbell, *Iron Lady*, p. 391; Nunn, *Thatcher, Politics and Fantasy*,
pp. 88-90; Filby, 'God and Mrs Thatcher', pp. 186, 201-205.

94. Thatcher, 'I Believe'.

95. Thatcher, 'I Believe'.

The function of evil worked on two levels for Thatcher: the personal level of individual duty and the level of the State, particularly the impact the State can have on the individual:

> ...it is one thing to say that the relief of poverty and suffering is a duty and quite another to say that this duty can always be most efficiently and humanely performed by the State. Indeed, there are grave moral dangers and serious practical ones in letting people get away with the idea that they can delegate all their responsibilities to public officials and institutions.[96]

Thatcher did not believe that 'Socialist theory and Socialist practice *as we know them*' (my italics) were 'contrary to the New Testament' and she did not claim to believe that 'you can't be a good and sincere Christian and a dedicated Social Democrat'.[97] However, the qualifications 'as we know them' and 'Social Democrat' are important because, for Thatcher, the most extreme manifestation of the intrusion of the State was Soviet or Soviet-inspired Communism – the Evil Empire. Yet Thatcher's thinking on such matters was not simply a practical reaction to the Cold War and her hostility to Soviet Communism, but a fundamental philosophical disagreement with Marxism and Socialism more generally. For Thatcher, 'whereas socialists begin with society, and how people can be fitted in, we start with Man' and because 'we see man as a spiritual being, we utterly reject the Marxist view, which gives pride of place to economics'.[98] Tyranny was, she argued, inherent in, or at least a consequence of, socialist thinking and its downplaying of the role of the individual. The Gulag 'only happened because socialism demoralised the whole nation, replaced the individual conscience by the party, right and wrong by what was good for the revolution'.[99] And these radically different philosophical assumptions were, for Thatcher, rooted in the Bible: 'Totalitarian Marxists will disagree with me in principle. They make no bones about rejecting all the assumptions from which I begin. I believe that their philosophy is utterly inconsistent with the Gospel.'[100]

As we saw, Thatcher did not stop with the placement of Communism in a Manichean framework and, despite her qualifications about Social Democrats, was prepared to extend her view of darkness to what was happening at home. 'What I believe is an evil', she argued in 1981, was

96. Thatcher, 'I Believe'.

97. Thatcher, 'I Believe'.

98. Thatcher, 'Dimensions of Conservatism'. Cf. Moore, *Margaret Thatcher*, pp. 348-50.

99. Thatcher, 'Dimensions of Conservatism'.

100. Thatcher, 'I Believe'. Cf. Filby, 'God and Mrs Thatcher', pp. 201-205.

sustained inflation.[101] It is worth contextualising this argument: it was made in the face of anxieties and criticisms over high unemployment and high unemployment was deemed an unfortunate by-product of combating high inflation in the emerging neoliberal thinking of the Thatcherite intellectual circle. Thatcher's response was to insist that her attack on inflation was both a moral and economic issue which required an alternative vision:

> For over thirty years the value of our currency has been eroding. It is an insidious evil because its effects are slow to be seen and relatively painless in the short run. Yet it has a morally debilitating influence on all aspects of our national life. It reduces the value of savings and therefore thrift, it undermines financial agreements, it stimulates hostility between workers and employers over matters of pay, it encourages debt and it diminishes the prospects of jobs. And that's why I put its demise at the top of my list of economic priorities. It is, in my view, a moral issue not just an economic one.[102]

On becoming leader of the Conservative Party it was statements similar to these that began to mark a more radical break with the economic past. She could be more emphatic still. 'The post-war Keynesian recipe of endless growth and full employment through high demand levels', she claimed to the Young Conservatives in 1977, had gone 'sour'.[103] While she still saw a role for the State in law, education, and protection of those most vulnerable, Thatcher argued that if people believe that the State is the answer to everything, they 'hand over' personal responsibility and charity becomes 'second-best'; in sum, 'the milk of human kindness' will dry up. In fact, Thatcher argued more dramatically (and 'biblically') that 'the time will come – indeed it is close at hand' (cf. John 4.21-23) when 'what the taxpayer is willing to provide for the good of humanity will be seen to be far less than what the individual used to be willing to give from love of his neighbour'. With an allusion to Luke 10.25-37 in place, Thatcher could prophetically warn: 'So do not be tempted to identify virtue with collectivism. I wonder whether the State services would have done as much for the man who fell among thieves as the Good Samaritan did for him?'[104] A long-standing favourite parable for Thatcher,[105] this foreshadowed Thatcher's more famous exposition of the

---

101.   Thatcher, 'Speech at St Lawrence Jewry'. Cf. Smith, 'Margaret Thatcher's Christian Faith', p. 243.
102.   Thatcher, 'Speech at St Lawrence Jewry'.
103.   Thatcher, 'Dimensions of Conservatism'.
104.   Thatcher, 'I Believe'.
105.   Campbell, *Grocer's Daughter*, p. 17.

Good Samaritan in an interview with Brian Walden in 1980 when she argued that 'no-one would remember the Good Samaritan if he'd only had good intentions; he had money as well'.[106]

The lack of concern for the rights of the individual and downplaying of self-help was in sharp distinction, Thatcher claimed, from a major emphasis of the Bible, and the New Testament in particular.[107] Indeed, even more fundamental to the Bible than the concept of the nation was 'the idea of personal moral responsibility'.[108] Further emphasising the point of contrast, she could likewise turn to an individualised notion of salvation: 'Our religion teaches us that every human being is unique and must play his part in working out his own salvation'.[109] Thatcher expressed such ideas (and not for the first time) in what we might generally label 'Pauline' language. 'What mattered fundamentally', she claimed, 'was Man's relationship to God, and in the last resort this depended on the response of the individual soul to God's Grace'.[110] The New Testament may be 'preoccupied with the individual' and 'his need for forgiveness and for the Divine strength which comes to those who sincerely accept it' but this was not alien to her Old Testament. The Ten Commandments (a passage, we might recall, aimed at the Israelites) were addressed 'to individuals': 'In the statements, "honour thy father and thy mother", "thou shalt not steal", "though shalt not bear false witness", and so on, the "thou" to whom these resounding imperatives are addressed is you and me'. Thatcher was also aware that 'we can deduce from the teachings of the Bible principles of public as well as private morality' but ultimately 'all these principles refer back to the individual in his relationships to others'. Again, this was dressed up in what would become classic Thatcherism: 'we must always beware of supposing that

---

106.   Transcript available at M. Thatcher and B. Walden, 'TV Interview for London Weekend Television *Weekend World* (1980)', *Margaret Thatcher Foundation*, http://www.margaretthatcher.org/speeches/displaydocument.asp? docid=104210. Thatcher had a distinctive take on 'loving your neighbour': 'You will note that it does not denigrate self, or elevate love of others above it. On the contrary, it sees concern for self and responsibility for self as something to be expected, and asks only that this be extended to others' ('Dimensions of Conservatism'). Filby ('God and Mrs Thatcher', p. 91) comments: 'The aim here was to counter the supposition that Christian duty to others should supplant or suppress personal responsibility, while the underlying political intention was to disprove the often-quoted Biblical basis for state socialism.' See also Raban, *God, Man and Mrs Thatcher*, p. 48.

107.   Cf. Filby, 'God and Mrs Thatcher', pp. 190-94.

108.   Thatcher, 'Speech at St Lawrence Jewry'.

109.   Thatcher, 'Dimensions of Conservatism'.

110.   Thatcher, 'I Believe'.

somehow we can get rid of our own moral duties by handing them over to the community; that somehow we can get rid of our own guilt by talking about "national" or "social" guilt. We are called on to repent our own sins, not each others' sins.' Notably the primary social needs in this Thatcherite take on Christianity and the Bible are not to be found in the State as she understood it but 'the family, the neighbourhood and the nation'.[111] 'You recall that Timothy was warned by St. Paul', she noted, 'that anyone who neglects to provide for his own house (meaning his own family) has disowned the faith and is "worse than an infidel"' (1 Tim. 5.8).[112]

Thatcher also believed that the solution to the tension between individual and society ('the whole of political wisdom consists in getting these two ideas in the right relationship to each other') was to be found in the New Testament. Her take on corporate thinking was (not for the first time) expressed in Pauline language: 'There is that great Christian doctrine that we are all members one of another expressed in the concept of the Church on earth as the Body of Christ. From this we learn our interdependence, and the great truth that we do not achieve happiness or salvation in isolation from each other but as members of Society.' This was 'one of the great Christian truths' which influenced her political thinking; the other was that 'we are all responsible moral beings with a choice between good and evil'.[113] Moreover, her individualism was, of course, part of that renewed spirit of the corporate entity of the nation, a combination which she also defended with reference to the Bible. Freedom, she argued, requires self-discipline and great responsibility which is not only tied in with 'glory and salvation' but also with 'our national greatness'. She looked to the book of Proverbs to provide support: 'Righteousness Exalteth a Nation' (Prov. 14.34).[114]

Some Church responses to Thatcher's individualist emphasis on choice and freedom and her take on the Protestant Work Ethic were effectively making claims that a Thatcherite Gospel was a false Gospel which enslaved as much as it freed.[115] If we were feeling theologically minded we might go further. There are times when Thatcher's rhetoric on individual *choice* might appear to be so strongly influenced by her

111.   Thatcher, 'Speech at St Lawrence Jewry'.
112.   Thatcher, 'Speech to the General Assembly of the Church of Scotland'. In the choice of the more archaic 'infidel', there may also be an echo of Thatcher's Orientalising contrast between West/Christianity/Judaism and East/Islam, as Raban suggested (Raban, *God, Man and Mrs Thatcher*, p. 54).
113.   Thatcher, 'I Believe'.
114.   Thatcher, 'I Believe'.
115.   Filby, 'God and Mrs Thatcher', p. 84, cf. pp. 206-11.

free-market philosophy that she came close to ideas of works-righteousness which would, of course, run clean contrary to some of the most famous ideas to emerge from the Reformation, though it could be argued that she retained the influence of the comparable importance of free will in anti-Calvinist Methodism and Wesleyan Arminianism from her own Protestant background. We already saw something of this in her Orientalising generalisations about religion East and West which were contrasted in terms of a 'limited role for free will and a very large role for fate' (East/non-Western) versus 'the creativity of man', the 'uniqueness of the individual', and 'respect for the value of work' (West). It naturally follows that Thatcher's exegesis would reveal the same sorts of emphases. For instance, the following claims are typical, if not memorable, for the connection made between the free-market and the crucifixion:

> from the beginning man has been endowed by God with the fundamental right to choose between good and evil... [W]e were made in God's own image and, therefore, we are expected to use all our own power of thought and judgement in exercising that choice... Our Lord Jesus Christ, the Son of God, when faced with His terrible choice and lonely vigil *chose* to lay down His life.[116]

She even hinted at earning eschatological salvation in her politicised use of Christian language: 'Christianity...also taught me that, in the final analysis, politics is about personal relations, about establishing the conditions in which men and women can best use their fleeting lives in this world to prepare themselves for the next'.[117]

Yet mixed in with these ideas are those of divine grace ('if we open our hearts to God, He has promised to work within us') and she did ultimately believe in Christianity over Judaism because, as she claimed, 'I do not, as a Christian, believe that the Old Testament – the history of Law – can be fully understood without the New Testament – the history of Mercy'.[118] Moreover, Thatcher did emphatically claim in a way long-familiar to Tory Christians that 'there is one heresy which it seems to me

---

116. Thatcher, 'Speech to the General Assembly of the Church of Scotland' (italics original). Cf. Raban, *God, Man and Mrs Thatcher*, p. 33: 'Christ dying on the Cross joins those folk who have exercised their right to choose – to buy their own council houses, to send their children to private schools, to occupy "paybeds" in NHS-funded hospitals'.

117. Thatcher, 'I Believe'. On Thatcher's emphasis on works over grace and its political connotations see R. Samuel, 'Tory Party at Prayer', *New Statesman* (January 28, 1983), pp. 8-10.

118. Thatcher, *Downing Street Years*, p. 510.

that some political doctrines embrace...the belief that Man is perfect-able'.[119] It is notable that this discussion was in the context of a criticism of Socialism and the idea that if education, health, and social welfare were correctly administered then 'we shall have exorcised the Devil'. This, she claimed, is 'bad theology' and, in her then recent past, a failure: 'we have expended vast efforts and huge sums of money on policies designed to make people better and happier. Have we really brought about a fundamental improvement in Man's moral condition?'[120] The Devil 'is still with us, recording his successes in the crime figures and in all the other maladies of this society, in spite of its relative material comfort'.[121] It is worth pointing out that this is from a speech given a year before she came to power and it again presumably functioned partly as an implicit criticism of Callaghan's Labour government.

But if Thatcher thought human perfection was heretical then the same logic had to apply equally to herself and free-market thinking. 'You must never be like the parable of the Pharisees as it were', she claimed while recalling her Christian upbringing in an interview with Miriam Stoppard in 1985, 'because you just really know how far you fall short of your ideal' (Luke 18.9-14).[122] Thatcher could therefore claim elsewhere that 'as a Christian' she was 'bound to shun Utopias on this earth and to recognise that there is no change in Man's social arrangements which will make him perfectly good and perfectly happy'. The 'free-enterprise system of itself' would not 'automatically...have these effects'. Of course, Thatcher believed in the necessity of the free market but it remained one aspect – a very important aspect – of *national recovery and prosperity* rather than leading to utopia. Indeed, the lack of utopia meant that she could likewise emphasise the need for charity and claim that the moral dimension of her vision for the recovery of the nation (a people with 'a purpose and an ethic') 'can only come from the teachings of a Faith'.[123] 'Remember the woman with the alabaster jar of ointment', she later warned.[124]

119.	Thatcher, 'I Believe'. See also Filby's discussion of Thatcher and Original Sin ('God and Mrs Thatcher', pp. 194-95).

120.	Thatcher, 'I Believe'. Or again in the Sermon on the Mound: 'To assert absolute moral values is not to claim perfection for ourselves. No true Christian could do that' (Thatcher, 'Speech to the General Assembly of the Church of Scotland').

121.	Thatcher, 'I Believe'.

122.	Stoppard and Thatcher, 'TV Interview'.

123.	Thatcher, 'I Believe'.

124.	Thatcher, 'Speech to the General Assembly of the Church of Scotland'.

Thatcher's individualist vision was also designed to generate 'wealth, well-being and freedom', while the State, as well as charitable individuals and organisations, could still provide a safety net for the more defenceless members of society. Thatcher believed that collectively the Ten Commandments, loving our neighbour as ourselves, the 'importance of observing a strict code of law', the New Testament 'record of the Incarnation', the 'teachings of Christ, and the establishment of the Kingdom of God', all provide 'a proper attitude to work' and 'principles to shape economic and social life'. In her Sermon on the Mound, she infamously used the example of Paul in 2 Thessalonians 3.10 ('If a man will not work he shall not eat') as justification of the view that 'we must work and use our talents to create wealth... Indeed, abundance rather than poverty has a legitimacy which derives from the very nature of Creation.'[125] This meant that the creation of wealth was, for Thatcher, a 'Christian obligation' and a fulfilment of 'our role as stewards of the resources and talents the Creator has provided for us'.[126] Here Thatcher turned to the seemingly lost idea that is 'inherent in Christ's parable of the talents'. Thatcherite exegesis would have it that the steward who 'simply did not use the resources entrusted to him' was 'roundly condemned' while the 'two who used them to produce more wealth were congratulated and given more'. She qualified this by immediately adding that to endorse the mediocre, to 'flinch from the challenge', or to complain that the government ought to be doing something, 'is not the way to rekindle the spirit of the nation'.[127]

But, if the Bible is to be part of wealth creation, it runs into one obvious difficulty: those biblical passages which appear to suggest an outright hostility to wealth (e.g. Mark 10.17-31; Luke 6.24-25; 16.19-31; Matt. 6.24//Luke 16.13; Matt. 11.8//Luke 7.25). Harking back to her father's exegetical views,[128] Thatcher dealt with such difficulties by interpreting them in a relative sense. 'Christ did not condemn riches as such', she argued, 'only the way in which they were used and those

---

125.   Thatcher, 'Speech to the General Assembly of the Church of Scotland'.

126.   Thatcher, 'Speech at St Lawrence Jewry'.

127.   Thatcher, 'Speech at St Lawrence Jewry'. See further the helpful discussion in Campbell, *Iron Lady*, pp. 391-93. On the Parable of the Talents, compare Raban, *God, Man and Mrs Thatcher*, p. 39: 'the Parable of the Talents is a fine example of His style at its most teasingly playful and paradoxical... [H]ere Mrs Thatcher appears to regard it simply as a divine sanction for the bond-broker and the arbitrageur.'

128.   Filby, 'God and Mrs Thatcher', p. 181. Cf. Smith, 'Margaret Thatcher's Christian Faith', pp. 245-47.

who put their trust in them'.[129] What the Church needs to do, she later added, is to guide us about our use of this world's wealth ('the spiritual dimension comes in deciding what one does with the wealth').[130] Again, Thatcher did argue that charity and social responsibility are ways in which wealth can be used in favour of good. But Thatcher was still aware of what might be seen as the selfish excesses of a neoliberal way of thinking and putting too much trust in money. The 'Tenth Commandment – Thou shalt not covet – recognises that making money and owning things could become selfish activities', she said. With her brand of Nonconformism coming through, she even claimed that adopting a 'philosophy' of 'eat, drink and be merry for tomorrow we die' (cf. Isa. 22.13; Eccl. 8.15; 1 Cor. 15.32), 'can result' in a 'grasping for wealth for its own sake and the pursuit of selfish pleasure'. Note that there is a degree of tension here. We get the less definitive 'can result' not 'does result' which contrasts sharply with her denunciations of collectivism. We also get the negative implications of this selfish attitude labelled a 'philosophy' with the implicit suggestion that it is not really quite biblical or Christian; indeed, the Bible is referenced to show that those who live for the moment are very much in the wrong.[131] Yet this would simultaneously overrule Ecclesiastes 8.15: 'So I commend enjoyment, for there is nothing better for people under the sun than to eat, and drink, and enjoy themselves, for this will go with them in their toil through the days of life that God gives them under the sun'. It is as if implicit exegetical tension were unconsciously reflecting the political tension of her individualism.

---

129.   Thatcher, 'I Believe'. Or again, 'it is not the creation of wealth that is wrong but love of money for its own sake (Thatcher, 'Speech to the General Assembly of the Church of Scotland'). It might be worth pointing out that Thatcher's interpretation of difficult texts concerning wealth is hardly new. Early Christian scribes also felt the need to alter biblical texts such as Mark 10.23-25 where there is a stark denunciation of wealth to imply, like the Thatcherite addition, that trusting in wealth rather than wealth per se was problematic. See J.G. Crossley, 'The Damned Rich (Mark 10.17-31)', *ExpTim* 116 (2005), pp. 397-401.

130.   Thatcher, 'Speech to the General Assembly of the Church of Scotland'.

131.   'On that day the Lord God of hosts called to weeping and mourning, to baldness and putting on sackcloth; but instead there was joy and festivity, killing oxen and slaughtering sheep, eating meat and drinking wine. "Let us eat and drink, for tomorrow we die". The Lord of hosts has revealed himself in my ears: Surely this iniquity will not be forgiven you until you die, says the Lord God of hosts' (Isa. 22.12-14); 'If with merely human hopes I fought with wild animals at Ephesus, what would I have gained by it? If the dead are not raised, "Let us eat and drink, for tomorrow we die"' (1 Cor. 15.32).

In fact it is at these points of tension that we find those disjunctions between ideals and reality, and even between Thatcher and certain manifestations of Thatcherism. She did not seriously impose the moral agenda of the outraged Christian right of the 1970s and 1980s, despite the perceptions of connections and similarity of public image. For whether she liked it or not, the Gekkoized and powerful subculture of self-centred, champagne-guzzling yuppies was quickly linked with the rise of Thatcherism.[132] As Filby has pointed out, Thatcher may have come from an austere Methodist background where her father sought the preservation of the Sabbath in Grantham, but she nevertheless aimed to put through the Shops Bill in 1986 and the deregulation of Sunday trading. Filby adds: 'she never reconciled the conflicting priorities of freedom of choice with the preservation of tradition. Over time, consumption became religion, the Sabbath like any other day, and the shopping centres the new churches and chapels.'[133] In retrospect, it seems that Thatcher herself was partly aware of such contradictions. Indeed, Frank Field recalled that Thatcher told him of the greatest disappointment of her premiership: 'I cut taxes as I thought it would generate a giving society. It didn't.'[134] Human charity may of course be imperfect and some of those with wealth may indeed feel social responsibility but Thatcher's decade was, as we all know, divisive. Social responsibility did not curb inner-city rioting, getting on bikes and looking for jobs was never a realistic solution to unemployment,[135] and thrift, personal creativity, and the safety net of charity did not make Poll Tax protestors feel particularly secure. And a good case could be made for healthy bonuses rather than social responsibility being the underlying motive for the Metropolitan Police to venture north and help Thatcher crush the miners who were, after all, defending a traditional community and close

132.   Campbell, *Grocer's Daughter*, p. 30: 'Alf Roberts would have been appalled by "Thatcherism"'.

133.   Filby, 'Margaret Thatcher'.

134.   F. Field, 'What would Thatcher do today about...the rich', *Times* (April 18, 2013). Field also mentioned this anecdote in the House of Commons tributes to Thatcher after her death.

135.   The Tebbitism was picked up in *Faith in the City*, p. 205: 'It is unrealistic to assume that even the skilled and mobile residents of our cities can all "get on their bikes" and move to the small towns and rural areas which are the focal points of economic growth to get a job – even if there were sufficient jobs (and housing) available for all. Certainly a middle-aged redundant shipyard worker in Gateshead cannot be expected to compete with a young school leaver in the South-East for a new service sector job.'

family relations and who received help from church support groups. This was a way of life that in another time Thatcher might have at least partly admired. Harmony, truth, and faith her reign did not always bring.[136]

But this brings us back to the beginning of this chapter: 'Thatcher' and 'Thatcherism' are labels that remain confrontational and 'toxic' while the key features of Thatcherism have been absorbed and taken up by all Prime Ministers since. As we will see, post-Thatcher readings of the Bible in the circles of the political elite and in parts of popular culture are not dramatically removed in the abstract, even if rhetorically they have had to be very careful not to become too closely associated with the Thatcher brand. Her exegesis, and her divisive and Manichean approach, might have since been softened and presented as far more inclusive, but she still crystallised a dominant understanding of the Bible in English politics and culture. Before we see how Thatcherism and Thatcher-ite exegesis became so embedded in popular biblical interpretation, we must first look at how the way was paved for Thatcher's Bible and its competitors, some influences, and failed alternatives in the light of the cultural changes of the 1960s.

136.   Compare the comments of Filby, 'Margaret Thatcher': 'Where critics go wrong with Thatcherism is to assume that there was no moral thinking behind the economics. Where admirers go wrong is to appreciate the moral underpinnings of Thatcherism without admitting that these often conflicted with its economic aims... Therein lies the great conflict within Thatcherism.'

Part III

CARRIERS OF CULTURAL CHANGE

Chapter 5

'WE'RE ALL INDIVIDUALS':
WHEN LIFE OF BRIAN COLLIDED WITH THATCHERISM[*]

1. Satire, Comedy, and Freedom

As David Harvey has shown, as part of the cultural shift towards neoliberalism in the 1960s and 1970s, the rhetoric of freedom, liberty, and individualism could be constructed in opposition to 'the stifling bureaucratic ineptitude of the state apparatus and oppressive trade union power'.[1] This rhetoric would manifest itself in a range of seemingly contradictory ways but, despite sharp differences and interests, the developing neoliberal consensus would harness some of the key similarities. On the one hand, Margaret Thatcher and her circle were pushing for radical economic change and challenging and reconfiguring traditional upper-class dominance and consensual politics, eventually paving the way for a new dominant class of sometimes provocative entrepreneurs. On the other hand, the youth movements, pop culture, and political satirists would mock politicians, the upper classes, the British class system, and union bureaucracy, and even provide a cultural and leisure resource for the new entrepreneurs. This attitude, Harvey added, would ground the later radicalism of the 'postmodern turn' and the scepticism would 'prepare the way for the suspicion of all metanarratives'.[2] The so-called 'Satire Boom' of the early 1960s would lead to some of the most significant examples of twentieth-century English antiestablishment comedy. It produced figures such as Peter Cook, Dudley Moore, Jonathan Miller, Alan Bennett, David Frost, John Bird, and John Fortune, and more collective ventures such as the TV programme *That Was the*

---

[*]   For earlier thoughts on *Life of Brian* and its uses of the Bible in the context of intellectual developments in the 1970s, see J.G. Crossley, 'Life of Brian or Life of Jesus? Uses of Critical Biblical Scholarship and Non-orthodox Views of Jesus in Monty Python's *Life of Brian*', *Relegere* (2011), pp. 95-116. For discussion of issues surrounding this, I would like to express my gratitude to Deane Galbraith

1.   Harvey, *Neoliberalism*, p. 57.
2.   Harvey, *Neoliberalism*, p. 51; see also p. 31.

Week That Was, the magazine *Private Eye*, and the increasing prominence of the more historic Cambridge Footlights club. Among the most internationally famous and enduring products of this period in terms of combining satire, comedy, youthful enthusiasm and iconic pop cultural status was Monty Python (Graham Chapman, John Cleese, Eric Idle, Terry Jones, and Michael Palin).

Monty Python's most famous and enduring legacy has, of course, been *Life of Brian* (dir. Terry Jones, 1979).[3] It is of some significance that the film was released in the same year that Thatcher was coming to power. Certainly, the secular humanism and morality underpinning *Life of Brian* would have been sharply at odds with Thatcher's own beliefs on a number of key issues. Likewise, the stance of Monty Python is hardly conservative or Conservative while *Life of Brian* itself, at times, borders on the anarchistic. Individually, Michael Palin would identify as a traditional Labour supporter while John Cleese was a prominent supporter of the SDP–Liberal Alliance in the 1980s and the Liberal Democrats in the 1990s, though Cleese's liberalism was open to certain Conservative views on entrepreneurship and defence.[4] Having said that, and no matter how perversely the presumably sometimes unintended overlaps were, some of the most memorable features of the satire in *Life of Brian* picked up on attacks that were associated with Thatcher. Indeed, Terry Jones could still make a loose comical connection between Jesus and Thatcher: 'My feelings towards Christ are that he was a bloody good bloke, even though he wasn't as funny as Margaret Thatcher'.[5]

More precisely, though, the film clearly satirises (as Cleese did for the SDP–Liberal Alliance) trade union and revolutionary leftist and Marxist groups in its portrayal of the wildly ineffective and overly bureaucratic People's Front of Judea, even if (unlike Thatcher) there was some lament over misguided focus and a loss of ideals. The British establishment and class system are implicitly satirised, whether through the strict Latin teacher, market traders, the tortured liberal crucifixion official, or the incompetent ruling classes and imperial administrators. But the anti-establishment satire has its limits, particularly in the case of imperialism,

3. All references to *Life of Brian* are from Monty Python, *The Life of Brian Screenplay* (London: Methuen, 2001). Page references to the screenplay will be included within parentheses in the main text.

4. H. Lacey, 'Python with no venom: Michael Palin profile', *Independent* (August 31, 1997). Cleese's party political broadcasts are available on YouTube. E.g. http://www.youtube.com/watch?v=VKp7HDv01hk and http://www.youtube.com/watch?v=9gv4Abt3sZU.

5. Quoted in R. Sellers, *Always Look on the Bright Side of Life: The Inside Story of HandMade Films* (London: John Blake, 2003), p. 5.

such as when the revolutionary Reg partly unintentionally listed its (not entirely historically accurate) benefits in his famous 'What Have the Romans Ever Done for Us' speech. As Philip Davies pointed out, 'The British...and especially the public-school class from which Monty Python comes, are content to poke gentle fun at its administrators, without condemning the system itself. The gifts of the Romans to the Jews point to the gifts of the British empire to large areas of the planet.'[6] But if the old is not totally thrown out, there is a degree of ideological reconfiguration and emphasis on what really matters. The alternative to the general criticism of religious interpretation in *Life of Brian* is found in the only real occasion when the film gets close to having a serious message: Brian's call for individualism and self-help over the collectivism of the crowd (p. 72). In the film this is a message of common sense (in both the popular and Gramscian meaning of the phrase) which ten years earlier could have been more naturally associated with anarchist and student voices from 1968.

2. The Radical Figure of Jesus/Brian

Life of Brian carries a number of ideological tensions in the aftermath of the 1960s which Thatcherism would attempt to harness, hold together, reconfigure, or transform. It did this partly by picking up on the Radical Jesus and transforming him into a figure more fit for late-twentieth-century Britain and, more specifically, through the figure of Brian. Moreover, through the figure of Brian, the film stealthily constructs a very different Jesus of history from the Christ of faith.[7] But does not *Life of Brian* attack the problematic interpretation, 'established religion', and even religious belief itself? Certainly, but using Jesus to make such a point is hardly new (see Chapter 1); even dedicated atheists or non-Christians as diverse as Proudhon, John Lennon, Douglas Adams, and Bill Hicks could see Jesus ultimately as someone misunderstood by his followers and who could be salvaged for radical or liberal sensibilities.

But there is another related problem with the idea that Monty Python used the figure of Jesus: the argument that Jesus and Brian are obviously two different characters in *Life of Brian* and that Jesus is portrayed

6. P.R. Davies, '*Life of Brian* Research', in *Whose Bible Is It Anyway?* (London: T&T Clark/Continuum, 2004), pp. 142-55 (152). This essay was first printed in J.C. Exum and S.D. Moore (eds.), *Biblical Studies/Cultural Studies: The Third Sheffield Colloquium* (Sheffield: Sheffield Academic Press, 1998), pp. 400-414.

7. For uses of the 'Christ of faith' and the 'Jesus of history' with reference to *Life of Brian* see Davies, 'Research', pp. 150-51.

respectfully and traditionally (certainly in terms of Hollywood Jesuses). Ever since opening in 1979 there have been consistent attempts to downplay the perceived blasphemous or disrespectful elements of *Life of Brian*. Eric Idle provided a standard defence of the film:

> Christ is in the movie twice. His birth's in there in the first place and then He's in the Sermon on the Mount. There's no denial of His existence, it's all about churches, that's what it is…it's about people interpreting, people speaking for God and people wanting to kill for God…[8]

Even Terry Gilliam's diligent churchgoing mother did not see what all the fuss was about because there was, after all, differentiation between Jesus and Brian right at the beginning in the stable scene.[9] Similar comments have been made by critical scholars such as Carl Dyke:

> *Brian* is not directly blasphemous. Nor would it have a prayer of mainstream acceptance and effectiveness if it were. It is not a broadside or even a shot across the bows so much as a nudge in the ribs. With respect to Jesus, who makes three brief tangential appearances, the movie is downright orthodox. In each case, the message is not that Jesus is wrong, or even that worshipping Jesus is wrong, but that fallible humans find all sorts of creative ways to get worshipping Jesus wrong… The Pythons' Jesus is not just behaviourally appropriate: he is divine… In terms of core Christian beliefs, the movie is reverent and unquestioning… Overall, by accepting the common sense of Jesus' divinity and ethical authority, *The Life of Brian* locates itself squarely within the hegemonic network of Christianity.[10]

These kinds of arguments are necessary partly because there have been, obviously, allegations of blasphemy and offensiveness aimed at the film and such allegations could be made, as we will shortly see, by audiences assuming Brian really is Jesus. Aside from the infamous attacks from Mervyn Stockwood (the then Bishop of Southwark) and Malcolm Muggeridge on the BBC 2 show *Friday Night, Saturday Morning* (BBC, 1979), there was uproar aplenty. In America, the film faced protests

8. The Pythons, *The Pythons' Autobiography* (London: Orion, 2003), p. 385.

9. Pythons, *Autobiography*, p. 355; Sellers, *Bright Side*, p. 21.

10. C. Dyke, 'Learning from *The Life of Brian*: Saviors for Seminars', in G. Aichele and R. Walsh (eds.), *Screening Scripture: Intertextual Connections between Scripture and Film* (Harrisburg: Trinity, 2002), pp. 229-50 (237-38, 240). See further R. Walsh, *Reading the Gospels in the Dark: Portrayals of Jesus in Film* (Harrisburg: Trinity Press International, 2003), pp. 29-33, 38-39; R. Walsh, 'Three Versions of ~~Judas~~ Jesus', in G. Aichele and R. Walsh (eds.), *Those Outside: Noncanonical Readings of the Canonical Gospels* (New York: T&T Clark/Continuum, 2005), pp. 155-81 (160 n. 11); R. Walsh, 'Monty Python's *Life of Brian* (1979)', in A. Reinhartz (ed.), *Bible and Cinema: Fifty Key Films* (London: Routledge, 2013), pp. 187-92.

outside cinemas in New York, it was not shown in parts of the Bible Belt, and one Texas cinema received a bomb threat. In the UK there were also the obligatory protests along with prayers encouraged for the film's downfall, arguments made for the imprisonment of the participants, and banning of the film in Harrogate, Swansea (until 1997), parts of Surrey, East Devon, and Cornwall. Channel 4 had to wait until 1991 to broadcast it on television, six years after it was originally intended for broadcast. It was also banned in Ireland, Norway, and Italy.[11] Film executives also had serious problems with the film. Bernard Delfont of EMI dropped *Life of Brian* just as filming was due to start because of the script's perceived blasphemous content, and meetings with potential backers in America were unsuccessful because of fears surrounding offense.[12]

The idea that Brian might be Jesus was, then, clearly controversial and deemed offensive by some groups. What is curious about this is that some of the ideas attributed to Brian have been, as we will see, attributed to the historical Jesus in scholarship for 200 years and they once had the power to destroy academic careers. Yet the scholarly quest for the historical Jesus had little wider impact by the 1970s and, when placed outside the universities, could clearly still have the power to shock when its ideas were presented, as least in coded form, to a wider audience. *Life of Brian* is part of this tradition in that it is offensive to those Christians who may personally find reconstructions of the historical Jesus blasphemous, as well as a mocking of central Christian beliefs, because an outright attack on the figure of Jesus himself it clearly is not.

The major way in which Monty Python can challenge the traditional Christ of faith is by making what should be an obvious intertwining of the lives of Brian and the Jesus of the gospels. Malcolm Muggeridge and Mervyn Stockwood recognised this when they suggested to John Cleese and Michael Palin that Brian was obviously Christ. However, Muggeridge and Stockwood had missed the first fifteen minutes of the film where the sort-of-distinction is made![13] Yet, pretentious though their evidence-lite posturing infamously was, Muggeridge and Stockwood still had a point: there *is* significant overlap between the characters. Jesus and Brian are born at the same time and at the same place. The baby Brian is even mistaken for the baby Jesus by the three wise men. The other key distinction scene is where Jesus gives the Sermon on the Mount. Yet even the Mount provides another notable similarity. In the screen version

---

11. For further details of various controversies see R. Hewison, *Monty Python: The Case Against* (New York: Grove, 1981); Sellers, *Bright Side*, pp. 14-21.

12. Pythons, *Autobiography*, pp. 365-68.

13. Pythons, *Autobiography*, pp. 384-85; Sellers, *Bright Side*, p. 19.

of the film a special cameo character is reserved for the film's eleventh-hour backer, ex-Beatle George Harrison. This character is Mr Papado-poulis who happened to reserve the Mount for Brian.

In fact, numerous aspects of the lives of Brian and Jesus have explicit similarities. Brian is also named with reference to the same hometown as Jesus (i.e. Brian of Nazareth; cf. e.g. Matt. 2.23). Both Brian and Jesus were, of course, proclaimed 'the Messiah' by followers. As people asked Jesus for a sign (e.g. Matt. 12.38; 16.1) which Jesus can refuse to give (e.g. Mark 8.12; Matt. 12.39; 16.4) so people ask for a sign which Brian does everything but give (pp. 59-60, 62-64).[14] Their use of language is often intimately similar and regularly laced with comic twists, at least in the case of Brian. This is particularly so when Brian has to pose as a prophet to avoid detection by the Romans using some quite straight-forward distorted parallels to some of the more famous sayings and parables of Jesus (pp. 53-55; cf. Matt. 5.1-12; Luke 6.20-26; Exod. 20.17; Deut. 5.21; Matt. 6.25-34; 7.1-2; 18.23-35; 21.28-32; 25.14-30; Luke 16.1-8; 19.11-27). The respective deaths of Jesus and Brian are also very similar. Not only are both crucified but both are crucified as revolutionary threats (cf. Mark 15.6-16, 27). These blindingly obvious parallels should immediately prick the ears of any viewer who wishes to know whether the film is trying to say something about Jesus.

So certain opponents of the film are in one sense right: Brian sort of *is* Jesus. In fact it is not just opponents of the film who pick up on this. This is obviously implied when Philip Davies notes the observation that 'Brian both *is* Jesus and is clearly *not* Jesus' which Davies shows was a particularly useful way of allowing the film 'to escape a certain amount of criticism for blasphemy or poor taste'.[15] From within the Python circle Terry Gilliam recalls the genesis of Brian after the completion of *Monty Python and the Holy Grail* (Terry Jones and Terry Gilliam, 1974): 'very quickly we came around to the feeling that Jesus was OK we weren't going to take the piss out of him, he was genuinely OK, so that's where Brian got created, he was a parallel'.[16] *Life of Brian* furthers this overlap-ping by applying to Brian controversial views about Jesus (and the historical Jesus in particular) which have been put forward both in mod-ern critical scholarship, as well as by ancient critics of what we would now call orthodox Christianity. That Monty Python created a 'real' historical figure of Jesus who was of relevance for the contemporary

---

14. For a list of the 'sign' passages in the gospels see Davies, 'Research', p. 147.
15. Davies, 'Research', p. 148; cf. p. 150.
16. Pythons, *Autobiography*, p. 353.

world is implied to some extent by Graham Chapman: 'That movie, if it said anything at all, said think for yourselves, don't blindly follow, which I think isn't a bad message and I'm sure Mr Christ would have agreed'.[17]

To create this dual focus on 'real' historical past and contemporary ideological relevance, the film used the latest, most famous or most provocative critical biblical scholarship which itself was very much a part of the intellectual, popular, and cultural milieu at the time when *Life of Brian* was being written, even if we cannot pin down precisely which books were read or the precise sources used for this or that theme. Indeed, not only did the Pythons read and re-read the Gospel texts and ancient literature, as several of those involved mention,[18] but, as Michael Palin recalled, the Pythons immersed themselves in the world of critical Gospel studies:

> …it was a very academic approach. We read books about the Bible story and that period, the Dead Sea Scrolls and *various new interpretations of the Gospels*, that sort of thing, just because we all felt, well, we can't just do silly jokes about people being knocked off donkeys, there's got to be a kind of philosophical approach as well.[19]

So, what sort of 'various new interpretations of the Gospels' influenced the writing and production of the film and enabled Monty Python to drill down to the 'real' historical Jesus?

3. He's Not the Messiah and He's Not the Resurrection

> Now if Christ is preached as raised from the dead, how can some of you say that there is no resurrection of the dead? But if there is no resurrection of the dead, then Christ has not been raised; if Christ has not been raised, then our preaching is in vain and your faith is in vain. (1 Cor. 15.12-14)

To drill back down to the historical Jesus, *Life of Brian* presented an attempted debunking of two of the biggest historical claims made about Jesus: that he was 'the Messiah' and that he was resurrected from the dead. Combined with this is the implicit denial in *Life of Brian* that death-by-crucifixion – which certainly did happen according to *Life of Brian* – has any theological significance.

---

17. Pythons, *Autobiography*, p. 370.

18. Pythons, *Autobiography*, pp. 355-56. Davies, 'Research', pp. 143-48, provides numerous parallels between *Life of Brian* and ancient sources, both biblical and non-biblical.

19. Quoted in Sellers, *Bright Side*, p. 4 (my italics).

To help with debunking messiahship, there already existed a respectable scholarly tradition that held that Brian was not the only one who did
not claim to be the Messiah while his followers went ahead and made
a dubious link. Given the absence of the term on the lips of Jesus in
Matthew, Mark, and Luke, it is often argued that Jesus never regarded
himself as 'the Messiah', at least in the titular sense, and that the title
was developed by the gospels or earlier post-Jesus tradition. This
'Messianic secret' theory provided by William Wrede in 1901 in relation
to the earliest of the gospels, Mark, provided the basis for the most
influential explanation of the transition from Jesus not thinking he was
'the Messiah' to the first Christians believing he was.[20] Despite criticisms
and qualifications, the 'Messianic secret' remains a very popular theory
to this day. It is one of the most basic theories taught in critical biblical
studies and was, significantly enough, translated into English in 1971.[21]
Put crudely, it was and is argued that the Messianic secrecy theme was a
theological device developed by the writer of Mark's Gospel to explain
the problem of why the historical Jesus was not believed to be, or did not
claim to be, the Messiah. The writer of Mark's Gospel, so dominant
forms of the argument go, made sure to construct a Jesus who kept his
true identity quiet and did not want it revealed until after the resurrection.
In other words, the messianic identity of Jesus was effectively a creation
of Jesus' followers and did not come from the historical Jesus himself.
The Messianic secrecy theme was and is built on the peculiar emphasis
in Mark's Gospel where Jesus commands demons to be silent because
they know who he really is (Mark 1.25, 34; 3.11-12), tells cured individuals to be quiet about what has happened (Mark 1.44; 5.43; 7.36;
8.26), and even asks his disciples not to tell anyone about grand claims
(Mark 8.30; 9.9). The disciples are frequently taught in private and
frequently misunderstand him. To add to the confusion the Markan Jesus
suggests that his parables were designed to confuse:

---

20. W. Wrede, *Das Messiasgeheimnis in den Evangelien* (Göttingen: Vandenhoeck & Ruprecht, 1901).

21. The English translation of Wrede, *Das Messiasgeheimnis in den Evangelien*
is by J.C.G. Greig, *The Messianic Secret* (London: James Clark, 1971). See further e.g. J.L. Blevins, *The Messianic Secret in Markan Research 1901–1976*
(Washington, DC: University Press of America, 1981); C.M. Tuckett (ed.), *The
Messianic Secret* (London: SPCK, 1983); H. Räisänen, *The 'Messianic Secret' in
Mark* (Edinburgh: T. & T. Clark, 1990); W.R. Telford, *The Theology of the Gospel
of Mark* (Cambridge: Cambridge University Press, 1999), pp. 41-54.

> When he was alone, those who were around him along with the twelve asked him about the parables. And he said to them, 'To you has been given the secret (or: mystery) of the kingdom of God, but for those outside, everything comes in parables; in order that 'they may indeed look but not perceive, and may listen, but not understand; so that they may not turn again and be forgiven.'(Mark 4.10-12)

We might also note that where the 1970s opened with the English translation of Wrede, it wound down with another prominent book on mystery in the Gospels: Frank Kermode's *The Genesis of Secrecy*. Kermode's book was initially delivered as the Charles Eliot Norton Lectures at Harvard between 1977 and 1978 and included an opening chapter on that classic problem of the riddle of Markan parable telling (Mark 4.11-12).[22] Whilst not positing direct sources, it is clear that ideas concerning secrecy, linked with Jesus' identity, were very much part of creative mainstream New Testament scholarship as *Life of Brian* was coming into being.[23]

Something roughly akin to the scholarly secrecy theory can easily be noted in a critical reading of the Gospel texts, at least in the sense that the first Christians were in the process of conveniently remembering great things about Jesus or neglecting to tell people certain dramatic events (cf. Mark 16.8). Look at the following Gospel texts and note the role of interpretation by followers (a key theme in *Life of Brian*, of course):

> The Jews said to him, 'What sign can you show us for doing this?' Jesus answered them, 'Destroy this temple, and in three days I will raise it up'. The Jews then said, 'This temple has been under construction for forty-six years, and will you raise it up in three days?' But he was speaking of the temple of his body. After he was raised from the dead, his disciples remembered that he had said this; and they believed the scriptures and the word that Jesus had spoken. (John 2.19-22)

> As they were coming down the mountain, he [Jesus] ordered them [certain disciples] to tell no one about what they had seen [the transfiguration of Jesus], until after the Son of Man had risen from the dead. So they kept the matter to themselves, questioning what this rising from the dead might mean. (Mark 9.9-10)

Rightly or wrongly, a hermeneutic of suspicion, coupled with a non-Christian perspective, might almost inevitably lead to slightly sarcastic mutterings that someone else might be making some remarkable claims

---

22. F. Kermode, *The Genesis of Secrecy: On the Interpretation of Narrative* (Cambridge, Mass.: Harvard University Press, 1979).

23. I owe this latter point on Kermode to Deane Galbraith.

on behalf of Jesus here and without his consent. Such a combination of scepticism and suspicion is clear in John Cleese's assessment of the Gospel miracles which, incidentally, is close to Geza Vermes' discussion of Jesus as a charismatic healer and exorcist from his book which seems to have directly or indirectly influenced *Life of Brian* (see below), and a view which has a long scholarly pedigree:[24]

> I don't know about the miracles, I mean a lot of the healing, the faith healing, I would imagine was absolutely sensible. I mean anyone who is suffering from the symptoms of something that's basically got a hysterical foundation then that could easily happen. I would have thought that just as much as faith healing is a fact of life. It all makes sense to me. Water into wine I would be very dubious about, frankly Brian [*laugh*]. Over the moon if it happened but...[25]

As Richard Walsh put it: 'One may remember that messianic acclamations are wrong more often than not, if not always. At least one laughs at the incongruity of an ordinary, Jewish, bastard, Messiah. Of course (wink wink) this is not the Gospel Jesus.'[26]

Life of Brian clearly has some very obvious parallels to followers who have made claims about their figurehead without permission and who have gone well beyond what was actually said. Miracles wrongly and stupidly get attributed to Brian and the crowd wrongly believe signs have been presented. And all along, of course, Brian wants nothing to do with the idea that he is the Messiah or indeed anything special but, for all his denials, he becomes the Messiah nonetheless (pp. 64-65). Note also the state in which Brian had just previously left the crowd by neglecting to finish off his parables once the Romans were out of sight, the very point where the crowd shake off their disdain and start getting interested. Paradoxically, it is Brian the hopeless storyteller who, without thinking, leaves his story tantalisingly unfinished and with his audience wanting more, the one narrative device which any storyteller worth their salt

---

24. G. Vermes, *Jesus the Jew: A Historian's Reading of the Gospels* (London: SCM Press, 1973), pp. 22-23: 'Four of them [exorcism stories]...describe as demonic possession what seems to have been mental or nervous illness... It ought to be mentioned at this juncture that the psychiatrist whom I have consulted on the question whether most of the diseases exorcised or healed in the New Testament could be recognized as hysterical, after giving a qualified affirmative reply, wished to know the success rate of the treatment and the state of health of the patients six months after discharge!' By the 1970s, the most prominent book on miracles in the Gospel tradition, H. van der Loos, *The Miracles of Jesus* (Leiden: Brill, 1965), was also entertaining similar ideas.

25. *The Pythons: A Documentary* (BBC/Python [Monty] Pictures, 1979).

26. Walsh, 'Monty Python's *Life of Brian*', p. 191.

might use. Now Brian has got the confused crowd hooked and wanting the explanations of his mysteries and secrets yet ultimately they remain confused by, but confident in, their new saviour (pp. 56-57). It is worth adding that in the gospels it is precisely after Jesus has given the Parable of the Sower (Mark 4.1-8), and precisely before he gives the explanation of the parable (Mark 4.13-20), that we get the above mentioned discussion of mysteries, explanations, and outsiders (Mark 4.10-12).

The resurrection of Jesus is of course *the* big miraculous action of Christian tradition and, despite virtually all other humanities subjects having long moved on from discussing whether such spectacular miracles can or cannot happen, the debates still rage fiercely in certain theological and biblical studies circles.[27] The sentiments of *Life of Brian*, it might reasonably be suspected, are on the side of those who would reject the view that Jesus was physically raised from the dead. The resurrection is implicitly challenged by providing no indication that Brian was to be resurrected from the dead, despite more-or-less following the Gospel narrative outline. In fact, *Life of Brian* implies the very opposite.[28] Whereas the Gospel stories end with Jesus being resurrected from the dead, *Life of Brian* conspicuously ends with Brian crucified, a notable contrast given the parallel lives of the two figures. If there is escape from death-by-crucifixion in the narrative world of *Life of Brian* it is not supernatural but very much this worldly and merely a temporary escape from the inevitability of death. One means of escape is by sheer cunning, by falsely claiming you are the one pardoned (pp. 96-97). Another is to have a rescue party arranged, perhaps led by your brother (p. 95). Yet another is to have some do-gooder take your place (pp. 89-90, 94; cf. Mark 15.21). Brian is clearly not so fortunate, emphasised by a sorry string of misunderstanding and incompetence, from the rendition of 'For He's a Jolly Good Fellow' to the crack suicide squad (compare Masada[29]) pointlessly killing themselves even *after* the guards have fled

27. For a recent overview of scholarship see G.R. Habermas, 'Resurrection Research from 1975 to the Present: What Are Critical Scholars Saying?', *JSHJ* 3 (2005), pp. 135-53. It is only fair to point out, however, that attempts to locate conservative approaches in mainstream interdisciplinary historical research have recently been strongly emphasised. See e.g. M.R. Licona and J.G. van der Watt, 'The Adjudication of Miracles: Rethinking the Criteria of Historicity', *HTR* 65 (2009), pp. 62-68; M.R. Licona, *The Resurrection of Jesus: A New Historiographical Approach* (Downers Grove, Ill.: InterVarsity Press, 2009).

28. Cf. R. Walsh, 'The Gospel according to Judas: Myth and Parable', in J.C. Exum (ed.), *The Bible in Film – The Bible and Film* (Leiden: Brill, 2006), pp. 37-53 (50).

29. Davies, 'Research', p. 144, further suggests a superficial parody of Japanese suicide squads.

in terror. Brian's stark fate is finally and conclusively underscored by Eric Idle's popular song, 'Always Look on the Bright Side of Life', where a full embrace of the joys of this life is the only challenge to the inevitability of an eternity in the dust (pp. 100-101).

As Hans Wiersma stressed, mocking and undermining the brutal nature of crucifixion – and implicitly Jesus' death and its theological significance – runs throughout *Life of Brian* and may be as jarring as any theme for Christians, or indeed anyone familiar with what actually happens to those crucified.[30] However, unlike the handling of resurrection and messiahship there is no significant indication that the crucifixion is denied as a historical event and nor is there any *influential* scholarly or popular tradition making such denials. There are certainly some relatively old traditions which have Jesus somehow avoiding crucifixion (cf. *Gospel of Barnabas* 217-18; Qur'an 4.157-58) and which may be hinted at in *Life of Brian* when the Simon of Cyrene-like saintly passer-by takes up Alfonso's cross and ends up taking his place.[31] However, this is not developed in any way relating to Brian or covered in any detail. Nevertheless, and clearly tied in with the denial of resurrection, is an undermining of any theological significance of the central symbol of Christianity. Monty Python's Jesus-Brian is not the Messiah, he is not resurrected from the dead, and the cross has no theological significance; he is just an ordinary misunderstood human being. This much puts Brian in a recognisable tradition of Jesuses in liberal and radical circles whose less-tainted ideological position can be found behind the later accretions of the church and interpretation. But, as with such Jesuses, they have a message for their time. Brian is no exception and his message is a recognisable one in the array of overlapping and often contradictory ideological views of post-1960s Britain and England in the build-up to Thatcherism.

4. Jesus and Brian, Revolution, and Trade Unions

We have seen some of the ways in which the 1960s, in general, and 1967–68, in particular, generated revolutionary enthusiasm – and eventual disappointment or rethinking. Alongside Christopher Hill's seventeenth-century radicals, the historical figure of Jesus would also prove useful for certain scholars to think through the contemporary social upheavals of the 1960s, though the influence in the field of biblical studies was not as

---

30. H. Wiersma, 'Redeeming *Life of Brian*: How Monty Python (Ironically) Proclaims Christ *Sub Contrario*', *Word and World* 32 (2012), pp. 166-77.

31. Davies, 'Research', p. 147.

significant as that of Hill on historians and the humanities. More specifically, and not unlike the disgruntled Brian, a revolutionary anti-Roman disposition has been attributed to the historical Jesus. By the time of *Life of Brian*, this was most famously (and then recently) argued by S.G.F. Brandon in the 1960s.[32] Brandon argued that the gospel traditions were edited after the failed Jewish revolt against Rome where there was much opposition to Judaism in Christianity and, consequently, the nationalistic overtones of a revolutionary Jesus were airbrushed from history. Brandon's revolutionary Jesus never gained a widespread following in academia and quickly led to an attempted debunking by leading New Testament scholars such as Martin Hengel.[33] Yet outside scholarship (even if Brandon's work was more popularising than most) the revolutionary Jesus had already gained enough popular acclaim among leftist groups during the Cold War to warrant a stern rebuke from another leading New Testament scholar of the twentieth century, Günther Bornkamm:

> Jesus' sayings are directed at two fronts, which are as relevant today as they were in the days of Jesus and the early Church. The first front of the fanatics who wish to claim Jesus for their own as the great revolutionary... Its threat is still with us. In Marxism and Bolshevism we have today, though greatly changed, an example of its historical reality...and these revolutionaries, when they wanted to claim Jesus as an ally in the struggle for a new world or social order, have had to learn again and again that they could not rely long on this ally... It is therefore not surprising that today this alliance, often enough attempted in revolutionary movements of the West, has apparently been definitely renounced...[34]

32. See e.g. S.G.F. Brandon, *Jesus and the Zealots: A Study of the Political Factor in Primitive Christianity* (Manchester: Manchester University Press, 1967); S.G.F. Brandon, *The Trial of Jesus of Nazareth* (London: B.T. Batsford, 1968).

33. E.g. O. Cullmann, *Jesus and the Revolutionaries* (New York: Harper Row, 1970); M. Hengel, *Was Jesus a Revolutionist?* (Philadelphia: Fortress Press, 1971). Interestingly though the idea of an anti-imperial Jesus and anti-imperial early church has begun to re-emerge in recent years and is popular at present among New Testament scholars. See e.g. R. Horsley, *Jesus and the Spiral of Violence: Popular Jewish Resistance in Roman Palestine* (San Francisco: Harper & Row, 1987); J.D. Crossan, *The Historical Jesus: The Life of a Mediterranean Jewish Peasant* (Edinburgh: T. & T. Clark; San Francisco: HarperCollins, 1991). Even conservative Christian scholars will now stress the Jesus movement as one in opposition to Rome. See e.g. N.T. Wright, *Jesus and the Victory of God* (London: SPCK, 1996).

34. G. Bornkamm, *Jesus of Nazareth* (London: Hodder & Stoughton, 1960), pp. 101-102.

In *Life of Brian* the revolutionary ambitions of Brian are absolutely explicit; or, to put it another way, he is a Brandon-esque Jesus and an un-Bornkamm-esque Jesus. Brian is desperate to join the general revolutionary movement and ends up as a member of the People's Front of Judea. But Brian's romantic hopes are undermined by the sheer incompetency of his fellow revolutionaries and the pedantic squabbles of the Judean People's Front, the People's Front of Judea, and the Campaign for Free Galilee, for which, of course, read twentieth-century trade unions and Marxist groups. Brian, with the partial exception of his lover Judith, is the only sane and reasonable figure with any inkling of how to get some kind of result – no mean feat when adrift in a sea of hopeless incompetence. Indeed, Brian's focus and anti-imperial hostilities transcend the childish revolutionary infighting during the attempt to kidnap Pilate's wife and mutilate or kill her if the quasi-Marxist demands to dismantle 'the entire apparatus of the Roman Imperialist State' (p. 27) were not met. And so when the fight breaks out between the Campaign for Free Galilee and the People's Front of Judea over who thought up the kidnap idea, Brian tries to unite the rebels against the common Roman enemy rather than the Judean People's Front (p. 32). And yet such ideals remain a romantic, albeit honourable, vision – this revolution was always doomed to fail because of general idiocy with a touch of cowardice and self-preservation.

As has been pointed out by Davies with reference to *Life of Brian*, revolutionary infighting was the kind of behaviour which the first-century CE Jewish historian Josephus highlighted around the time of the failed Jewish revolt against Rome in 66-70 CE, and which according to Josephus was, if anything, more likely to cause disaster than the Romans.[35] For readers who are familiar with Monty Python, the following recollection from Josephus concerning Jewish internecine fighting could almost inevitably be read as a proto-Pythonesque narrative:

> The conspirators against the city being now divided into three camps, Eleazar's party, having the keeping of the sacred first-fruits, directed their drunken fury against John; the latter with his associates plundered the townsfolk and wreaked their rage upon Simon; while Simon also to meet the rival factions looked to the city for supplies. Whenever John found himself attacked on both sides, he would face his men about in opposite directions, on the one hand hurling missiles from the porticoes upon those coming up from the town, on the other repelling with his engines those who were pouring their javelins upon him from the temple… [A]nd upon his retreat Simon advanced and did the same; as though they were

35. E.g. Davies, 'Research', pp. 143-45.

> purposely serving the Romans by destroying what the city had provided
> against a siege and severing the sinews of their own strength... [T]he
> brigand chiefs, divided on all else, put to death as their common enemies
> any in favour of peace with the Romans or suspected of an intention to
> desert, and were unanimous only in slaughtering those deserving of
> deliverance... The rival parties...were at grips, trampling over the dead
> bodies that were piled upon each other, the frenzy inhaled from the
> corpses at their feet increasing their savagery; and ever inventing some
> new instrument of mutual destruction. (Josephus, *War* 5.21-34; cf. 5.5-20;
> see also Tacitus, *Hist.* 5.12.4)

We can only begin to speculate about what might have happened had
someone suggested that the factions unite against the common enemy.
But, unlike the tragi-comic portrayals of these revolutionary figures
of both screen and (Josephus' version of) first-century history, Brian
actually manages to get something done on his first revolutionary outing:
the anti-Roman graffiti act. This small act of antiestablishment rebellion,
like Jesus' overturning of the tables of the moneychangers and dove-
sellers (Mark 11), directly leads to Brian's crucifixion.

We might make a further suggestion about one possible ramification
of the idea of Brian the revolutionary and, by implication, Jesus. What
Life of Brian does is show that crucifixion is far from being a unique
punishment effectively reserved for Jesus (and perhaps the two bandits)
in human history. Rather, Brian is just one of many people crucified
at the end of the film, including people being crucified for little more
than a casual punch-up. Crucifixion is referenced commonly enough in
ancient sources, including, or especially, in Josephus. It is perhaps worth
noting that when the relatively successful bandit, Eleazar ben Dinai, was
finally captured under Felix (c. 52–60 CE) after twenty years on the run,
indiscriminate crucifixions were meted out according to Josephus: 'Of
the brigands whom he crucified, and of the common people who were
convicted of complicity with them and punished by him, the number was
incalculable' (*War* 2.253; cf. *Ant.* 20.160-161). If the arguments presented in this chapter are correct, including the idea of a revolutionary
Jesus underlying Brian, then could *Life of Brian* be further suggesting
that Jesus too was little more than just another victim of indiscriminate
Roman punishment in a world where people follow any old Messiah and
any old prophet (cf. Josephus, *War* 2.258)?

However, what is left of Brian's revolutionary thinking is of most
significance for our purposes. Brian ultimately thinks that revolutionary
after revolutionary who appear at his crucifixion are misguided fools
with ultimately absurd ideas. A horrified Brian labels his comrades
'bastards' after Reg, on behalf of the revolutionaries of the People's

Front of Judea, offers up congratulations on the occasion of his apparent martyrdom (p. 96). But it is not just the ever-ineffective revolutionaries of the People's Front of Judea: Brian can only sigh at the absurdity after the crack suicide squad kill themselves despite the Romans fleeing in fear (p. 97) and even his lover Judith finally succumbs to the absurd worldview of Reg and his similarly deluded revolutionary siblings. In addition to the revolutionary failures, the film itself does not really have a wholly negative view of the Roman Empire, for which, of course, we can also read the British Empire (see above). With the revolution more-or-less as debunked as messiahship and resurrection are, Brian leaves us with his one enduring message from the film: you are all individuals. Is this story from revolution to being an individual who can do it for themselves not a textbook post-1960s case?

5. Thinking about Sex

One way 1960s individualism was expressed was, of course, through the famed free-love and sexual liberation which might have been enthusiasti-cally embraced or viewed with outrage depending on your perspective on such matters. While Brian did not get the chance to marry he was hardly uncomfortable with the idea of a pre-marital dalliance with probably the only other revolutionary who comes close to being sensible: Judith. And it is undeniably clear that they engaged in an enjoyable night which moved well beyond heavy-petting. This is clearer still in the script which explicitly refers to seemingly naughty behaviour during the night (p. 66) while the script emphasises further that Brian has his mind on the quality of their nocturnal activities while Judith has her mind on Brian's teach-ings (p. 77). This, combined with full-frontal nudity, was not just a product of provocative and playful attitudes nurtured in the1960s; the Monty Python team would almost certainly have known that the image of Jesus had been given a free-love makeover. The question of Jesus having erotic thoughts has a long history and today typically, perhaps inevitably, gets raised in the secularised or less conservative quarters of theological reflection on the humanity of Jesus. The canonical Gospels and Christian orthodoxy do not explicitly entertain the idea that Jesus had sexual feelings for another human being. But the view that Jesus was in love in some way or other with Mary Magdalene has been a subver-sive and provocative view of Jesus which dates back to the first few centuries after Jesus' death and has recently proven popular, if the success of the *Da Vinci Code* and a whole host of sensationalist literature is anything to go by. This tradition also has a major cinematic moment, of course, in Martin Scorsese's *The Last Temptation of Christ* (Universal Pictures, 1988) which was released less than ten years after *Life of Brian* and based on the 1950s novel by Nikos Kazantzakis.[36] The key ancient text for the tradition of Jesus' relationship with Mary Magdalene, even if it has or has not been misread, is the apocryphal *Gospel of Philip*. Here Mary was Jesus' consort, favoured among the disciples and the woman whom Jesus used to kiss on the mouth (*Gospel of Philip*, Saying 59; cf. Saying 36).

But erotic tendencies and naïve thoughts of love were also a family trait, at least in the case of Brian. Mandy may have protested too much at Judith and her son's sleeping arrangements. Brian's father, we learn from Mandy, was not in fact Mr Cohen (not that this surprised Brian) but the Roman centurion, Nortius Maximus. The disbelieving Brian asks whether she was raped to which his mother replies that this was the case...at first (p. 18). By the time the issue of Mandy's virginity explicitly arises in *Life of Brian* it is already crystal clear that she is not a virgin and that the story of her virginity gets falsely attributed to her by Brian's pious-but-stupid followers (pp. 72-73). We even get clear echoes of one of the pinnacles of Mariology, the 'Hail Mary', chanted in unison by the crowd to the Mother of Brian (p. 71; cf. John 19.27). This sort of reasoning has a not-so-subtle parallel with certain views of Jesus' origins. In fact from the second century CE (and no doubt before) opponents of Christianity have tried to explain Gospel stories of the virgin birth (Matt. 1–2; Luke 1–2) differently. One explanation was that the story of Mary's virginity was designed to cover up a dark secret, namely that the real father was not even the saintly Joseph but a not-so-saintly Roman soldier called Panthera. The following is the relatively famous attempted refutation by Origen (c. 182–251 CE):

> But let us now return to where the Jew is introduced, speaking of the mother of Jesus, and saying that 'when she was pregnant she was turned out of doors by the carpenter to whom she had been betrothed, as having been guilty of adultery, and that she bore a child to a certain soldier named Panthera'. And let us see whether those who have blindly concocted these fables about the adultery of the Virgin with Panthera, and her rejection by the carpenter, did not invent these stories to overturn his miraculous conception by the Holy Spirit: for they could have falsified the history in a different manner, on account of its extremely miraculous character, and not have admitted, as it were against their will, that Jesus was born of no ordinary human marriage. (Origen, *Contra Celsum* 1.32).

---

36. N. Kazantzakis, *The Last Temptation* (London: Faber & Faber, 1975).

Another version of this tradition occurs, for example, in the *Toledoth Yeshu*, a Jewish anti-Christian polemic which parodies the life of Jesus:

> Near his house dwelt a widow and her lovely and chaste daughter named Miriam. Miriam was betrothed to Yohanan, of the royal house of David, a man learned in the Torah and God-fearing. At the close of a certain Sabbath, Joseph Pandera, attractive and like a warrior in appearance, having gazed lustfully upon Miriam, knocked upon the door of her room and betrayed her by pretending that he was her betrothed husband, Yohanan. Even so, she was amazed at this improper conduct and submitted only against her will. Thereafter, when Yohanan came to her, Miriam expressed astonishment at behaviour so foreign to his character. It was thus that they both came to know the crime of Joseph Pandera and the terrible mistake on the part of Miriam... Miriam gave birth to a son...[37]

In addition to these ancient polemical traditions, countless modern-day biblical critics have suggested that the gospel stories of the virgin birth are pious fictions like other stories of miraculous or unusual origins in the history of religions, such as stories in Israelite tradition (e.g. Gen. 17.15-18; 21.1-2) or stories of major figures like Alexander the Great (Plutarch, *Alexander* 2.1–3.4), while scholars such as Jane Schaberg and Gerd Lüdemann have taken extremely seriously the idea that Mary was raped in their historical reconstructions of Jesus' birth.[38] The development of Mariology was in many ways a pious creation of religious admirers (cf. Luke 1.39-56) and a big step on the way to high Mariology which was eventually to become associated with the Catholic Church in particular. By the 1970s, this sort of reasoning had, of course, a long academic history, and would have been among the most obvious scholarly traditions for any budding sceptic to exploit. For what it might be worth, we might add that, in 1977, Raymond Brown published his massive and influential commentary on the infancy narratives.[39] Even if the Monty Python team had not consulted this comprehensive commentary

37. M. Goldstein, *Jesus in the Jewish Tradition* (New York: Macmillan, 1950), pp. 148-54.

38. J. Schaberg, *The Illegitimacy of Jesus: A Feminist Theological Interpretation of the Infancy Narratives* (San Francisco: Harper & Row, 1987 [reprinted and expanded for Sheffield: Sheffield Phoenix Press, 2006]); G. Lüdemann, *Virgin Birth? The Real Story of Mary and Her Son Jesus* (London: SCM Press, 1998).

39. R.E. Brown, *The Birth of the Messiah: A Commentary on the Infancy Narratives in Matthew and Luke* (rev. edn; London: Chapman, 1993 [1977]). Any number of conservative, radical, and liberal explanations of the virgin birth stories could be cited from the history of critical scholarship but the usual starting point, with discussions of the key positions, remains Brown's massive work of reference.

(and even if they had, they might not have found it entirely agreeable), the ideas accepted and critiqued by Brown were at the forefront of, and 'in the air' around, mainstream New Testament scholarship of the time.

This is, of course, another aspect of Monty Python debunking stories later attributed to Jesus (and Mary), just like the resurrection and messianic claims. But there is another aspect to this view of how Brian/Jesus was conceived: sexuality and single-parenthood is more-or-less out in the open in a way we might not expect from previous Jesus-films. Even Mandy, who relentlessly complains about Brian's apparent obsession with sex, is still happy enough giving oral relief to a Roman solider and only just after Brian has left their house. Indeed, Brian appears perfectly comfortable with the notion that his father was not Mr Cohen; his problem was when he found out his father was not Jewish but Roman. Mandy may have hidden the ethnicity of Brian's father but the only thing resembling potential social tension was Brian's anti-Roman imperialism which might also land them in trouble. And, of course, and in part as a reaction to increasing cultural prominence, Mandy was to foreshadow that negative stereotype of the political right in the 1980s: the single mother.

6. The Multicultural Jewish Brian of History

Another point of historical Jesus research which influenced *Life of Brian* is the seemingly banal fact that Jesus was a Jew. We might illuminate the once surprising nature of this point by simply recalling the clichéd cinematic and visual images of the blond-haired, blue-eyed Christ. Brian is, of course, anything but the Christ of faith and is a fairly 'ordinary' Jew who wears a skull cap as a matter of routine. His surname, 'Cohen', is as recognisably Jewish as could be imagined. Indeed, one of Brian's particular concerns in the face of Roman occupation is his Jewish identity and he only attempts to use his Roman connections to escape crucifixion (p. 40). When stunned about the news of his father being a Roman, Brian throws an adolescent tantrum, proclaiming his Jewishness through a number of slang terms (p. 19).[40]

In modern historical Jesus scholarship the phrase 'Jesus the Jew' is a well-known scholarly cliché but in the early 1970s it was anything but a banal fact. In 1973 Geza Vermes published one of the most famous

---

40. See also A. Reinhartz, 'Jesus in Film: Hollywood Perspectives on the Jewishness of Jesus', *JRF* 2 (1998), http://www. unomaha.edu/~jrf/JesusinFilmRein.htm.

books in historical Jesus studies with the then revolutionary title, *Jesus the Jew*. Some reviewers – but far from all – were suitably outraged at this suggestion, although some of the criticisms appear to follow the route of being more indirectly critical of the theory and more critical of the abilities of the scholar. As Vermes recalls in his autobiography,

> A Jewish critic, violently resenting my refusal to classify Jesus as a Pharisee, put me among the anti-Semites. A well-known English Jesuit now deceased described the book's learning as 'at times…oppressive'. He blamed the 'overcrowded' character of the volume on my 'apparent desire' to show off my familiarity with Christian biblical criticism! An American Bible expert, taking exception to my light-hearted remark that New Testament scholars often wear the blinkers of their trade, haughtily dismissed the book with 'Jesus the Jew deserves better than this'. A French woman writer, contributing to a right-wing magazine, settled for the double denunciation of 'scandal and blasphemy'.[41]

Yet, as Vermes also realised, the phrase would soon ease into scholarly language with little additional difficulty.

Vermes' Jesus was not the Christ of conventional Christian faith. He was a charismatic holy man of Jewish tradition who observed the biblical commandments such as Sabbath and food laws, or at least in ways paralleled in early Judaism, and happened to be crucified through being in the wrong place at the wrong time. He did not think of himself as the Messiah or anything too grand. In fact most of the titles the historical Jesus might have used (e.g. son of man, son of God, etc.) are shown by Vermes to have a more this-worldly frame of reference as opposed to indicating anything like the second person of the Trinity. Despite the consistent scholarly rhetoric that Jesus was a Jew, this emphasis has caused some problems for Christian academics. There are endless scholarly constructions of Jewish identity as effectively fixed and stable, which has a key function of providing 'the Jewish background' to be transcended by Jesus (who rhetorically remains 'very Jewish' in doing so), no doubt in part because of a socio-religious pressure to show to the faithful that he was still something a bit more spectacular than just a charismatic holy man.[42]

---

41. G. Vermes, *Providential Accidents: An Autobiography* (London: SCM Press, 1998), pp. 213-14.

42. For discussion see esp. Arnal, *The Symbolic Jesus*; Crossley, *Jesus in an Age of Terror*, pp. 143-94; Crossley, *Jesus in an Age of Neoliberalism*.

It is important to put this scholarly and cultural tradition into wider historical and cultural perspective. Prior to Vermes the dominant position in critical scholarship (and more broadly in popular understandings of Jesus) – influenced by nearly 2000 years of church teaching – was sharply to differentiate Jesus from Judaism. In the context of Nazi Germany this reached new depths with some now truly bizarre sounding claims, such as Walter Grundmann's argument that Jesus was more likely to have been of Aryan descent.[43] Grundmann belonged to the Nazi party and was a supporting member of the SS yet, despite the obvious antisemitic influences on his work, continued to be regarded as a serious scholar well beyond 1945. Grundmann was far from the only Nazi involved in New Testament scholarship.[44]

Even though Nazi Christians were discredited after the Second World War, anti-Judaism was a constant feature of post-war New Testament scholarship. But, despite the discrediting of Nazi Christian scholars, the lack of interest in the 'Jewishness' of Jesus, the clear differentiation of Jewish Christians like Paul from Judaism, and the generally negative construction of early Judaism, remained firmly rooted in New Testament scholarship and the churches, even among those who were opponents of antisemitism and the Nazi party.[45] Buoyed along by a sea change in dominant Anglo-American attitudes towards Israel, the Holocaust, and Judaism after the Six Day War and the emergence of liberal multi-culturalism,[46] Vermes' *Jesus the Jew* in turn paved the way for the positive reception of E.P. Sanders' *Paul and Palestinian Judaism*, which

43. For further discussion see e.g. S. Heschel, 'Nazifying Christian Theology Walter Grundmann and the Institute for the Study and Eradication of Jewish Influence on German Church Life', *CH* 63 (1994), pp. 587-605; Heschel, *The Aryan Jesus*; Casey, 'Anti-Semitic Assumptions'; Head, 'Nazi Quest', pp. 55-89.

44. Gerhard Kittel, for instance, was not only a Nazi propagandist but also editor of the *Theological Dictionary of the New Testament*. This work is still recommended to undergraduates and still utilised by leading professors despite many of the early contributions being riddled with and distorted by antisemitism and anti-Judaism. G. Kittel and G. Friedrich (eds.), *Theologisches Wörterbuch zum Neuen Testament* (10 vols.; Stuttgart: Kohlhammer, 1933–79). Grundmann also participated in the *TWNT* project. For further discussion see e.g. Casey, 'Anti-Semitic Assumptions'.

45. See further e.g. D. Boyarin, *A Radical Jew: Paul and the Politics of Identity* (Berkeley: University of California Press, 1994), pp. 212-14; Casey, 'Anti-Semitic Assumptions'; Kelley, *Racializing Jesus*; J.G. Crossley, *Why Christianity Happened: A Socio-Historical Account of Christian Origins, 26–50 CE* (Louisville: WJK, 2006), Chapter 1.

46. Crossley, *Jesus in an Age of Terror*, pp. 177-94.

perhaps more than any work in New Testament studies made scholars aware of the extent to which Judaism was cast in a negative light.[47] Without this context it is easy to underestimate the then unusual nature of Vermes' portrait of Jesus the Jew, even if it was starting to become partly domesticated (at least in scholarship) by the 1980s.

An aside on Thatcher and the emergence of Thatcherism might illuminate the point further. As we saw in the chapter on Thatcher, she believed that Judaism and Christianity were representative of 'western religions' with their shared emphasis on the value of work and the creativity of the individual, as well as seeing Jews, Judaism, and her Old Testament as epitomising the basic values of Thatcherism. Her closest ally from the religious establishment was the Chief Rabbi, Immanuel Jakobovits. Already present in her engagement with Jewish voters in Finchley, Thatcher's attitude towards Jewish people was noted by high profile Tories, and with some surprise given the levels of disdain towards Jewish people in the decades leading up to Thatcherism. As the former Chancellor, Nigel Lawson, described Thatcher, 'there was not the faintest trace of anti-Semitism in her make-up: an unusual attribute'.[48] From the leadership of the older generation on Jewish ministers in Thatcher's cabinet, there was the notorious remark (attributed to Harold Macmillan) that there were 'more Estonians than Etonians'.[49] Yet, for all Thatcher's philosemitism, and like dominant trends among New Testament scholars and in Anglo-American politics and culture more generally, a note of difference and superiority remained. As we saw, for instance, she was clear that she did not equate Judaism and Christianity and that the Old Testament could only be understood in light of the New Testament and its message of mercy.

Vermes' major point that Jesus was a Jew and was very different from the Christ of faith is certainly reflected in *Life of Brian* (released only six years after the publication of *Jesus the Jew*) and the popularity of such ideas were partly a product of shifting attitudes towards Judaism, Israel, and multiculturalism. Such shifting attitudes even had a more direct impact on the making of *Life of Brian*. One character who did not make the final cut was the Jewish revolutionary, Otto (pp. 74-75). Otto had hopes for a thousand-year, racially purified, Jewish state ('ridding [Israel] of the scum of non-Jewish people, making it pure, no foreigners, no gypsies, no riff-raff') with the film due to show his Star of David

47. Sanders, *Paul and Palestinian Judaism*.

48. Lawson, *The View from No. 11*, p. 256.

49. A. Connor, 'Top of the class', *BBC News* (October 17, 2005), http://news.bbc.co.uk/1/hi/magazine/4349324.stm.

morphing into a swastika. Otto's character was withdrawn for obvious political, cultural and personal reasons.[50] Nevertheless, there is also evidence of constructed difference, or downplaying of Jewish difference, in that Brian retains a little Gentile-ness for the audience, or at least Brian is not entirely alien to a Gentile audience, or indeed British or English audiences. His forename and those of his mother and others in the film were hardly distinctively Semitic and were common English names.[51] And he is, of course, the bastard son of a Roman soldier in a move that provides a link with the coded British imperial past while simultaneously complicating and questioning the connection. As Mandy warned a stunned Brian while explaining why his nose is the shape it is: don't forget you really are a Roman (p. 19).

7. A Brian for His Times

Like Thatcher herself, *Life of Brian* was a culturally popular critique of post-war consensuses. But *Life of Brian*, like the roughly contemporaneous punk movement, is hardly ideologically pure Thatcherism and its cultural provocation was clearly out-of-step with Thatcher's morally upright, good Christian housewife, Mary Whitehouse-style, 'Tory woman' image of the 1970s.[52] Individual Pythons may well be horrified – arguably rightly so – with the idea that the central message of individualism and the punk-like thinking for yourself could be deemed compatible with Thatcherism. But at the same time, all those who voted for Thatcher were not necessarily in agreement with everything Thatcher believed and promoted. Clearly, the famous statistic that only 39% of union members voted Labour in the 1983 General Election (32% Conservative and 28% Liberal/SDP) says something about the appeals, tensions, and contradictions involved in voting generally and in voting for Thatcher in 1983.[53] And nor was there a precise ideological match between Thatcher and champagne-guzzling yuppies, celebrity entrepreneurs, or Duran Duran, all of whom were obviously products of Thatcherism, irrespective of whether Thatcher would have approved of the video for 'Girls on Film'.

50. Sellers, *Bright Side*, p. 14.
51. Davies, 'Research', pp. 150.
52. Nunn, *Thatcher, Politics and Fantasy*, pp. 26-63; Filby, 'God and Mrs Thatcher', pp. 142-45, 185-87.
53. R. Hague, 'Confrontation, Incorporation and Exclusion: British Trade Unions in Collectivist and Post-Collectivist Politics', in H. Berrington (ed.), *Change in British Politics* (London: Cass, 1984), pp. 127-59 (149); A.L. Booth, *The Economics of the Trade Union* (Cambridge: Cambridge University Press, 1995), p. 28.

But, as we saw in Chapter 1, what we are dealing with are matters of significant overlap and how disparate ideological phenomena can be unconsciously brought together or harnessed as part of broader social and cultural change in an age of neoliberalism. As David Harvey summarised this post-1968 tension: 'By capturing ideals of individual freedom and turning them against the interventionist and regulatory processes of the state, capitalist class interests could hope to protect and even restore their position'.[54] And for all its secular humanist values and liberal-leftist writers, *Life of Brian* did lampoon the trade unions, as well as right-wing loudmouths, and did advocate a form of individualism in the dying embers of revolutionary ideals. By analogy, we might note that many – though certainly not all – of the ideas surrounding the historical Jesus and applied to Brian in the film have been accepted by some critically minded members of the various Christian churches. Indeed, a good sign of its ideological significance in the late twentieth century is that it may once have been banned but it now finds itself non-controversially at the top of 'most popular comedy film' lists.[55] As Carl Dyke points out via Gramsci and the usual Christ–Brian distinction, *Life of Brian* may not, after all, be as counter-hegemonic as some, like Dyke's younger self, might like to think.[56]

54. Harvey, *Neoliberalism*, p. 42.

55. See e.g. 'Life of Brian named best comedy', *BBC News* (January 1, 2006), http://news.bbc.co.uk/1/hi/entertainment/4573444.stm.

56. Dyke, 'Learning from *The Life of Brian*', pp. 240-41, 248-50. See also Walsh, 'Gospel according to Judas', pp. 49-50.

Chapter 6

SAVING MARGARET FROM THE GUILLOTINE:
INDEPENDENT MUSIC IN MANCHESTER FROM THE
RISE OF THATCHER TO THE RISE OF BLAIR*

1. From Punk to Britpop: Manchester 1976–1994

Amidst the shifts in mass communication of the mid-late twentieth century, Perry Anderson emphasised the importance of the growing use of the colour television in the cultural shift towards postmodernity.[1] These radical pop cultural changes in the 1960s meant that pop music, fashion, and television became key media for carrying cultural change and challenging traditional authority, particularly in the form of established religious authority, as Callum Brown has shown, to which we could equally add political and most forms of establishment authority.[2] Of course, cultural change and challenges to traditional authority almost inevitably lead to a changing of the guard and we have seen this most strikingly in the emergence of Thatcherism, more specifically, and neoliberalism, more generally. Changes in television, fashion, and pop music are dependent on a number of subcultural trends and movements which are likewise part of the generation of wider cultural changes, as well as epitomising the tensions between challenging the traditional authority and becoming the new authority. Such tensions were picked up

---

* For earlier reflections on Manchester music in the context of emerging Thatcherism, see J.G. Crossley, 'For EveryManc a Religion: Uses of Biblical and Religious Language in the Manchester Music Scene, 1976–1994', *BibInt* 19 (2011), pp. 151-80.

1. Anderson, *Origins of Postmodernity*, pp. 88-89.

2. Brown, *Religion and Society in Twentieth-Century Britain*, pp. 224-77. See also D. Galbraith, 'Drawing Our Fish in the Sand: Secret Biblical Allusions in the Music of U2', *BibInt* 19 (2011), pp. 181-222 (189-90).

in Dick Hebdige's influential and now classic analysis of subculture.[3] Subcultures modify, develop, and absorb images of the surrounding culture in order to construct identities and relative autonomy in the face of the fragmentation of capitalist culture. Subculture can function as both resistance to, and interaction with, market forces from above. The rise of the distinctive Manchester music scene between 1976 and 1994 is a case in point: it emerged at the same time as Thatcherism and reached its peak as Thatcherism became increasingly embedded in English politics. One way or another, this musical scene was always going to tell us something about cultural change in this period; it is an added bonus that the leading musicians were regularly citing the Bible.

Before we turn to such use of biblical language, an overview of the Manchester music scene of this period and what made it distinctive is probably required. The early post-punk period (late 1970s) saw the emergence of bands such as Joy Division, The Fall, and Buzzcocks. While The Fall still remain with us (after numerous changes in line-up), the mid-1980s was dominated by other bands. Joy Division became New Order and The Smiths would become one of the most critically acclaimed bands of the Thatcher era. By the late 1980s, New Order remained but the mantle was passed to The Stone Roses and Happy Mondays, who in turn would give way to Oasis by the mid-1990s. What partly made this overall period distinctive was that by the late 1970s bands were starting to construct a particularly Mancunian identity in contrast to bands which came before them.[4] Manchester groups from the 1960s certainly existed and were certainly successful (e.g. Freddie and the Dreamers, The Hollies) but were typically reliant on professional songwriters or went to America and cracked the American market.[5] Other 1960s and 1970s bands with Manchester connections (e.g. 10cc, Sad Café, Bee Gees) were not notably Mancunian in their identity, lacking both the cityscapes in their lyrics and an emphasis on local accent in their singing.[6]

3. D. Hebdige, *Subculture: The Meaning of Style* (London: Methuen, 1979) and *Hiding in the Light: Images and Things* (London: Routledge, 1988).

4. P. Morley, 'Manchester: The Truth behind the Bizarre Cult Sweeping a City's Youth', *New Musical Express* (July 30, 1977), reprinted in *Joy Division: Piece by Piece: Writing about Joy Division 1977–2007* (London: Plexus, 2008), pp. 37-38, 44.

5. D. Haslam, *Manchester, England: The Story of the Pop Cult City* (London: Fourth Estate, 1999), p. 105.

6. Cf. Haslam, *Manchester*, p. 143.

The Big Bang moment/Creation Story for this distinctively Mancunian music scene came from London, Manchester's great cultural Other,[7] and a performance by the Sex Pistols at the Lesser Free Trade Hall on June 4, 1976. Pete Shelley and Howard Devoto, soon to be of Buzzcock's fame, invited the Sex Pistols to Manchester for their first non-London performance. What became significant about this performance was the showcasing of a do-it-yourself punk attitude which would inspire some of the most influential figures in the Manchester music scene. In addition to Shelley and Devoto, luminaries included Mark E. Smith (The Fall), Bernard Sumner and Peter Hook (Joy Division and later New Order), Morrissey (The Smiths), alongside the music promoter, local celebrity, Granada TV presenter, and the soon-to-be co-founder of Factory Records, Tony Wilson.[8]

The rise of independent record labels (such as Factory Records) would soon follow the Sex Pistols-inspired musical revolution, beginning with Buzzcocks' successful self-released four-track EP, *Spiral Scratch* (1977).[9] Buzzcocks would sign for a major label (United Artists) but not before they ushered in the era of the independent labels.[10] Factory Records was certainly the most famous of the independent labels from Manchester and probably from throughout the UK. Factory began life in 1978 when Alan Erasmus and Tony Wilson organised regular music nights at the Russell Club and would house some of the most influential Manchester bands of the period (e.g. Joy Division, New Order, and

7. Compare the comments of Simon Reynolds, '*24 Hour Party People*', *Film Comment* (2002), reprinted in S. Reynolds, *Totally Wired: Post-Punk Interviews and Overviews* (London: Faber & Faber, 2009), pp. 358-66 (358): 'No British city has a greater sense of self-mystique than Manchester. Populous enough to swagger convincingly as a counter-capital to London, yet still eclipsed by the latter's concentration of political, financial and media power, Manchester has developed a retaliatory superiority complex: northern suss and spirit versus those smug, effete "southern wankers".'

8. There are numerous recollections of this crucial event and the follow up gig at the Lesser Free Trade Hall on July 20, 1976, where Buzzcocks supported the Sex Pistols. For summaries see e.g. J. Savage, *England's Dreaming: Sex Pistols and Punk Rock* (London: Faber & Faber, 1991), pp. 174-76; J. Savage (ed.), *The Haçienda Must be Built!* (London: IMP, 1992), pp. 30-32; M. Middles, *From Joy Division to New Order: The True Story of Anthony H. Wilson and Factory Records* (London: Virgin, 1996), pp. 14-16, 23-26, 40-41; Haslam, *Manchester*, pp. 110-11; Ford, *Hip Priest*, pp. 14-17.

9. S. Reynolds, *Rip It Up and Start Again: Postpunk 1978–1984* (London: Faber & Faber, 2005), pp. 92-93.

10. For a fuller discussion see Reynolds, *Rip It Up*, pp. 92-109.

Happy Mondays). Peter Saville provided the distinctive stark and modernist-influenced Factory artwork,[11] while the producer Martin Hannett brought sonic innovation in his distinctive pared-down, minimalist Joy Division 'sound'. Though these aesthetic credentials are not self-evidently 'Mancunian' in themselves, Factory did set out to be, as Paul Morley put it, 'not just a revolutionary independent label but to be above all a Manchester record label'.[12] Hannett and especially Wilson would certainly bring their Mancunian biases but neither as violently so as the DJ Rob Gretton, manager of Joy Division and New Order, and hater of London and travelling to London.[13] His anti-London attitude was partly behind the comparatively generous idea of a 50–50 profit split between label and band.[14] Wilson provided greater publicity and exposure on regional television. From the early 1970s onwards, Wilson was a presenter on Granada TV, working on news, current affairs, and debate-based programmes, as well as unsubtly promoting his musical interests, particularly on arts programmes such as *So It Goes* and the musical finales to *Granada Reports*.[15] Wilson's earlier television presence had already attracted interest and requests from Morrissey and Howard Trafford, aka Buzzcock's Howard Devoto.[16]

By the end of the 1980s, Happy Mondays and The Stone Roses were redirecting Manchester music towards the crossover between rave/dance and guitar music, sometimes referred to generally as 'baggy' or the even-more-dated label, 'Madchester', and brought to a national audience in Happy Mondays' EP: *Madchester Rave On* (1989).[17] The late 1980s would also mark another shift in the fortunes of the Factory club run by Tony Wilson and New Order: the Haçienda. The Haçienda opened in

---

11.   Reynolds, *Rip It Up*, p. 95. For a full collection of Factory art and design see M. Robertson, *Factory Records: The Complete Graphic Album* (London: Thames & Hudson, 2006).

12.   Morley, *Joy Division*, p. 46.

13.   Middles, *From Joy Division to New Order*, p. 35, 108.

14.   Middles, *From Joy Division to New Order*, pp. 108, 110, 279; J. Robb, *The North Will Rise Again: Manchester Music City (1976–1996)* (London: Aurum, 2010), pp. 112-15.

15.   Middles, *From Joy Division to New Order*, pp.121-22.

16.   Middles, *From Joy Division to New Order*, pp. 20-26.

17.   For the origins and influence of the term 'Madchester' see M. Middles, *Shaun Ryder: Happy Mondays, Black Grape and Other Traumas* (London: Independent Music Press, 1997), pp. 93-94. On the famous Top of the Pops show featuring both Happy Mondays and The Stone Roses, and links with Mancunian identity, see e.g. Robb, *North*, pp. 309-10 and M. O'Connell, *Ian Brown: Already in Me: With and Without the Roses* (New Malden: Chrome Dreams, 2006), pp. 109-12.

1982 and would spend the early and mid-1980s as a half-full venue for bands but the rapidly growing rave scene of the late 1980s and early 1990s would effectively make it the first superclub and central to the collective memory of those in and around the Manchester music scene.[18]

But the mid-1990s was the beginning of the end of this Manchester music scene as something distinctively and famously Mancunian. Predictably, drug use saw off Happy Mondays as a significant cultural force, assisted by unconventional acts such as Shaun Ryder angrily wielding a Magnum and shooting a mirror in the Factory-run Dry Bar. Happy Monday's 1992 album, *Yes Please*, was not widely deemed a success by critics (nor indeed by some band members) and was effectively the end, though Shaun Ryder and Bez did briefly make a brief successful Britpop reappearance with Black Grape.[19] Drugs likewise put an end to The Stone Roses' hope of chart domination. But their rise was also halted by a legal dispute with record labels which started in 1990 and meant that their highly anticipated second album in 1994 missed its moment and did not achieve the critical acclaim of their first. The acrimonious split predictably followed, though Ian Brown did achieve some success in his solo career.

Of course, this was not the end of Mancunian musicians constructing a Mancunian identity and dance music would continue to be associated with Manchester. However, from the mid-1990s Manchester pop music, especially in its guitar-based manifestations, became popularly associated with one band: Oasis. One of the key reasons for this association was the media presentation of, and obsession with, the apparent rivalry between The North versus The South, Working-Class versus Middle-Class, Mancunians versus Mockneys, epitomised (in media terms) by Oasis versus Blur.[20] And in distinction from the musical developments of the 1980s and 1990s, the self- and popular perception was that there was nothing new about Oasis. Of course, what band does not borrow heavily from the past? However, the rhetoric was different; Oasis *wanted* to be like The Beatles (or even Slade). In fact, they also sounded like a direct continuation of the 'baggy' Madchester scene (especially The Stone Roses) but without the dance influences. Yet what is also significant is that Oasis were constructing themselves as something bigger than Manchester, something much more *national* (and, if they had their way, international). Liam Gallagher put this transcending of Manchester a

18. E.g. Savage (ed.), *Haçienda*, pp. 17, 19, 20.

19. Middles, *Shaun Ryder*, pp. 132-57; Robb, *North*, pp. 277-80.

20. See J. Harris, *The Last Party: Britpop, Blair and the Demise of English Rock* (London: HarperPerennial, 2004), for all the details.

different way: 'I wanted to go to the top. To be the next Beatles, bigger than The Beatles. I didn't want to be the next Mondays, 'cos that's (holds finger and thumb slightly apart) that big.'[21]

Significantly, Oasis became synonymous with *Britpop* rather than *Madchester*. Of course, Oasis showed off their Mancunian and North-Western credentials but they still made the symbolic and physical shift to London (Noel Gallagher even moved to Camden). As John Robb pointed out, Oasis were 'perhaps the first band of any note for years to buck the stay-in-the-north trend'.[22] There is a telling comparison to be made between the defining moments of The Stone Roses and Oasis. At their peak, The Stone Roses played to 30,000 at a special one-off performance in the North-West, at Spike Island near Widnes (May, 1990); at their peak, Oasis played to a total of 250,000 in two shows at Knebworth Park, Hertfordshire (August, 1996), the heart of Middle England.

The emergence of Oasis' transcendence of Manchester was accompanied by other symbolic events marking the End of an Era. 1992 saw the end of Factory Records with the Haçienda following suit in 1997 after well-publicized troubles with finances, violence, and drugs. As dance superclubs took off throughout the UK, the Haçienda (especially) and other clubs in Manchester became more associated with drugs and gangs, with 'Madchester' acquiring a new nickname: 'Gunchester'.[23] Illustrating the End of an Era as much as anything else, the Haçienda is now home to plush city centre flats, bearing the same brand name and glaring at anyone on the train between Deansgate and Manchester Oxford Road stations.

2. 'For EveryManc a Religion'

Late twentieth-century British youth culture has long been noted for being particularly 'secularised' or having a hostile or indifferent attitude towards Christianity (at least as traditionally understood). The punk, post-punk, and independent music scene with which the main Manchester bands were associated was no exception. The hostility towards, critique of, playing around with, or sheer indifference to religion and Christianity in such subcultural circles can be found in songs as seemingly diverse as Sex Pistols' 'Anarchy in the UK' (1977), Depeche Mode's 'Blasphemous

---

21. Quoted in Robb, *North*, p. 369.
22. Robb, *North*, pp. 363-64, 373.
23. On the problems around the late 1980s/early 1990s see further S. Redhead and H. Rietveld, 'Down at the Club', in Savage (ed.), *Haçienda*, pp. 71-77; Middles, *From Joy Division to New Order*, pp. 233-40; Haslam, *Manchester*, pp. 191-219.

Rumours' (1984), The Shamen's 'Jesus Loves Amerika' (1988), and Morrissey's 'Everyday Is Like Sunday' (1988). As Deane Galbraith has shown, it was thoughts of mainstream and subcultural embarrassment, potential career destruction, and a lack of credibility that Christianity might bring to an aspiring band which led U2 (big fans of Joy Division) to provide more veiled references to their faith.[24] However, while hardly producing Christian bands, and indeed while retaining a strand of anti-religious rhetoric, Christianity did form part of the backdrop to the Manchester bands and not simply as a point of contrast. Catholicism in particular played a significant role in the construction of identities among Mancunian families, as it likewise did in Liverpool. Manchester's industrial past was built on both cotton and immigration, including Irish and Irish Catholic immigration which would become so prominent in twentieth-century Greater Manchester culture and English pop music and culture more generally.[25]

Among others, Tony Wilson, The Smiths, Happy Mondays, and Oasis all had close Irish connections and the impact of this background is rarely far from the surface, even if sometimes thinly veiled. Morrissey would sing about his heritage in relationship to nationalism and patriotism in 'Irish Blood, English Heart' (2004). Shaun Ryder remembered his grandfather, Big Billy Carroll, in a different manner: 'One big, Irish motherfucker, cock of the estate... He'd go to church every fuckin' night, say a prayer, and then be up to his old fuckin' ways.'[26] This Catholic and Irish Catholic background was not always nostalgic and could provide a context for reaction. Una Baines, an early influential member of The Fall, identified as a feminist and rejected her Catholic upbringing when she was at her all-girls school because she thought the Bible was anti-women.[27] Whether audiences in Manchester and beyond would take note of the influence of this Irish Catholic background is not easy to determine but it does to some extent explain why biblical and religious language occurs throughout the output of prominent Manchester bands (see below).

Irish Catholicism was not the only source of such language for Manchester bands. A notable Jewish population in Prestwich may have indirectly or directly influenced The Fall, particularly as they encountered a young Mark E. Smith. Smith also remembered forming an

24. Galbraith, 'Drawing Our Fish in the Sand', pp. 189-95.
25. See further S. Campbell, *Irish Blood, English Heart: Second Generation Irish Musicians in England* (Cork: Cork University Press, 2011).
26. Quoted in Middles, *Shaun Ryder*, p. 25.
27. Reynolds, *Rip It Up*, p. 178.

ecumenical gang with members identified as Catholics, Jews, and Protestants.[28] Elsewhere, Ian Curtis (from Macclesfield) had gained an 'O' Level in Religious Knowledge. According to his widow, Deborah Curtis, he was awarded prizes 'in favourite subjects': History and Divinity. Curtis also intended to continue his study of History and Divinity at 'A' Level but left college after arguing with teachers. Curtis' interest got increasingly intense. He would, for instance, claim to have a 'religious experience', which consisted of a drunken gouging of the book of Revelation, and he was reluctant to marry Deborah in a church because he believed she would be struck down when walking down the aisle.[29] Ian Brown was more of an outsider, initially hailing from Warrington. Brown sung 'for everyman a religion' in 'F.E.A.R.' and has described his beliefs in terms of universalistic spirituality, which is said to involve a belief in a higher force and the use of 'natural' psychedelic drugs for greater spiritual insight. Brown attends different places of worship and will challenge parts of any religion he deems problematic.[30] He is also a regular reader of the Qur'an and the Bible, the latter certainly coming through in The Stone Roses' songs. Brown has claimed to read the Bible 'for the stories' and sees Exodus as particularly influential while claiming to be obsessed with the figure of Moses.[31] Brown or any of the other Manchester musicians hardly share the evangelical zeal of U2 but the description 'secular' does not perhaps do justice to these avid users of the Cultural Bible.

3. Biblical Language: Joy Division and The Fall

After bemoaning the portrayal of Manchester pop musicians as little more than borderline hedonistic louts in the film *24 Hour Party People* (dir.: Michael Winterbottom, 2002), Simon Reynolds pointed out that the 'canon of existentialist literature (Kafka, Conrad, Camus, Dostoevsky) was massively influential on post-punk bands like Joy Division', adding that it was 'a hyper-literate time, when singers went around with Penguin Modern Classics poking out of the pockets of their long black over-coats'.[32] Reynolds is undoubtedly correct but one additional resource for

28. Middles, *From Joy Division to New Order*, p. 52; N. Blincoe, 'Mark E. Smith: wonderful and frightening', *Telegraph* (April 26, 2008).

29. D. Curtis, *Touching from a Distance: Ian Curtis and Joy Division* (London: Faber, 1995), pp. 6, 20, 29, 103-104.

30. L. Baker, 'The unsinkable Ian Brown', *Guardian* (February 2, 2002).

31. O'Connell, *Ian Brown*, p. 269.

32. S. Reynolds, 'Joy Division: Two Movies', in Reynolds, *Totally Wired*, pp. 358-66 (363).

those with cultural pretentions that he did not include was the Bible, or what we might call the Cultural Bible. In fact, the connections between Manchester pop music and the (Cultural) Bible were seemingly obvious in Easter 2006 and the public presentation of the Manchester Passion. The Manchester Passion featured music from a familiar list of high-profile bands (e.g. The Smiths, Joy Division, New Order, The Stone Roses, Happy Mondays) and personalities (e.g. Bez, Tim Booth) from the past 30–40 years. And there was a readymade song for the climax: The Stone Roses' 'I Am the Resurrection'. This was not the first time Manchester pop music had joined forces with theatrical performance. David Yallop's retelling (*In God's Name*, 1984) of the mysterious demise of Pope John Paul I and his thirty-three days in office provided the inspiration for the play and song *Hey! Luciani* (1986) written and performed by Mark E. Smith and The Fall.[33]

From the 1970s to the 1990s there was a marked shift in the use by Manchester bands of biblical, quasi-biblical, and religious language which in many ways was, as we will see, embedded in the cultural, political, and social changes in Manchester and Britain more widely. In the early post-punk period, biblical and related language was used regularly by the most prominent performers for dark introspection, cynical observation, nihilism, and pessimism. Misery and cynicism could sometime affect bands like The Stone Roses and Happy Mondays but by the end of our period biblical and related language was more typically being used for self-congratulation, self-importance, hedonism, and optimism, even if short-lived in certain instances.

At the beginning of our period, for instance, in 'Passover', from Joy Division's 1980 album *Closer*, Curtis looks to an imminent but uncertain personal crisis which appears to be merged with the life of Moses and the exodus from Egypt. Curtis' retelling countered a dominant received tradition of the exodus as a positive heroic story. Instead, Curtis viewed Moses' behaviour and leadership of the Israelites much more ambiguously, even to the point that it might even have been disastrous. The song can look to times when there was security, such as in youth when protection given to the infant Moses is recalled and when God was present with Moses in the burning bush. But moving to Moses' adult life, security gives way to insecurity. The Passover, the blood on the doorpost, death, and the plagues are obvious cause for concern and an ambiguous legacy to leave (cf. Exodus 11–12). Likewise, the wilderness wanderings and the destruction of Pharaoh's army are used to hammer

---

33. See further, S. Ford, *Hip Priest: The Story of Mark E. Smith and The Fall* (London: Quartet, 2003), pp. 164-67.

home the destructive consequences of personal actions. Of course, for personal destructive actions we can read 'Curtis' and much as 'Moses'. Curtis would kill himself the same year and his potential for suicide is hinted at throughout *Closer* and the previous album, *Unknown Pleasures*. Curtis' own torments and suffering were complicated further by trying to come to terms with his ongoing affair with Annik Honore and family life, the combination of which also come through in numerous Joy Division songs. In this context, 'Passover' is a relentless reflection on the possible consequences of Curtis' actions.

Various destructive scenes relating to the Bible and Christian history are part of Curtis' dystopian vision in 'Wilderness' (1979), where the narrator travels far and wide throughout time. Typically in Curtis' vision, there is no redemption. Christ's blood is merely the blood shed of another innocent and so, unlike the Pauline vision of Christ's death and the Lord's Prayer, the power and glory of sin rules without end. With the centre-point of Christianity removed, saints become nothing more than destroyers of knowledge and tearful martyrs die unfairly with their names not remembered. Depersonalised the lyrics may have been, but they are, again, not-so-easily removed from the guilt-ridden Curtis' personal agonising, presumably itself seen as a continuation of the dominance of sin.

The Fall began as Manchester's other dominant early post-punk band. Known for their 'social surrealism',[34] Mark E. Smith and The Fall constructed a world of distorted cityscapes, eccentric people, and supernatural paranoia. Close to being a plague on all your houses, few escape the cynicism, including those moving in similar circles to The Fall: working-classes, middle-classes, pretentious music critics ('Hip Priests'), and punk and musical purists ('New Puritans') are all targets. Blake's 'Jerusalem' is now a distorted vision full of surreal horrors and new verses are added which concern a man slipping on a discarded banana skin and hurting his head who then thinks of moving to Sweden or Poland to get proper attention after the government refuse to give him a sizeable hand-out. A New Jerusalem traditionally understood this unpleasantly absurdist and unpleasant world is not.

In 'Spector vs Rector 2', Smith added extra words to his possession song, 'Spectre vs Rector', and referenced another of their songs, 'New Puritan', in its furious end-is-nigh prophetic critique and a further attack on certain musical types. The embellishment of the earlier version included this ominous opening warning about the state of the nation,

---

34. Reynolds, *Rip It Up*, p. 178.

decadent sins, and a puritan who remain unclean. And in an equally ominous ending, Smith screeched in prophetic-like anger a repetition of the righteous judgment facing decadent sinners at the hands of the New Puritan. A related vision of apocalyptic decay was also developed in the 1984 album opening song, 'Lay of the Land' and its opening distorted chant. As with Joy Division, the end times do not contain the hope and optimism of films of the 'apocalyptic genre' or the political rhetoric of the Labour tradition. The survey in 'Lay of the Land' has the beaten last Briton against the backdrop of a fuzzy radio and no longer reflecting on the absurdities of human fate. The only ones present are thieves, death, and the worst kind of kerb crawlers. As also found with Joy Division, cultural decline is everywhere. The airwaves are full of the ordinary and the pinnacle of culture is nothing more than a bad stew. There is even mention of one of the most dated of English situation comedies, *On the Buses*. And in the midst of this dystopia is reference to 'the good book of John' surrounding the Son.

4. Biblical Language: Happy Mondays and The Stone Roses

If we compare the apocalyptic bleakness with the use of biblical language in the Madchester era then there are some striking differences. The surrealism of Happy Mondays can pose problems for interpretation but it is still clear that there is the idea of self-replacement for Jesus in their not-too-subtly titled song 'Kuff Dam', from the 1987 debut album, *24 Hour Party People Plastic Face Carnt Smile (White Out)*. Shaun Ryder sings about his authority to speak truth to people. This sentiment stands in direct contrast to the ineffectiveness of Jesus who is no longer the supreme healer. In fact, the singer replaces Jesus (denounced as a 'cunt') and is a superior healer of 'furry tongue'. 'Messianic' claims were furthered more explicitly in one of Happy Mondays' breakthrough singles, the 'hedonistic manifesto',[35] 'Hallelujah' (1989). 'Hallelujah' continued the Jesus-replacement with an even more explicit self-identification of a kind of Messiah, one of drug-fuelled hedonism. While the singer exclaims 'hallelujah!' there is the constant reminder that this is not a traditional Saviour. Instead Shaun William Ryder will be filling you with 'junk'.

Ian Brown has long been a dedicated reader of the Bible and biblical and quasi-biblical allusions are unmistakable in The Stone Roses' songs and are more wide-ranging than in any of the artists covered in this

---

35. A. McGee, 'Happy Mondays are back. Hallelujah!', *Guardian* (August 27, 2007).

chapter. The Stone Roses' 1989 eponymous debut album appears vaguely to follow the structure of Gospel narratives, at least in terms of beginning and ending. The album's opening song is 'I Wanna Be Adored' (often thought to be an allusion to the Adoration), and closes with 'I Am the Resurrection'. The self-identification is a match for Happy Mondays in terms of grandeur; as Michael O'Connell claimed of this album structure: 'To say both tracks are daunting affirmations of the Roses' unshakable self-belief would be an understatement'.[36]

Such 'unshakeable self-belief' and more came in the form of satanic possession in 'I Wanna Be Adored'. The language of adoration and adoring the singer are repeated constantly accompanied by the enticement of a near-whisper, in what has become another landmark of Madchester individualism and egotism. Again, it is worth comparing this with what came before. The Fall were likewise known for singing about the supernatural but, for instance, in 'Elves' (1984) the emphasis is darker and paranoid where the world of the fantastical is against the singer. Exorcism, possession, and selling the soul to the devil were taken up in 'Spectre vs Rector' (1979). Here, only the character of the Hero is able to take up the challenge of possession. Yet even in this instance, we are still far removed from The Stone Roses' positive embrace of possession for there is much ambiguity surrounding the 'last scene' where the Inspector is going mad, where it is questioned whether the Spectre has gone forever and where the exhausted exorcist has had to retreat to the mountains. Indeed, in the live version on *Totale's Turns (It's Now or Never)* (1980), Smith's addition was more ominous as the Hero sings that the Spectre remains omnipresent.

While retaining an element of the satanic, the theme of possession was treated differently in The Stone Roses' 'Breaking into Heaven' (1994), itself from the hardly understatedly entitled album, *The Second Coming*. According to 'Breaking into Heaven', it would be simple to saw through the gates of heaven (as popularly understood) and all the icons should listen because the singer is coming. The message is that the old vision of heaven needs to be replaced with a more inward-looking 'spiritualised' kingdom. There is an obvious allusion to Luke 17.20-21 about the kingdom being inside as the singer emphatically claims that this kingdom is there for the taking in the here and now. Ian Curtis' take on things relating to the afterlife stands in stark contrast. In 'Heart and Soul' (1980), the inevitable end brings no glorious kingdom, nor is there one among us, nor is there hope. There is an abyss laughing at creation combined

---

36. O'Connell, *Ian Brown*, p. 93.

with a destructive unfurling of world history, both intertwined, of course, with the fate of the individual. Indeed, there is no personal salvation or chance of forgiveness and, ultimately, heart and soul will burn. 'Heart and Soul' was sung in near-whispering and accepting tones which, as the first song on the second side *Closer*, set the scene for the rest of the album. As Reynolds put it, the second side 'is even more disturbing…on account of its serenity. It's as though Curtis has stopped struggling altogether.'[37] By way of contrast here, we only need recall the understatement of 'unshakeable self-belief' involved in The Stone Roses' take on eschatology.

There may have been implicit self-importance in Curtis' use of the persona of Moses but it was, nevertheless, an attempt to understand depression and the consequences of his decisions. There are, however, no such obvious qualifications for The Stone Roses who, as part of their 'unshakeable self-belief' would use the persona of the raised Jesus or even Jesus-as-God, most famously in the final song on their eponymous debut album, 'I Am the Resurrection'. After a series of anticipated choruses, Ian Brown finally ends the lyrical section of 'I Am the Resurrection' with the double repetition of the 'real chorus' about being the resurrection and not, ultimately, hating the implied recipient of the singer's lyrics.[38] The allusions to John 11 are obvious enough, and this sort of Johannine allusion is found elsewhere, for instance on the b-side of 'One Love' which includes an explicit reference to the singer being the vine and the implied recipient being the branches. After the anticipated final chorus is repeated at the end of 'I Am the Resurrection' the lyrical section of the song ends and is followed by nearly 5 minutes of upbeat instrumental, borrowing from 60s psychedelia, Hendrix, funk, Motown, and contemporary dance music. Before the anticipated final chorus and the famous instrumental section, the song builds up to its climax(es) with biblical language of repentance (and, ultimately, acceptance/forgiveness) with the singer appearing to take on the persona of God or Jesus-as-God. The song begins with a clear enough allusion to Jesus' ambiguous stories of knocking on doors and the different responses this might bring. Hope remains for those who knock persistently, no matter what the responses might be along the way (Luke 11.5-10; cf. Matt. 7.7-11; John 10.1-10). Yet elsewhere, the one knocking can remain

37. Reynolds, *Rip It Up*, pp. 187-88.
38. Cf. O'Donnell, *Ian Brown*, p. 92: 'Stunningly, the real chorus is revealed at the end of three verses, a majestic, magical howl of triumph: "I am the resurrection and I am the light [*sic*?]".'

an evildoer (Luke 13.23-27). In 'I Am the Resurrection', we find the Luke 11.5-10 version of the door-knocking tradition (eventual redemption), though the door-knocker has much in common with the rejected ones of the Luke 13.23-27 version. 'I Am the Resurrection' also draws on the prophetic literature and the theme of the stubbornness of Israel (and God), including the apparent inability of Israel to repent of her sins. The song even used the Semitic language of repentance ('turn') in the context of not being able to stand the company of the implied recipient. The final graceful acceptance is only given once it is clear that the singer's great Other is seemingly rejected entirely.

Implicit throughout, of course, is that the song is *really about* a human–human (rather than God–human) relationship, though it could theoretically be (and has been) taken as an attack on a particularly egotistical individual. However, the song itself provides no indication of it being an obvious polemic against this hypothetical egotist and it does end an album which began with more than 'unshakeable self-belief'. Indeed, the sentiments expressed in 'I Am the Resurrection' tally with the swagger of Ian Brown's public persona. For instance, in 2002 Lindsay Baker asked Brown if he had a 'Messiah complex' to which Brown's reported answer was that he 'couldn't take it on' before then adding that 'I did sing about angels, I did sing "I am the resurrection" but I felt righteous in them days'.[39] Baker further reported that 'he says he never feels weighed down by gravity when he walks down the street, that he reads the Bible and the spirit breathes life into him, that he has a recurring dream where he has a gold crown, and he's sitting under a tree, with a lion under one arm and a lioness under the other'. It is not difficult, then, to see why people might understand 'I Am the Resurrection' as something other than a simple retelling of biblical stories.

The title of The Stone Roses' long-awaited second album hardly downplayed such confident pretentions: *The Second Coming* (1994). Guitarist John Squire effectively confirmed this when he told *Melody Maker* in May 1995 that 'I thought it was cocky and tongue-in-cheek at the same time'.[40] The language on the album tracks might not be quite so elevated but the marked difference from Joy Division and The Fall is still strong. 'Love Spreads' opens the album and has Jesus being crucified and portrayed as a black woman. This is a forgiving Messiah who is both the singer's queen *and* sister. This 'messianic' sister appears to have turned up previously in The Stone Roses' lyrics. In the single 'She Bangs

39. Baker, 'The unsinkable Ian Brown'.
40. P. McAuley, 'Where cherubim play', http://www.thisisthedaybreak.co.uk/.

the Drums' (also from The Stone Roses' debut album), the singer gets eased by both passion fruit and holy bread and the female figure gets the quasi-biblical language treatment of 'coming to pass' and 'the first and the last'.

But, as with the queen in 'Love Spreads' also being 'my sister', there are also some 'messianic' claims implicit in 'She Bangs the Drums', particularly when The Stone Roses were becoming the latest Mancunian saviours rather than their older rivals. The Smiths had previously announced their arrival by claiming that the sun shines from their behinds ('Hand in Glove' [1983]) but now The Stone Roses were singing about the past kissing where the sun doesn't shine because the future belongs, presumably, to them ('She Bangs the Drums' [1989]). As part of the comparison between post-punk Manchester and Madchester, we could recall Joy Division's 'Heart and Soul' where the past becomes part of the future and a present out-of-control. Alluding to their Joy Division past but now with disco-inspiration, we might further note New Order's 'Confusion' (1983). Here Bernard Sumner sings about the past as present but now owning the future. But even New Order, it seems, were superseded by The Stone Roses.

But instead of world domination, The Stone Roses' second album effectively marked their end and Oasis would follow with their own brand of supersessionism. Probably Oasis' most famous song with biblical allusions is 'Live Forever' (1994). Despite apparently having Noel Gallagher's mother in mind, one obvious context in which to view this song is the time it was released and became popular (rather than when it was actually written). By 1994 Oasis had achieved public notoriety for their drug use at a time when a fetishized 'lad culture' had almost effortlessly merged with Britpop, epitomised by the rise of *Loaded* magazine (launched May 1994) and its cocaine-snorting editor James Brown.[41] It is difficult not to see the confident quasi-biblical language as a part of this backdrop, irrespective of the song's 'true meaning'. Put slightly differently, in such a context it would certainly not have been difficult to associate such a background with lyrics couched in terms of wanting to fly and wanting to live forever.

For all their bravado and swagger, Oasis, and Noel Gallagher in particular, were capable of referencing the bleak past. 'Live Forever' was in fact released when the angst of American-based grunge had a central

---

41. T. Hulse, 'James Brown: the latest edition', *Independent on Sunday* (October 5, 1997); D. Teather, 'Father of lads' mags still loaded with ideas', *Guardian* (August 24, 2007).

role in British youth subculture and alternative music in the early 1990s and when Noel Gallagher had personally felt the impact of unemployment. 'Live Forever' is a sufficiently general song to leave the 'meaning' open-ended but it is extremely optimistic in its escape from problems past and present. After all, the song ends by echoing those biblical traditions of end times and life eternal (cf. 1 Thess. 4.16-17; John 3.16; 5.24; 11.25-26).

As noted, 'Live Forever' was said to be written with the Gallagher brothers' mother, Peggy, in mind. It is perhaps worth mentioning that Peggy Gallagher (nee Sweeney) was no stranger to Christianity and the Bible having spent over six years being brought up in a convent and later, when in Manchester, she sent her sons to a Catholic school and had problems with the church over a separation from her violent husband.[42] 'Live Forever' is another important example when we compare the output from the beginning of our period. Where Joy Division and The Fall would also reference the problems past and present, there was little chance of escape. Indeed, in Curtis' lyrics, and in his life, death was the only thing close to an escape. With Oasis, when problems are acknowledged, the escape is nothing less than life eternal.

There were, then, some sharply different uses of biblical language by the most high-profile Manchester bands between the late 1970s and the late 1980s/early 1990s. As an aside, we might note that The Smiths, falling somewhere in the middle (1982–87), in some ways provide a bridge in their use of religious language. Morrissey certainly embraced the misery of the early post-punk years but, inspired as he was by Wilde, wit and irony are constantly present. For instance, 'Vicar in a Tutu' (1986) tells the story of a vicar from the Holy Name Church who also happens to wear a tutu. We are told that he is not strange and that he just wants to live his life that way with the song exiting by the singer repeating that he is the living sign. Tragi-camp would become part of Morrissey's public presentation, particularly through his self-pitying, Christ-crucified, or Sacred Heart kitsch poses.[43] In his later solo career, Morrissey would even write the song, 'I Have Forgiven Jesus' (2004), where he took on the role of a priest and developed the play between angst and humour.

42. Harris, *Last Party*, pp. 116-19.
43. Harris, *Last Party*, p. 5.

5. Taking the Rain out of Manchester? Cityscapes and Personalities between 1976 and 1994

A range of factors can explain this shift from misery to hedonism and, as we will see, they intersect with the emergence and consolidation of Thatcherism. The expected individual influences are clear enough. For instance, it is not difficult to make connections between Curtis' bleak lyrics and his epilepsy, his interest in epileptics, his marriage break-down, and his suicidal depression. As we have seen, Curtis' lyrics are certainly not woodenly autobiographical and are typically 'depersonal-ised'; Reynolds uses the term 'existentialist' over 'autobiographical', pointing to influences from Kafka and Camus among others, to which, of course, we can add the Bible.[44] Equally, however, 'autobiography' and 'existentialism' are not easily separated, as the example of 'Passover' showed, and so Curtis' life was obviously a significant influence on his particular use of biblical language.

Mark E. Smith was not like Curtis and his own quirks and peculiarities have been an important influence on his use of biblical language. Smith – the grumpy, misanthropic armchair-critic *par excellence* – also had a diverse range of literary influences with a tendency towards horror (e.g. H.P. Lovecraft, Edgar Allan Poe, Philip K. Dick), and to which we can likewise add the Bible. Or, as Simon Ford put it, Smith's interests veer towards 'the off-beat *noir* of non-mainstream genre fiction'.[45] Smith may not have been tortured like Curtis but his interests too were not those of the hedonism of late 1980's Manchester.

Crucially, Smith and Curtis shared the Manchester and Salford city-scape during the mid–late 1970s. Combined, Manchester and Salford (the home of Tony Wilson, Peter Hook, and Bernard Sumner) had provided imagery for the stereotypical dour, northern working-class city, most popularly through soap operas such as *Coronation Street*, films such as *Love on the Dole* and *A Taste of Honey* (a major influence on Morrissey, as was the playwright Shelagh Delaney), and songs such as Ewan MacColl's 'Dirty Old Town'. Industry had played a significant part of these popular images but by the 1970s Manchester was in serious industrial decline and this was being noticed in connection with the emerging musical scene. According to Tosh Ryan of Rabid Records in 1977, 'The area is so neglected, so economically deprived and full of

---

44. Reynolds, 'Joy Division: Two Movies', p. 358. See also Reynolds, *Rip It Up*, pp. 180-83; S. Reynolds, 'Music to brood by, desolate and stark', *New York Times* (October 7, 2007).

45. Ford, *Hip Priest*, pp. 12-13.

massive housing complexes, that the mood of the place was right and ready for a new movement in music with a markedly different criteria of success. What has developed is peculiar to Manchester.'[46]

Desolate and decaying cityscapes are common to both The Fall and Joy Division, with 1970s urban Manchester an integral part of the bleak backdrop for promotional photographs. As if to hit the greyness home, Joy Division's first television performance (of 'Shadowplay') on *Granada Reports* in 1978 was introduced by Tony Wilson who emphasised the Manchester and Salford origins of the band before the performance itself was interspersed with 'monochrome footage of a dire cityscape'.[47] Even the name 'Factory' was linked with the state of urban Manchester. Paul Morley commented that

> The name Factory was as much out of the Lancashire mills, the local industrial past, as it was a knowing nod to Warhol's Manhattan community of freaks and dreamers. Also, when most factories in the area had closed down, here was one that was opening.[48]

Yet, as the opening of this Factory implies, Manchester of the late 1970s was also vaguely pointing towards the urban regeneration that Manchester would eventually receive, or, more visibly, its more central areas would receive. The Manchester skyline today is marked but the Hilton skyscraper, while even a casual glance around the city centre will take in glitzy bar after glitzy bar. Between the 1970s and the present, the rave scene was likewise contributing to the earlier urban changes with some of the dominant figures taking advantage of cheap old buildings. 'The Joy Division years were over', claims Dave Haslam, and the new clubs were now starting to 'impose a new image on the city'.[49] This context would also produce Happy Mondays and The Stone Roses, and Manchester groups of this period explicitly wanted to repackage the image of the city from one where the inhabitants wallow in the misery into the hedonism of Madchester.[50]

Musical trends were, then, tied in with social, economic, and even architectural developments. In this vein, it is not difficult to see connections between the simultaneous emergence of Madchester with the

46. Quoted in Ford, *Hip Priest*, p. 20, and originally from 'New Wave Devolution: Manchester Waits for the World to Listen', *Melody Maker* (May 14, 1977). See also Haslam, *Manchester*, pp. 109-10.

47. Curtis, *Touching*, p. 61. The *Granada Reports* performance is available at http://www.youtube.com/watch?v=FzTw4PYfROU.

48. Morley, *Joy Division*, p. 15.

49. Haslam, *Manchester*, pp. 188-89.

50. Robb, *Stone Roses*, p. 5.

unashamed hedonism of the acid house and rave scene, which also owed much to Manchester dance music in the form of, for instance, 808 State and A Guy Called Gerald. New Order were arguably most suited to these crossovers because they had been one of the key British influences on electronic and dance music which would explode in the rave era. Uses of, and changes in, dance genres are particularly notable because crossovers with more conventional rock music were, in fact, being pioneered earlier in the post-punk era. Joy Division embraced drum beats and electronica by way of disco, though this was, of course, lacking the hedonism of later New Order experiments with dance music. Disco was arguably as crucial as punk in early post-punk experimentation and Donna Summer's 'I Feel Love' (1977), with its entirely electronically synthesised backing music, would be as influential on the darker visions of Joy Division and Public Image Ltd as it would on the long-term future of dance music hedonism.[51] But this was not alien to disco; disco had embraced the tragic as well as the fun, as did another important influence on Joy Division (and The Fall) from dance music: Northern Soul. Before the profound influence of the Northern Soul clubs on the hedonism of the rave scene (including a number of the same DJs turning up in the Haçienda), Joy Division were sampling the guitar from N.F. Porter's gritty Northern Soul classic, 'Keep On Keeping On' in their 1979 track, 'Interzone'.

If post-punk extracted near-pure misery from disco, then rave extracted near-pure joy. New Order are a case in point, straddling, as they did, the post-punk and rave eras. Listen to any electronic track from their earlier incarnation as Joy Division and compare it with New Order's 1988 acid house/rave and Ibiza-inspired anthem, 'Fine Time', and the difference is striking. But even as New Order, there are striking contrasts. For instance, compare 'Fine Time' with their earlier dark disco classic, 'Blue Monday' (1983). Bernard Sumner's monotone vocals and the opening lyrics do not conjure up images of San Antonio clubs in the way the cocky 'Fine Time' might. The rapid beats of the drum machine in 'Blue Monday' and electronic sounds are militarised which the accompanying video emphasised further still with additional marching, explosions, tanks, helicopters, beach landings, missiles, and, most significantly, the

---

51. Reynolds, *Rip It Up*, p. 266; S. Reynolds, 'Interview: Steven Morris', in *Totally Wired*, pp. 229-43 (234). Cf. Haslam, *Manchester*, p. 150. Worth a comparative mention are Joy Division and New Order Factory stable-mates, A Certain Ratio, who were also developing funk but, despite their penchant for wearing shorts, likewise with a distinctly dark edge

Harrier Jump Jet which had risen to cultural prominence through the Falklands War. The usual guesses as to what the song is actually 'about' (e.g. Falklands War, a series of Swedish student suicides in the 1950s, or Curtis' suicide on the eve of Joy Division's American tour) may or may not hit the mark but they all support John Harris' claim that Blue Monday might be the bleakest disco record ever released.[52]

In terms of fame and cultural significance, it would be The Stone Roses and Happy Mondays who would benefit most from the growing prominence of dance/rave in the late 1980s. Ian Brown would claim that 'pop music was saved by the advent of acid house and rap because whites have done nothing for ten years' and he thought it natural that their fans would like dance music.[53] The Stone Roses would also find themselves temporarily reversing the typical influence of dance on guitar music when the famous bassline from 'I Am the Resurrection' was sampled by the North West's rap/dance/electronica specialists MC Tunes and 808 State in 'Tunes Splits the Atom' (1990). The standard dance influence was embraced by Happy Mondays, not only in their musical output but also by having their songs remixed by leading DJs. And, after all, it was Happy Mondays who gave the world the party-anthem, '24 Hour Party People'.

When dealing with pop and rock music generally, and dance, post-punk, Northern Soul, or Madchester more specifically, drug use can hardly be ignored in musical and social changes. The cultural prominence of certain types of drugs used or referenced is particularly important. Acid/LSD hardly died out with the hippies but it was amphetamines that became associated with Northern Soul, punk, and post-punk, particularly in the songs of The Fall.[54] Amphetamines may be a stimulant but are also known for inducing paranoia, a side-effect which turned up in the songs of The Fall and Joy Division. Incidents involving the use of drugs and downers to pacify patients on the psychiatric ward were further reported by The Fall's Una Baines while Curtis himself would receive downers and tranquilizers for his epilepsy, although they only appear to have worsened his depression.[55] By the late 1980s and early 1990s, ecstasy had risen to cultural prominence and media notoriety and

52. Harris, *Last Party*, p. 17. For discussion of the different interpretations of 'Blue Monday' see Middles, *From Joy Division to New Order*, pp. 247-49.

53. Quoted in Robb, *Stone Roses*, p. 213.

54. Middles, *From Joy Division to New Order*, p. 48; Haslam, *Manchester*, p. 145; Reynolds, *Rip It Up*, pp. 176-77.

55. Reynolds, *Rip It Up*, p. 177.

became synonymous with rave. Ecstasy would retain the sleep-defying element of amphetamines but could also make the user highly friendly, euphoric, and conducive to hours of dancing without inhibitions. It was relatively cheap (approximately £10–£15 per tablet) and rarely consumed with alcohol which further kept costs down. As if marking this narcotic shift, Mark E. Smith sang on The Fall's 1990 album, *Extricate*: 'Remember when you needed three caps of speed/To get out of bed/And now you're on ecstasy' (The Fall, 'Hilary').

The impact of ecstasy on British dance music was almost immediate. DJ Mike Pickering described the importance of ecstasy for post-1987 Haçienda dance nights:

> It [dance music] changed almost overnight... The noticeable thing was that it went a lot more white, immediately. You could see the black kids who were dancers were getting moved over a bit... People were going fucking mad... It was the best scene I've ever been involved in, there were people from all backgrounds and walks of life, all getting on, and it was so creative when it first started... One of the things that made it so special was that it was going on in the ignorance of the authorities. They thought everyone was in a good mood. It was only when the usual seedy southerners let *News at Ten* in, overnight it just died. Suddenly it got sleezy cos of the coppers, and the hoods.[56]

Its significance was also noted by the main Madchester bands. The Stone Roses openly acknowledged using ecstasy and were aware of its emergence at the same time as the band. Indeed, John Squire recalled that he first took ecstasy as The Stone Roses were on the rise. However, there was a degree of ambivalence. Band members have also tried to distance themselves from the direct influence of ecstasy on the band's creativity and ambition.[57] Yet, we should still follow The Stone Roses' awareness that there were broader cultural trends which accompanied ecstasy and the increasing prominence of Madchester.

Happy Mondays were not so coy and openly embraced the ecstasy phenomenon. Bez – Happy Mondays' dancer who hid his taste for ecstasy the least – would effectively incorporate it into his act and ecstasy would become one focal point for the hedonistic agenda associated with Happy Mondays. Ryder even sang explicitly, positively, and satirically. In 'God's Cop' (1990), from the telling entitled album, *Pills 'n' Thrills 'n' Bellyaches*, the singer mocks the then Greater Manchester Chief of Police, James Anderton. Anderton was untypically open about

---

56. Interviewed in Savage (ed.), *Haçienda*, pp. 30-32 (32).
57. O'Connell, *Ian Brown*, pp. 142-43; cf. Robb, *North*, pp. 241-42.

his faith and accompanying illiberal views on homosexuality which gave him the nickname God's Cop or God's Copper. In 'God's Cop', Ryder jokingly accused Anderton of theft and pictured a scene where 'me and the chief got slowly stoned'. The chorus, as became typical of musical encomiums to ecstasy, took the highly controversial ecstasy culture to divine levels by referring to God's acceptance and God raining down of the drug on the singer.

6. Margaret's Guillotine

But for all the hedonism and reimagining of the cityscape, Madchester was also covering up deeper social problems. Shaun Ryder and Bez viewed the use of LSD, alcohol, amphetamine, and cannabis as a means of escaping the boredom and hopelessness of 1980s urban life (one rumour is that the name 'Happy Mondays' came from the day for benefits collection).[58] Ecstasy provided even more escapism; according to Bez, when 'the E scene came along' it was, 'ironically, one of the biggest out-cries from the young in recent times that they were not happy with their lot, even though, strangely enough, everyone appeared to be ecstatic at the time… [I]t took the monotony out of bein on the dole or sinkin under the pressure of tryin to cope on criminally low wages in a desperate bid to maintain dignity.'[59] The developments in Manchester music, and its use of biblical language, can obviously be seen as a reaction against Thatcherism. But they were also a by-product of Thatcherism. Some of the issues surrounding hedonism and do-it-yourself agendas already suggest that there are clear connections with developing Thatcherism, even if Thatcher would no doubt have personally disapproved of much of what was happening in Manchester's music scene, not least the drug taking and drug references. Such tensions and contradictions were, of course, picked up in Hebdige's analysis of subculture and equally apply here. So, on the one hand, rave and ecstasy use certainly had communal tendencies and they were certainly remembered in terms of escapism from the individualism and isolation of the Thatcher years. On the other hand, rave, like other youth movements, had significant commercial potential (as seen in the redevelopment of Manchester) and a hyper self-confidence, both so integral to Thatcherite neoliberalism.

---

58. See e.g. Middles, *Shaun Ryder*, pp. 22-24, 27. For a different account see J. Warburton with Shaun Ryder, *Hallelujah! The Extraordinary Return of Shaun Ryder and Happy Mondays* (London: Virgin, 2000), pp. 5-6.

59. Bez, *Freaky Dancin': Me and the Mondays* (London: Pan Books, 1998), p. x.

A notable example of the rave culture's commercial potential was its close association with designer and labelled clothing and a serious poseur culture. Certain expensive labels became synonymous with the rave scene and were worn, embraced, and endorsed by the leading Manchester bands of the rave era, whether through spending sprees or performances in promotional videos.[60] A poseur culture may not be new in youth movements but in the case of Madchester, it was a striking contrast with what had come before, particularly the deliberately scruffy 'anti-labels' of the alternative music scene which had generated bands like Happy Mondays and The Stone Roses. For instance, an anti-fashion stance and dour demeanour was integral to the image of The Fall while Joy Division were presented in bleak greys and created 'a monochrome austerity and discipline redolent of totalitarianism'.[61] But then, as ever, the fashionista seeds were already planted in the 1970s: after all, was not the most long-lasting influence of punk on mainstream fashion?

The tensions within Thatcherism between traditional morality and extravagant wealth creators also played their part in Manchester. In some ways, cocaine might be deemed to be the ultimate Thatcherite drug, associated as it was and is with boosts of supreme confidence and the yuppies. In fact, cocaine would replace ecstasy as the more culturally prominent drug of the 1990s and would become synonymous with mid-1990s 'Britpop' just as ecstasy had been with Madchester. And it was Oasis in particular who were most famously associated with cocaine, both in use and allusions. Cocaine was beginning to make a cultural impact as the rave scene developed (Prodigy's 'Charly' reached number three in 1991) and even The Stone Roses began to indulge: guitarist John Squire became a heavy cocaine user in the early 1990s (and this might even be connected with his interest in guitar solos and dominance of the guitar). Ian Brown, a hostile opponent of cocaine use, claimed that Squire's use contributed to the band's downfall.[62] There is almost certainly an allusion to cocaine use in The Stone Roses' 'Breaking into Heaven' (written by Squire) which gives the singer considerable confidence and power.

60. Harris, *Last Party*, pp. 20-21; Middles, *Shaun Ryder*, pp. 101, 127-31; O'Connell, *Ian Brown*, p. 112; Robb, *Stone Roses*, p. 9. Cf. New Order performing 'Fine Time' on Top of the Pops at http://www.youtube.com/watch?v=TCgwiIjfQ5E.

61. Reynolds, *Rip It Up*, p. 181. Cf. Middles, *From Joy Division to New Order*, pp. 66-67.

62. O'Connell, *Ian Brown*, pp. 143-44, 153-54.

Late 1980s music from independent labels was arguably more suscep-
tible to Thatcherite rhetoric than their immediate predecessors from the
post-punk explosion. From the late 1970s until 1987, independent music
was strongly associated with the Left and anti-Thatcherism. In the 1980s
such thinking was focused on the Red Wedge movement which included
a number of alternative and independent musicians in uncomfortable
alliance with the opposition Labour Party. However, Thatcher's third
consecutive victory in 1987 and leftist disillusionment effectively broke
up this opposition. Musicians connected with Red Wedge were prepared
to accept the need for a new generation and there was little hostility
when this new generation were largely a-political by comparison.[63] But
the a-political attitude could become counter-revolutionary: Shaun Ryder
would even utter the unutterable when he provocatively claimed that he
admired Margaret Thatcher. Gender politics could also be turned on its
head in ways that would have been anathema for early 1980s independent artists; Ryder and Bez, for instance, posed with models in a bath for
Penthouse.[64] Unlike the fashionable puritanism of the 1980s, Happy
Mondays and The Stone Roses actually *wanted* to conquer the charts and
wanted success. This could be rationalised in ways other than mere
materialism, of course. Ian Brown, for example, thought The Stone
Roses' music was more aesthetically worthy of topping the charts at the
expense of less worthy pop music.[65]

As Thatcherism was taken up by Blair and New Labour, Oasis would,
as we saw, desire even greater musical success. Perhaps the most-hyped
example of the 1990s was the race between Oasis' 'Roll with It' and
Blur's 'Country House' for the number one spot in 1995. It was now
taken as natural that sales and popularity were at least as important as
aesthetics for the two dominant bands from independent and alternative
music backgrounds. Probably the defining moment of ideological syn-
chronisation with the establishment was in 1997 when Noel Gallagher
accepted an invitation to Tony Blair's victory party at 10 Downing Street
and was pictured chatting to Blair with a glass of champagne in hand.
Tony Wilson did not approve and saw this as an example of how pop
music could become part of the cultural and ideological elite.[66] Of
course, Blair at the time lacked the 'toxicity' of Thatcher, even if he had

---

63. See Harris, *Last Party*, pp. 4, 22-23.

64. Harris, *Last Party*, pp. 16, 20-21. But cf. Middles, *Shaun Ryder*, pp. 130-31.

65. Harris, *Last Party*, p. 17.

66. B. O'Neill, 'Me and my vote: Anthony H. Wilson', *Spiked Politics* (June 1,
2001), http://www.spiked-online.com/Articles/00000002D0FF.htm.

accepted key aspects of Thatcherism, and the presence of the vocally anti-Thatcher Gallagher was not as shocking as praising Thatcher. However, acceptance of Blair's soft-Thatcherism helps us partly understand how Gallagher could re-interpret the aggressively class-critical lyrics of the Sex Pistols to mean that they were little more than an agenda for having a good time.[67] Gallagher's depoliticising of the ferocious anti-Thatcherism of The Smiths is equally striking in his claim that he is, rather, just strictly interested in the music rather than politics, adding, 'Morrissey was going on about poetry and vegetarianism and... Johnny [Marr] was going on about the Rolling Stones and T-Rex and The Stooges and I think, hmmm, yeah'.[68] The range of once interconnected poetic and political elements were at one time deemed integral to The Smiths as the quintessential anti-Thatcher 1980s band, but have now been given the familiar postmodern treatment of replacing the political sting with presentational and stylistic 'cool'.

Irrespective of whether Gallagher or any other Manchester musician would approve, crucial aspects of neoliberalism and Thatcherism had become part of the cultural assumptions.[69] This intentional tension of anti-Thatcherite Thatcherism-in-the-making was present in the early post-punk period and the emergence of the independent record labels. As we have seen with the aftermath of the post-1968 contradictions, Reynolds argued that these post-punk independent labels were in fact an attempt at providing an alternative to the arrival of Thatcher and Reagan who themselves were part of a backlash against 1960s counter-culture.[70] Independent labels and independent bands were most readily associated with the Left, leftist movements such as Rock against Racism, and various leftist philosophies, such as Situationism and Gramscian Marxism.[71] Manchester may not have been the most political post-punk city (with the high-profile exception of The Smiths) but leftist connections were certainly present. Tony Wilson and Factory would play around with Marxist, anarchist, and Situationist allusions (including the very names of the band, The Durutti Column, and the club, Haçienda). The Fall were

---

67. Harris, *Last Party*, pp. 144-45.

68. 'The Smiths: Not Like Any Other Love', *BBC Culture Show Special* (May 13, 2013), available at http://www.youtube.com/watch?v=wrsGewHZA3U.

69. The influence of broader commercial trends of the changes in Manchester come through in Morley, *Joy Division*, pp. 45-56, including the ways in which the music might have influenced these changes, but without emphasis placed on the ways in which these commercial trends influenced the music.

70. Reynolds, *Rip It Up*, pp. xxv-xxvi. See also Harris, *Last Party*, pp. 3-10.

71. Reynolds, *Rip It Up*, pp. 76, 96-97, 110-12.

initially perceived to be a band with strong leftist sympathies and political agendas, as Paul Morley's famous and not-entirely-accurate assessment in 1977 made clear:

> The Fall have prompted quotes like 'I thought the Clash were political until I saw you'... Their words are voiced, clipped ideologies, entertainment for radicals maybe... The Fall could stand alone as a genuinely committed, politically agile rock 'n' roll band.[72]

Morley was not the only person to misunderstand The Fall in this way but what is more significant is that there was the assumption that they simply *were* a politicised and leftist band.

The leftism was pushed further still. Aesthetically, independent labels and independent musicians were trying to provide an alternative to more commercial pop and rock music. This could take different and seemingly extreme forms. A standard cover from independent labels would be in the style of a cheap black-and-white photocopy.[73] But other labels, such as Factory, had a high, even anti-business, aesthetic. The most notorious example of this aesthetic was New Order's single 'Blue Monday' (1983) which was so expensively designed that the Biggest Selling 12 Inch Record of All Time initially sold at a loss. Not helping profits, the 12" cover had neither band name nor song title on the front sleeve, at least not in the conventional sense. The design was based on the 5.25 inch floppy disks used for the production of electronic music and details of what the 12" actually was could be established by working out the colour coding on the front of the record sleeve in conjunction with the colour wheel on the reverse of the New Order album *Power, Corruption & Lies* (1983).[74]

What is clear, then, is that there was a strong counter-cultural, anti-mainstream, and anti-corporate tendency in the emerging independent labels just as British and American politics and mainstream culture was tending towards the exact opposite. Yet for all the playing around with radical ideas, independent labels did not escape the prevailing economic thinking. Reynolds' qualification is significant in that the agenda of independent labels began to echo the rhetoric of emerging Thatcherism:

> Independent labels represented a sort of anti-corporate micro-capitalism based less on left-wing ideology than the conviction that major labels were too sluggish, unimaginative and commercially minded to nurture the most crucial music of the day.[75]

72. Morley, *Joy Division*, pp. 41-42.
73. Reynolds, *Rip It Up*, pp. 99-100.
74. Robertson, *Factory*, pp. 62, 65.
75. Reynolds, *Rip It Up*, p. xxvi.

Independent labels were not inherently hostile to wealth creation and they clearly represented a niche and sometimes successful market. It is further telling that independent music is now more associated with a genre ('indie') than labels and almost all 'indie' bands are now on major non-independent music labels. And, in a reference for the connoisseur, was not the fall of the old independent labels symbolically confirmed in 2009 when Selectadisc – Nottingham's iconic music shop and retailer for independent labels – closed in the face of longer-term pressure from corporate expansion (e.g. HMV, Fopp) and the shift away from vinyl?[76]

The Cultural Bible and the seemingly depoliticised individualist hedonism of Madchester's Bible were crucial ways of carrying, or even masking, this cultural and political change. A fully blown Thatcherite rhetoric would not have worked as Thatcher and Thatcherism lacked sufficiently wide-ranging credibility in 1980s alternative youth-driven subcultures (despite certain flirtations, such as Curtis voting Tory in 1979). By contrast, Manchester music carried a great deal of (sub)cultural capital between the mid-1970s and mid-1990s and was an ideal carrier of cultural change (in 1990 the University of Manchester was famously believed to be the most in-demand British university thanks to the popular credibility of Happy Mondays and The Stone Roses).[77] With the help of the Bible to ease the change and transition, the Manchester music scene was able to modify and recreate itself in its negotiations with the changes brought about by neoliberal capitalism until a form of Thatcherism was assumed the norm despite all the fierce hatred of Thatcher and a range of ideological contradictions. 'The Jones Boy' illustrated this point differently in *Viz*'s 'Top Tips': 'MORRISSEY: Stop chirping on about the USA and capitalism in your songs when a) you live over there and b) you go on chat shows just to promote your new album you fucking charlatan'.[78]

76. M. Atkinson, 'Brief encounters: Sleccy's vinyl countdown', *Guardian* (March 13, 2009).

77. Compare the suggestions made in Morley, *Joy Division: Piece by Piece*, pp. 45-46: 'It's crazy, although oddly it can be done, to map a journey, some muffled, defiant adventure, from the suicide of Ian Curtis to the opening of a Manchester Harvey Nichols... It's just as crazy...to chart a course from the shorts A Certain Ratio wore as they danced to their own barking, grievous dance music to the number of boutique hotels that existed in Manchester by the early years of the 21st century... [T]he story began when the Sex Pistols visited the city in June and July 1976... Johnny Rotten's immaculate glare, his burning, fanatical stare of fury, pointed just one way – into the future.'

78. 'Top Tips', *Viz* 139 (October 2004).

Part IV

FROM THATCHER'S LEGACY TO BLAIR'S LEGACY

Chapter 7

YOUR OWN PERSONAL JUDAS:
THE REHABILITATION OF JEFFREY ARCHER

1. Thou Shalt Not Get Caught

Despite Thatcherism-without-Thatcher becoming the political norm by the mid-1990s, this period would simultaneously mark a decline of the Conservative Party in British politics, and in no small part due to the 'toxic' image that Thatcher had come to represent. Thatcher was brought down in 1990 by a combination of her confrontational style of running cabinet, Michael Heseltine's leadership ambitions, the long-serving Geoffrey Howe's devastating resignation speech, and the deeply unpopular Poll Tax. Her apparently consensual replacement, John Major, had surprisingly managed to win the 1992 General Election outright, but it would be downhill for the Tories from then on. The issue of Europe and the EU was ripping the party apart while, among other things, the BSE crisis, recession, and political 'sleaze' all but made a crushing defeat in the 1997 election inevitable and one from which they have only just (about) recovered. 'Sleaze' was *the* word that stuck with the Conservative Party throughout the 1990s. This was the era that the Conservatives were embroiled in arms sales to Iraq, cash for parliamentary questions, and perjury trials, not to mention several sex-related stories in which the tabloids happily wallowed. Several Conservative figures became synonymous with 'sleaze' in popular imagination, such as David Mellor, Neil Hamilton, and Jonathan Aitken, the latter imprisoned for perjury. Against this backdrop, the sight of several high profile Tories spectacularly losing their parliamentary seats in the 1997 General Election became one of the more striking television moments of late twentieth-century Britain.

When the Conservative Party was trying to rebrand and 'detoxify' its image in the early post-1997 years, the behaviour of Jeffrey Archer (born 1940) would never let us forget this era of Conservative politics. As his biographer Michael Crick put it, he 'never does anything ordinary or dull; every Archer move seems to have that extra twist, and so often an

ingredient of deception and trickery… [He is] one of the most colourful characters in British public life, and…the most dishonest politician
in post-war British history.'[1] Few among a British audience would
disagree with this assessment. However, his collaborator on Archer's
work on the figure of Judas, the Australian New Testament scholar
Francis J. Moloney, was initially unaware of Archer's reputation in the
UK. Moloney claimed that 'I really admire his honesty and integrity'
while having to acknowledge that his assessment was 'the exact opposite
of what everybody says about him'. Nevertheless, even someone as
sympathetic as Moloney had to concede (either with naivety or understatement) that 'I am sure he is a bit of a villain – I would not doubt
that'.[2] This sort of spectacular understatement or naivety perhaps fails to
do full justice to Archer's life which has been one of a series of dramatic
rises and falls – often accompanied by creative financial decisions, flings,
mistresses, and a patchy record of remembering the truth.

There are numerous stories of dubious factuality surrounding the early
life of Jeffrey Archer, whether these are claims made by him or others on
behalf of him. A book on Archer himself can only do full justice to the
range of stories and fictions surrounding him and so it is most fortunate
that the journalist Michael Crick has provided the most comprehensive
account of which the following is a mere summary.[3] It is not always
entirely clear the degree of involvement that Archer had in claims about
whether his father was a decorated war hero or someone who engaged in
criminal behaviour, whether his early athletic achievements were quite as
impressive as had been pronounced, whether he gained quite as many
'O' Levels as Oxford University (or the Oxford Department of Education, to be precise) were led to believe or from where the claim about
non-existent 'A' Levels originated, or the validity of an award from the
International Federation of Physical Culture (IFPC) for teaching PE and
entering higher or further education. Archer also claimed to have been
the youngest-ever member of the Greater London Council (GLC) in 1967
(aged 27) but even in 1967 a fellow Conservative colleague, Anthony
Bradbury, was 25, and in 1964 Gordon Dixon had been a member at 26.[4]

1. M. Crick, *Jeffrey Archer: Stranger than Fiction* (rev. edn; London: Forth
Estate, 2000), p. xiii; cf. p. 431. Or again, P. Kelso, 'Mendacious, ambitious, generous and naïve', *Guardian* (July 20, 2001): 'He is by turns mendacious, egotistical,
ambitious, pushy, resilient, tactless, gullible, funny, charming, reckless, hard
working, generous, self-obsessed, loyal and naïve'.

2. Maloney quotations are collected in R. Gledhill, 'Jesus was no miracle
worker: the Gospel of Jeffrey Archer', *Times* (March 21, 2007).

3. Crick, *Jeffrey Archer*.

4. Crick, *Jeffrey Archer*, p. 120.

Despite claims made on book covers and by Archer himself, he was not, at 29 years of age, the youngest MP when elected in a 1969 by-election. Earlier in 1969, Bernadette Devlin, then aged 22, was also elected in a by-election, and others such as John Ryan, Les Huckfield, and the Conservative Christopher Ward were all younger, thereby making Archer the fifth youngest.[5]

These seemingly minor issues would foreshadow greater scandal and controversies. As a GLC councillor, as Crick would later document, he would assist colleagues with expenses for a 10 percent cut.[6] However, the first major scandal-in-the-making involved his charity work for the United Nations Association (UNA) and more claims of extravagant and misleading approaches to expenses. The chair of UNA was Humphrey Berkeley who challenged whether Archer was fit to be selected as a Conservative MP for Louth in the 1969 by-election. These doubts were dismissed and Archer sued Berkeley for libel in a case which would continue for three years. This was eventually settled out of court: Berkeley did not have to retract his claims or apologise, Archer had to cover the costs for both himself and Berkeley, and the terms of the settlement were not to be disclosed.[7] Murky though the outcome of the Berkeley case was, Archer's first serious fall came in 1974 and this time it did cost him his Louth seat. Guilty more of bad judgment, Archer was the victim of the Aquablast fraud which led to massive financial losses and near bankruptcy. This loss forced Archer to step down as MP for Louth but it was also the catalyst (and even inspiration) for his unstoppable rise as a novelist with his first book, *Not a Penny More, Not a Penny Less* (1976). It was this side (or perhaps main) career which would go on to make him a multi-millionaire. Yet, in the aftermath of the Aquablast scandal the seeds of another fall were sown: Archer would tell another story that would, like many of his explanations, grow uncontrollably in later decades. While he denied the allegation of theft, he was accused of stealing suits from a store in Toronto whilst he was serving as a witness.[8] Some twenty years later he would try to explain the situation by claiming that he had accidentally taken the suits but thought he was still in the shop. Furthermore, he had claimed that he had crossed a bridge to another shop while thinking he was still in the same one. And therein lay another problem: the bridge did not exist at the time of the alleged theft (see below).

5. Crick, *Jeffrey Archer*, pp. 147-48.
6. Crick, *Jeffrey Archer*, pp. 122-23, 141.
7. Crick, *Jeffrey Archer*, pp. 124-27, 140-46
8. P. Foot, 'Those Suits', *London Review of Books* 17 (May 1995), p. 14.

Despite reservations of leading Tories, Archer was made Conservative Party Deputy Chairman in 1985 but a year later resigned due to a scandal that would mark the rest of his career. The *News of the World* led the way with a story accusing Archer of organising a payment for the sex-worker, Monica Coghlan, to leave the country. The *Daily Star* went further still by claiming what had previously been implied: Archer had had sex with a prostitute. Archer sued the *Daily Star*, claiming that his payment to Coghlan was a charitable act. Archer won the case and £500,000 in damages. This cost the editor of the *Daily Star* his job, even though the journalist Adam Raphael would find evidence of Archer's perjury. But with his stunning victory, newspapers were now reluctant to risk challenging Archer's reputation.

This was not the last Archer would hear of the Coghlan case but in the meantime another infamous allegation of financial irregularity would emerge in 1994 when it was revealed that the Department of Trade and Industry were investigating Archer – now Baron Archer of Weston-super-Mare of Mark in the County of Somerset – over allegations of insider dealing. It had been alleged that Archer had attempted to buy shares in Anglia Television, a company which boasted his wife, Mary Archer, as a non-executive director, around the time when there was an agreed takeover bid by MAI plc. Archer vigorously denied the claims.[9] Archer pleaded ignorance and lack of evidence meant there would be no prosecution. Crick claimed that 'no other politician would have got away with Anglia on top of everything that had gone before. The press got to him but only over the things that weren't the serious things – the mistresses and the gaffes.'[10]

In October 1999 Archer won the vote to become the Conservative candidate for the newly formed post of Mayor of London. However, now the mustard seed would bloom in full. The endless financial arrangements and the Coghlan affair story would eventually come to include attempts to round-up various people to cover for him with some massive financial incentives, deals over intellectual property rights and information about Archer, convenient holidays, and, for Terence Baker (who appeared to have lied for Archer), film and TV rights for his books.[11] But, more specifically, Ted Francis (who claimed he was owed money by Archer) and Angela Peppiatt (Archer's former secretary) claimed

9. Financial and political staff, 'Archer in DTI Shares Inquiry', *Guardian* (July 8, 1994); Crick, *Jeffrey Archer*, pp. 405-18.

10. L. Jury, 'The fall of Jeffrey Archer: the media-enemies ensured that the whiff of scandal lingered', *Independent* (July 20, 2001).

11. Cf. Crick, *Jeffrey Archer*, pp. 296-312.

Archer's alibi in the 1987 trial was a lie based on Peppiatt's diary which she had kept at the time. Despite initial staunch support from the Tory leader William Hague, in 2000 Archer was removed as the Conservative candidate for London Mayor and expelled from the Conservative Party. The difference a month makes in politics is clear enough:

> This candidate [Jeffrey Archer] is a candidate of probity and integrity. I am going to back him to the full. (William Hague, October 1999)[12]

> This is the end of politics for Jeffrey Archer. I will not tolerate behaviour like this in my party. (William Hague, November 1999)[13]

Shortly after, Scotland Yard charged Archer with perjury and perverting the course of justice. Presumably with unintentional comic timing, he was charged during the running of his play, *The Accused*, in which Archer starred as a man accused of murdering his own wife and where the audience act as jury by casting their verdicts of guilty or not guilty.[14] On July 19, 2001 Archer was finally sentenced to four years' imprisonment before being released after two years on July 21, 2003. Judge Mr Justice Potts described the case, which included everything from bribery to Archer pressuring his secretary to forge diary entries, 'as serious an offence of perjury as I have had experience of and have been able to find in the books'.[15] In 2002, Archer had to repay the *Daily Star*, as well as cover legal costs.

This was not quite the end of matters. During his imprisonment his charity work was being scrutinised further and the cause with which he has become most associated: the fate of the Kurds. After seeing what was happening to 800,000 Kurds after the Gulf War, Archer proposed a targeted fund-raising programme under the name Simple Truth which involved the British Red Cross, £10 million of British government money, Chris de Burgh, and a multi-location international rock concert which would include such inviting luminaries as MC Hammer, Rod Stewart, Sting, New Kids on the Block, Gloria Estefan, and Peter Gabriel. But there were the inevitable difficulties such as doubts about

12. *Channel 4 News* (October 4, 1999), quoted in Crick, *Jeffrey Archer*, p. 444.

13. 'I had to top Archer', *BBC News* (November 23, 1999), http://news. bbc.co.uk/1/hi/uk_politics/533362.stm.

14. J. Archer, *The Accused* (London: Methuen, 2000). For the details surrounding Archer's arrest see P. Kelso and N. Hopkins, 'Archer takes refuge on stage from a real life drama', *Guardian* (September 27, 2000).

15. 'Archer jailed for perjury', *BBC News* (July 19, 2001), http://news.bbc. co.uk/1/hi/uk/1424501.stm. Reports of the trial are collected on the *Guardian* website. See http://www.guardian.co.uk/archer/subsectionmenu/0,5667,522617,00. html.

whether the funds from different governments were actually generated by Archer and Simple Truth, Archer's non-disclosure of all the information about donations, and a lack of clarification on whether most of the £57 million raised had reached Kurdistan. Among many other things (including potentially upsetting delicate geopolitical balances)—Archer's behaviour led to direct public criticisms from the Kurdish Disaster Fund—were reports that relief supplies had unfortunately ended up in the hands of Iraqi troops and Saddam Hussein's family as well as allegations surrounding Archer's behaviour in potential oil deals.[16]

2. Abel, Not Cain

After his release from prison, Archer made some explicit attempts at purifying his name and image, with his prison diaries being just one example.[17] Archer's public purification was also carried out elsewhere in the British media. Roy Hattersley wrote a profile of Jeffrey Archer for the *Sunday Times*, adding that Archer was constantly wanting to be rehabilitated in the public eye. Indeed, Archer spoke to Hattersley of his worry that the British public would be sceptical of him after 'what *seems* to be a long pattern of dubious behaviour'![18] The most popular vehicle for public rehabilitation in recent years has, of course, been television. Despite the sheer amount of celebrity-centred reality television readily available for Archer to parade himself, his television choices might still

16.   For the details of Archer and his involvement with Kurds, see Crick, *Jeffrey Archer*, pp. 367-82. See also M. Tempest, 'Archer fraud allegations: the simple truth', *Guardian* (August 16, 2001). The Archerean absurdities ran throughout this episode. Compare Crick, *Jeffrey Archer*, pp. 367-69, 376: 'And the story of his efforts to help the Kurds would encapsulate many of Archer's best and worst qualities. On the one hand he brought to the Kurdish appeal his compassion, energy and unquenchable self-belief; yet at the same time his efforts suffered from his customary lack of attention to detail, bad judgement, and exaggeration of his own achievements... He was joined by two young Kurds based in London, Brook Saib and Nadhim Zahawi... Archer dubbed the two friends Bean Kurd and Lemon Kurd...attempting a little Kurdish, he tried to get the crowd to chant "Long Live Kurdistan!"; due to a slight mispronunciation, however, his words came out as the equivalent of "Bastard Kurdistan!"'

17.   J. Archer, *A Prison Diary. Vol. 1, Belmarsh: Hell* (London: Macmillan, 2002); J. Archer, *A Prison Diary. Vol. 2, Wayland: Purgatory* (London: Macmillan, 2003); J. Archer, *A Prison Diary. Vol. 3, North Sea Camp: Heaven* (London: Macmillan, 2004).

18.   R. Hattersley, 'The Big Dipper: an interview with Jeffrey Archer', *Sunday Times* (February 19, 2006) (my italics). Hattersley also pointed this out on BBC 1's *Heaven and Earth Show* (April 15, 2007).

be said to constitute a bizarre Archerean twist. Archer – alongside minor celebrities such as the rapper MegaMan from So Solid Crew, the pop star and cheese-maker Alex James, *Eastenders'* Patsy Palmer, and the former footballer Stan Collymore – found himself on the more reputable side of the courtroom as part of a jury who had to decide on a fictional court case in the BBC2 programme, *The Verdict* (first aired: December 2006).[19] In yet *another* bizarre Archerean twist, Archer even managed to reinvent himself further still as the morally upstanding 'goodie' judge on the ITV programme, *Fortune: Million Pound Giveaway* (first aired: January 2007), where members of the public make a case to a panel of million-aires, like Archer, for 'worthy cause' money.[20]

But it was also the cultural power of the Bible, combined with his own success as a novelist, to which Archer turned in his attempted rehabilita-tion. In particular, Archer, in collaboration with Moloney, wrote *The Gospel according to Judas by Benjamin Iscariot* (2007).[21] Biblical allu-sions would have been nothing new to devotees of Archer's fiction or anyone even casually aware of Archer's novels, or at least those not suffering Bible-blindness. Archer's fondness for popular idioms almost inevitably means that these idioms will include biblical or quasi-biblical idioms (see further Chapter 9) and the biblical basis of these idioms are sometimes loosely woven into the plot structure, as we see, for instance, in *Kane and Abel* (1979), *The Prodigal Daughter* (1982, following on from *Kane and Abel*), *The Eleventh Commandment* (1998), and *The Sins of the Father* (2012). In a nod to Dante, his three-volume prison diaries also have the subtitle titles, *Hell* (2002), *Purgatory* (2003), and *Heaven* (2004). However, the *Gospel according to Judas* is something altogether different: it is presented and written as if it *were* a Bible or a book of the Bible. It is complete with mock-leather Bible cover, red-letters for Jesus' words, chapters and verses, gold-coloured page edges, and attached tassel book-mark. This obviously plays on the idea of the Bible as having some sort of cultural power (see Conclusion) and, among other things, already tells us how much importance is being placed in the story Archer is going to present us.

19. The homepage is: http://www.bbc.co.uk/pressoffice/pressreleases/stories/ 2006/12_december/12/bbctwo_verdict.shtml.

20. See also C. Brooker, 'Screen Burn', *Guardian* (February 3, 2007). The homepage for *Fortune: Million Pound Giveaway* is: http://www.itv.com/page. asp?partid=7130.

21. J. Archer with F.J. Maloney, *The Gospel according to Judas by Benjamin Iscariot* (London: Macmillan, 2007).

In this fictional gospel, Judas' son, Benjamin, recounts his father's story because Judas' name has been horrendously blackened and so it is up to Benjamin to set the record straight. Judas was a follower of Jesus but mistakenly thinks Jesus was to be a more nationalistic Messiah who would drive out the Romans. Despite doubting, Judas continually felt a tremendous sense of loyalty – in contrast to certain disciples, and Peter in particular – and sought to get Jesus out of Jerusalem to safety. This would have given Judas a unique position, for 'he alone among the disciples could now save his Master, and with him the fate of Israel'.[22] Unfortunately, a scribe was to take advantage of Judas' caring side by pretending to help but this scribe really wanted details of location in order to kill Jesus. The scribe then betrayed Judas, labelling him the betrayer. A heartbroken Judas retired to Qumran whilst various documents and Christian figures invented lies about him. Obviously, the Gospel images of Judas-as-betrayer (at least according to popular and most academic readings) would be problematic for Archer's agenda, hence the explicit rejection or retelling of the Gospel accounts in the *Gospel according to Judas*.

The artistic rehabilitation of Judas is nothing new but there was no doubt a more immediate influence on Archer's choice of subject. One year prior to the publication of the *Gospel according to Judas* was the sensational publication of the ancient *Gospel of Judas* which would have provided Archer with an obvious and immediate source of inspiration. Two major interpretations of this ancient text have involved the guilt of Judas. Put simply, one (associated with Marvin Meyer and others) claimed that the *Gospel of Judas* defended Judas's role as necessary (in line with some modern and implicitly Christianizing Judases); the other (associated with April DeConick and others) claimed the *Gospel of Judas* is in line with the traditional interpretation that Judas was to be blamed. However, the initially proposed view that Judas was largely innocent was the one that made all the headlines across the world and has been the dominant interpretation reported across the mainstream British media, including a documentary on the National Geographic Channel on Sunday, April 9, 2006.[23]

---

22. Archer, *Gospel according to Judas*, p. 64.

23. E.g. 'Judas "Helped Jesus Save Mankind"', *BBC News* (April 7, 2006). http://news.bbc.co.uk/1/hi/world/americas/4882420.stm; J. Borger and S. Bates, 'Judas: this is what really happened', *Guardian* (April 7, 2006); J. Petre, 'Gospel of Judas presents traitor as Jesus's favourite', *Telegraph* (April 7, 2006); P. Vallely and A. Buncombe, 'History of Christianity: The Gospel according to Judas', *Independent* (April 7, 2006).

Some of the more modern Judases in film and literature, which are, of course, free to move away from the starkly negative portrayals of Judas-as-arch-betrayer, provide a more recent tradition into which Archer's Judas can generally slot.[24] Probably more than any other film portrayal of Judas of immediate or more broadly 'unconscious' relevance for studying Archer's *Gospel according to Judas* is Martin Scorsese's controversial 1988 film, *The Last Temptation of Christ*, where several issues broadly echoed in Archer's *Gospel according to Judas* can be found. Scorsese's Judas is not naïve and innocent like Archer's Judas but Scorsese does, crucially, have a degree of sympathy in his portrayal of Judas. Scorsese's ginger Judas picked up on certain modern rethinkings of Judas in that he is an anti-Roman revolutionary who also feels a sense of betrayal in his accusation levelled at the crucifix-making Jesus effectively being a Roman collaborator. Scorsese's pragmatic and thoughtful Judas is smarter and more decisive than the other disciples, and even shoots Peter down in one heated argument. Jesus and Judas discuss their different messianic theologies and even have the odd scene of intimacy, bordering on the homoerotic. An intrigued Judas thinks hard about whether to follow a Zealot command to kill Jesus and openly discusses with Jesus that he will kill him should he step out of line. Clearly, Scorsese's Judas is no cardboard baddie and there is some thought gone into Judas' understandable motivations. Like Archer's *Judas*, *Last Temptation* explicitly distances itself from the official orthodox line by prefacing the film with a statement that the film is *fictional* and *not* based on the Gospels.

3. First among Equals

These examples provide a general cultural context in which *Gospel according to Judas* was written and could be written. But there is that other hugely significant influence on *Gospel according to Judas*: Archer's own life. Most non-British readers may not be so familiar with the career of Jeffrey Archer beyond Archer-the-novelist. However, the biographical profile of the authors in *Gospel according to Judas* may not be the most helpful in the case of Archer, though it is not too difficult to imagine readers and reading communities up and down the UK filling in at least some of the gaps. The profile merely tells us how Archer is an Oxford-educated, international best-selling author who was a former Member of

24. See e.g. Pyper, *An Unsuitable Book*, Chapter 6; Walsh, 'The Gospel according to Judas', pp. 37-53; R.G. Walsh, *Three Versions of Judas* (London: Equinox, 2010).

Parliament and who is currently a Member of the House of Lords, adding that he lives with his wife Mary at the Old Vicarage, Grantchester.

What Archer's biographical profile did not give, then, were all the reasons for why Archer became such a well-known figure in the UK. But given that the reader of this chapter now has no excuse for not knowing about Archer's colourful life, how could we not already claim what looks to be the blindingly obvious conclusion that *Gospel according to Judas* is more-or-less Archer's own view of Archer's plea of relative inno-cence? How Britain's most infamous politician has been misunderstood, just like Judas before him! If the hypothetical reader of this chapter is not prepared to make this kind of casual connection, it does not mean others did not in some of the early reactions to *Gospel according to Judas* (in some cases, even before it was read). Mark Goodacre's then *NT Gateway* blog reported the publishing of *Gospel according to Judas* and this led to several comments. 'Mike', for instance, commented:

> Not only a new gospel, also a new parable? the parable of Jeffrey Archer:

> Watch you say (about me), the vilain [*sic*] is never who one thinks.
> Even in your Good Book: Juda is innocent, but the Evangelists were spin doctors![25]

On his blog, *Thought Experiments*, journalist and author Bryan Apple-yard had had enough when (January 8, 2007) he heard of the publication of *Judas*: 'The rehabilitation of Jeffrey Archer has gone too far'. One of the comments makes the crucial connection even more explicit. James Hooley said, 'Do I detect a sneaky allegorical undertone to this publication? I mean, let's face it, Judas fell in with the wrong crowd and some dirty money changed hands.'[26] On his blog, *Cultural Snow*, music and culture writer Tim Footman admitted (March 26, 2007) that he had not read the book but, like many journalists, he still felt he could say something analytical. 'Archer's new book is blatantly autobiographical', he added, 'a fact that will be obvious to all but the most clueless reader'.[27] Strong words indeed from someone who openly admitted to not having read the book. On Archer's blog, where the moderated comments are unashamedly overflowing with staggeringly high praise for Archer's

---

25. M. Goodacre, 'Archer and Moloney's Gospel of Judas', *NT Blog* (March 20, 2007), http://ntweblog.blogspot.co.uk/2007/03/archer-and-moloneys-gospel-of-judas.html. I have retained the original typographical errors.

26. B. Appleyard, 'Jeffrey and Judas', *Thought Experiments* (January 8, 2007), http://bryanappleyard.com/jeffrey-and-judas/.

27. T. Footman, 'By Request: Thirty Pieces of Archer', *Cultural Snow* (March 26, 2007), http://culturalsnow.blogspot.com/search/label/Jeffrey%20Archer.

life and work, he announced (January 9, 2007) the publication of *Gospel according to Judas*, much to the delight of his loyal followers. And here too there were questions – though Archer obviously could not give answers prior to the publication – relating to the connections between Judas and Archer. For instance, 'the pixie' asked, 'Reading between the lines, do you identify a little with Judas? In that you've both been treated, some might argue, unfairly.'[28]

The world of the mainstream British media had a similar cynical reaction to the non-Archer blogs. The review of Archer's book by Ann Widdecombe – one of the few members of the contemporary British Conservative party to rival Archer's fame in the British media – ran with the deliberately ambiguous title: 'Can a Reputation Be Rescued?' Tellingly, Archer's former colleague added, 'Archer wrote this book knowing that everyone would draw parallels with his own life'. 'Come on, Jeffrey', Widdecome exclaimed more colourfully, 'he had just betrayed the Messiah, not the Conservative party'.[29] In a television interview, Andrew Pierce, deputy editor of the long-time Conservative-supporting British broadsheet, the *Daily Telegraph*, saw the book as a 'metaphor' for Jeffrey Archer's life with the intention of the rehabilitation of both Judas *and* Archer, a view echoed in the studio by the former Deputy Leader of the Labour Party, Roy Hattersley.[30]

Inevitably, spoofs based on the overlap between Judas and Archer got developed in the press. A *Guardian* take outrageously overlapped the lives of both, with more than a little poetic license and little concern for the details of *Gospel according to Judas*.[31] In the *Sunday Telegraph*, Oliver Pritchett sent up *Gospel according to Judas* with a mock-reconstruction of a great archaeological find and, once again, the humour was based more on Archer's life than the details of *Gospel according to Judas*:

28. J. Archer, 'The Gospel according to Judas', *Jeffrey Archer's Official Blog* (January 9, 2007), http://jeffreyarchers.blogspot.com/2007/01/gospel-according-to-judas.html.

29. A. Widdecombe, 'Can a reputation be rescued?', *Guardian* (April 7, 2007).

30. Comments again made on the *Heaven and Earth Show* (UK), BBC1, April 15, 2007, to the cheery husband and wife team, Carrie and David Grant, briefly known for their Sunday morning theological analysis in addition to, among other things, their singing and dancing expertise on BBC1's *Fame Academy*.

31. J. Crace, 'The Gospel according to Judas by Benjamin Iscariot and Recounted by Jeffrey Archer and Prof. Francis J Moloney', *Guardian* (March 27, 2007).

> In a sensational development, archaeologists have found some ancient scrolls in a remote cave and they believe these may have been written by Judas Iscariot. This could well change our perception of one of the most reviled men in history. The work appears to be an account of the life of Jeffrey Archer.
>
> The author of these scrolls (thought to be Judas) describes how he managed to piece together the story, using an ancient papyrus of a publisher's blurb found in a dried-up riverbed near Grantchester... The story of his downfall now appears to be a myth. It has been assumed that Archer was found guilty of perjury, but this was almost certainly the result of a mishearing in oral history. His crime was actually perfectionism.[32]

The lack of concern for the details of the *Gospel according to Judas*, even among those who have read the book, is a common thread across the popular claims that Judas is really Archer.

At this point, the shooting down of popular mob mentality might be expected, particularly as most arguments for the identification of Archer with Judas lack details and serious evidence. But if Archer does one thing well, it is his sheer predictability of trying to establish his innocence to the Great British Public.[33] So, instead, what I will do is to show that all the detailed evidence in fact *confirms* the instinctive evidence-lite/free, knee-jerk reaction of those among the trolls, newspaper readers, politicians, and broadsheet hacks who were right to think that the *Gospel according to Judas* was in fact Archer's transparent attempt at resurrecting his public persona.

4. A Matter of Honour

So how did the art itself really reflect the man? Well, obviously, the correspondence is not always one-for-one. Archer may have many faults but, unlike his Judas, he surely would never have difficulties sleeping under the roof of an 'impure man who owed his wealth and position to a

---

32. O. Pritchett, 'What Would Judas Make of Jeffrey?', *Sunday Telegraph* (March 25, 2007).

33. The predictions of two journalists who investigated Archer are worth citing in this respect. Crick, *Jeffrey Archer*, p. 467, foresaw as follows: 'Even if he follows Jonathan Aitken to jail as a result of the current perjury investigation by the police, Archer will work all the harder to redeem himself, perhaps with a huge charity campaign, or a project in one of his favourite fields – the theatre, art or sport'. According to Adam Raphael, 'His guilt was writ large', *Observer* (July 22, 2001): 'I have little doubt that he [Archer] will bounce out of jail in two years' time... [T]he odd spot of adversity will not dent his ability to entertain and flatter the famous.'

race of disbelievers'.[34] Yet, on the other hand, is it really possible for anyone, at least a British audience or anyone familiar with Archer's life, to read the opening chapter of Judas and not think, *this is Archer according to Archer*?

> This gospel is written so that all may know the truth about Judas Iscariot and the role he played in the life and tragic death of Jesus of Nazareth… Indeed, they have blackened my father's name to the point where he is now thought of as the most infamous of all Jesus' followers. He has been branded a traitor, a thief and a man willing to accept bribes… The Christians continue to spread the word throughout Galilee that Judas was a man of violence, a hanger-on and someone who could not be trusted. Despite contrary evidence, these libels are still abroad and often repeated by the followers of Jesus, even to this present day… [M]y father became a follower of Jesus of Nazareth, and was so trusted by the Master that he was later chosen to be one of his twelve disciples… My father has now returned to the God he loved and served so faithfully.[35]

No matter how strong the allegations made against Archer, this does not mean, of course, that Archer accepts them all. What is most significant for our purposes is how Archer reacted to criticisms levelled at his reputation. In his prison diaries, Archer stresses that he was not given a fair trial, that Justice Potts' summary was extremely one-sided and biased in advance, and that numerous allegations were simply false.[36]

With such general comments in mind, we might add that there are some fairly transparent Judas-as-Archer themes. One is *money*, and in particular Judas' role as treasurer of the Jesus movement: Judas gets the common purse, makes sure all get something to eat, are clothed, have shelter, and so on.[37] However, like Archer himself, Judas gets accused of financial improprieties, even though the explanations given are innocent misunderstandings (e.g. running out of money). Of course, Archer does not think Judas has done wrong in his important position and so it is no surprise that when Benjamin complains that the jar of precious ointment could be sold for three hundred denarii, a couple of disciples 'murmured' that Judas was going to retain the money (cf. John 12.6).[38]

We all know that we should always be looking out for deeper meanings and not read texts woodenly but if ever there were an exception then this must be it. The theme of general innocence over all things financial is as much a theme in Archer's life as it is in the *Gospel according to*

---

34. Archer, *Gospel according to Judas*, p. 54.
35. Archer, *Gospel according to Judas*, pp. 1-3.
36. E.g. Archer, *Hell*, pp. 86, 87-88, 93, 115; Archer, *Purgatory*, p. 155.
37. Archer, *Gospel according to Judas*, p. 42.
38. Archer, *Gospel according to Judas*, p. 66.

Judas. In his prison diaries, for instance, Archer attacked Emma Nichol-
son 'for hinting that the millions of pounds I helped raise for the Kurds
didn't reach them, with the twisted implication that some of the money
must therefore have ended up in my pocket'.[39] But perhaps most
remarkably, Archer gave a telling reaction in his 2007 interview with
Roy Hattersley in answer to a question about the Humphrey Berkeley
affair when, after claiming that there has never been any suggestion of
financial impropriety in his life, he repeated that he could not remember
whether he had paid Berkeley's legal costs. Staggering though such
comments might ordinarily seem, in the context of Archer's life and
consistent behaviour, perhaps they are not. Indeed, Hattersley claimed
that he did not doubt that Archer was convinced of his own innocence.[40]

Of course, not even Archer believes he is always sweet and innocent.
As he proclaimed in the run-up to the mayoral elections: 'if you're only
going to have a saint for this job, I'm certainly not your man'.[41] With all
the above in mind, Judas' narrative role gets highlighted at some very
notable places. In Chapter 9, one of the most obvious Judas-is-really-
Archer chapters, issues of forgiveness and the dangers of hypocrisy get
hammered home (read: *you lot are at least as bad as me!*). For example,
Judas is curious about Jesus' prayers to his 'Father in heaven' and it is
Judas who asks Jesus to teach the disciples how to pray, rather than the
anonymous disciple of Luke 11.1. And, of course, Jesus then delivered
the Lord's Prayer which includes those famous words, 'Forgive us our
sins, as we forgive the sins of others'.[42] Just prior to this, Judas wept
when Jesus preached about how easy it is to love those who love you but
trickier to be compassionate and bring unity in contexts of division and
so the mercy of the Father must be imitated.[43] Jesus continued by telling
people not to condemn or judge others because everyone was guilty of
some offence. In case you did not get that, Judas reinforced these words
by passing them on to those not present to hear, all the while, of course,
reinforcing these words to the reading audience. And, to cap things off,
Jesus then speaks more on how bad it is to be *judgmental* (Luke 6.41;
Matt. 7.3), wise words which Judas enthusiastically endorses.[44]

You do not need me to connect the obvious.

39. Archer, *Hell*, p. 89; cf. pp. 113, 145, 146, 149.
40. Hattersley, 'The Big Dipper'.
41. 'I'm no saint, says Lord Archer', *BBC News* (September 5, 1999), http://
news.bbc.co.uk/1/hi/uk_politics/438941.stm.
42. Archer, *Gospel according to Judas*, p. 31.
43. Archer, *Gospel according to Judas*, p. 29.
44. Archer, *Gospel according to Judas*, p. 30.

5. False Impression: Who Betrayed Whom?

Peter plays a crucial role in Archer's narrative by making some serious errors and is consistently compared to, and contrasted with, Judas. Chapter 14 is a notably anti-Petrine section. When Judas warned Peter that the coffers were running low and that Jesus ought to be informed, Peter refused and told Judas to continue to do Jesus' bidding without question.[45] This would lead to a problem covering costs when they all arrived in Jerusalem.[46] When Judas wanted to question Peter about Jesus' apparently troubling teachings Peter ignored poor Judas.[47] Peter was not supposed to tell anyone about the Transfiguration but could not hide his joy and blurted it out to Judas.[48] Peter is also the one who suspected Judas of financial irregularities.[49] When Jesus says that someone will betray him at the Last Supper,[50] it is clear what Judas thought: he was innocent of betraying Jesus as all he wanted to do was to save Jesus from a pointless death. However, immediately following, we are told that Peter was the most vehement in his denial and protested, saying he would lay down his life for Jesus. Jesus, of course responded with the famous cock crowing saying (Mark 14.30; Matt. 26.34; Luke 22.34) before an even more passionate response.

After Jesus was arrested, Judas, wanting to see if he could rescue Jesus, started to approach Peter, 'confident' that together they could save Jesus' life. But at that moment he witnessed Peter denying Jesus three times. The *Gospel according to Judas* makes the parallelism between the two crystal clear: both failed the Master but, Judas thought, both could still be redeemed.[51] But Peter says it would have been better had Judas not been born and, not for the first time, Judas felt 'betrayed'. After all, (and how about this for an emphatic nod to the knowing reader), *he* did not flee when Jesus was arrested and, unlike Peter, *he* had not denied Jesus (three times!) so why was *he* the one branded a sinner?[52]

---

45. Archer, *Gospel according to Judas*, p. 48.

46. Archer, *Gospel according to Judas*, pp. 52-53.

47. Archer, *Gospel according to Judas*, pp. 48-49.

48. Archer, *Gospel according to Judas*, pp. 49-50.

49. Archer, *Gospel according to Judas*, p. 66. Peter is not *entirely* bad. For instance, like Judas, he wonders why Zacchaeus only has to give away half his money while the rich young man had to give all of his away (p. 54).

50. Archer, *Gospel according to Judas*, p. 70.

51. Archer, *Gospel according to Judas*, p. 76.

52. Archer, *Gospel according to Judas*, pp. 76-77.

Forty years after the crucifixion, Benjamin informs his now Qumran-dwelling Essene father that there was a gospel being spread around the world, saying *Peter* had given the direction to strike Judas' name off the list of disciples originally chosen by Jesus. Moreover, *the disciples* invented all the stories of Judas we know (e.g. the hanging, the thirty pieces of silver). Consequently, Judas demanded that his story should be put forward to provide a record of the truth and was, fortunately enough, able to recall every detail from forty years previous.[53]

There should be little doubt, then, that *Gospel according to Judas* deliberately highlights the sins of Peter and other disciples to show that Judas was not deserving of his fate. Indeed, Archer has been quite explicit about this. In one recent interview, Archer said that Judas had a 'rough deal' and, given that disciples like Peter made serious mistakes, why is it that Judas has to be the biggest sinner in history?[54]

Yet, once again, it is difficult not to see parallels in Archer's life and the treatment he received compared to others. Recall the 1990s and the Golden Era of Sleaze for the Conservative Party. During Archer's downfall, even his staunch supporter, William Hague, had to distance himself from Archer in particular in an attempt to rid the Conservative Party of its sleazy image, adding that Archer had let the party down.[55] Hague's successor, Iain Duncan Smith, said that Archer would not be welcome back in the Conservative Party on his release while in 2005 a spokesperson for the now Conservative leader, David Cameron, made it clear that Archer was still not welcome, emphatically stressing that 'Lord Archer's days as an active politician are over'.[56]

---

53.   Archer, *Gospel according to Judas*, pp. 88-89.

54.   Interview with Jeffrey Archer on the *Heaven and Earth Show* (UK), BBC1 (April 15, 2007).

55.   P. Wintour, 'Disgraced Archer quits over plot to lie in court', *Observer* (November 21, 1999).

56.   Press Association, 'Tory leader: Archer not welcome', *Guardian* (July 22, 2003); N. Temko, 'No way back for Archer, says Cameron', *Observer* (November 27, 2005). Notably, in the comments section of Archer's blog, Cameron comes in for some criticism by 'David': 'Glad you are still going strong with your book tour. I am afraid the UK is also guilty of voting on looks rather than ability… I think William Hague would have been a fine PM but wasn't given the chance…and now the Torys have gone with what they perceive as the right look with David Cameron' (https://www2.blogger.com/comment.g?blogID=29716984&postID=5467280395729419147).

But, from Archer's perspective at least, why single him out? There were plenty of other disciples who misbehaved: the Mellors, the Aitkens, the Hamiltons, and so on. Mellor, like Archer, was involved in a sex scandal, but Aitken was involved in arms deals while Hamilton was involved in cash for parliamentary questions, both of which could easily be seen as morally more questionable. Yet Archer remains the most infamous of them all.[57] It is also worth mentioning Archer's main rival to be Conservative candidate for London Mayor, Steven Norris. Norris had served in Thatcher's government as a Parliamentary Private Secretary but had been one of the many MPs who persuaded Michael Heseltine to stand against her, ultimately bringing Thatcher's reign to an end. As for Thatcher's successor, John Major, Norris famously said in the 1995 leadership campaign that he was the 'least worst option'! Archer, on the other hand, had been a staunch supporter of both Thatcher and Major – publicly, privately, and personally – yet several figures within the Conservative party were deeply suspicious of Archer and unsuccessfully tried to stop him for fear he was an 'accident waiting to happen'.[58]

There is also the useful supporting evidence from Archer's prison diaries of people who had not deserted him. Indeed, the diaries are, notably, dedicated to 'foul-weather friends', clearly implying that the opposite type of friends were not there for him. Furthermore, Archer makes sure he name checks those who stood by him, supported him, or were at least not harshly critical when he was imprisoned: MPs, David Faber, John Gummer, and Peter Lilley; members of the Lords, Bertie Denham and Robin Ferrers; former Prime Minister, John Major; and the former Archbishop of Canterbury, George Carey.[59] A list of supporters was even drawn up, with Archer commenting in his prison diaries that this 'news gives me such a lift, and makes me feel guilty that I had ever doubted my friends would stand by me'.[60] Naturally, the opposite is also important: those-who-betrayed-Archer is another theme in his prison diaries. For instance, when lying on his prison bed, Archer mused:

57. Cf. H. Young, 'Honest John Major landed his party with Lord Archer', *Guardian* (November 23, 1999).

58. The 'accident waiting to happen' is how Willie Whitelaw, the former Conservative Deputy Leader, described Archer in a warning to Margaret Thatcher. The phrase is also the title of Crick's chapter on the topic of Archer, Norris, loyalty, and the race for London Mayor. See Crick, *Jeffrey Archer*, pp. 422-44.

59. Archer, *Hell*, pp. 62, 92.

60. Archer, *Hell*, p. 92.

I think about the verdict, and the fact that it had never crossed my mind
even for a moment that the jury could find Francis innocent and me guilty
of the same charge. How could we have conspired if one of us didn't
realize a conspiracy was taking place? They also appeared to accept the
word of my former secretary, Angie Peppiatt, a woman who stole thousands
of pounds from me, while deceiving me and my family for years.[61]

Loyalty and betrayal clearly meant a lot to Archer.

While there are some fairly obvious connections between, on the one
hand, Peter and the disciples and, on the other, a range of fallible politicians, themes of loyalty and betrayal surround the other major character
to get rough representation in *Gospel according to Judas*: an unnamed
scribe who (significantly?) becomes the Scribe with a capital 'S'. The
Scribe gets riled at being tricked by Jesus' Parable of the Good Samaritan into having to accept that Samaritans might be good neighbours after
all. Judas and the Scribe get to know one another and, while Judas has
some reservations about Jesus, all he wanted to do is make sure Jesus
was safe and got out of Jerusalem alive. The Scribe agreed but all along
he was duping the naïve, well-intentioned Judas into giving away the
location of Jesus. Consequently, the Scribe went off to the Sanhedrin and
double-crossed Judas (yes, it was someone else's fault!) in order to sort
out the finer details of killing Jesus. 'How flattering the press can be
when they want something', claimed Archer in his prison diary and in
sentiments hardly alien to the role of the Scribe.[62]

In the climax to the Judas–Scribe subplot, the theme of betrayal
reaches its peak, with Judas as the betrayed, innocent victim. Even
Judas' kiss that gave Jesus away was more accidental than not. When
Judas heard Jesus agonising, he hoped Jesus would leave Jerusalem, and
threw his arms around Jesus before kissing him. Then the band of
officers appeared and a horrified Judas had realised what he had (accidentally) done.[63] And how does the horrified Judas act? He charges at the
Scribe with fists and spit flying, screaming about *betrayal*.[64] Worse still,
when people wanted to know who betrayed Jesus, the Scribe steps
forward and declares that it is Judas Iscariot.[65] After this revelation the
crowd repeatedly chants that Judas is a 'betrayer' and as Judas pleads
with the Scribe to tell the truth the Scribe responds with a smile and
repeats the allegation of 'betrayer'. All Judas can now do is weep.

61. Archer, *Hell*, p. 11.
62. Archer, *Purgatory*, p. 222.
63. Archer, *Gospel according to Judas*, pp. 73-74.
64. Archer, *Gospel according to Judas*, p. 74.
65. Archer, *Gospel according to Judas*, p. 77.

This is *the* key narrative device for the shifting of the blame away from Judas in Archer's book. And the choice of a scribe as the arch-betrayer is not accidental. One of Archer's real-life problems has been those modern day scribes – the press and unauthorized biographers – and so it is no surprise that it was a profoundly dishonest *Scribe* who manipulated the innocent and naïve Judas into giving away Jesus to the bad guys. In general terms this has connections with Archer's political life: John Major's Conservative government was notorious for complaining about bad press and campaigning journalists, though this is, of course, a common complaint of any party in power and was at least matched by the New Labour government. As Crick put it:

> After the battering that John Major and his party had suffered during the 1990s, there was something of a siege mentality about the party. Weren't the papers and the journalists going after Archer the very same people who had unfairly attacked the Tories in the past? To many activists, public criticism of Archer was just a further example of the way the untrustworthy media had it in for the Conservatives.[66]

But more specifically, and more significantly, Archer had far more personal problems than most with the press.

The British tabloids, for instance, have been crucial in Archer's downfall. It was the *News of the World* which, in 1986, ran the fateful multi-page story on Archer's involvement with, and payment to, Monica Coghlan which was picked up by other newspapers and led to Archer resigning his governmental position. It was the *Daily Star* which went further and implied Archer was involved sexually with Coghlan, prompting Archer to sue. But in another twist to our story, Archer was duped by an elaborate *News of the World* trap involving secret tape-recorders, Coghlan, a London train station, a posse of disguised journalists, and a touch of farce.[67] Interestingly, Archer, in a statement that might have come from Archer's Judas, admitted to 'lack of judgement' but added, 'foolishly, as I now realise, I allowed myself to fall into what I can only call a trap in which a newspaper, in my view, played a reprehensible part'.[68]

Intriguingly, Archer initially responded to the editor of the *News of the World* with both threats and emotional appeals in last-gasp attempts to prevent the publication of the story in order to save his career. And this was not the first or last time Archer had combined threats and emotion to

---

66. Crick, *Jeffrey Archer*, p. 442.
67. For the full story see Crick, *Jeffrey Archer*, pp. 262-76.
68. S. Trotter, 'Archer claimed he fell into trap over pay-off', *Glasgow Herald* (October 27, 1986); Crick, *Jeffrey Archer*, pp. 263-64.

journalists.[69] During the Berkeley affair, John Clare, then of the *Times*, was sent to Louth to investigate the allegations levelled at Archer and grilled him on a train journey to King's Cross. As Clare went through the allegations, Archer did not dispute them and pleaded with Clare not to publish the story claiming it would upset his wife. When that failed, Archer then threatened legal action.[70]

But more specifically, three major journalistic figures were central to Archer's downfall: Paul Foot, Adam Raphael, and Archer's *bête noire*, his biographer Michael Crick.

Adam Raphael, the former political editor of the *Observer*, described himself as belonging to 'a not very select band of journalists who over the years have become obsessed by the fact that such an obvious charlatan should have been allowed to play a prominent role in British public life'. Raphael was forced under subpoena to give evidence for the *Daily Star* in Archer's successful 1987 libel trial but the jury evidently did not believe Raphael's claim that Archer had admitted to him that he had met Coghlan, clean contrary to Archer's claims in court. The result of the 1987 case led Raphael to research the details further, concluding that Archer had 'repeatedly perjured himself throughout the trial' and had conspired to pervert the course of justice. But more crucially for present purpose, Raphael's involvement in the Archer case led to allegations emanating from the Garrick Club that he had 'betrayed Archer'.[71]

By the time of the doomed mayoral election bid, Paul Foot had emerged as a prominent journalist investigating Archer's truth claims in the *Daily Mirror* and the *Evening Standard*, as well as in the satirical magazine, *Private Eye*. The *Evening Standard* vigorously opposed Archer's candidacy for the mayoral elections. In reaction, Archer accused the *Evening Standard* of holding a vendetta against him.[72] In March 1998 when Archer was 3/1 favourite to become mayor of London, Foot wrote a damning article listing issues from Archer's past under the blunt title, 'Why this man is unfit to be mayor'.[73] Prior to this Foot had been journalistically involved in various parts of Archer's colourful life:

69. Jury, 'Fall of Jeffrey Archer: The Media'; Crick, *Jeffrey Archer*, pp. 275-76.

70. Crick, *Jeffrey Archer*, p. 142.

71. Raphael, 'His Guilt Was Writ Large'. See also Raphael's book on high-profile libel cases with one particular case most prominent: *My Learned Friends: An Insider's View of the Jeffrey Archer Case and Other Notorious Libel Actions* (London: W.H. Allen, 1989).

72. Jury, 'Fall of Jeffrey Archer: The Media'.

73. P. Foot, 'Why this man is unfit to be mayor', *Evening Standard* (March 25, 1998), reprinted in P. Foot, *Articles of Resistance* (London: Bookmarks, 2000), pp. 170-74.

when Archer first stood as an MP Foot was contacted at *Private Eye* by Humphrey Berkeley; when confronted on the missing suits episode in Toronto Archer wrote to Foot 'confirming' that the man was not even him; in 1987, while working for the *Daily Mirror*, Foot was sent a document relating to Archer's shoplifting charges in Toronto with a description closely resembling Archer's details, right down to his address. On the suits episode, the *Daily Mirror* would not run with the story as Archer had recently won £500,000 compensation from the *Daily Star*, but the story would re-emerge in Crick's biography. The Crick version stated honest mistakes and confusion (unchallenged by Archer) yet Foot was told by Archer that there was no incident. Foot would print this inconsistency in his *Evening Standard* article challenging Archer's suitability for London mayor. Archer did respond to allegations made by Foot yet, in classic Archer style, there remained some damaging errors in his response, including citing the bridge in the Toronto store that did not then exist![74]

Finally, Michael Crick, the political journalist, and arguably *the* ultimate modern-day Scribe in Archer's life, collected Archer's lies in well-documented detail in his biography of Archer, and had even written to the Conservative leader at the time of the London mayoral elections, William Hague, warning him that there was more scandal to come.[75] The Archer–Crick controversy was captured on television for all to see. After Archer was elected Conservative candidate for Mayor of London, just before the next wave of scandal, Crick was prevented from asking questions. Crick recalls the moment he was pushed aside by Archer's spokesperson, Stephan Shakespeare, before being dragged by the shoulders by Archer's driver, David Crann. It followed that no questions could be posed by the press to Archer and his beaten opponent Steven Norris, much to the press's fury.[76] The investigative documentary programme, *Panorama*, caught Archer on camera angrily criticising Crick and the television portrayal of Archer, accompanied by the ominous threat: 'You wait till I'm Mayor. You'll find out how tough I am.'[77]

In the more immediate context of the genesis of the *Gospel according to Judas*, Archer's dislike of the British press is not difficult to find. In his prison diaries, it should be no surprise that another recurring topic is Archer's hatred for what he saw as the lies and manipulation of the British press and how they discredited him and others, both throughout

74. See further Crick, *Jeffrey Archer*, p. 435.
75. Crick, *Jeffrey Archer*, p. 431.
76. Crick, *Jeffrey Archer*, pp. 443-44.
77. 'Jeffrey Archer: A Life of Lies'.

his life and while he was in prison.[78] It is significant that Archer's first press interview after his release from prison was with a fellow member of the House of Lords, Roy Hattersley, and here he again betrayed a deep distrust for the press. Hattersley recalled that the interview would bring up painful topics but that Archer accepted this because Hattersley, being a privy councillor, could be trusted![79] Even in the publicity accompanying the publication of the *Gospel according to Judas*, Archer could not help but get a dig in at his home press; in one press conference Archer noted that the questions from the floor 'were all serious and considered' but with 'the exception of one English newspaper – it was a delight to hear the groans that followed his question'.[80]

In this light, it is extremely difficult to read the *Gospel according to Judas* with its damning of the manipulative Scribe at the expense of the manipulated Judas and not think of Archer's big problems with the British press, certain campaigning journalists, and his unauthorized biographer.

6. Speculative Archerisms

With there being enough powerful evidence to suggest that the *Gospel according to Judas* has deliberate parallels with Archer's life, it is highly tempting to read such things into other details in the book. We might label these 'speculative' because they are more in the realm of educated guesses and cannot be proven with any degree of certainty. But collectively they start to make this reader at least feel a little suspicious that Archerisms are indeed coming through (consciously or unconsciously) so the argument is worth presenting for others to make their judgments.

Perhaps a hermeneutic of suspicion starts to take over any interpreter of Archer, but is there not a striking parallel in the formatting of the first two title pages? The first title page has *THE GOSPEL ACCORDING TO* and *BY BENJAMIN ISCARIOT* sandwiching *JUDAS*, with *JUDAS* in a notably larger font and different colour. The format is identical for the second title page. For reasons of greater clarity we may reconstruct and parallel them both in the following way:

---

78. E.g. Archer, *Hell*, pp. 81, 92, 97, 122-23; Archer, *Purgatory*, pp. 2, 13, 25, 76, 105, 150, 222, 240, 260, 308. Note, however, positive readings of the press when they side with Archer e.g. *Heaven*, pp. 435-36.

79. Hattersley, 'The Big Dipper'.

80. Archer, 'Gospel according to Judas'.

THE GOSPEL ACCORDING TO
JUDAS
BY BENJAMIN ISCARIOT

RECOUNTED BY
JEFFREY ARCHER
WITH THE ASSISTANCE OF PROFESSOR FRANCIS J. MOLONEY
SDB, AM, STD, DPHIL (OXEN)

Coincidence? I think we should be told, to steal a regular phrase from an old enemy of Archer, *Private Eye*.

Another speculative Archerism is when the *Gospel according to Judas* provides an emphatic nod to the women in Jesus' ministry. These women were loyal to him from the beginning, had scarified everything for him, and given up time and money. And the women listed are: Mary, from the village of Magdala who, it is emphasised, is otherwise known as Mary Magdalene; Joanna, the wife of Chuza, Herod's steward; and a generic and unspecified reference to others dedicated to the cause.[81] Moreover, Judas felt shame when he realised that Mary Magdalene, Mary the mother of James and Joseph, and the generic other women had remained loyal all along, that the women had wept when Jesus appeared in the square, and that they remained nearby when Jesus was on his way to be crucified and loyally stood by the cross.[82]

It can only be speculated as to how many readers would have blinked if Archer had inserted 'Mary Weedon from Cheltenham Ladies' College, who came to be known as Mary Archer' or 'Mary the mother of William and James Archer' into these lists. Indeed, Mary Archer is a significant presence in Archer's prison diaries, in ways that clearly carry echoes of the Gospels (biblical and Archerean). Volume 2 (*Purgatory*) has for its epilogue Kipling's 'The Thousandth Man' which, of course, has the theme of rare loyalty, and was dedicated to 'Mary: The thousandth woman'. It is also worth noting Archer's comments at the beginning of his prison diaries: 'I turn and glance at my wife Mary seated at the back of the court, head bowed, ashen-faced, a son on either side to comfort her'.[83] Archer's comments on Mary in his first British interview (February 2007) after his release from prison, and just a year before the *Gospel according to Judas* was published, are perhaps more significant still. He praised Mary's 'remarkable stoicism with which she faces everything'.

81. Archer, *Gospel according to Judas*, p. 26.
82. Archer, *Gospel according to Judas*, pp. 79-81.
83. Archer, *Hell*, p. 1.

He went on to answer the question of whether his 'recovery' would have been impossible or virtually impossible without her:

> I often think about that. It's having a sheer anchor. Someone there who is reliable and solid the whole time... The answer to the question is, of course, I don't know. But it would certainly have been 10 times as hard.[84]

Similarly, the role of women in general gets highlighted in his prison diaries. The method of doing so may be somewhat clunky and patronising but for these reasons it shows that Archer wanted to highlight the point:

> I turn my attention to the letters. Like my life, they are falling into a pattern of their own, some offering condolences on my mother's death, others kindness and support. Many continue to comment on Mr Justice Potts's summing-up, and the harshness of the sentence. I am bound to admit they bring back one's faith in one's fellow men...and women.[85]

Finally, Archer once had clear ambitions to be leader of the Conservative Party and has regularly seen himself as a figure of some importance, though he is hardly the only individual analysed in this book who might be deemed to hold a Messiah Complex. With typical Archerean flourish, the book launch for the *Gospel according to Judas* included a press conference chaired by the head of the Pontifical Biblical Institute in Rome and located at Westminster Cathedral, London.[86] Archer also enlisted the help of his collaborator Francis Moloney, himself an internationally recognised Catholic scholar with links to the Vatican. Hyperbole aside, Ann Widdecombe had a point when she says 'he doesn't bother with the local priest, but goes to the Vatican and one of the greatest living scriptural scholars'.[87] Equally spectacular is that a figure no less than Archbishop Desmond Tutu, apparently Archer's first choice,[88] narrated the audio version of *Gospel according to Judas*! Examples of Archer's interest in the grandeur of Archer are not difficult to find. For instance, Archer did not hide his light in presenting his relationship with

---

84. Hattersley, 'The Big Dipper'.

85. Archer, *Hell*, p. 87 (elliptical dots original). Also worth mentioning is the art-imitating-life example of the importance of Benjamin as a loyal son in *Gospel according to Judas* and the theme of the loyalty of Archer's real-life sons in his prison diaries (e.g. Archer, *Hell*, pp. 10-11).

86. J. Hooper, 'Archer attempts to rehabilitate Judas', *Guardian* (March 21, 2007); Gledhill, 'Gospel of Jeffrey Archer'.

87. Widdecombe, 'Can a Reputation Be Rescued?'

88. J. Archer on his 'official' blog: http://jeffreyarchers.blogspot.com/2007/03/voice-of-archbishop-desmond-tutu.html.

'my Kurds'. Crick reported: 'But yet again Archer couldn't help adopting the air of an imperial governor. "My Kurds", he would describe them to accompanying reporters; and to the Kurds the press were "my senior journalists".' And on his clear popularity among Kurds, Archer would say 'See how they love me'.[89] So what else might this background tell us about the self-identity of Judas/Archer in the *Gospel according to Judas*? Obviously, there is a lack of self-doubt but in terms of precise detail the following speculative connection (and note the eerily similar verses) is too difficult to resist as it would appear to imply that we put Judas (and therefore Archer) in an even greater light:

> Jesus wept (John 11.35)
> Judas wept (*Judas* 22.35)

Archer couldn't be implying…could he?[90]

7. Not a Penny More, Not a Penny Less

While the use of Judas in art, film, and literature may provide an implicit criticism of traditional Christian readings, this invariably results in a reworking of Christian myths and ideals in order to give them contemporary relevance. Richard Walsh, for instance, argued that the greedy Judas is excluded or removed from American Jesus films in part because he 'raises uncomfortable questions for capitalist Americans and is more likely to turn up in Marxist or anti-consumption Judas films', thereby allowing audiences to remain 'comfy Christian capitalists'.[91]Archer himself would not be immune to such difficulties; he became very rich, has an entrepreneurial background, is a self-confessed 'free enterprise merchant',[92] and he was close ideologically and personally to Thatcher,

89. Crick, *Jeffrey Archer*, p. 381.

90. To add to the motley crew of anti-Archer readings online, even the conspiracy theorist end of blogging can note the obvious connection between the biblical verse and *Gospel according to Judas*. See N. Godfrey, 'Gospel of Judas (Archer/Moloney) fantasy verses', *Vridar* (September 4, 2007), http://vridar.wordpress.com/2007/04/09/gospel-of-judas-archermoloney-fantasy-verses/#more-263.

91. Walsh, 'Gospel according to Judas', pp. 44, 46. We might add that Walsh pointed out that (pre-Patriot Act) nationalist-revolutionary Judases can redirect questions away from consumer capitalism towards other political questions, thereby resonating with Zionist and ideals of freedom. While Walsh's focus was mainly on American films, this could be one (conscious or unconscious) influence on Archer's choice of a nationalist-revolutionary Jesus.

92. Archer, *Hell*, p. 149.

all issues which come through in his novels.[93] However, rather than ignore questions implicitly challenging the tenets of capitalism, Archer's Judas tackles them head-on. The *Gospel according to Judas* shows the problems Judas had with the story of the rich young man and in particular Jesus' command for the rich man to sell all he had and give it to the poor in order to buy treasure in heaven.[94] For Judas, Jesus could not function as a king overthrowing the Romans while a wandering prophet but, worse still, this was out-of-step with what are described as Israel's greatest traditions of measuring God's glory through wealth and national success. Judas then proceeds to quote Psalm 72.15-17, and a Solomonic tribute to the material blessings of a 'great king'.[95] In other words, and in a move carried out by other political figures covered in this book, one aspect of the Bible is used to trump another deemed problematic. This section ends by Archer's rich young man responding simply, warning them that they follow a dangerous man who will lead to the fall of many in Israel (Luke 2.34), a view later accepted by Judas.[96] Notably, the Gospel reason that the money could be used for the poor (Mark 10.21) gets dropped in the *Gospel according to Judas*. While capitalist popular culture may well have absorbed anti-capitalist critique,[97] we can always rely on Archer, and his exegesis, to come to the defence of the capitalist system that has ultimately rescued him from all the betrayals and personal financial disasters.

Archer's exegetical support for the joys of material blessings is not one that carries much clout in a post-2008 political climate where austerity and hostility to corporate avarice and greedy bankers is prominent. Unlike our next heir-to-Thatcher, Tony Blair, and the Thatcherite heirs-to-Blair, Michael Gove and David Cameron, Archer's take on Thatcher's Bible is *too* greed-is-good, *too* attached to an electorally toxic brand of Thatcherism and Conservatism, *too* close to the idiosyncratic Jeffrey Archer, and *too* far removed from an exegetical tradition with cultural credibility to be deemed successful in terms of party political influence. Unlike that presented by Gove and Cameron (see Chapter 9), the nationalism presented by the *Gospel according to Judas* is that of a

93. Foot, 'Why this man is unfit to be mayor', p. 172.
94. Archer, *Gospel according to Judas*, p. 46.
95. Archer, *Gospel according to Judas*, p. 47.
96. Archer, *Gospel according to Judas*, p. 55.
97. S. Žižek, 'Return of the Natives', *New Statesman* (March 4, 2010); M. Fisher, *Capitalist Realism: Is There No Alternative?* (Winchester, UK: Zero Books, 2009); C. Cremin, *Capitalism's New Clothes: Enterprise, Ethics and Enjoyment in Times of Crisis* (London: Pluto Press, 2011).

revolution for Israel, and material blessings are Judas-themes that have resonated more in America than in a nation where, despite the best efforts of Christopher Hill, revolution is often deemed to have been something that foreigners have done and do. After all, is Cromwell not ambiguously celebrated and commonly known as a Christmas-banning killjoy? But amidst all this, is there not a heart-warming story about a Bible-inspired rehabilitation of a disgraced politician? Should we not end with a rousing moralistic finale on the importance of giving someone a second chance? Probably not; for in one sense, this curious variant of the Neoliberal Bible *is* the ultimate hyper-Thatcherite success story of an ambitious individual who has picked himself up again and again. There is no moral to this latest episode in Archer's colourful life, other than that crime probably pays. Archer will sell more books, make more TV appearances, rake in more filthy lucre, and possibly even get himself involved in another reinvigorating scandal. But did you really expect *piety* when the main argument here has shown that a rowdy mob of trolls, bloggers, hacks, and television-friendly politicians were right all along?

Chapter 8

45 MINUTES FROM DOOM!
TONY BLAIR AND THE RADICAL BIBLE REBRANDED

1. Spiritual *and* Religious: The Political Theology of Tony Blair

By the turn of the millennium, the Thatcher revolution in political thinking was over, both in the sense that she was now a figure often deemed
'toxic' and that the general tenets of Thatcherism had simultaneously
been accepted by the main political parties and culturally normalised.
Indeed, Thatcher famously claimed that her greatest legacy was New
Labour. By the time Tony Blair (b. 1953) came to power in 1997, issues
surrounding Christianity and the Bible had changed.[1] Thatcher faced a
Church of England prepared to confront her on issues of social justice,
inner-city tensions, and welfare. After her third election victory in 1987,
and the final stage of her embedding of Thatcherism, the Church shifted
its attention more abstractly towards the worries about the perils of
materialism. In the longer term, high-profile concerns with poverty
would become more internationally focused (e.g. Make Poverty History,
Jubilee 2000) and more consensual, with politicians walking side-by-side
with anti-poverty campaigners, in addition to more specialised concerns
for issues of human rights and ethics. While the relationship between
Church and State became less antagonistic, the 1990s and the 2000s saw
identity politics become more of a serious problem for the very authority
of the Anglican Church, in particular the rise of those most polarising of
debates: women priests (and later bishops) and homosexuality. Such
issues were of increasing prominence, of course, because of the wider
acceptance of more liberal attitudes towards homosexuality and gender
equality. Questions about 'Englishness' in relation to race and immigration had also changed. Whereas questions of colour and race were
pushed to the fore, not least by Enoch Powell, liberal multiculturalism
had become much more firmly embedded in English politics by the time

---

1. For a more detailed summary of what follows see e.g. Filby, 'God and Mrs
Thatcher', pp. 212-31. See also Steven, *Christianity and Party Politics*, pp. 105-20.

Blair took office. Of course, this still meant tolerance on the assumption that liberal capitalist democracy is the norm, and a stark reminder of this qualification came on September 11, 2001. And September 11 now brought 'religion' and Islam to the fore in the dominant discourses surrounding debates on immigration as well as international politics. The Cold War was certainly over; the War on Terror was about to begin.

A product of a private education, socialist-cum-Tory atheist father, Protestant mother of Irish descent, rock music, music management, and the legal profession, Blair grew up wearing his Christianity and politics lightly, at least in public. It was only from his time at St John's College, Oxford (1972–75), that Blair began to start thinking more seriously about politics (even Marxism) and religion ('I was brought up as one, but I was not in any real sense a practising Christian until I went to Oxford').[2] Confirmed as an Anglican at St John's, here he would articulate the importance of Christianity in terms of social relevance, social change, and social mobility, but stressing the relationship between the individual and the community as Thatcherism was in the ascendancy. There were a number of formative influences on Blair's political and social theology, typically coming from a centre-left form of Christian Socialism, and including Peter Thomson, John Burton (Labour Councillor and Blair's agent for 25 years), Cherie Booth whom he would of course marry, and the ideas of communitarian thinkers such as John Macmurray,[3] though whether communitarian ideas were rigorously implemented or properly understood is moot.[4] But it was Thomson who Blair would describe as probably the most influential person in his life.[5] Thomson was a Christian

2. R. McCloughry, 'Practising for Power: Tony Blair', *Third Way* (September 14, 1993), http://web.archive.org/web/20070927142102/http://www.thirdway.org.uk/past/showpage.asp?page=43.

3. For summaries see e.g. J. Rentoul, *Tony Blair* (London: Warner, 1996), pp. 36-48, 72-75, 293-95; A. Seldon, *Blair: The Biography* (London: Free Press, 2004), pp. 32-46, 515-32; F. Beckett and D. Hencke, *The Blairs and their Court* (London: Aurum, 2004), pp. 28-44; P. Stephens, *Tony Blair: The Making of a World Leader* (London: Viking, 2004), pp. 15-36; J. Burton and E. McCabe, *We Don't Do God: Blair's Religious Belief and its Consequences* (London: Continuum, 2009), pp. ix-47.

4. S. Hale, *Blair's Community: Communitarian Thought and New Labour* (Manchester: Manchester University Press, 2006). Cf. Beckett and Hencke, *The Blairs*, pp. 27-31.

5. T. Blair, *A Journey* (London: Hutchinson, 2010), p. 78. Cf. Burton and McCabe, *We Don't Do God*, p. 8: 'Tony hadn't really thought deeply about religion and politics until he met Peter'. For further detail on the influence of Thomson on Blair see e.g. Rentoul, *Tony Blair*, pp. 36-45; Burton and McCabe, *We Don't Do God*, pp. ix-xi, 4-13, 58.

Socialist and Australian Anglican priest and was a mature student at St John's when Blair met him. He helped Blair articulate the fusion of what Blair would categorise as religion and politics in that 'religion' is deemed something which comes first and prioritises humankind and values while 'politics' prioritises the analysis of society and how it can be changed. Blair overlapped both categories but still stressed that for him and Thomson religion would always come first.[6]

Andrew Rawnsley claimed that 'No Prime Minister since William Gladstone read the Bible more regularly'.[7] Even so, prior to becoming Labour leader in 1994, Blair was fairly quiet about his Christianity and love of the Bible, though under the influence of the then Labour leader John Smith he joined the Christian Socialist Movement in 1992.[8] On becoming leader, Blair was still relatively quiet, particularly after the experience of the media jumping on his religious beliefs in reaction to an infamous interview with the *Sunday Telegraph* in 1996. Alastair Campbell claimed in his diaries:

> I could see nothing but trouble in talking about it. British people are not like Americans, who seem to want their politicians banging the Bible all the time. They hated it, I was sure of that. The ones who didn't believe didn't want to hear it; and the ones who did felt the politicians who went on about it were doing it for the wrong reasons... I felt fully vindicated. As I said to TB...Never talk about God... GB [Gordon Brown] called and we agreed God was a disaster area.[9]

But intense media interest in Blair's Christianity would resurface again during the 'war on terror', particularly because of Blair's close association with the evangelical Christian, Republican, and American president, George W. Bush.

As this might already imply, precisely what the 'socialism' was in Christian Socialism would change over time and the stress on individual responsibility and social mobility would bring his political Christianity and exegesis close to Margaret Thatcher's. Prior to becoming a Labour Party MP in 1983, Blair had certainly read Marxist literature and was

---

6. Blair, *Journey*, p. 78. A typical Blair soundbite is as follows: 'Blair said politicians should not ignore religion, calling for a "religion-friendly democracy and democracy-friendly religion"'. See 'Tony Blair, former Prime Minister, did order Number 10 staff to pray', *Huffington Post* (July 24, 2012), http://www.huffingtonpost.co.uk/2012/07/24/tony-blairm-former-prime-prayer_n_1699362.html.

7. A. Rawnsley, *The End of the Party: The Rise and Fall of New Labour* (London: Penguin Books, 2010), p. 447.

8. Rentoul, *Tony Blair*, pp. 47, 293.

9. A. Campbell, *The Blair Years* (London: Hutchinson, 2007), pp. 111-12.

interested in Marxism. But ultimately he would not become (or remain?) a Marxist in the sense that he perceived it to be a useful resource rather than an ideology requiring absolute fidelity. By the early 1980s Blair would be regarded as something of a 'soft' leftist of the Kinnock variety. Like other Labour MPs of his generation, he was influenced by the peace movement and was a supporter of CND. Yet his general drift to the right of the Labour Party was becoming gradually clear and he firmly opposed Benn's bid for the deputy leadership in 1981, though only supporting the candidate of the right, Dennis Healey, as an anti-Benn option.[10] But, accompanying the electoral failures of the 1980s and 1992, Blair would look into ways of attracting the non-traditional Labour voter and move further to the right of the party, particularly on becoming leader after the death of John Smith in 1994. Along with Gordon Brown and Peter Mandelson, Blair would develop a form of social democracy that would embrace Thatcherite economics, reject a number of iconic Labour policies from the 1980s such as unilateral disarmament, rethink the role of the welfare state, and, most noisily, drop Clause 4 (a commitment to common/public ownership or nationalisation) from the Labour Party constitution – all of which reflected the Giddens-inspired 'Third Way'. With the inclusion of the former journalist Alastair Campbell among the core group, an obsession with PR and controlling or limiting the influence of the media (seen to be a key factor in the loss of the 1992 election) became a marked feature of Blair's leadership. By the time of his landslide election victory in 1997 at the age of just 43 (then the youngest Prime Minister since 1812), Labour had become New Labour and, assisted by three electoral victories, Blair became increasingly prominent on the global stage, particularly in his enthusiasm for military interventions in Kosovo, Sierra Leone, Afghanistan, and, of course, Iraq. And as we saw in the chapter on Thatcher, the ideological shift from the Evil Empire/Cold War to the Axis of Evil/War on Terror was smooth enough.

Nevertheless, Blair would still articulate himself in what he understood to be communitarian terms in his shift towards New Labour.[11] In a 1993 interview, when he was Shadow Home Secretary, Blair might allude to a critique of Thatcher's 'there's no such thing as society' and he may still be using the language of 'socialism' but it is reinterpreted in a way that was hardly alien to her way of thinking, particularly in the language of community support, morality, and individualism:

10. Rentoul, *Tony Blair*, pp. 73-77.

11. J. Kampfner, *Blair's Wars* (London: Free Press, 2004), pp. 73-75; Burton and McCabe, *We Don't Do God*, pp. 62-66, 77, 91, 133; Stephens, *Tony Blair*, pp. 19-20.

> You are what you are in part because of others, and you cannot divorce the individual from the surrounding society. That idea is to me the distinguishing philosophical feature of the Christian religion. But the notion of the individual within a community is not a substitute for individual responsibility... Christianity is a very tough religion, and there are certain imperatives of individual conduct that it is very, very strong on. It is not a religion that makes easy excuses for people. My reinterpretation of the socialist message is that social responsibility is important to reinforce personal responsibility, not as a substitute for it.[12]

Indeed, even when explaining the 2008 financial crisis Gordon Brown could articulate the government's position with reference support from the Bible (and beyond) combining individualism, personal morality, entrepreneurialism, and the significance of capitalism, with virtually no reference to the public sector and state interventionism, and in a way not entirely alien to a Thatcher speech:

> [Adam Smith] argued the flourishing of moral sentiments comes before and is the foundation of the wealth of nations. And when people ask, 'Can there be a shared global ethic that can lie behind global rules', I answer that through each of our heritages, traditions and faiths, there runs a single powerful moral sense demanding responsibility from all and fairness to all. Christians do not say that people should be reduced merely to what they can produce or what they can buy – that we should let the weak go under and only the strong survive. No: we say, 'Do to others what you would have them do unto you'.
>
> ...When Judaism says, 'Love your neighbour as yourself', when Muslims say, 'No one of you is a believer unless he desires for another what he desires for himself', when Buddhists say, 'Hurt not others in ways that you find yourself hurtful', when Sikhs say, 'Treat others as you would be treated yourself', and when Hindus say, 'The sum of duty is not do unto others what would cause pain if done to you', they each and all reflect a sense that we share the pain of others, we believe in something bigger than ourselves, that we cannot be truly content while others face despair, cannot be completely at ease while others live in fear, and cannot be satisfied while others are in sorrow. I believe that we all feel, regardless of the source of our philosophy, the same deep sense, a moral sense, that each of us is our brothers' and sisters' keeper.
>
> ...Winstanley called it 'the light in man'. Call it duty or simply call it conscience, it means we cannot and will not pass by on the other side when people are suffering and when we have it within our power to be both responsible and to support fairness, and endeavour to help.
>
> So, I believe that we have a responsibility to ensure that both markets and governments serve the public interest, to recognise that the poor are

---

12. McCloughry, 'Practising for Power'.

our shared responsibility, and that wealth carries unique responsibilities too... Now that people can communicate so easily and instantaneously across borders, cultures and faiths, I believe we can be confident that, across the world, we are discovering that there is a shared moral sense.[13]

Likewise, Blair may have rhetorically distanced himself from the hyper-individualist interpretation of Thatcherism and high levels of unemployment associated with it, but, as we will see below, Brown's words could equally have come from Blair.[14]

The concern for personal responsibility, the individual, and the community was developed further in Blair's ideas of societal and liberal tolerance. Given that Blair is a longstanding social liberal – at least in his parliamentary behaviour, as evidenced by voting patterns and matters of conscience (e.g. pro-choice on abortion, supported stem-cell research, promoted the 'morning after' pill, introduced legislation for civil partnerships)[15] – it is no surprise that this ecumenicalism was developed more broadly in terms of interreligious harmony and dialogue, nor that it played a role in his handling of Northern Ireland. After his interviews with Blair, Andrew Rawnsley recalled that Blair would often talk about the 'latest inter-faith book that he had read on holiday or was keeping by his bedside' and that Blair believed that Christians, Jews, and Muslims 'were all essentially children of the same God'.[16] But it was the interest

---

13. G. Brown, 'Speech and Q&A at St Paul's Cathedral: Transcript of speeches by the Prime Minister and Australian Prime Minister Kevin Rudd at St Paul's Cathedral' (March 31, 2009), http://webarchive.nationalarchives.gov.uk/+/number10.gov.uk/news/speeches-and-transcripts/2009/03/pms-speech-at-st-pauls-cathedral-18858.

14. Blair's anti-Thatcher (/Major) Christian rhetoric is found in e.g. T. Blair, 'Preface', in Bryant (ed.), *Reclaiming the Ground*, pp. 9-12 (10): 'Central to Christianity is the belief in equality... It is shameful that millions of our fellow citizens are out of work, that many young of our people are left without hope and opportunity... [I]t is about the union between individual and community.' See also Seldon, *Blair*, p. 519.

15. Burton and McCabe, *We Don't Do God*, pp. 67-68, 180-82; Stephen, *Tony Blair*, pp. 27-28.

16. Rawnsley, *End of the Party*, p. 448, cf. p. 410. See also p. 173 where it is reported that Blair said the Jewish God and the Christian God is 'the same God'. There are a number of similar anecdotes reported. For example: '...he would always ask what was the best way to do things, not because of his Christian beliefs but because of a strict set of values that apply to all religions, Muslims and Jews, as well as Christians' (Burton and McCabe, *We Don't Do God*, p. 9); 'He told one friend on holiday: "The main religions are all about the same thing"' (Kampfner, *Blair's Wars*, p. 74); '"Jews, Muslims and Christians...all children of Abraham." Barry

in Islam in particular that was to be intensified after September 11, and with the following 'war on terror', when he became increasingly (and, for some of his supporters and some of his enemies, uncomfortably) associated with Bush and the kind of American evangelical Christianity Bush continues to represent in the popular imagination. As we will see, this provoked further, more globally framed thinking about ecumenicalism, involving global interaction among religions, the ways in which religions relate to liberal democracy, and the significance of all this for the exegesis of both the Bible and the Qur'an.

Indeed, Blair has embraced traditions beyond the 'Abrahamic faiths', including those which might be regarded as 'spiritual' and which are popularly perceived, or even caricatured, as the kinds of beliefs associated with a certain strand of affluent liberal 'New Age' thought.[17] This has typically been portrayed in the press through the relentless focus on Cherie Blair and her spiritual companion, Carole Caplin. However, there were telling sans Caplin moments. For instance, the *Times* reported that in August 2001, the Blairs stayed at the plush Maroma Hotel, near Cancún, where Tony and Cherie took part in a Mayan 'rebirthing ritual' which, according to the brochure, 'is equally beneficial for the mind and spirit… [P]articipants are invited to meditate, feel at one with Mother Earth and experience inner feelings and visions.' Sporting only bathing costumes, the couple approached the Temazcal pyramid containing the steam bath (and also representing 'the womb'), bowed, and prayed to the four winds. Once inside, it was reported, the herb-infused steam generated a 'cleansing sweat' in order to balance 'energy flow'. As Mayan songs were chanted, the Blairs had to imagine animals in the steam and explanations of their visions were given. Then their hopes and fears were confronted in order to facilitate the rebirth. The pain of (re-) birth was symbolically enacted by screaming out loud. They were given melon and papaya to eat and told to rub the remains, along with mud from the Mayan jungle, on one another's bodies. They also spoke their wishes. Tony Blair's wish was for world peace.[18]

Cox, a close friend, says the theme has long been part of his private conversation: "He will say to you that if you look beyond the rituals, almost all religions share the same fundamental values"' (Stephens, *Tony Blair*, pp. 25-26).

17. Cf. Beckett and Hencke, *The Blairs*, pp. 278-79, 337. It is tempting to contrast Thatcher on theosophy: 'Theosophy was a mixture of mysticism, Christianity and "the wisdom of the East", sense and nonsense' (Thatcher, *The Path to Power*, p. 7).

18. T. Baldwin, 'Cherie stops Blair being stick in mud', *Times* (December 15, 2001). The Downing Street response strongly suggests that this story was at least roughly accurate: 'I've no idea whether all this is true. The Prime Minister, as you

In 2007, shortly after stepping down as Prime Minister, Blair converted to Catholicism. This had been long expected, not least because Cherie Blair and their children are baptised Catholics and Blair had been attending Catholic Mass.[19] What is notable is that during his political career Blair did not accept the official Catholic line on a number of key issues such as contraception, homosexuality, and abortion, and he did not follow Pope John Paul II's opposition to the Iraq War.[20] As we will see, political, social, or cultural liberalism – in many ways a logical outworking of his take on communitarian thinking – as well as the guiding centrality of parliamentary democracy, continues to be a significant feature of Blair's belief and exegesis. Nor did Blair drop his ecumenicalism when he converted. On the contrary, ecumenical and communitarian concerns got more global still when, in 2008, he founded the Tony Blair Faith Foundation. At the launch in the Time Warner Centre, New York, Blair claimed that one of the goals of the Foundation was to counter extremism 'in all six leading religions'.[21] However, it also has goals framed in more positive terms, claiming to promote 'understanding and respect between the world's major religions' which is deemed 'central to a policy to secure sustained peace'. Despite globalisation and an 'increasingly interconnected world', 'faith has remained at the core of life for billions' and 'underpins systems of thought and behaviour... [uniting] people around a common cause.'[22]

Blair also wanted to continue his influence at the level of policy making and so the Foundation also includes the Faith and Globalization Initiative which brings together a 'network of leading research universities analysing the interaction of faith and globalisation' and 'presenting the findings to public policy makers and the wider world.'[23] The Faith and Globalization Initiative received a considerable level of academic

know, is in Belgium for the European summit. However, what I can tell you is that, like any other couple on holiday abroad, they enjoyed doing what the Romans do.' According to the *Times*, 'those close to him' suggested that he 'probably went along with it to please Cherie'. Blair's symbolic rebirth was deemed too ecumenical for some Christians who were not happy at this perceived idolatry. See e.g. L. Gunter, 'Tony Blair and wife perform chant ritual to lizards/pyramid in Mexico', *Edmonton Journal* (December 2001–January 2002).

19. See further Seldon, *Blair*, pp. 516, 521-23.

20. Rawnsley, *End of the Party*, p. 449.

21. 'Blair launches faith foundation', *BBC News* (May 30, 2008), http://news.bbc.co.uk/1/hi/uk_politics/7427809.stm. The big six are Christianity, Islam, Judaism, Buddhism, Hinduism, and Sikhism.

22. http://www.tonyblairfaithfoundation.org/page/about-us.

23. http://www.tonyblairfaithfoundation.org/. See also http://www.fgi-tbff.org/.

support. In addition to the Foundation having a significant presence at the annual American Academy of Religion meeting, the Faith and Globalization Initiative was initially taken up by Yale University, Durham University, and the National University of Singapore,[24] and now counts among its global 'Lead Universities' and 'Associate Universities' the University of Winchester, St Mary's University College, McGill University, Tecnológico de Monterrey, University of Western Australia, Peking University, University of Prishtina, Banaras Hindu University, Pwani University College, and Wheaton College.[25] The Yale collaboration involved the Divinity School and School of Management, with Blair appointed a Howland Distinguished Fellow. The Faith and Globalization seminar was 'organized by Yale's Divinity School, led by Dean Harold Attridge' and Blair would even co-teach with Miroslav Volf.[26]

In his memoirs, Blair discusses the role of the Foundation in further detail and, concerning the future of global harmony in particular, in highly optimistic language. In this context he gives a number of general statements about the global importance of religious tolerance. In order to create peaceful coexistence in a context of globalisation, he argues, practitioners of different 'faiths' must learn from and respect one another. For Blair, the Foundation was designed to do just this and the focus is on youth and the future. So, for instance, new technology can bring together children of different faiths (including of Christian, Muslim, Jewish, Buddhist, Hindu and Sikh faiths) from twelve different countries.[27] Blair does not believe that young people are merely self-absorbed and gadget-obsessed. On the contrary, he sees the young people working for him in Africa and the legions of volunteers in his Foundation as 'dynamic', dedicated, and with an unprejudiced religious commitment. Blair claims that even young Israelis and Palestinians can come together as they strive for 'fulfilment' and opportunities to better themselves and their situation. This, for Blair, illustrates that while there may be acts of hate, there are always these benign sentiments, and actions of such faith-driven people can bring change for the better.[28]

24. 'Tony Blair launches Faith and Globalisation programme at Durham University' (July 10, 2009), http://www.dur.ac.uk/news/newsitem/?itemno=8243.

25. http://www.fgi-tbff.org/.

26. 'Yale and Tony Blair Launch Faith and Globalization Initiative' (September 18, 2008), http://news.yale.edu/2008/09/18/yale-and-tony-blair-launch-faith-and-globalization-initiative. See further http://faithandglobalization.yale.edu/.

27. Blair, *Journey*, p. 690.

28. Blair, *Journey*, p. 691.

If we translate this into the categories used in this book, we might reasonably expect that this sort of thinking would reflect overlapping aspects of the Liberal Bible and the Radical Bible (and who would disagree with global peace and harmony?). But there are parts of Blairite and New Labour thought that are not-so-compatible with the Radical Bible (and radicalism more generally) of the Labour tradition.[29] The 'war on terror' isolated a lot of (often grudging) supporters on the Left (and elsewhere), though we will return to Blair's attempt to incorporate and transform traditions from the Radical Bible in the aftermath of September 11. But there were other means which would make it difficult for Blair and New Labour to be associated with the class-confrontational aspects of the Radical Bible and easy to become associated with a popular understanding of Thatcherism: certain individuals did not hide (some of) their close associations with wealthy capitalists. Perhaps it was Peter Mandelson, one of Blair's closest confidants, who best epitomised New Labour's love of capitalism. He has (legitimately) been described as someone who 'swanked around the salons of the wealthy, the powerful and the right-wing',[30] and he notoriously claimed in 1998 that New Labour was 'intensely relaxed about people getting filthy rich' before quickly adding, 'as long as they pay their taxes'.[31] But, especially since he stepped down as Prime Minister, the British media regularly makes guesses about Blair's not insignificant personal wealth (with estimates even reaching £60,000,000), and column inches are taken up by discussion of his numerous properties, private jet travel, public speaking fees, business interests, and fraternising with the rich and famous. And this upward mobility has even been performed in biblical terms, albeit probably too publicly for Blair's liking. In 2011, after a summer dominated by the phone hacking scandal, it was discovered that Blair is godfather to Rupert Murdoch's daughter, Grace, and that he was present at her Christening on the banks of the River Jordan where all the participants – including celebrities such as Nicole Kidman, Hugh Jackman, and Queen Rania of Jordan – were garbed in gleaming white cotton. There was no indication that Blair was present when the story and photographs were

29. Cf. Stephens, *Tony Blair*, p. 16: 'Gladstone, too, had kept a Bible by his bedside... Blair preferred to place himself in the company of these Liberals rather than in the pantheon of previous Labour leaders.'

30. A. Rawnsley, *Servants of the People: The Inside Story of New Labour* (London: Penguin Books, 2000), p. 214.

31. J. Rentoul, 'Intensely relaxed about people getting filthy rich', *Independent Blog* (February 14, 2013), http://blogs.independent.co.uk/2013/02/14/intensely-relaxed-about-people-getting-filthy-rich/.

presented in the magazine *Hello!* (April 2010); it was only in a later interview that Murdoch's then wife, Wendi Deng, stated that Blair was one of Murdoch's closest friends.[32] After years of associating with the rich and famous, the shift away from Old Labour was now symbolically complete; Blair may or may not see himself as a prophet but surely he now walks among the kings.

2. 'This Money and Bloodshed'

Blair has written and spoken a lot about tolerance, interfaith harmony, and world peace but, as we all know, religions have not always got along and, if we were to consistently foreground religious identity, we could even follow those who argue that the Christian Blair remains a high-profile advocate of the invasions of largely Islamic Afghanistan and Iraq. Blair has long been aware of such inter-faith difficulties as the flip side of religious compassion, and to tackle the historic problem of religions not always peacefully coexisting is, of course, part of Blair's vision. But there is a steelier edge to the hope for the future and it is revealed almost in passing in the discussion of religion in his memoirs. In a typically vague manner, Blair describes how new technologies may join up differ-ent faiths but, through their youthfulness, children can learn about different faiths and cultures based on 'truth' rather than 'deeply mis-guided preconceptions'.[33] This assumption of 'truth' and the possibility of 'deeply misguided perceptions' reveals the essentialist notion of True Religion and False Religion that runs throughout Blair's thinking, particularly on Islam, and it is a notable feature of the rhetoric of the Tony Blair Faith Foundation.[34] Yet it was, of course, the 'war on terror', including the invasions of Afghanistan and Iraq, which framed Blair's thinking on Islam, both in his own words and in popular imagination and memory. Only the most naïve would assume that Blair's vision of interfaith harmony does not come at a cost, as Blair himself was only too aware when trying to rethink his justification of the Iraq war. 'This

32. 'Tony Blair "godfather to Rupert Murdoch's daughter"', *BBC News* (September 5, 2011), http://www.bbc.co.uk/news/uk-politics-14785501; D. Sabbagh, 'How Tony Blair was taken into the Murdoch family fold', *Guardian* (September 5, 2011); D. Dumas, '"I had never been in a supermarket before I came to America": Wendi Murdoch on her childhood, her daughters and being best friends with Nicole Kidman', *Daily Mail* (September 10, 2011).

33. Blair, *Journey*, p. 690.

34. E.g. on the opening of the Tony Blair Faith Foundation in 2008, Blair noted 'extremism associated with the perversion of the proper faith of Islam'. See 'Blair launches faith foundation'.

money and bloodshed', he argued, was predominately expended because of the consequences of extremism which did not reflect the will of Iraqis.[35]

This is why it is important to approach the liberalism and tolerance of Blairite theology with a hermeneutic of suspicion. And we should not forget that we are dealing with the leader of a party famed for its obsession with controlling – or at least limiting – the influence of the mass media. There are a range of ideological trends relating to geopolitical factors partly responsible for the more essentialist binaries of Blair's understanding of True Religion/Islam and False Religion/Islam. By and large, these were probably articulated unintentionally by Blair but they are deeply embedded ideological trends underpinning liberal interventionism which also form the continuity with Thatcher's Cold War thinking on related matters of ideological- and civilisation-difference (see Chapter 4) which Blair developed. There are, for instance, historic links between nationalism, interventionism, cultural superiority, and differentiation which contribute to the perpetuation of markets and underpin the 'war on terror'.[36] There are also the ideas crystallised by Samuel Huntington in his influential thesis of a 'Clash of Civilisations', which in turn owes a debt to Bernard Lewis' essay, 'The Roots of Muslim Rage'.[37] While assessing a range of competing global 'civilisations' (Western, Confucian, Japanese, Islamic, Hindu, Slavic-Orthodox, Latin American, and possibly African), Huntington argued that with the fall of the Soviet Union, 'Islam' and the 'Arab world' have become a threat to 'the West'. According to Huntington, Western ideas such as individualism, liberalism, human rights, equality, liberty, democracy, free markets, and so on are not found in other civilisations and Islam has taken on the oppositional role, not least, as he infamously claimed, because it has 'bloody borders'. While there are seemingly endless portrayals of a stark

35. Blair, *Journey*, p. 479.

36. See e.g. N. Chomsky, *Pirates and Emperors, Old and New: International Terrorism in the Real World* (London: Pluto, 2002); A. Callinicos, *The New Mandarins of American Power* (Cambridge: Polity Press, 2003); D. Harvey, *The New Imperialism* (Oxford: Oxford University Press, 2003); D. Gregory, *The Colonial Present: Afghanistan, Palestine, Iraq* (Oxford: Blackwell, 2004); R. Fisk, *The Great War for Civilisation: The Conquest of the Middle East* (London: Fourth Estate, 2005); G. Achcar, *The Clash of Barbarisms: September 11 and the New World Disorder* (2nd edn; London: Saqi, 2006); Klein, *The Shock Doctrine*.

37. S.P. Huntington, 'The Clash of Civilizations?', *Foreign Affairs* 72 (1993), pp. 22-49; S.P. Huntington, *The Clash of Civilizations and the Remaking of World Order* (New York: Simon & Schuster, 1996); cf. B. Lewis, 'The Roots of Muslim Rage', *The Atlantic* (September 1990), pp. 47-60.

'Islam versus the West' in politics, intellectual thought, and the media,[38] Blair (and Bush) attempted to nuance this and downplay the grand differences in civilisation ('a clash not so much between civilisations but rather one about the force and consequence of globalisation'),[39] trying to make arguments about interventionism more along the lines of a liberal imperialism with a soft Orientalist twist.[40] In the immediate aftermath of September 11, Blair, echoing Thatcher, believed that the problem was particularly manifested in the form of 'extremism', rather than Islam as a whole, though he would modify this further on reflection. Indeed, Blair developed his thinking extensively on this issue, just as Thatcher did, with reference to the Bible and religion, on the Cold War.

After September 11, Blair argued that the 'war on terror' would indeed be a war but that it was 'in a profound sense' an ideological battle: 'the mores and modus vivendi of religious fanaticism versus those of an enlightened, secular system of government that in the West, at least, incorporated belief in liberty, equality and democracy'.[41] Blair may have come to believe that the two sides are more complicated than a simple binary might suggest but a strict binary still guides his thinking through-out, even when the language of a 'spectrum' of beliefs in Islam is introduced. At one end are 'the extremists who advocate terrorism to further the goal of the Islamic state' who may be 'few in number' but 'their sympathisers reach far further along the spectrum than we think'. At this point, Blair seemed to have one eye also on the (typically) liberal-left opposition in the UK (at least as understood by certain liberal interventionists) because among these 'sympathisers' are 'many [who] do not agree with the terrorism' but who nevertheless (and note the scare quotes) 'understand' why it is happening. Likewise, and a little further along the spectrum, 'are those who condemn the terrorists, but in a curious and dangerous way buy into bits of their world view'. These people 'agree with the extremists' that America is 'anti-Islam', they see the invasion of Afghanistan or Iraq 'as invasions of Muslim nations', and they view Israel 'as the symbol of Western anti-Islamic prejudice'. These people stretch 'uncomfortably far into the middle of the spectrum'. On the other side, however, are 'a large number, probably the majority' who 'condemn terrorists and their world view'. This group 'find the terrorism

38. Crossley, *Jesus in an Age of Terror*, pp. 25-52, 58-142.

39. Blair, *Journey*, p. 346.

40. On the general history of which see e.g.; R. Seymour, *The Liberal Defence of Murder* (London: Verso, 2008); M. Dillon and J. Reid, *The Liberal Way of War: Killing to Make Life Live* (New York: Routledge, 2009). See also, of course, E.W. Said, *Orientalism* (3rd edn; London: Penguin Books, 2003).

41. Blair, *Journey*, p. 346.

repugnant' and 'they wish to be in alliance with the Western nations against it'. However, for Blair, this group have yet to articulate confidently 'a thoroughly reformed and modernising view of Islam'. They are stuck, he suggests, because common in 'the Arab and Muslim world' is a problematic choice on the one hand between a potentially well-meaning ruling elite (but which the people are concerned about promoting), and on the other, a popular movement with the wrong intentions (but which the people are too keen to promote).[42]

Blair's view of Islam and extremist Islam is, therefore, and by his own admission, thoroughly mixed in with his political ideas, democracy, and the modern nation-state which has further echoes of Thatcher's Cold War thinking. The Blairite view would have it that True Religion (and Politics) must be in line with an enlightened, secular system of government' and a 'belief in liberty, equality and democracy', whereas False Religion (and Politics) must not. More precisely still, True Religion (and Politics) would see nations such as America, Britain, and Israel as forces of good, whereas False Religion (and Politics) would not. This is a universalist vision of liberal democracy to which the world, presumably, must ultimately conform.[43] This is why Scripture and reading Scripture for instruction is important for Blair because his logic suggests that we must trace religion back to its true, essential origins in order to get behind the later 'corruptions'. Once we do this, we find that True Religion is not only based on scriptures but also tolerant and necessarily compatible with the secularised nation state and the correct foreign policy. This was a view implicit in Thatcher's handling of Islam and religion; we will see it developed much further still by Blair.

This is also a view implied in Obama's liberalising exegesis of Christian, Jewish, and Muslim sacred texts in his famous speech delivered in Cairo in 2009, which we might label Liberal Holy Scriptures rather than Liberal Bible,[44] a kind of foreign policy equivalent of Gordon Brown's handling of the 2008 financial crisis with reference to what 'Judaism…Muslims…Buddhists…Sikhs…Hindus say'. 'Scriptural' language (from 'Holy Koran', 'Holy Bible', the Talmud) was brought to the fore by Obama, bringing together Christianity, Islam, and Judaism under the umbrella of peace and the general term 'God':

42. Blair, *Journey*, p. 348.

43. H. O'Shaughnessy, 'Tony Blair's Faith Foundation inspires ridicule', *Guardian* (May 13, 2009).

44. B. Obama, 'Remarks by the President on a New Beginning', *The White House: Office of the Press Secretary* (2009), http://www.whitehouse.gov/the-press-office/remarks-president-cairo-university-6-04-09.

> We have the power to make the world we seek, but only if we have the
> courage to make a new beginning, keeping in mind what has been written.
> The Holy Koran tells us, 'O mankind! We have created you male and a
> female; and we have made you into nations and tribes so that you may
> know one another.'
> The Talmud tells us: 'The whole of the Torah is for the purpose of
> promoting peace'.
> The Holy Bible tells us, 'Blessed are the peacemakers, for they shall be
> called sons of God'. [Matt. 5.9]
> The people of the world can live together in peace. We know that is
> God's vision. Now, that must be our work here on Earth. Thank you. And
> may God's peace be upon you.

Just prior to this Obama spoke of 'one rule that lies at the heart of every
religion', that 'we do unto others as we would have them do unto us' (cf.
Matt. 7.12; Luke 6.31). 'This truth', he adds, 'transcends nations and
peoples – a belief that isn't new; that isn't black or white or brown; that
isn't Christian, or Muslim or Jew'. When Obama referred to 'do unto
others as we would have them do unto us', he vaguely interpreted the
admittedly already vague saying and sentiment as 'a faith in other
people', adding it was 'what brought me here today'. Faith in people to
do precisely what was not fully expanded but in the same context Obama
mentioned that 'we should choose the right path, not just the easy path',
the former presumably being the path Obama's administration choose.

We should not forget the importance of the geopolitical and religious
contexts that are of obvious importance when giving a major speech in
Cairo shortly after the end of the Bush administration. This early post-
Bush speech was light on detail about foreign policy but it maintained a
standard American line on the Middle East, albeit in general terms.
'America', Obama claimed, 'respects the right of all peaceful and law-
abiding voices to be heard around the world, even if we disagree with
them. And we will welcome all elected, peaceful governments – provided they govern with respect for all their people.' While Obama was
careful to distance himself from Bush in this speech, there was little
difference in general aims. After all, who decides what are 'peaceful
governments', governing 'with respect'? At this point it is worth remind-
ing ourselves that Obama was the guest of Mubarak, who would –
eventually – not be deemed a friend but at this time was running a police
state.[45] While Obama might have been reaching out to Muslims in the
Middle East, he made the same move as Blair, namely, to reach out to

---

45. *Amnesty International Report 2009: Egypt*, http://thereport.amnesty.org/en/
regions/middle-east-north-africa/egypt; R. Fisk, 'Police state is the wrong venue for
Obama's speech', *Independent* (June 3, 2009).

those who would agree with (Anglo-)American foreign policy in the Middle East. While there may have been a rhetorically anti-Bush move, we are not really too far from 'you're either with us or against us'. Moreover, the Obama speech defended the actions in Afghanistan and praised the international support for the pursuit of violent extremists which is not far from the 'coalition of the willing'. In this context Obama implied another aspect of this coalition when he mentioned 'the enduring faith of over a billion people is so much bigger than the narrow hatred of a few. Islam is not part of the problem in combating violent extremism – it is an important part of promoting peace'.

Blair heaped praised on Obama's Cairo speech, seeing it as an exceptional case for peace and coexistence and effectively combining soft and hard power.[46] What we will now see is that these sorts of sentiments were effectively worked out in Blair's own version of the Liberal Bible but a Liberal Bible – or indeed Obama-style Liberal Holy Scriptures – which had to deal with the influence of the Radical Bible in the Labour tradition.

3. Doing God? The Iraq War and the Apocalyptic Bible

But did Campbell – Blair's Director of Communications and Strategy – not famously claim 'we don't do God' when Blair was asked a question about religion by *Vanity Fair* journalist, David Margolick? Campbell's response has typically been taken to refer to New Labour's queasiness on issues relating to religion and public presentation of policy, or even that the New Labour government were not prepared to entertain religious questions at all. However, Alastair Campbell has claimed that this 'was not a major strategic statement' but rather an attempt to end the interview when Margolick kept asking a 'final question' and the last example happened to be about his faith. Even so, he still argues that 'we don't do God' was 'simply part of a view that in UK politics, it is always quite dangerous to mix religion and politics, not least because the electorate are not keen on it, and the media and politicians tend to misrepresent it whenever it happens'.[47] However, it is certainly clear that God – and the

46. Blair, *Journey*, p. 673.

47. A. Campbell, 'Baroness Warsi misses point of "we don't do God", writes a pro faith atheist', *Alastair's Blog* (September 16, 2010), http://www.alastaircampbell. org/blog/2010/09/16/baroness-warsi-misses-point-of-we-dont-do-god-writes-a-pro-faith-atheist/. Recall, of course, Campbell's reaction to Blair giving the controversial 1996 *Sunday Telegraph* interview on God and the Bible. See Campbell, *The Blair Years*, pp. 111-12. See also the comments in Steven, *Christianity and Party Politics*, p. 105.

Bible – did play a role in Blair's thinking, even if they were not always out in the open.[48] After all, it was God, claimed Blair on *Parkinson*, who would ultimately judge him over Iraq,[49] while Campbell recalled that Blair 'often' read the Bible 'when the really big decisions were on'.[50] It was not without reason that Private Eye could parody Blair as the trendy Vicar of St Albion.

While Blair might have wanted to foreground his Christianity more in his political career, what we instead saw was a more carefully managed downplaying of such beliefs with the intention of not scaring off parts of the electorate (he famously feared people would assume him a 'nutter' for talking about religious convictions).[51] Indeed, it seems that the biblical references Blair wanted in his speeches were given the red pen treatment by Campbell (or at least those that Campbell spotted).[52] However, biblical phrases, allusions, and quasi-biblical language still remained present in his writings and speeches. But they are even more than the vague, faintly Judaeo-Christianised, biblical citation found among successful American politicians such as Clinton, Bush and Obama and designed (ideally) to speak to believers without (ideally) alienating non-Christians and non-believers.[53] Frank Field's reported claims about Blair's understanding of Anglicanism and politics might apply equally to Blair's use of the Bible: 'the Church of England survived because it realises how much religion the English will take, which is not very much'.[54] Blair was, and remains, vague in using precise biblical allusions publicly and even now, free from electoral politics, he is still not likely to provide notification that a biblical allusion or quotation is imminent or has just passed.[55]

48. Rawnsley, *End of the Party*, pp. 446-49; Burton and McCabe, *We Don't Do God*, p. xv.

49. The remarks to Michael Parkinson were made on the March 4, 2006, edition of ITV's *Parkinson*. The footage is available at 'PM attacked on Iraq "God" remarks', *BBC News* (March 4, 2006), http://news.bbc.co.uk/1/hi/4773124.stm.

50. A. Campbell, *Power and the People 1997–1999: The Alastair Campbell Diaries, vol. 2* (London: Arrow, 2011), p. 596.

51. 'Blair feared faith "nutter" label', *BBC News* (November 25, 2007), http://news.bbc.co.uk/1/hi/7111620.stm.

52. Burton and McCabe, *We Don't Do God*, pp. 61-62.

53. On which see Berlinerblau, *Thumpin' It*.

54. Rawnsley, *End of the Party*, p. 448.

55. This might further explain the relative degree of Bible-blindness (though certainly not to the extent of some of the people covered in this book) and lack of appreciation of thoroughgoing 'religious' issues in Blair's rhetoric and thinking by his biographers. See E.L. Graham, 'Doing God? Public Theology under Blair', in

The following are famous enough biblical examples of the language of 'light' from the Sermon on the Mount and Johannine literature:

> You are the light of the world. A city built on a hill cannot be hid. No one after lighting a lamp puts it under the bushel basket, but on the lampstand, and it gives light to all in the house. In the same way, let your light shine before others, so that they may see your good works and give glory to your Father in heaven. (Matt. 5.14-16)

> The true light, which enlightens everyone, was coming into the world. (John 1.9)

> Again Jesus spoke to them, saying, 'I am the light of the world. Whoever follows me will never walk in darkness but will have the light of life'. (John 8.12)

> Yet I am writing you a new commandment that is true in him and in you, because the darkness is passing away and the true light is already shining. (1 John 2.8)

When this language turns up in his memoirs, Blair does not mention chapter and verse, or even the Bible, and certainly not Christ, but the allusions to such thinking are clear enough, even if woven in a relatively loose manner in support of the ideals of the American nation and as a justification for the invasion of Iraq in 2003. While George Bush's Manichean view of the world may appear simplistic, Blair claims, it was a blunt analysis which could not really be disputed because certain nations continued to be run by corruption and oppression and lacked a bright future:

> There is no house on the hill which makes the present struggle worthwhile; just a horizon full of deeper despair as far as the eye can see. For those people in that bleak wilderness, America does stand out; it does shine; it may not be a house in their land they can aspire to, but it is a house they can see in the distance, and in seeing, know that how they do live, is not how they must live. So when I look back and I reread all the documents and the memories flood back to me...I know that there was never any way Britain was not going to be with the US at that moment...[56]

The convenient vagueness of the language of light is sufficiently widespread as an assumption of Good that it could, in theory, be embraced by all, or at least those who want to be on the side of Good, whether

P.M. Scott, E.L. Graham, and C.R. Baker (eds.), *Remoralizing Britain? Political, Ethical and Theological Perspectives on New Labour* (London: Continuum, 2009), pp. 1-18.

56. Blair, *Journey*, p. 434.

Christian or not. Future hope marks Blair's use of such biblical or quasi-biblical language, which is perhaps not a surprise when the implied language of binaries is invoked; indeed, and again like Thatcher's Cold War thinking, Blair had seen Christianity in strict terms of 'right and wrong, good and bad' long before the 'war on terror'.[57] Blair's future hopes are also marked by a use of language we might generally describe as 'apocalyptic', if by contemporary implications of that slippery term we mean dramatic global changes in the not-too-distant future, the inevitability of war, and the ultimate overcoming of suffering, injustice, hunger, and oppression. While Blair attributed the Manichean outlook to Bush, this would also be a fair way of categorising Blair's outlook too (as he came close to implying in his assessment of Bush),[58] and certainly when he uses vague biblical, quasi-biblical, and theological language. But this outlook cannot be understood apart from its contemporary political ramifications, in particular the Blair doctrine of liberal interventionism and, especially, the post-September 11 'war on terror'. As his agent and close friend John Burton claimed, Blair 'believed strongly, although he couldn't say it at the time, that intervention in Kosovo, Sierra Leone – Iraq too – was all part of the Christian battle; good should triumph over evil'.[59] That said, Blair was explicit on September 11, 2001: 'This is not a battle between the United States of America and terrorism, but between the free and democratic world and terrorism... [W]e, like them, will not rest until this evil is driven from our world.'[60]

But in whatever form Blair constructed a threat associated with Islam – whether a question of extremists or the deep roots of an extremist worldview – it is still one that is constructed in opposition to, and in distinction from, liberal democracy. With Saddam Hussein on the horizon, Blair combined this concern with 'rogue states' who, Blair would argue, might provide more firepower for those extremists. And so the Manichean outlook was more precisely contextualised in terms of Weapons of Mass Destruction (WMDs) in the build-up to the Iraq war. The following is Blair's preface to the 2002 government document on Iraq's alleged WMDs:

57. In his preface to the 1993 book on Christian Socialism Blair wrote: 'Christianity is a very tough religion... It is judgemental. There is right and wrong. There is good and bad...when we look at our world today and how much needs to be done, we should not hesitate to make such judgements' (Blair, 'Preface', p. 12).

58. See e.g. Rawnsley, *End of the Party*, p. 42.

59. Burton and McCabe, *We Don't Do God*, p. xv.

60. T. Blair, 'Blair's statement in full', *BBC News* (September 11, 2001), http://news.bbc.co.uk/1/hi/uk_politics/1538551.stm.

...in light of the debate about Iraq and Weapons of Mass Destruction (WMD), I wanted to share with the British public the reasons why I believe this issue to be a current and serious threat to the UK national interest.

In recent months, I have been increasingly alarmed by the evidence from inside Iraq that...Saddam Hussein is continuing to develop WMD, and with them the ability to inflict real damage upon the region, and the stability of the world.

What I believe the assessed intelligence has established beyond doubt is that Saddam has continued to produce chemical and biological weapons, that he continues in his efforts to develop nuclear weapons, and that he has been able to extend the range of his ballistic missile programme.

...his [Saddam's] military planning allows for some of the WMD to be ready within 45 minutes of an order to use them.

In today's inter-dependent world, a major regional conflict does not stay confined to the region in question. Faced with someone who has shown himself capable of using WMD, I believe the international community has to stand up for itself and ensure its authority is upheld.

The threat posed to international peace and security, when WMD are in the hands of a brutal and aggressive regime like Saddam's, is real. Unless we face up to the threat, not only do we risk undermining the authority of the UN, whose resolutions he defies, but more importantly and in the longer term, we place at risk the lives and prosperity of our own people.[61]

Whether it was Blair's intention or not, this assessment would provide the basis for the infamous '45 minute' claim made by sections of the English press which in turn only heightened the idea of impending apocalypse. For instance, the *Sun*'s headline on September 25, 2002, was 'BRITS 45mins FROM DOOM: Cyprus within missile range'.[62]

This globalizing rhetoric of the Clash of Civilisations (whether openly acknowledged or not by Blair), and the more precise allegations of WMDs, were given a distinctive nationalizing spin by picking up on the myth of Churchill.[63] But the Churchill–Hitler/Blair–Saddam parallel runs into obvious difficulties (as any attempt at precise historical paralleling is

61. *Iraq's Weapons of Mass Destruction – The Assessment of the British Government* (September 24, 2002), available at http://www.number-10.gov.uk/output/Page271.asp.

62. Compare also: '45 MINUTES FROM ATTACK: dossier reveals Saddam is ready to launch chemical war strikes', *London Evening Standard* (September 24, 2002); 'MAD SADDAM READY TO ATTACK: 45minutes from a chemical war', *Star* (September 25, 2002).

63. Cf. J.G. Crossley, Defining History', in J. G. Crossley and C. Karner (eds.), *Writing History, Constructing Religion* (Aldershot: Ashgate, 2005), pp. 9-29 (15-17); Fisk, *Great War for Civilisation*, pp. 1140-44.

wont to do[64]) in its application, certainly in distribution of power between the nations involved. In his speech to Parliament on the eve of the Iraq war, Blair was aware that the analogy could not be developed too precisely and acknowledged that there were 'glib and sometimes foolish comparisons with the 1930s... [H]istory does not declare the future to us so plainly'. But develop the historical analogy he did, albeit developing its 'lessons' more generally. Blair discussed a newspaper editorial from 1938 which declared that peace was upon the nation and from this we learn: 'It is that, with history, we know what happened. We can look back and say, "There's the time; that was the moment; that's when we should've acted".' But the 1930s became more decontextualised and, like Churchill versus Hitler, is placed firmly into a Manichean framework. Moreover, it is at this crucial point in his argument ('why I believe that the threat we face today is so serious and why we must tackle it') that Blair brings in quasi-biblical and primordial language of chaos and order:

> The threat today is not that of the 1930s... [T]he world is ever more interdependent... The key today is stability and order. The threat is chaos and disorder – and there are two begetters of chaos: tyrannical regimes with weapons of mass destruction and extreme terrorist groups who profess a perverted and false view of Islam.[65]

We should not forget that this speech was not only given on the eve of the Iraq war but that it was also an attempt to persuade the Labour Party in particular to endorse the invasion. This is important because the idea of what we might even call messianic interventionism was previously developed in Blair's speech to the Labour Party conference in September 2001 where the quasi-biblical and apocalyptic language was, if anything, even more emphatic (e.g. 'an act of evil', 'we were with you at the first. We will stay with you to the last', 'the shadow of this evil', 'lasting good', 'hope amongst all nations', 'a new beginning', 'justice and prosperity for the poor and dispossessed', 'the starving, the wretched, the dispossessed, the ignorant, those living in want and squalor'):

64. As Blair himself claimed in 1982: 'Historical analogies can be superficially attractive, but on close analysis, plain wrong'. See T. Blair, 'The full text of Tony Blair's letter to Michael Foot written in July 1982', *Telegraph* (June 16, 2006), http://www.telegraph.co.uk/news/uknews/1521418/The-full-text-of-Tony-Blairs-letter-to-Michael-Foot-written-in-July-1982.html.

65. 'Iraq', Hansard: Commons Debates (March 18, 2003), Columns 767-68, http://www.publications.parliament.uk/pa/cm200203/cmhansrd/vo030318/debtext/30318-07.htm.

In retrospect, the Millennium marked only a moment in time. It was the events of September 11 that marked a turning point in history, where we confront the dangers of the future and assess the choices facing human-kind. It was a tragedy. An act of evil...We [the British nation] were with you [the American people] at the first. We will stay with you to the last... It is that out of the shadow of this evil, should emerge lasting good: destruction of the machinery of terrorism wherever it is found; hope amongst all nations of a new beginning where we seek to resolve differ-ences in a calm and ordered way; greater understanding between nations and between faiths; and above all justice and prosperity for the poor and dispossessed, so that people everywhere can see the chance of a better future through the hard work and creative power of the free citizen, not the violence and savagery of the fanatic. I know that here in Britain people are anxious, even a little frightened. I understand that... Don't kill innocent people. We are not the ones who waged war on the innocent. We seek the guilty... Today the threat is chaos... The starving, the wretched, the dispossessed, the ignorant, those living in want and squalor from the deserts of Northern Africa to the slums of Gaza, to the mountain ranges of Afghanistan: they too are our cause. This is a moment to seize. The kaleidoscope has been shaken. The pieces are in flux. Soon they will settle again. Before they do, let us re-order this world around us.[66]

Of course, we cannot entirely rule out the influence of apocalyptic thinking in American evangelical Christianity and Christian Zionism, particularly among those groups with which Bush associated and in the language that found its way into the rhetoric of the 'war on terror'.[67] But, while there are some general overlaps, this form of evangelical Christi-anity does not have much emotional currency in the UK. Likewise, there may be the influence of Thatcherite thinking on the Cold War, but directly invoking the 'toxic' Thatcher brand would always be problem-atic, even for Blair. In fact, given that Blair's speeches were designed to persuade the Labour Party – much of which was jittery or at least ambivalent about Bush and the invasion of Iraq[68] – there is a more important 'apocalyptic' influence to be found here.

66. Available at http://politics.guardian.co.uk/labour2001/story/0,,562006,00. html (part 1) and http://politics.guardian.co.uk/labourconference2001/story/0,1220, 561988,00.html (part 2).

67. On the general background to which see e.g. M. Northcott, *An Angel Directs the Storm: Apocalyptic Religion and American Empire* (London: I.B. Tauris, 2004); M.L. Taylor, *Religion, Politics, and the Christian Right: Post-9/11 Powers and American Empire* (Minneapolis: Augsburg Fortress, 2005); Crossley, *Jesus in an Age of Terror*, Chapter 5.

68. Cf. Kampfner, *Blair's Wars*, pp. 122-23.

The Beveridge Report famously spoke about 'evil giants' of 'want', 'squalor', 'disease', and 'ignorance', and was the kind of language that influenced the famous 1945 manifesto of (what would become) arguably the most widely admired Labour government of arguably the most widely admired post-war Labour leader, Clement Attlee. The 1945 manifesto was written in the aftermath of the Second World War against 'Japanese barbarism' and 'Nazi tyranny and aggression', claiming 'Victory in war must be followed by a prosperous peace' and that 'we should build a new United Nations, allies in a new war on hunger, ignorance and want'.[69] Order and chaos – key terms in Blair's speech to Parliament on the eve of the Iraq War – likewise echo the 1945 manifesto, albeit to be given a notably Blairite reinterpretation. As the manifesto stated, 'The Labour Party stands for order as against the chaos which would follow the end of all public control. We stand for order, for positive constructive progress as against the chaos.'

As we saw in Chapter 1, a long-established strand of the English radical tradition, from Winstanley and the seventeenth-century radicals through Blake to the Nonconformist influence on the modern Labour movement and figures such as E.P. Thompson (who became critically engaged with the Labour Party), has long been infused with biblical, quasi-biblical, and even millenarian language of utopianism and heaven-on-earth. In fact, 'Jerusalem', based on Blake's poem 'Milton', was also invoked by Attlee and the Attlee government which has since become almost synonymous in British political discourse with the idea, which has a long history in the Radical Bible tradition, of building a New Jerusalem (Rev. 3.12; 21.3).[70] Indeed, 'Jerusalem' is still sung at the end of post-war Labour Party conferences and the language of New Jerusalem is still invoked in Labour debates.[71] While invoking the precise phrase 'New Jerusalem' might have been fraught with some difficulties in a speech inaugurating the war on terror, apocalyptic language of dramatic social transformation for the victims of want, squalor, disease, and a new life for the poor, oppressed, dispossessed, ignorant, and wretched of the earth, is clearly something that has an emotional hold on the Labour Party. That said, as we also saw in Chapter 1, Winstanley,

69. '1945 Labour Party Election Manifesto: Let Us Face the Future', http://www.labour-party.org.uk/manifestos/1945/1945-labour-manifesto.shtml.

70. On 'New Jerusalem' and the Radical Bible see e.g. J. Kovacs and C. Rowland, *Revelation: The Apocalypse of Jesus Christ* (Oxford: Blackwell, 2004), pp. 21-22, 72-74, 226-43.

71. E.g. J. Cruddas, 'On building the new Jerusalem', *New Statesman* (September 30, 2012).

Blake, Thompson, and other representatives of this apocalyptic and utopian strand of the Radical Bible were part of revolutionary thinking in the old fashioned sense of opposing the dominant powers – including those at home. Clearly, that is not something Blair would entertain – whether in party political terms or capitalist ownership – and so with Blair we have the transformation of this aspect of the Radical Bible which may use its language but, significantly, is in line with the Liberal (-interventionist) Bible and its generic emphases on democracy, rights, tolerance, and freedom. While the idea of facilitating the radical trans-formation was retained, it was now the radical transformation of other societies into one like ours. As we have seen and will see again, what we have here is an important moment in shifting the Radical Bible away from mainstream politics by adopting its language but ultimately rejecting, or at least displacing, its revolutionary ideology.

Yet like an occasional Tony Benn, Jeremy Corbyn, or Alan Simpson remaining somewhere on the Labour back benches post-1997, the Radical Bible could still be heard, as it still would be through the reference to Winstanley in Gordon Brown's speech on international capitalism cited above. In fact it was an echo of the Radical Bible in the 'prophets versus kings' tradition that apparently caused Blair's 'wobble' in his handling of the British and American bombing of Iraq in 1998 and where, presumably, John the Baptist confronting the court of Antipas was not sufficiently analogous to a Prime Minister and President of major world powers confronting what by now was effectively a third-world, tin-pot dictatorship. According to Alastair Campbell's diary entry:

> **Wednesday 16 December** [first day of bombing] TB was clearly having a bit of a wobble. He said he had been reading the Bible last night, as he often did when the really big decisions were on, and he had read something about John the Baptist and Herod which had caused him to rethink, albeit not change his mind.

Campbell explains in the accompanying footnote: 'After John the Baptist denounced the marriage of Herod Antipas, Herod ordered him to be imprisoned and later beheaded'.[72] But, as with other big decisions, biblical stories about challenging power did not change Blair's mind. Like Labour's reassessment of Clause 4 before it, the Radical Bible was going to change in the hands of New Labour. It is of some significance that for someone as powerful as Blair to make claims about challenging power, he instead has to adopt the language of benign power, such as

72. Campbell, *Power and the People*, p. 596.

establishing order from chaos or bringing peace through destruction. John the Baptist was thought to be a prophet; is this one not implying that he is more than a prophet?

4. As Is Written: Pure Democracy

Blair is still regularly mocked for behaving like a 'Messiah' or accused of having a 'Messiah complex'.[73] But, widespread though they undoubtedly are, it is not just his detractors in the media who have made such remarks. Of his post-prime ministerial work as special envoy and representative for the Middle East Quartet, a 'long-time associate' is reported to have said, 'Tony acquired a Messiah complex after the Good Friday agreement in Northern Ireland... He brings the same optimism to the Quartet job.'[74] If it were not Blair's intention to present himself in such elevated terms, his speeches and soundbites, particularly when coupled with military intervention and peace negotiations, do not help. And nor does some of his more recent behaviour help, even if he did not expect to it to become public. For instance, when prompted to write the location of 'home' in the VIP visitors' guest book at the British Embassy in Washington, Blair wrote not 'London' or 'Buckinghamshire' (the locations of his townhouse and mansion respectively) but 'Jerusalem', where he spends occasional time at the American Colony hotel as part of his work for the Quartet.[75]

If Blair is the Messiah, then he is a thoroughly modern, liberal, multicultural, interfaith Messiah, who might still vanquish evil and his enemies but never on grounds of race, ethnicity, gender, sexuality, or even religion. In many ways this is a typical position within the liberalism and multiculturalism of the past forty years and one which has been

---

73. E.g. (among many), R.D. North, *Mr Blair's Messiah Politics: Or What Happened When Bambi Tried to Save the World* (London: Social Affairs Unit, 2006); B. Budowsky, 'Tony Blair's messianic justifications for the Iraq war', *The Hill* (February 1, 2010), http://thehill.com/blogs/pundits-blog/international-affairs/79041-tony-blairs-messianic-justifications-for-the-iraq-war#ixzz2R0MXgtxz; D. Owen, *The Hubris Syndrome: Bush, Blair and the Intoxication of Power* (New York: Methuen & Co., 2012); D. Sandbrook, 'Hubris and a man who thinks he can only be judged by God', *Daily Mail* (September 28, 2012).

74. L. Barber, 'Tony Blair: An Exclusive Interview', *Financial Times Magazine* (June 29, 2012). Even Campbell claimed that 'Joking aside, I warned him against world-leader-it is' (Campbell, *Power and the People*, p. 67).

75. S. Walters, 'An identity crisis for Blair: Former PM describes Jerusalem as "home"', *Daily Mail* (April 12, 2009).

associated with neoliberalism. This kind of liberal multiculturalism has the constant qualification that the Other has to be both embraced and yet understood in terms of dominant liberal discourses with anything problematic removed or stigmatised.[76] Or, as Slavoj Žižek memorably put it in his summary of the limited toleration of multiculturalism in relation to contemporary capitalism: 'On today's market, we find a series of products deprived of their malignant property: coffee without caffeine, cream without fat, beer without alcohol…'[77] The more crushing aspect of this embrace has been that liberal tolerance typically reinscribes difference and, as in the contemporary case of the 'war on terror' and the Clash of Civilisations rhetoric, can be employed as part of a liberal imperialistic and interventionist agenda to remove any global illiberal Otherness. We will return to this point in more detail in Chapter 9 and it should already be clear that Blair's understanding of 'religion' is a prime example of such an ideological position. Unsurprisingly, then, we also get what we might call decaffeinated exegesis. For example, rather than emphasise Gospel texts which talk about how a Gentile woman and her daughter represent dogs eating crumbs of the food given to the children (Mark 7.24-30; Matt. 15.21-28), Blair instead claimed that 'an abhorrence of prejudice based on race, class, gender or occupation is fundamental to the Gospels. It is what draws so many Christians into politics, across the political spectrum.'[78] In terms of scriptural assumptions, it is significant that Blair claims to read both the Bible *and* the Qur'an 'every day'. This is in part to understand global events ('to be faith-literate is crucial in a globalised world') but 'mainly just because it is immensely instructive'.[79]

76. See e.g. S. Žižek, 'Multiculturalism, or, the Cultural Logic of Multinational Capitalism', *New Left Review* I/225 (1997), pp. 28-51; S. Žižek, 'Liberal multiculturalism masks an old barbarism with a human face', *Guardian* (October 3, 2010); W. Brown, *Regulating Aversion: Tolerance in the Age of Identity and Empire* (Princeton: Princeton University Press, 2006); D.T. Goldberg, *The Threat of Race: Reflections on Racial Neoliberalism* (Oxford: Wiley-Blackwell, 2009); A. Lentin and G. Titley, *The Crises of Multiculturalism: Racism in a Neoliberal Age* (London: Zed Books, 2011); J.G. Crossley, 'The Multicultural Christ: Jesus the Jew and the New Perspective on Paul in an Age of Neoliberalism', *BCT* 7 (2011), pp. 1-9; Crossley, *Jesus in an Age of Neoliberalism*.

77. Žižek, *The Puppet and the Dwarf*, p. 96.

78. T. Blair, 'Faith in Politics', Speech to the Christian Socialist Movement (London, 2001), http://www.britishpoliticalspeech.org/speech-archive.htm?speech= 280.

79. T. Adams, 'This much I know: Tony Blair Interview', *Observer* (June 12, 2011). See also Rawnsley, *Servants of the People*, p. 276, and Rawnsley, *Last Party*, p. 36.

This is a crucial move because there is good reason why scriptural texts are so central for Blair: they come to represent the pure form of tolerant, liberal, democratic religion which can always be found behind the later corruptions of history.

However, in his quest for purer origins, Blair can condemn parts of Christian history in the distant past for persecuting non-believers and heretics because this kind of behaviour is a distortion of Christianity which is a religion, he suggested, based on compassion and love.[80] But, according to this logic with a Blairite spin, it is Islam that needs addressing in the present. Blair gives a potted history of Islam which is one of gradual decline into dictatorship and, ultimately, the deeply entrenched political stance today of those on the 'wrong' side of Blair's spectrum. For Blair, his appreciation of this history has helped him understand what he did not in 2001 when he thought it was just a few fanatics who could be defeated with ease and he would have been deeply disturbed if he knew fighting would still be taking place in Afghanistan (though claimed he would still have made the same decisions about Afghanistan and Iraq).[81] It is significant for understanding Blair's argument – as well as for understanding the arguments of a number of anti-theistic public intellectuals like Richard Dawkins – that he does not consider, at least in this context, the history of the battle-hardened Mujahedeen of the 1980s, the history of imperial disasters in the Afghanistan region, or the histories of different groups in Iraq and Afghanistan as part of his understanding for the ongoing fighting in the 'war on terror'. Instead, the idealist distortion of 'religion' provides the most crucial explanatory factor for Blair, a view repeated throughout the 'war on terror', including Blair's response to the July 7 attacks which infamously did not address the issue of the wars in Afghanistan and Iraq.[82] However, once we peel back to, or contrast with, the heart of Islam – True Islam in Blairite terms – we learn that it is in fact entirely compatible with enlightened government featuring morally upright leaders. Within twenty years of Islam beginning, Blair explains, it developed a government but it was also an attempt to bring the Abrahamic faiths back to their roots with an emphasis on principles,

80. Blair, *Journey*, p. 347. Blair long held such views. E.g. Blair, 'Foreword', p. 9: 'Christianity has been used for dubious and sometimes cruel purposes wholly at odds with its essential message. But at its best, it has inspired generations of people throughout almost 2000 years to believe in and work for a better, more humane and more just world.'

81. Blair, *Journey*, p. 347.

82. 'In full: Blair on bomb blasts', *BBC News* (July 7, 2005), http://news.bbc.co.uk/1/hi/uk/4659953.stm.

rationality and morality. In fact, he adds, merciful and devout Islam initially provided a sharp contrast with Christianity which, at the time, so Blair suggests, was tending to butcher enemies and contained priests more interested in debauchery and vice.[83]

In fact, Blair developed the argument that this form of Islamic government could even justify intervention into less enlightened countries, and not just any country but one which has particular relevance for Blair: he claimed that as Islam grew and spread geographically it was even seen as a liberator, even by some Christians such as the Nestorians in…Iraq. And the justification for, and ultimate origins of, this tolerant, rational, and principled system of government in Blair's argument is God-given scripture, the revelation given to the Prophet from God via the angel Gabriel, that is, ultimately, the direct word of God.[84] In keeping with his quest for pure origins, Blair has even claimed to have read three versions of the Qur'an in order to find passages to counter extremist positions.[85]

Of course, Blair is aware that there is plenty in the Bible – and 'religion' more generally – which is not so easy to boil down to the essentials required for a modern liberal democracy and so he focuses on 'the values like love of God and love of your neighbour' as the core features of religion rather than 'doctrine and practice': 'one of the things I do through my Foundation, through trying to bring different religious faiths together, is to show how, actually, there is a huge common space around these values between the different religious faiths.'[86] This, inevitably perhaps, means that Blair is comfortable reading scriptures 'less literally' and 'more metaphorically'. But, in a hermeneutical move again made by Obama, there is a flexibility with the biblical texts whereby those controversial aspects for modern liberal democracies can also be problematised, attributed to radically different ancient social contexts, and compared with other alien practices that are not readily endorsed by contemporary Christians in liberal democracies. So, for instance, Blair can claim, in language curiously reminiscent of the so-called antithesis in Matthew (Matt. 5.21-48) and his own relentless political rhetoric of 'modernising' Labour from Old to New, that,

83. Blair, *Journey*, p. 347.
84. Blair, *Journey*, p. 347.
85. Rawnsley, *End of the Party*, p. 44.
86. J. Hari, 'A Civil Partnership: Interview with Tony Blair', *Attitude* (April 8, 2009), pp. 50-52 (52).

when people quote the passages in Leviticus condemning homosexuality, I say to them – if you read the whole of the Old Testament and took everything that was there in a literal way, as being what God and religion is about, you'd have some pretty tough policies across the whole of the piece…and you've got the Old Testament kings with hordes of concubines, and so on. There's no way that you could take all of that and say, we in the 21st century should behave in that way.[87]

Yet there are still hermeneutical controls for Blair, even within the biblical (and quranic) texts, though they are effectively general concepts compatible with liberal democratic values, and they involve that classic move towards the figure of Jesus, though Blair now logically has to extend this to include Mohammad. Again, Blair uses an antithetical argument and again these figures are, crucially for Blair's hermeneutic, tolerant and progressive so, no matter what the rest of the biblical and quranic texts say, the core figures retain the essence of True Religion (and Politics):

And actually, what people often forget about, for example, Jesus or, indeed, the Prophet Mohammed, is that their whole raison d'être was to change the way that people thought traditionally. Christianity was very much about saying, no, 'an eye for an eye, a tooth for a tooth' is not the right way to behave. And the Koran was, of course, an extraordinary, progressive – revolutionarily progressive – document for its time. That's why many of the old pagan practices that the Prophet was keen to wean people away from were dispensed with.[88]

One of the notable things about Blair's hermeneutics is that echoes of the Radical Bible again remain, in this instance the kind of idea of communal checks on interpretation that so fascinated the Marxist Christopher Hill (see Chapter 2), though inevitably the potential for conflict is downplayed by Blair. So, for instance, Blair can praise the Catholic Church and religious leaders like the Pope but, echoing the main lesson he has claimed to have learned in politics, he ultimately echoes David Brent in seeing hope in 'the people' ('What makes me optimistic? People. Since leaving office, I have learned one thing above all: the people are the hope').[89] Again with echoes of his own rebranding of Labour as New Labour and presentation of his own fresh-faced rise to

87. Hari, 'Interview', p. 52.
88. Hari, 'Interview', p. 52.
89. Blair, *Journey*, p. 691. Blair is therefore also able to make the claim that a Muslim leader – crucially an *elected* leader – could be open to gay rights because ultimately 'people will find their way to a sensible reformation of attitudes' (Hari, 'Interview', p. 52).

power in the 1990s, Blair is regularly insistent, as we saw above in his own echoes of 'The Greatest Love of All' (the Whitney version), that the younger generation are the ones most likely to bring change and ensure the 'evolution' of biblical interpretation. In this instance, the younger generation likewise do not share official or traditional views on homosexuality more typical of an older generation (especially the leaders) but even so Blair appears to extend the communal wisdom to the whole congregation:

> what is interesting is that if you went into any Catholic Church, particularly a well-attended one, on any Sunday here and did a poll of the congregation, you'd be surprised at how liberal-minded people were… On many issues, I think the leaders of the Church and the Church will be in complete agreement. But I think on some of these issues, if you went and asked the congregation, I think you'd find that their faith is not to be found in those types of entrenched attitudes. If you asked 'what makes you religious?' and 'what does your faith mean to you?' they would immediately go into compassion, solidarity, relieving suffering. I would be really surprised if they went to 'actually, it's to do with believing homosexuality is wrong' or 'it's to do with believing this part of the ritual or doctrine should be done in this particular way'.[90]

Note again that for Blair change comes through general principles of 'faith' compatible with liberal democratic ones ('compassion, solidarity, relieving suffering').

As it happens, we have some indication that Blairite hermeneutics are now established within the Labour Party and this is shown precisely on the issue of homosexuality and the parliamentary debate over same-sex marriage in February 2013.[91] Two now perhaps expected examples of biblical support came up: loving the neighbour and the singling out of Jesus. Toby Perkins (Labour, Chesterfield) claimed that 'as a Christian' he had 'no worries about voting for this Bill' because 'what greater example of the equalities agenda could there be than Jesus Christ himself?… Jesus Christ led the way on promoting equalities.' Notice also that there are echoes of the Radical Bible but the confrontational element is now more about defending victims of oppression which in turn provides the justification for equality: 'There are any number of stories in the Bible that make it absolutely clear that Jesus stuck up for groups that had been oppressed over the years'. The other use of Jesus came from

90. Hari, 'Interview', p. 52.

91. 'Marriage (Same Sex Couples) Bill', Hansard: Commons Debates (February 5, 2013), Columns 125-230, http://www.publications.parliament.uk/pa/cm201213/cmhansrd/cm130205/debtext/130205-0001.htm.

David Lammy (Labour, Tottenham) and likewise we get the shift from Jesus the state criminal to Jesus defending victims of oppression: 'the Jesus I know was born a refugee, illegitimate, with a death warrant on his name, and in a barn among animals. He would stand up for minorities. That is why it is right for those of religious conviction to vote for this Bill.' Lammy also made sure that alternative understandings of the Bible which are not compatible with liberal democracies were assumed to be highly irrelevant: 'those on the extremes of our faith have poisoned what is an important debate with references to polygamy and bestiality'.

But this Liberal Bible is not restricted to Labour (or the Liberal Democrats). Minus the echoes of the Radical Bible, the Conservative MP Peter Bottomley argued in favour of same-sex marriage with biblical support. The 'primary commandment is to love the Lord my God with all my heart, soul, mind and strength' and this 'should be used as a way of defining the second great commandment, which is to treat my neighbour as myself'. This was interpreted to mean that 'we are asking whether we can remove the barriers that stop same-sex couples enjoying the commitment—the "at one" meaning—of marriage. That is what the Bill comes down to. It does not redefine marriage; it just takes away barriers.' The Bible of Perkins, Lammy, and Bottomley is a Bible deprived of its malignant properties, the Bible shorn of any Otherness problematic for liberal democracy, tolerance, and equality.[92] This is a development of Thatcher's Bible of tolerance but now further applied to issues Thatcher's government would not become associated with,

---

92. As we will see in the final chapter, homosexuality and the Bible remains a strand in the Radical Bible tradition. However, when we contextualise Perkins, Lammy, and Bottomley, it is clear that they are not in this tradition. The most obvious point is that they are all arguing in favour of opening up access to, and potentially promoting, a traditional institution: marriage. Bottomley is, obviously, a Tory and not part of the Radical Bible tradition. Though not entirely to the right of the Labour Party, Perkins was elected in 2010 and supported the New Labour candidate, David Miliband, in the Labour leadership race. Lammy's voting pattern on key issues since 2001 has been a checklist of New Labour policies removed from its radical tradition, as we see from TheyWorkForYou.com (http://www.theyworkforyou.com/mp/david_lammy/tottenham):

Voted *very strongly for* introducing *foundation hospitals*.
Voted *very strongly for* the *Iraq war*.
Voted *very strongly against* an *investigation* into the Iraq war.
Voted *moderately for* a *stricter asylum system*.
Voted *very strongly for* introducing *ID cards*.
Voted *very strongly for* Labour's *anti-terrorism laws*.

although Thatcher herself had a history of a more liberal position on homosexuality.[93] Yet Blair's modified version of the Thatcher Bible is, as we will now see, the Bible most influential among the political classes running the Conservative-led Coalition government but, as we will also see, not quite the same Radical Bible of those who have a different take on same-sex marriage.

93. Untypically of Conservative thinking of the time, Thatcher had voted in favour of legalising homosexuality. See e.g. 'Sexual Offences (No. 2)', Hansard Commons Debates (July 5, 1966), Columns 259-67, http://hansard.millbanksystems. com/commons/1966/jul/05/sexual-offences-no-2; Thatcher, *The Path to Power*, pp. 150-53; Campbell, *The Grocer's Daughter*, p. 192. However, Section 28 (and the so-called promotion of homosexuality in schools) was tied in with concerns for a 'Christian' perception of 'traditional morality' and was a controversial feature of her time as Prime Minister.

Chapter 9

THE GOVE BIBLE VERSUS THE OCCUPY BIBLE

1. 1611 after 2008: The Bible in an Age of Coalition

The 2008 recession – itself a result of longer-term issues in neoliberal deregulation – made its near inevitable impact on British party-politics. A strong case is often made that it cost Gordon Brown and Labour the 2010 election, though the new Coalition government showed that there was not a strong alternative for an outright winner. Tellingly, the Thatcherite and neoliberal rhetoric was intensified, particularly in the form of public sector cuts, alongside a decreasing popular respect for welfare, as the key tenets of Thatcherism became increasingly embedded in younger generations (see Chapter 4). However, political and public discourse also witnessed an increasing social liberalism on issues such as gender equality and gay rights.[1] As some vocal and sizeable Tory opposition to same-sex marriage continued to show (more Tories voted against the bill than for it), such social liberalism is not typically part of traditional Conservatism but it was, nevertheless, brought in by David Cameron and gained degrees of support from leading Tories touted as future Prime Ministers, Boris Johnson and Michael Gove. Alongside broader cultural changes over the past thirty years, the New Labour government (which introduced civil partnerships) had injected greater social liberalism into Thatcherism and just as Blair became known as the heir to Thatcher so Blair now had his own heirs in Cameron and Gove. Cameron was believed to have coined the phrase 'heir to Blair' while in 2013 Gove would repeat his unambiguous admiration for Blair proclaimed in a 2003 *Times* article entitled, 'I can't fight my feelings any more: I love Tony':

> You could call it the Elizabeth Bennett moment. It's what Isolde felt when she fell into Tristan's arms... By God, it's still hard to write this, but I'm afraid I've got to be honest. Tony Blair is proving an outstanding

1. Harris, 'Generation Y; Ipsos-MORI, 'Generations'.

Prime Minister at the moment... I just look at who's enraged by the Thatcherite stance that Mr Blair has adopted towards Iraq... And Mr Blair's policy has more than just the right critics. It has the merit of genuine moral force. As the Prime Minister has pointed out, all those opposed to him have no solution to the problem of proliferating weapons of mass destruction, they offer no hope to the people of Iraq... My admiration for the Prime Minister's bravery in making this case is, I have to add, only increased when I listen to the sneering condescension with which broadcasters treat Government policy on Iraq. Jeremy Paxman is just one of several who seem determined never to give the elected head of our Government the benefit of any doubt, cheerily mocking Mr Blair's Christian beliefs and brazenly maintaining that the last inspections regime failed because of Western, not Iraqi, bad faith.[2]

But this sort of praise and mimicking of Blair was not simply because of Blair's right-of-centre politics; as we will see, both Cameron and Gove would, if anything, be more explicit in their use of the Bible in public discourse than the man they apparently want to emulate.

But the Age of Coalition brought the Liberal Democrats back to a position of power and in many ways they were perfectly suited to a post-Thatcher and post-Blair fusion of economic and social liberalism, both in their political message and their use of the Bible. In 2013, Jo Latham and Claire Mathys published a collection of essays with the notable title, *Liberal Democrats Do God*, bringing together a number of prominent Liberal Democrat politicians.[3] This was a potentially important moment for the Liberal Democrats because despite their Nonconformist history and Gladstone himself, they have gained a reputation as a 'secular' party with an openly atheist leader in Nick Clegg and recently having one of Parliament's most active atheists in Evan Harris. While a number of other participants also raised the issue of 'secularism' and the Liberal Democrats, Greg Mulholland's essay in particular addressed such issues head-on and polemically.[4] Nevertheless, *Liberal Democrats Do God* provides the clearest contemporary use of the Bible by leading

2. M. Gove, 'I can't fight my feelings any more: I love Tony', *Times* (25 February, 2003). See also A. Pierce, 'Horror as Cameron brandishes the B-word', *Times* (October 5, 2005); T. Shipman, 'I should never have called myself "the heir to Blair"', admits Cameron', *Daily Mail* (May 5, 2010); T. Ross, 'Michael Gove aims to be the heir to Tony Blair', *Telegraph* (May 15, 2013).

3. J. Latham and C. Mathys (eds.), *Liberal Democrats Do God* (Kindle edn; London: LDCF, 2013).

4. G. Mulholland, 'Liberalism, the Liberal Democrats and the Dangerous Drift towards Moral Conformity', in Latham and Mathys (eds.), *Liberal Democrats Do God*, Chapter 3.

Liberal Democrats. Unsurprisingly, the Liberal Bible features prominently, often paralleling the Blairite spin on social liberalism. While his
views on same-sex marriage may differ in nuance from Blair and his
followers, Greg Mulholland used the examples of persecution and
'Christ's teaching' (as well as a personal story of abuse while campaigning) to illustrate the classic liberal concern for the experience of others:
'As a Christian, if I am to follow Christ's teaching, I must be grateful to
those who abuse me in his name… [I]t has given me a much better
understanding of what it is like to face hatred as a result of what you are,
and an appreciation of the experiences of others who face racial, sexist,
homophobic or nationalist hatred.'[5] It is notable that when issues of
discrimination and poverty emerge, the confrontational edge of the
Radical Bible is again not present in these uses of the Liberal Bible. For
Sarah Teather, Christianity demands particular attention 'to the most
vulnerable members of society' and asks that Christians 'seek and find
the face of Christ in the poor, the hungry, the sick, the imprisoned and
the stranger', based on the 'idea of Jesus identifying himself with the
least amongst people'. But 'what follows logically', Teather added, 'is a
perspective on policy-making which is inclusive and not exclusive'.[6]

   Indeed, there are a number of readings of the Bible which closely
resemble policies popularly associated with the Liberal Democrats and
which are implicitly based on a (politically) liberal interpretation of all
human beings created in the image of God and equally deserving of
respect, as some of the participants point out.[7] Alan Beith claimed that
'the concept of forgiveness, properly examined, offers insights into what
we need to do with our criminal justice system'. Beith was more precise
still, claiming that 'restorative justice [is] an approach which is firmly
rooted in New Testament thinking' and that restorative justice processes
'work to bring offenders and victims into communication, allowing
victims to express the impact an offence has had upon them, as well as
getting answers to their unanswered questions about the crime. It also
gives the offender the opportunity to make amends.'[8] Another favourite
Liberal Democratic theme likewise gets some attention. According to
Duncan Hames, and using a passage which we have seen used a number

   5. Mulholland, 'Liberalism', Chapter 3.
   6. S. Teather, 'Liberal Language and the Christian Calling', in Latham and
Mathys (eds.), *Liberal Democrats Do God*, Chapter 11.
   7. J. Pugh, '"Doing God" in the Liberal Democrat Party', in Latham and Mathys
(eds.), *Liberal Democrats Do God*, Chapter 1; Teather, 'Liberal Language'.
   8. A. Beith, 'Should the State Forgive?', in Latham and Mathys (eds.), *Liberal
Democrats Do God*, Chapter 5.

of times by politicians, 'Jesus' appeal to "love your neighbour as your-self" has clear applications for any Christian's approach to the environ-ment'. Hames wanted to challenge, through exegesis, potentially prob-lematic interpretations of Genesis 1.28 ('God said to them, "Be fruitful and multiply, and fill the earth and subdue it; and have dominion over the fish of the sea and over the birds of the air and over every living thing that moves upon the earth"') in relation to environmentalism. He argued that for him and probably 'most Christians', the term 'dominion' should be 'interpreted as responsible stewardship rather than exploitative tyranny', before adding that further evidence of 'man's duty to protect the earth abounds throughout the Bible, from God's order to Adam and Eve to work and keep the garden to the instruction in the Leviticus that "you shall not strip your vineyard bare", to Jesus's observation of the Father's care for even the smallest sparrow'.[9] Completing the Liberal Democrat bingo-card, Baroness Brinton, looked at Deuteronomy 10.18, Leviticus 19.33-34, and Hebrews 13.2 to defend certain voices on immi-gration, as well as attacking others: '…our modern world has become increasingly xenophobic, and it can be hard for the biblical voice to be heard. How many of us have heard the shrill voice on the doorstep, complaining that all the best jobs are taken by immigrants, or that "they" are getting free health services and welfare despite not contributing to the tax system.'[10]

But, at some point, someone was bound to note that it is not always so easy to equate the contents of the Bible with liberalism and modern sensibilities and so – as we saw when Blair confronted socially illiberal biblical passages in the Bible – hermeneutical guidelines are required for separating the wheat from the chaff. Lord Tyler made the common move of having the seemingly liberal Jesus overrule anything illiberal or anachronistic, including the liberal bogeyman, Paul: 'Above all, I hope those of us who remain Anglicans can soon find a way to return to Christ's own teaching, and stop agonising over the dated views of my namesake Paul of Tarsus, let along the washing up requirements of the Book of Leviticus.'[11] However, Andrew Stunell went further still and effectively downplayed the Liberal Bible in favour of what might be called the Liberal Holy Spirit which allows illiberal biblical verses to be

9. D. Hames, 'It's Good to be Green', in Latham and Mathys (eds.), *Liberal Democrats Do God*, Chapter 10.

10. Baroness Brinton, 'Immigration: "…I was a stranger and you took me in"', Latham and Mathys (eds.), *Liberal Democrats Do God*, Chapter 8.

11. Lord Tyler, 'Faith, Society and the State', in Latham and Mathys (eds.), *Liberal Democrats Do God*, Chapter 6.

overturned. For Stunell, the 'biggest challenge' is to explain 'why Wilberforce was right about slavery, and St Paul was wrong'. Paul, in this and the role of women, 'hadn't fully discerned the Spirit' and 'the Holy Spirit did not stop work when the Book of Revelation was sealed'. Indeed, Stunell, in arguably the most direct challenge to conventional political readings of the Bible, went even further still and claimed that:

> No Christian should have as their goal the recreation of some mythical olden days society where Christian values were understood and universally acknowledged, where lambs and lions sat down together, and harmony reigned supreme. It never existed. Neither the first Century in Judea nor the 19th Century in England provides that model.

Instead, 'thanks to the vigorous and continuing work of God's Holy Spirit, we know better than they did', including how to understand issues of children's rights, care of the disabled, respect for differences, being a lot more relaxed about women wearing hats and veils in church. The Holy Spirit, Stunell added, continues to show 'how God wants our society, nationally and internationally to be shaped', with 'full rights' for gay people, disabled people, and women worldwide. As with Blair (and indeed Obama), Stunell also used problematic biblical verses against others: if Christians want to oppose rights for homosexuals, why not oppose rights for people committing adultery? However, despite all the concerns about the Bible being outdated, Stunell's views ultimately remain grounded in the Bible and, at least on the basis of *Liberal Democrats Do God*, a favoured Lib Dem biblical passage, 'the recognition that if all six billion of us are made in God's image, we must all be treated equally and honestly by each other'.[12]

However, one essay received particular media mockery: the Introduction by Steve Webb (Minister of State for Pensions) and its claim that God is a liberal.[13] Webb acknowledged how Labour and Conservatives can corner the market on political engagement and Christianity but now wants to see the Liberal Democrats as having an important role:

> The most fundamental reason why a Christians should feel at home in the Liberal Democrats is that the character of God, as revealed in the Christian Gospel, would suggest that God must be a liberal! This assertion will

12. A. Stunell, 'Three Reasons to Thank God – and Not the Usual Ones', in Latham and Mathys (eds.), *Liberal Democrats Do God*, Chapter 4.

13. E.g. P. Dominiczak, 'Pray consider: would God be a Lib Dem or a Somerset Tory?', *Sunday Telegraph* (August 25, 2013); J. Groves, 'God? He's a Liberal, says (Lib Dem) minister who claims party has support of the Almighty despite languishing in the polls', *Daily Mail* (August 26, 2013); N. Lezard, 'In the beginning God said – Let there be Lib Dems', *Independent* (August 26, 2013).

shock or offend some, but I believe that there is no other conclusion that can be drawn from a reading of the New Testament. The Gospel makes it clear that human beings have freedom. Jesus makes it clear that God does not seek slaves, but sons and daughters. And God gave us the most extraordinary freedom – the freedom to reject and crucify his Son. There must be something very precious about freedom, a value dear to the heart of every liberal.[14]

Yet, this is not distinctively Liberal Democrat, even if it is entirely compatible with the Liberal tradition. Party-political name-dropping aside, Webb's formulation, intended or not, is close to how Thatcher understood the Bible. Even if Webb's assertion will 'shock or offend' the political and media establishment, perhaps it should not. As we saw with Thatcher (and Blair), fundamental to the Bible were ideas of personal moral responsibility, freedom, and individualism. Furthermore, like Webb, Thatcher even saw the crucifixion, and the idea that Jesus *chose* to die, as part of her take on individualism. Indeed, Thatcher's Bible is present elsewhere in Webb's Introduction:

> If the Almighty Creator of the universe does not impose his will on his creation, then we flawed individuals who are involved in the political process should be deeply cautious about using the power of the state to impose our will on others. Clearly there have to be frameworks and boundaries, and the state is right to impose those. But beyond this, our faith surely teaches us that we should be very wary of anything more coercive. Those who recognise in the Gospel a deep reverence for human freedom and self-determination will find a natural home in the Liberal Democrats.[15]

These ideas also echo Thatcher's interpretation of the Bible framed in terms of her opposition to socialism, Marxism, and Soviet Communism. Unlike some of the figures from the Radical Bible tradition (e.g. Tony Benn), but in common with a Tory tradition, original sin was important, as indeed it is elsewhere in *Liberal Democrats Do God*.[16] For Thatcher

14. S. Webb, 'Introduction', in Latham and Mathys (eds.), *Liberal Democrats Do God*. See also Mulholland, 'Liberalism', Chapter 3: '…anyone who denies me my right to believe in Jesus Christ is denying me of my right to believe in liberalism. That philosophical path is the road to intolerance, to undermining freedom of conscience, a road no true liberal would proceed along.'

15. Webb, 'Introduction'.

16. E.g. Tim Farron, 'What Is Christianity, Do I Need to Take It Seriously, and Can I Be a Liberal Democrat and a Christian?', in Latham and Mathys (eds.), *Liberal Democrats Do God*, Chapter 2: 'The Bible says many things that society will feel uncomfortable about with regards to personal morality. Given that Christians accept that the Bible is the word of the perfect God and that we are extremely

original sin and human imperfection were important, if only because of her dislike of the assumed opposite: the idea that human beings were able to achieve perfection. It is significant that for Thatcher that this sort of discussion was generated in the context of a criticism of socialism and state interventionism which, she argued, could not improve the 'moral condition' of the human being. This was not just part of Thatcher's attack on the role of the state but also her perception of utopian thinking that, she argued, marked socialism and which she thought inevitably led to the suppression of the individual and, ultimately, to the Gulag. For Thatcher, the Bible (or 'the Gospel'), and its apparent concerns for freedom and individualism, were part of the antidote to state-heavy thinking, even if, like Webb and other Liberal Democrats in the collection, she still saw a role for the state, albeit limited.

Among the louder echoes of Thatcher's Bible are comments about free trade and wealth, as might be expected from those grounded in the nineteenth-century Liberal tradition. John Pugh, for instance, claimed that 'all Liberals are passionate about free trade' and 'sceptical but supportive of state action'. But, like Thatcher, there is the issue of wealth which might be used irresponsibly. For Pugh, 'Liberals to a man and woman bemoan the unfairness of wealth distribution in our country and indeed the world' before noting two different types of Liberals: 'those reconciled to appreciable wealth inequality' and 'those who…remain unhappy about the wide distribution of wealth – extremes of wealth and poverty'. Blunt biblical verses may seem to attack inequality of wealth harder still by condemning wealth and the wealthy outright. However, as with Thatcher, and indeed Powell, these have to be interpreted differently. Pugh suggested that 'Christian Liberals of whatever hue have traditionally seen "wealth" itself as morally problematic' and in support cites arguably the most difficult passages but in a notably vague manner: 'the parable of Dives and Lazarus, the eye of the needle proverb etc.'. Echoing Powell, Pugh suggests that 'Christians are taught to be sceptical and indeed humble about any clear link between worldly achievement and genuine personal merit', adding that 'this isn't a simple matter' and that 'it doesn't necessarily follow that Christian Liberals would favour higher tax rates for the wealthy rather than the encouragement of philanthropy, or disown utterly any concept of "undeserving poor"'.[17]

---

imperfect human beings, then we should not be surprised if the Bible doesn't make us uncomfortable! But I also believe that we must never seek to legislate to force people who are not Christians to live as if they were.'

17. Pugh, 'Doing God'.

For all the mockery received at the hands of the press, the Liberal Democrat Bible, at least as presented in *Liberal Democrats Do God* and certainly in Webb's Introduction, is largely in line with Thatcher's Bible after the Blairite socially liberal qualification, and with occasional Liberal Democrat twists. Cameron likewise did not escape the gaze of the British press for his use of the Bible, though he has, as yet, failed to receive the mockery that Steve Webb did for *Liberal Democrats Do God*. Two of Cameron's most high-profile uses of the Bible were in his messages at Easter 2011 and Christmas 2012. These were a surprise to the British press, provoking comments such as 'an unusually Christian tone' (*New Statesman*), 'a little pious' (*Guardian*), and 'rare in British politics' (*Telegraph*). The *Daily Mail* claimed that Cameron has 'regularly ignored advice that politicians in the modern age should not "do God"' but 'went further than ever…when he quoted from the Bible'.[18] Perhaps such direct mention of the Gospels and Jesus were in contrast to what might have happened with Blair but Cameron's use of the Bible should by now be familiar in its general vagueness and broad consensual sentiment in that the Christmas story is about 'hope', that John's Gospel preaches grace, truth, love, and peace, that Easter is about God's mercy, and that Jesus' teaching on love remains relevant today:

> But Christmas also gives us the opportunity to remember the Christmas story – the story about the birth of Jesus Christ and the hope that he brings to the countless millions who follow him. The Gospel of John tells us that in this man was life, and that his life was the light of all mankind, and that he came with grace, truth and love. Indeed, God's word reminds us that Jesus was the Prince of Peace.[19]

> Easter is a time when Christians are reminded of God's mercy and celebrate the life of Christ. In the Gospel of Mark, Jesus taught us to love God and love our neighbour. He led by example and for millions of us his teachings are just as relevant now as they were in his lifetime.[20]

18. N. Watt, 'David Cameron ignores Alastair Campbell's advice as he does God', *Guardian* (April 27, 2011); J. Bingham, 'Cameron's olive branch to the Church in Christian Christmas message', *Telegraph* (December 24, 2012); C. Crampton, 'David Cameron's Christmas message', *New Statesman* (December 24, 2012); T. Shipman, 'PM's Christmas bid to calm Christian anger at gay marriage: David Cameron quotes Gospel of St John in annual message', *Daily Mail* (December 24, 2012).

19. Text available at: 'A Christmas message from David Cameron (December 25, 2012)', http://www.conservatives.com/News/News_stories/2012/12/A_Christmas_message_from_David_Cameron.aspx.

20. D. Cameron, 'David Cameron's Easter Message (April 24, 2011)', https://www.gov.uk/government/news/david-camerons-easter-message.

Cameron's premiership also coincided with a significant celebration that would take place on his watch: the 400th anniversary of the King James Bible in 2011. At the closing of the anniversary Cameron gave a speech where the major features of the Liberal Bible and the exegetical emphases of politicians such as Thatcher and Blair were present. Cameron suggested that Britain can still be understood as a *Christian* nation. What Cameron did not mean was equally important. He did not mean that Britain is, or should become, a theocracy nor that the British people should all be going to church, singing hymns, praying to God, fasting, dealing with heretics appropriately, vigorously converting non-believers, and so on. It would be a great surprise if Cameron did advocate such things given that he described his 'religious faith' as a 'typical member of the Church of England': it 'is a bit like the reception for Magic FM in the Chilterns: it sort of comes and goes'.[21] Instead, Cameron's vision of a Christian nation with the King James Bible at its heart is, as with Blair and Thatcher, a thoroughly liberalised notion of what a multicultural and multi-faith 'Christian country' ought to be, with anything unpalatable to this idea of the nation-state removed:

> [From] human rights and equality to our constitutional monarchy and parliamentary democracy...the first forms of welfare provision... language and culture... [T]he Judeo-Christian roots of the Bible also provide the foundations for protest and for the evolution of our freedom and democracy... [They form] the irrepressible foundation for equality and human rights, a foundation that has seen the Bible at the forefront of the emergence of democracy, the abolition of slavery and the emancipation of women... Responsibility, hard work, charity, compassion, humility, self-sacrifice, love, pride in working for the common good and honouring the social obligations we have to one another, to our families and our communities...these are the values we treasure. Yes, they are Christian values. And we should not be afraid to acknowledge that. But they are also values that speak to us all – to people of every faith and none.[22]

21.   The full quotation is: 'I believe, you know. I am a sort of typical member of the Church of England. As Boris Johnson once said, his religious faith is a bit like the reception for Magic FM in the Chilterns: it sort of comes and goes. That sums up a lot of people in the Church of England. We are racked with doubts, but sort of fundamentally believe, but don't sort of wear it on our sleeves or make too much of it. I think that is sort of where I am.' See N. Watt and P. Wintour, 'Interview: How David Cameron is trying to reinvent the Tories', *Guardian* (July 16, 2008).

22.   D. Cameron, 'Prime Minister's King James Bible Speech (December 16, 2010)', Number 10 Downing Street, http://www.number10.gov.uk/news/king-james-bible/. Cameron has since been more vocal in his more explicit Thatcherite use of the Bible to support the downplaying state provision and the promotion of charitable acts in their place, including his claim that 'Jesus invented the Big Society 2,000

Again, it would, presumably, be pointless asking what Cameron would have made of the details about Abishag the Shunammite keeping the ageing David warm in his bed, Joshua's conquest, posting parts of a chopped-up concubine, the cave of Adullam, smashing babies heads against rocks, labelling Gentiles 'dogs', condemning the rich to Hades, destroying idols, the weeping and gnashing of teeth, or, perhaps more pertinent still, using the King James Bible itself to convert heathens. Instead, the King James Bible and Christian values have to be understood in terms of liberal parliamentary democracy.

In the Age of Coalition, the King James Bible has also continued to survive through an emphasis on the Cultural Bible which was brought to the fore in the 400th anniversary celebrations. The following are the main aims of the King James Bible Trust, as found in their Mission Statement:

> Reflect the global importance of the King James Bible and the role it has played in spreading the English language around the world.
> Promote events and celebrations throughout 2011 to ensure that as many people as possible can encounter the King James Bible by the year's end.

The Mission Statement concludes:

> The Trust, an education and arts Trust, will highlight and debate the significant contribution that the King James Bible continues to make. Fundamentally the Trust is here to leave a lasting legacy for future generations, by ensuring that this great work of literature and learning is still read and taught in years to come.[23]

Developing her own views on the Liberal Bible, Yvonne Sherwood has noted the lack of concern in this Mission Statement for the historic role of the King James Bible in the combination of evangelism and empire.[24] And when the King James Bible Trust mention the King James Bible (and 'religion'), it is not about altars, blood, or sacrifice but a very contemporary form of liberal multiculturalism in the form of Liberal or Cultural Holy Scripture: 'The Trust is hard at work developing projects which will include…[d]iscussions about similar values in the texts of the world's major religions'.[25] The aesthetic and heritage angle was the position taken up by Richard Dawkins (a contributor to the promotional

---

years ago; I just want to see more of it'. I have discussed this in more detail at http://sheffieldbiblicalstudies.wordpress.com/2014/04/17/david-camerons-latest-bible/.

23. Available at http://www.kingjamesbibletrust.org/about-us/mission-statement.

24. Y. Sherwood, 'This Is Not a Bible/Ceçi n'est pas une Bible', unpublished paper delivered to the Biblical Literacy and the Curriculum Conference, University of Sheffield, May 25–28, 2011.

25. Available at http://www.kingjamesbibletrust.org/about-us.

material of the Trust). Whereas the decaffeinating of the Bible – the King James Bible in this instance – is culturally implicit, Dawkins, following a standard New Atheist line, remained happy to be explicit in wanting to highlight any problematic moral elements in the Bible and 'religion'. But once this can be accepted, Dawkins argued:

> I must admit that even I am a little taken aback at the biblical ignorance commonly displayed by people educated in more recent decades than I was... The King James Bible of 1611 – the Authorized Version – includes passages of outstanding literary merit in its own right... But the main reason the English Bible needs to be part of our education is that it is a major sourcebook for literary culture... Surely ignorance of the Bible is bound to impoverish one's appreciation of English literature... We can give up belief in God while not losing touch with a treasured heritage.[26]

The present and the immediate, coupled with culturally short attention spans, and mapped on to a rapidly changing yet increasingly standardised world, may indeed be a distinctive feature of our postmodern and neo-liberal age.[27] However, and probably because of this combination of unsettling, fragmentation, and homogenization, it is also an age of individual and collective nostalgia; or, as Mark Fisher put it, 'an age given over to retrospection, incapable of generating any authentic novelty'.[28] Such uses of the King James Bible are clearly present in Cameron's speech, the Mission Statement of the King James Bible Trust, and Dawkins' fight against what he perceives to be cultural ignorance.

Such fragmented memories, simultaneously nostalgic whilst forgetting other seemingly important, uncomfortable, and even dangerous issues, have a ready-made cultural icon in the King James Bible with its antiquated language and gold lettering on a leather-bound cover, not to mention numerous cultured supporters of its historic and aesthetic qualities. In May 2012, Gove, in his role as Education Secretary, and with the backing of private donors, took advantage of this cultural icon when he sent out copies of the King James Bible to English state schools with the following printed in gold on the spine: PRESENTED BY THE SECRETARY OF STATE FOR EDUCATION. Following the typical endorsements of the King James Bible in the 400th anniversary celebrations and beyond, Gove explained that he wanted this sent to schools because 'The King James Bible has had a profound impact on our

---

26. Dawkins, *The God Delusion*, pp. 340-41, 343, 344.

27. Harvey, *Condition of Postmodernity*, pp. 201-323; F. Jameson, *Seeds of Time* (New York: Columbia University Press, 1994).

28. Fisher, *Capitalist Realism*, p. 59; Harvey, *Condition of Postmodernity*, pp. 85-87.

culture... Every school pupil should have the opportunity to learn about this book and the impact it has had on our history, language, literature and democracy.'[29] It is worth noting that the Gove Bible neatly complements one of the most controversial aspects of Gove's time at the Department for Education, namely his early draft proposals for the History curriculum, which placed a strong emphasis on a patriotic narrative history of Britain and the importance of this history for national (effectively English) identity.[30]

The Gove Bible gained some weighty support. Once again Dawkins got partly in the mood by declaring his double-edged support for the Gove Bible. 'A native speaker of English who has never read a word of the King James Bible is verging on the barbarian,' proclaimed Dawkins, even if adding that his 'ulterior motive' was to expose the Bible for what it is: 'not a moral book and young people need to learn that important fact because they are very frequently told the opposite'.[31] The Gove Bible gained further endorsement in a 2012 Westminster discussion on Religion in Public Life featuring Tony Blair and Rowan Williams and chaired by the leading *Telegraph* journalist, Charles Moore.[32] Once again, all the familiar positions from the Liberal Bible and Cultural Bible were present. Moore (who also mentioned the 400th anniversary) called the Gove Bible 'a good politicised gesture' and added that the King James Bible represented a 'vital political act that helped unite the kingdom of Scotland and the kingdom of England and it helped to forge the United Kingdom and became the key text of our social order... [T]his is an essential part of how we come to be, what we are, and why we believe what we believe.' Williams acknowledged that the Gove Bible was an 'iconic gesture' but wanted to go further and see such a 'big, complicated text' in the hands of young people be given the support of wider investment in 'resources and energy in the whole educational establishment to

29. 'Schools get King James Bible to mark 400th anniversary', *BBC News*.

30. See e.g. A. Philipson, 'Leading historians back reforms to history curriculum', *Telegraph* (February 15, 2013); R.J. Evans, 'The Wonderfulness of Us (the Tory Interpretation of History)', *London Review of Books* 33 (March 17, 2011), pp. 9-12; R.J. Evans, 'Michael Gove's history curriculum is a pub quiz not an education', *New Statesman* (March 21, 2013); R. Garner, '"Jingoistic and illegal" – what teachers think of Michael Gove's national curriculum reforms', *Independent* (June 12, 2013); W. Mansell, 'Michael Gove redrafts new history curriculum after outcry', Guardian (June 21, 2013).

31. R. Dawkins, 'Why I want all our children to read the King James Bible', *Observer* (May 19, 2012).

32. The full debate (from which I have transcribed) is available at http://www.youtube.com/watch?v=1jE5z8UC_nk.

make it possible for the imagination of a child to respond fully to all that that means'. He wondered, 'What are the conditions that will make this work in a really constructive way, a really educating way?' Blair denied that the Gove Bible was 'an act of proselytization… [W]e're not trying to convert anyone by doing it'. Rather, he claimed that it's 'part of our tradition and history as a country… It's good that people understand it.'

2. Surviving Cynicism and the Noble Big Other

> Such then, I said, are our principles of theology—some tales are to be told, and others are not to be told to our disciples from their youth upwards, if we mean them to honour the gods and their parents, and to value friendship with one another.
>
> Yes; and I think that our principles are right, he said.
>
> But if they are to be courageous, must they not learn other lessons besides these, and lessons of such a kind as will take away the fear of death? Can any man be courageous who has the fear of death in him?
>
> Certainly not, he said.
>
> And can he be fearless of death, or will he choose death in battle rather than defeat and slavery, who believes the world below to be real and terrible?
>
> Impossible.
>
> Then we must assume a control over the narrators of this class of tales as well as over the others, and beg them not simply to revile but rather to commend the world below, intimating to them that their descriptions are untrue, and will do harm to our future warriors.
>
> That will be our duty, he said.
>
> Then, I said, we shall have to obliterate many obnoxious passages, beginning with the verses,
>
> 'I would rather be a serf on the land of a poor and portionless man than rule over all the dead who have come to nought.'
>
> …And we must beg Homer and the other poets not to be angry if we strike out these and similar passages, not because they are unpoetical, or unattractive to the popular ear, but because the greater the poetical charm of them, the less are they meet for the ears of boys and men who are meant to be free, and who should fear slavery more than death. (Plato, *Republic*, Book 3)

And yet…do plenty of schools not already have King James Bibles? Does or will anyone actually read them at those schools where Gove's Bible is present? Was not Rowan Williams being implicitly cynical in arguing for the need for wider educational resources to understand such a complicated text? Would it be overly cynical to suggest that donating King James Bibles to schools is an exercise in PR, or a further exercise in promoting Govian history? In fact, comments of sceptical inner-city teachers who will not be using the Bible or those who see through the apparent PR purposes of the exercise are (predictably?) found in the same newspaper reports as Gove's plan, as well as among sceptical liberal journalists and comedians, all providing outlets of cynicism in the same newspaper as the reports.[33] It would probably not be a great surprise if Cameron or Gove did not privately believe that the King James Bible would be taken up and read by even a handful of children in a given school. There is indeed a touch of scepticism when Dawkins wrote, 'I am a little shocked at the implication that not every school library already possesses a copy. Can that be true? What do they have, then? Harry Potter? Vampires?... But does anybody, even Gove, seriously think they will [read it]?'[34] Gove or Cameron would hardly write or speak openly like this at present but if one day they were able to speak openly, who knows? Yet all the while the official narrative of a grand, democratic, cultured English civilization associated with the King James Bible continues comparatively unchallenged despite the popular cynicism over readership. Presumably this is the real ideological function of this story.

Broadly speaking, this perpetuation of the official story despite the cynicism can be tied in with the unconscious fiction of the Big Other, which we can in turn tie in with the more overtly cynical tradition of the Noble Lie, associated (rightly or wrongly) with figures from Plato through Machiavelli to Leo Strauss. Much of the Lacanian work on the Big Other has been carried out by Slavoj Žižek and others and applied

33. J. Shepherd, 'Michael Gove's King James Bible plan rescued by millionaire Tory donors', *Guardian* (May 15, 2012); D. Mitchell, 'Michael Gove's biblical zeal is a ruse', *Observer* (May 20, 2012). A more dangerous level of exposing the emperor's nakedness is when it moves beyond the legitimate channels for holding power to account (e.g. liberal media). This was particularly clear in the WikiLeaks controversies. Here Žižek wrote of the 'shameless cynicism of the existing global order whose agents *only imagine that they believe in their ideas of democracy, human rights*, etc., and, through moves like the WikiLeaks disclosures, *the shame (our shame for tolerating such power over us) is made more shameful by publicizing it*' (S. Žižek, *Living in the End Times* [rev. edn; London: Verso, 2011], p. 410, italics original). WikiLeaks did not really reveal what was previously unknown ('The only truly surprising thing about the revelations is that there was no surprise in them: didn't we learn *exactly* what we expected to learn?' [Žižek, *Living in the End Times*, p. 408, italics original]). If there is any doubt about the potential dangers involved, if the revealing of the emperor's nakedness is not done through the correct channels and by the correct people, just recall what has since happened to Julian Assange, Bradley Manning, and Edward Snowden, all of whom have, in different ways, found their very lives threatened.

34. Dawkins, 'Why I want all our children'.

to contexts of postmodern capitalism (as well as Soviet Russia). We can think of this Big Other symbolically functioning as a figure who 'believes' the official, expected, or accepted public narratives, even if individuals really do not. Cynicism towards, disintegration and fragmentation of, and belief in, this Big Other have been a hallmark of postmodernity for Žižek.[35] Another feature of a reliance on the Big Other who 'really believes' involves a definition and function of 'culture', something particularly relevant to the King-James-Bible-as-heritage arguments. Žižek has argued that 'culture' has emerged as 'the central life-world category'. What this means is that when we deal with the topic of religion (or the public presentation of the Bible), people do not necessarily 'really believe' but rather 'just follow (some) religious rituals and mores as part of respect for the "lifestyle" of the community to which we belong (nonbelieving Jews obeying kosher rules "out of respect for tradition", etc.)'. As Žižek has suggested,

> 'I don't really believe in it, it's just part of my culture' effectively seems to be the predominant mode of the disavowed/displaced belief characteristic of our times. What is a cultural lifestyle, if not the fact that, although we don't believe in Santa Claus, there is a Christmas tree in every house, and even in public places, every December? ... '[C]ulture' is the name for all those things we practice without really believing in them, without 'taking them seriously'... Today, we ultimately perceive as a threat to culture those who live their culture immediately, those who lack a distance toward it. Recall the outrage when, two years ago, the Taliban forces in Afghanistan destroyed the ancient Buddhist statues at Bamiyan: although none of us enlightened Westerners believe in the divinity of the Buddha, we were outraged because the Taliban Muslims did not show the appropriate respect for the 'cultural heritage' of their own country and the entire world. Instead of believing through the other, like all people of culture, they really believed in their own religion, and thus had no great sensitivity toward the cultural value of the monuments of other religions – to them, the Buddha statues were just fake idols, not 'cultural treasures'.[36]

A distanced concern for 'our culture' and the cynical keeping up of appearances helps explain in part the function of Gove's Bible in schools and without, of course, recourse to anything too problematic like weighing up the merits of casting out Girgashites, debating whether ageing rulers should be warmed in bed by young women, discussing the impor-

35. E.g. S. Žižek, *The Ticklish Subject: The Absent Centre of Political Ontology* (London: Verso, 1999); S. Žižek, *For They Know Not What They Do: Enjoyment as a Political Factor* (2nd edn; London: Verso, 2008); Fisher, *Capitalist Realism*, pp. 44-50.

36. Žižek, *Puppet and the Dwarf*, pp. 7-8.

tance of speaking in tongues, or using the King James Bible to convert and colonise. After all, if a politician is deemed to believe *too much* it might, as Steve Webb found out, lead to the idea that a politician really believes in all the illiberal and alien material we all really know is in the Bible, and sometimes even practiced privately behind closed doors on a Sunday. The tension between enough God/Bible and too much God/ Bible – indeed a public God/Bible versus private God/Bible – is what a politician must negotiate and with no guarantee they will be represented fairly. Recall Gove's explanation of the need for the King James Bible in schools: 'Every school pupil should have the opportunity to learn about this book and the impact it has had on our history, language, literature and democracy'. Recall too Cameron's vocal support for the cultural heritage of the King James Bible. Fortunately for Gove and Cameron, their views tally with Dawkins' worries about the barbarianism of a life apart from the King James Bible and are an important indicator that they will not be ridiculed for believing in the more peculiar bits of the Bible we all know really exist, even if a politician can ill afford to admit it.

There is an assumption, then, that the King James Bible is, or should be, or must be, an obvious part of British and English cultural heritage. But in the case of both Dawkins and Gove there is clearly a fear that the ideological hinterland of the King James Bible could be under threat or even lost. In one sense, after going centuries unchallenged, the ongoing survival of the King James Bible is hardly a given and it could be seen as an unlikely survival story. The King James Bible is, after all, problematic in terms of its underlying Greek text-critical history, it is written in antiquated English, and it could potentially evoke scare stories of KJV-only 'fundamentalism'. Indeed, the standard explanation for the loss of its near monopoly in the English-speaking world is not particularly conducive to longer-term survival: by the turn of the twentieth century there was an increasing concern that the language of the King James Bible was too archaic for congregations and new Greek manuscript discoveries called into question *Textus Receptus*, thereby resulting in the King James Bible becoming one Bible among many by the end of the twentieth century. Moreover, the idea of the King James Bible as *the* Bible – or indeed *the* Book – of the British Empire may have left its mark on the colonies, but the decline of the Empire might be another reason to think that its days of influence in Britain were always going to be numbered.

And yet the King James Bible has continued to survive, even if in radically different ways from its pre-twentieth-century dominance. There are a number of general ideological reasons for its survival in Britain and in an era of postmodernity, commercialisation, and neoliberalism. As we saw in Chapter 1, the postmodern era has seen an explosion in different types of Bible with an accompanying fetish for the (re-)packaging of already existing biblical translations for a target audience or market, neatly replicating the relentless postmodern interest in multiple identities and a relentless quest for more markets. As we further saw in Chapter 1, image has played a crucial role in the survival or perpetuation of the Neoliberal Bible. As Katie Edwards has shown, the Bible in advertising only needs a split-second image to convey a range of 'common sense' meanings involving the intersection of (among other things) branding, gender, and nationalism.[37] As an embedded cultural icon, the King James Bible was ready to survive the numerous different Bibles on the market and in one sense it can take its place among, or alongside, the *Queen James Bible, The Soldiers' Bible, The Teen Bible for Girls*, or any number of the Zondervan specialised Bibles whose true meaning is instantly understood on sight. The distinctively branded King James Bible has managed to stand out and is instantly recognisable as a leather-bound text, with two columns, and a gold-coloured typesetting of 'Holy Bible' – possibly understood as *the* Bible – that might be bought for Christenings. Whether we know precisely that it was a Bible published in 1611 is another issue – its branding and image retains a certain ancient and nostalgic mystique while, explicitly or implicitly, remaining the authoritative Bible of English or British nationalism.

Throughout this book we have seen that the actual content of the Bible is not always significant for understanding what it 'really means' and in a world of instant imaging the content might be thought especially irrelevant. But we should qualify this, at least in terms of the survival of the King James Bible, as such well known, albeit isolated, verses continue to survive. Perhaps as much as anything it is the language of the King James Bible that has allowed it to survive and it has done so, in no small part, by a removal or downplaying of anything perceived to be too 'religious'. A major feature of David Crystal's book on the continued uses of King James Bible idioms is a relentless perpetuation of 'secularizing' and playful use of that which might be deemed 'religious' language.[38] Crystal has provided a wide range of famous phrases from the King James Bible (or King James 'sounding' phrases), from low and high culture, including those which have had a 'permanent influence on the development of the English language' (*Let there be light, My brother's keeper, Begat, Bread alone, Heal thyself*, and so on). He has

---

37. Edwards, *Ad Men and Eve*.

38. D. Crystal, *Begat: The King James Bible and the English Language* (Oxford: Oxford University Press, 2010).

shown that idioms are adapted, often with comical intent, with all sorts of unexpected language play (e.g. *Am I my brothel's keeper?*).[39] All these points are central to his analysis of the extent to which King James Bible idioms have 'permeated genres of modern spoken or written English', such as, for instance, marketing, journalism, sport, theatre, punk music, computing, and so on.[40] Likewise, one of the key reasons for survival of idioms (and not necessarily in the same form found in the King James Bible) is a range of phonetic properties, such as iambic rhythms (e.g. *...how the mighty have fallen!*) and rhyme, or indeed words which lend themselves to rhyme and thus adaptation (e.g. 'grave' as in *From the cradle to the grave*).[41] Crystal simultaneously pointed out that there is little evidence for lexical innovation and grammatical innovation and so, in this sense, the King James Bible is little more than a book of witty or useful idioms.

3. Surviving Postcolonialism

A dominant and important result from the analysis of Crystal's collection of idioms is that 'the items discussed...are not quotations: they are every-day expressions used by speakers and writers of modern English, most of whom will have no religious motivation for their use'.[42] Being so embedded in a wide range of cultural contexts should alert us to ways in which the Bible continues to survive in Western cultural contexts, striving to come to terms with secularism, nationalism, and global capital-ism. However, using a selection of texts from the King James Bible in the contemporary British media, R.S. Sugirtharajah argued that 'From the use of these quotations it is sometimes difficult to assess whether the sacred text of Christians is held in veneration or being mocked... [O]ne is often baffled as to whether the Sacred Word is held in reverence or taken for its comic value.'[43] Indeed; and yet playful or cynical irony is one way of maintaining and repackaging a dominant ideological position for our postmodern times whilst seemingly transgressing the traditional narratives and assumptions.[44] Sugirtharajah referred to the use of the

39. Crystal, *Begat*, p. 2.
40. Crystal, *Begat*, p. 261.
41. Crystal, *Begat*, pp. 75, 85, 261.
42. Crystal, *Begat*, p. 257.
43. R.S. Sugirtharajah, 'Loitering with Intent: Biblical Texts in Public Places', *BibInt* 11 (2003), pp. 567-78 (572-73).
44. S. Žižek, *The Sublime Object of Ideology* (London: Verso, 1989); S. Žižek, *Welcome to the Desert of the Real! Five Essays on September 11 and Related Dates*

King James Bible in sports reports and one example he gave comes from the *Guardian* and concerns the 'ritualized form of football results aired after the matches'. This example illustrates how the cultural capital of the King James Bible is maintained through playfulness and witty quasi-intellectual allusion:

> And these are the kings of the land whom Joshua and the children of Israel smote beyond Jordan westwards...
>> King of Jericho, one; the king of Ai, which is beside Beth-el, one.
>> The king of Jerusalem, one, the king of Hebron, one;
>> The king of Jarmuth, one; the king of Lachish, one;
>> The king of Eglon, one; the king of Gezer, one.
>> The king of Debir, one; the king of Geder, one[45]

We might note an even more irreverent example (among others) of the Bible in the British tabloids: the *Sun* (September 17, 2010) and its topless 'page three girl', Hollie, 22, from Manchester. Hollie, we are informed, 'was intrigued to see the Pope downing Fanta yesterday. She said: "Pontiffs have traditionally favoured fine wines. In fact, appellations were first mentioned in the Bible, and Pope John XXII was key in developing the renowned Châteauneuf-du-Pape in the 1300s."'[46] There may well be a comical element: a topless women explaining papal history is not, to my admittedly limited knowledge of such matters, common in traditional accounts. This Bible is not (necessarily) the King James Bible but it still implicitly suggests the Bible is part of our heritage and tradition. With such thoughts in mind, it is significant that in a study of the construction of 'religion' and the use of the Bible in the contemporary British press there was plenty of comedy, plenty on the Bible and Christianity as part of our cultural heritage, but very little in the way of directly attacking the Bible or even 'religion'.[47]

After reading a sample of examples from the British Press, Sugirtharajah suggested that 'the founding totem of the western world has now ended up in the popular press as "an erratic" and "an eccentric" cultural artifact sans religious authority or theological clout'.[48] Yet is this not

---

(London: Verso, 2002), p. 71 ('When we think we are making fun of the ruling ideology, we are merely strengthening its hold over us'); Crossley, *Jesus in an Age of Neoliberalism*, pp. 32-34.

45. Sugirtharajah, 'Loitering with Intent', p. 570, quoting Matthew Engel, 'Dark Angel', *Guardian*. Sugirtharajah was unable to supply the date of the *Guardian* article but estimated that it is from the 'middle 1990s'.

46. I owe this reference to Sarah Hussell.

47. Crossley and Harrison, 'Mediation'.

48. Sugirtharajah, 'Loitering with Intent', p. 577.

precisely the point? It *should* have lost its theological clout and religious authority *as traditionally understood.* The King James Bible, and the Bible and 'religion' more generally, still serve nationalism but have modified as capitalist liberal democracy has changed. This background should make us particularly aware of the nuanced ways in which biblical literacy might have functioned in a postmodern age. Dawkins' symbolic older generation (real or imaginary) may bemoan the lack of biblical literacy in the sense that people do not understand our 'treasured heritage' or have a detailed knowledge of its contents but on another level biblical literacy continues to function in such ways supportive of heritage whether individuals know it or not and whether they like it or not. Biblical literacy and/or the survival of the Bible work in part thanks to fast-paced recognition of certain biblical types and pithy sayings. The Bible has been marketed in endless ways and this has, to some extent, provided a means for its potential medium-term future. It has been adapted and adopted nostalgically as the text of liberty, freedom, democracy, gender equality. Of course, everyone knows that the King James Bible is not *really* going to be read chapter-by-chapter and cover-to-cover and that, for all the concerns about heritage, it is not without reason that it is precisely the book we might proverbially expect to prop up a table leg or gather dust. But the discourse of 'our heritage' retains its symbolic and nostalgic power, despite all the accompanying cynicism. Outside the realm of 'fundamentalist' readers, a dominant form of biblical literacy may now be said to reflect this decaffeinated Bible.

Yet, the seriousness of the imperial and globalising significance of the English Bible, sometimes assumed to be the King James Bible, was shown in the recent controversies over the announcement of the Patois Bible. The Patois Bible is part of a translation project that has been overseen by the Bible Society and designed to provide a translation for five million patois speakers in Jamaica and Britain.[49] Some of the reactions have been significant because there is the assumption that (a certain form of) English is the only language for worship and understanding. Prudence Dailey, chair of the Prayer Book Society, was reported to have claimed that 'I can see that a translation of this type could be useful, but I'd have reservations about its use in the context of public worship... I would want to encourage a style of worship which elevated people above the everyday and my fear with this is it might lose some of the sense of awe that we should have.' Conservative MP Ann Widdecombe was

49. J. Wynne-Jones, 'Bible to be turned into patois', *Telegraph* (October 11, 2008).

reported to have said that 'It's one thing to turn the Bible into modern vernacular, but to turn it into patois is utterly ridiculous. When you dumb down you take away any meaning it might have.'[50] God, it would seem, really does speak English but additionally, as Tim Footman put it, sports an MCC tie with the word of God enunciated in the cut-glass accent of Tonbridge Wells.[51]

Yet one critic was perhaps more of a surprise. Diane Abbott, the Labour MP for Hackney North and Stoke Newington and on the left of the party, claimed that in a British context the Patois Bible would imply that 'Jamaicans are not literate enough to understand the Bible in Standard English' despite the 'one book ordinary Jamaicans are brought up to read…is the Bible'. Abbott argued that it is an insult to 'ordinary Jamaicans' to claim that 'of all books, they cannot understand the Bible'. Abbott added further reasons against the Patois Bible. Patois, she claimed, 'is not essentially a written language', that translation of an English text 'loses half the vigour and charm of attempting to relate a Bible story in patois', and that for those who take 'the Bible and its theological meaning seriously' patois is unsatisfactory because it is 'a style of speaking which was never meant to be set out on paper and convey precise theological concepts'. However, Abbott added an argument based on the global economic significance of the English Bible:

> I also think that Jamaicans, whilst they should cherish patois, should also value Standard English. In economic terms, the fact that Jamaicans speak English as their first language is enormously important. English is the language of world commerce. In India, millions of dollars are poured into making sure educated Indians can speak good English, in order that they can compete in the call centre market. Jamaicans already speak English. But sometimes they seem to take this huge asset for granted. Patois is charming, but it will not help Jamaica compete in the international marketplace. Standard English will.[52]

In response to Abbott, Paul Williams made a number of counter-arguments. He pointed out that the majority of Jamaicans do not speak English and claimed that the implicit suggestion that the 'sanctity' of the Bible can only be upheld in Standard English downgrades Jamaican Creole. In one sense, Williams shares a similar assumption to Abbott on

---

50. Wynne-Jones, 'Bible to be turned into patois'.

51. T. Footman, 'The gospel according to Widdecombe', *Guardian* (October 14, 2008).

52. D. Abbott, 'Cherish J'can dialect, but please, no Patois Bible', *Jamaica Observer* (January 16, 2011).

the more global significance of translation for a standardised language (in this case the potential for Jamaican Creole). He noted, for instance, how widespread use of the mass media will perpetuate Jamaican Creole. In addition to Williams' claim that Abbott's views are 'tantamount to language discrimination', this sentiment brings Williams' Patois Bible also into line with the Liberal Bible or even the Neoliberal Bible. As Williams put it, 'discrimination in any way or form is not what we are striving for in this age of globalisation'.[53]

However, for all the movement towards the Neoliberal Bible, there is something ambiguous implicit in these turns to standardised and global-ised language that faintly echoes a more radical tradition in relation to colonisation and resistance. In her argument about the importance of the English Bible for global capitalism, Abbott's argument tacitly assumes the Patois Bible has a potentially counter-cultural function. Williams argued (citing R. Anthony Lewis) that European Christian colonisation primarily involved biblical texts and Bible translation and that all the talk about the Bible and Standard English is problematic because what is really at stake is the King James Bible and its antiquated language:

> Yes, many ordinary Jamaicans cannot read the Bible, especially the English of the King James Version, which is not Standard British English, much less Standard Jamaican English. There are problems with many of the words and phrasings, but even more important, many people are at a loss with the metaphoric and poetic language in which it is written.[54]

Williams did not explicitly connect the King James Bible with imperial-ism but it was, and is, the King James Bible that is the Bible of both the coloniser and the colonised. This tension was picked up by the Jamaican-born poet Linton Kwesi Johnson who, on the occasion of its 400th anniversary, noted that the King James Bible is simultaneously 'a most effective tool of colonisation' and '[was] the only [book] in my illiterate grandmother's house when I was a child in Jamaica'.[55]

As a poet, Johnson's recollections of the King James Bible are unsurprisingly in the tradition of the Cultural Bible. He pointed out, for instance, its influence on Jamaican popular music and oral culture. 'Used

---

53. P.H. Williams, 'Abbott, Patois Bible and language discrimination', *The Gleaner* (March 27, 2011).

54. Williams, 'Abbott, Patois Bible and language discrimination'.

55. L.K. Johnson, 'The King James Bible's language lessons', *Guardian* (February 19, 2011). See also B. Caesar, 'Interview: Linton Kwesi Johnson talks to Burt Caesar at Sparkside Studios, Brixton, London, 11 June 1996', *Critical Quarterly* 38 (1996), pp. 64-77.

with dexterity and wit', he added, 'biblical sayings are very powerful tools in the rhetoric of everyday discourse, and a rich repository of metaphor, simile, aphorism and imagery'. He recalled 'the language' of the Old Testament and the Psalms, some of which he could recite from memory, as his 'first real introduction to written verse' and so, he argued, 'it's not at all surprising that my verse has some biblical references'.[56] But when we turn to Johnson's poetry we see that he has used the Cultural Bible in line with the Radical Bible. 'Di Great Insohreckshan' and 'Mekkin Histri' both pick up on a long tradition, found in reggae, dub, and the Radical Bible tradition more generally, of a demonised power labelled 'Babylon'.[57] Both poems contain strongly confrontational anti-Babylon, anti-establishment sentiments, set up in dramatic 'apocalyptic' contexts and language use that comes close to the politically revolutionary. Both poems were written in the aftermath of the 1981 Brixton riots and explicitly contain settings in contemporary England. Furthermore, 'the tone', he argued, 'is celebratory because I wanted to capture the mood of exhilaration felt by black people at the time'. However, Johnson made further connections with the 2011 riots which began in Tottenham after Mark Duggan was killed by the police. When the riots began, Johnson was performing in Belgium with the Dennis Bovell Dub Band and recalled two particular performances, of 'Di Great Insohreckshan' and 'Mekkin Histri'. Bovell, a Tottenham resident, called Johnson on the night of August 6, 2011, to inform him of what was happening. Johnson reflected that if anything had changed some of the problems had worsened since the days of 'Di Great Insohreckshan' and 'Mekkin Histri':

> I was not at all surprised that the riots began in Tottenham in the light of the killing of Mark Duggan by a police officer and the history of conflict between the police and the black community in that part of London… It is clear to me that the causes of the riots are racial oppression and racial injustice, as well as class oppression and social injustice. The most widespread expression of discontent that I have ever witnessed in this country has to be seen in the context of the marginalisation of sections of the working class and the ideologically driven austerity measures of the Tory-led government.[58]

56. Johnson, 'King James Bible's language lessons'.

57. On Babylon and the Radical Bible, see e.g. C. Rowland and J. Roberts, *The Bible for Sinners: Interpretation in the Present Time* (London: SPCK, 2008).

58. L.K. Johnson, 'Trust between the police and the black community is still broken', *Guardian* (March 28, 2012).

Clearly, Johnson's ideological position is firmly in opposition to the political status quo, particularly on issues of race, class, and economics ('the Thatcher decade, was one of class struggle and racial conflict'[59]) and he has long identified with radical politics (he had joined the Black Panthers while at school). He is reported to have claimed that there 'doesn't seem to be a radical left anymore', that politics is now 'at the centre or right of centre', and that he does not vote in national elections.[60] When Thatcher died, he called her 'a ruthless class warrior for the ruling class' whose 'ignominious achievement was the tearing up of the post-World War Two "settlement", clawing back the gains the working class had won'. But he saw Thatcher as epitomising the political establishment: 'Her cross-party admiration stems from the fact that she is regarded as the architect of the neo-liberal orthodoxy to which they all subscribe, notwithstanding the dire straits in which the free market dogma has taken the British economy'.[61] Elsewhere he has reportedly gone further still, arguing that 'I think this government is the most extreme I have experienced in the nearly 50 years that I've lived in this country', and that they are 'using the financial crisis as a way of implementing neoliberal policies that even Mrs Thatcher in her heyday would not have contemplated'.[62] On issues of race, he claimed that 'Thatcher will be remembered by many black people of my generation as a bigot and a xenophobe who fanned the flames of racial hatred, giving succour to the fascists who were emboldened to carry out terrorist attacks against black and Asian people'.[63] The language Johnson used to explain advances in black integration since the 1980s in his reflections on the 2011 inner city riots is significant because it is openly that of the radical tradition: 'We had to resort to insurrection to integrate ourselves into British society'.[64]

Johnson has also located himself in distinction from black leaders in the political establishment, notably in the context of recalling the 2011 riots. Against the former chair of Equality, and Human Rights Commission and former chair of the London Assembly for the Labour Party, Trevor Phillips, Johnson argued that on the issue of policing and

---

59. L.K. Johnson, 'Thatcher and the inner city riots', *Huffington Post* (April 16, 2013), http://www.huffingtonpost.co.uk/linton-kwesi-johnson/margaret-thatcher-inner-city-riots_b_3081167.html.

60. S. Morrison, 'Linton Kwesi Johnson: "Class-ridden? Yes, but this is still home"', *Independent on Sunday* (December 2, 2012).

61. Johnson, 'Thatcher and the inner city riots'.

62. Morrison, 'Linton Kwesi Johnson'.

63. Johnson, 'Thatcher and the inner city riots'.

64. Johnson, 'Trust between the police and the black community is still broken'.

young black people nothing has changed since the uprisings of 1981, adding, 'Never mind what Trevor Phillips says'. He also endorsed comments by Joseph Harker, further commenting that 'the dozen or so black members of parliament are one step removed from their communities'.[65] Harker had previously claimed that,

> Today we have a dozen black MPs, including some in the Conservative party, but their backgrounds are a million miles from the community activism of their predecessors. Today's crop, well groomed in spin, ensure they remain on message. 'I'm not a black MP, just an MP who happens to be black', is their common refrain. Aside from Diane Abbott (also of the class of 87), can anyone imagine them speaking with the passion of a Grant or Boateng?[66]

Johnson's ideological position is significant in terms of the Radical Bible because, as his endorsement of Harker and his dismissal of Phillips further show, he is firmly outside Parliamentary and party-political discourse. While the King James Bible is so widely spread that it can still be utilised in a range of ideological positions and not so easily tied down to the political establishment alone, the Radical Bible, at least in this instance, would have no place in contemporary party-political discourse. Indeed, Johnson's Radical Bible is one example among others of the marginalisation of the Radical Bible which was once so central to the origins of the Labour movement.

4. What Ever Happened to the Radical Bible?

> Many peoples shall come and say, 'Come, let us go up to the mountain of the LORD, to the house of the God of Jacob; that he may teach us his ways and that we may walk in his paths'. For out of Zion shall go forth instruction, and the word of the LORD from Jerusalem. He shall judge between the nations, and shall arbitrate for many peoples; they shall beat their swords into ploughshares, and their spears into pruning-hooks; nation shall not lift up sword against nation, neither shall they learn war any more. (Isa. 2.3-4)

> Beat your ploughshares into swords, and your pruning-hooks into spears; let the weakling say, 'I am a warrior'. (Joel 3.10)

> He shall judge between many peoples, and shall arbitrate between strong nations far away; they shall beat their swords into ploughshares, and their spears into pruning-hooks; nation shall not lift up sword against nation, neither shall they learn war any more. (Mic. 4.3)

---

65. Johnson, 'Trust between the police and the black community is still broken'.

66. J. Harker, 'For black Britons, this is not the 80s revisited. It's worse', *Guardian* (August 11, 2011).

In Labour Party politics, the Radical Bible lost its power once the Bennite Left lost any serious influence with its defeat ultimately confirmed by the symbolic removal of Clause 4 and the rise of Blair. The Radical Bible was effectively pushed outside Parliament and party-politics, only retaining some connections on the fringes of the Labour Party, or its language brought into the fold of the Liberal Bible (see Chapter 8). However, just as radical politics survived outside Parliament and mainstream party politics, most notably the high-profile 'anti-globalisation' protests associated with, for instance, Seattle in 1999 or Genoa in 2001, so the Radical Bible was able to re-emerge in different, often independent and non-affiliated groups, albeit with more typical postmodern fragmentation than it had been when associated with the Labour and Communist parties. While 2008 may have brought about the Coalition it also generated a global movement in many ways at odds with dominant understandings of liberal democracy, at least in its relationship to capitalism: Occupy. In the post-2008 era, the Occupy movement provided an outlet for sustained, high-profile radical politics (as well as more liberal-reformist politics). The Occupy movement in the UK became geographically associated not only with the world of finance but also the Church: Occupy London Stock Exchange was located at St Paul's cathedral on land co-owned with the City of London Corporation. The presentation of the Anglican Church agonising about who to support was presented in terms of the radical tradition versus the establishment tradition, Giles Fraser versus the Bishop of London Richard Chartres, and ultimately picking up on what Roland Boer has argued is a political tension at the heart of Christianity and the Bible.[67] Or, as Marina Hyde put it with tongue partly in cheek, Fraser might imagine Jesus born in the camp but 'I could imagine St Paul siding with health and safety'.[68]

In addition to his claims that he 'could imagine Jesus being born in the camp',[69] Fraser, who resigned as canon chancellor of the cathedral after a vote to seek out possible legal advice on the eviction of the protestors, wanted to stress that St Paul's is 'not the parish church of the city, with

67. In addition to Boer's multi-volume project, *Criticism of Heaven and Earth* (2007–13), see e.g. Boer, *Rescuing the Bible*; R. Boer, *Political Grace: The Revolutionary Theology of John Calvin* (Louisville: WJK, 2009); R. Boer, *Political Myth: On the Use and Abuse of Biblical Themes* (Durham: Duke University Press, 2009).

68. M. Hyde, 'Jesus may be with Occupy London, but St Paul would have sided with health and safety', *Guardian* (October 28, 2011).

69. A. Rusbridger, 'Canon of St Paul's "unable to reconcile conscience with evicting protest camp"', *Guardian* (October 27, 2011).

its banks and livery companies' but rather 'the cathedral church for the whole of London... Its constituency includes some of the most deprived inner city estates in the whole of Europe.' He even framed this in language which became synonymous with Occupy: 'It does not exist as a gilded dressing-up box for the 1%, nor simply as a place of protest for the 99%, but a place of prayer for the 100%'. Fraser further inverted ownership of the biblical stories in making the comparison between the 'middle-class Englishmen' who wanted 'to address the financial crisis with well-meaning seminars and reports' and the 'nonviolent direct action...angry...scruffy...loud' Occupy camps who were 'much more like John the Baptist than your average Anglican cleric, who can be too easily conscripted within the bosom of the establishment'.[70] But for all the portrayal of the Occupy events in the media, Fraser (a former Trotskyite) tried to stress that he was not in fact an anti-capitalist campaigner and he remained on the liberal reformist wing of those sympathetic with Occupy. He has even been reported to have claimed that Jesus would have taken a more extreme position on modern capitalism; for Jesus, he claimed, 'the love of money is the root of all evil'.[71]

As it turned out, the Radical Jesus was indeed present in the protests. One of the enduring images from Occupy London Stock Exchange was a protester dressed up as Jesus (complete with white robe, beard, long hair, and crown of thorns) with a sign bearing an allusion to a favourite story from the Radical Bible tradition: I THREW OUT THE MONEY-CHANGERS FOR A REASON.[72] The story of Jesus and the money-changers (Matt. 21.12-13; Mark 11.15-17; Luke 19.45-46; John 2.13-22) was repeated throughout the reporting on Occupy London, particularly in the left-leaning *Guardian*. Terry Eagleton, for instance, picked up on Jesus' actions in the Temple as a point of comparison to Occupy London, adding that cathedral staff were lucky that the demonstrators did not behave as badly as their master. Jesus would have probably 'understood what those currently shivering outside St Paul's are up to' and by throwing the 'ruling caste of a holy place into an unholy panic, just as he did', the protestors are, to that extent, followers of Jesus, even if they 'despise religion'. In fact, Eagleton went as far as claiming that Jesus' actions in the Temple showed that he 'was at one with a later Jewish prophet, Karl Marx, whose concept of alienation involves just such a

70. G. Fraser, 'Occupy London's eviction is a failure for the church, not the camp', *Guardian* (January 31, 2012).

71. Rusbridger, 'Canon of St Paul's'.

72. S. Hill, 'Would Jesus kick the Occupy London protesters off St Paul's grounds?', *Guardian* (October 20, 2011).

break between the product and the producer'.[73] Worth comparing here is one Liberal Democrat use of the story of Jesus and the moneychangers which is given a more reformist spin: 'All Liberals are passionate about free trade... Christians, perhaps following the example of Christ in the Temple, are more prone to question the scope and place of market behaviour and to encourage the state to do likewise.'[74]

And Jesus was not just in London. On the main outward-facing tent at Occupy Sheffield (located on the forecourt of Sheffield Cathedral) the words FORGIVE US OUR TRESPASSES were visible in large letters, topped only in size by OCCUPY SHEFFIELD and with the notable (and popular) variant of 'trespasses' over 'debts' or 'sins' (cf. Matt. 6.12; Luke 11.4) which may sound like a KJVism (and which may be the point) but was in fact made famous from the version in the Book of Common Prayer and the Tyndale Bible before it. A curious aside on Occupy Sheffield is worth mentioning. I spoke to some of those camped outside Sheffield Cathedral and asked them about the significance of using the Bible and locating themselves in front of a cathedral. The constant answer was that the biblical references simply appeared appropriate given the location and that the location was only significant because it was one of the few places that provided ample space in the city centre and emphatically not because of any symbolism involved in a cathedral. Of course, this may not have been the view of all those at Occupy Sheffield but there is a potentially significant issue concerning the lack of intentionality among those participants I had spoken to. It is precisely because the *cathedral* (rather than any number of privately owned shops and spaces) has the symbolic advantage of such city central, publicly accessible space that arguably gave Occupy Sheffield its high-profile locally and presumably facilitated or generated, to some degree, the prominent use of the Bible in its visual protests.

Of course, Occupy has its precursors and has grown out of a range of significant leftist movements which had come to, or gained further, prominence post-1968. As we saw in Chapter 2, in their English and British manifestations such groups did not necessarily (though some, of course, did) have strong ties to the Communist Party or even to Marxist groups (e.g. direct action, anarchism, environmentalism, feminism, animal rights activism, CND, Greenham Common Women's Peace Camp, various radical leftist religious movements, McLibel, Stop the War Coalition). One of the most high-profile English examples of the past

---

73. T. Eagleton, 'Occupy London are true followers of Jesus, even if they despise religion', *Guardian* (November 3, 2011).

74. Pugh, 'Doing God'.

twenty-five years was when Andrea Needham, Joanna Wilson, and Lotta
Kronlid broke into a British Aerospace factory at Warton, Lancashire, in
January 1996. They caused an estimated £1.7 million damage to a Hawk
jet destined to be used by the Indonesian government against East Timor
after a deal signed by the British government in 1993. Another colleague,
Angie Zelter, was later arrested after she claimed she would continue the
actions of the others.[75] The group were known as 'Seeds of Hope – East
Timor Ploughshares' which invoked the prophetic language of Isaiah
2.3-4, Joel 3.10, and Micah 4.3 in support of their aims and which was
further emphasised when a 'Swords into Ploughshares' banner was
unfurled on the jet. The case was brought to Liverpool Crown Court
where, due to legal planning of their actions, the Ploughshares Four were
acquitted. During the protests and support surrounding the trial at
Liverpool Crown Court, a Bible was placed outside on a mini-altar-like
small box with Father Fitzgerald from St Michael's Church, Liverpool,
praying, and with the protests and support visually dominated by a
procession of crosses.[76]

  With inspiration from the Catholic Worker Movement, the largely
American-based Plowshares Movement which began in 1980 became a
non-violent, direct action group typically associated with issues relating
to the nuclear arms race and nuclear war. It grew out of direct action and
protests against the Vietnam War in the late 1960s by the Catholic priest
Daniel Berrigan and his brother and former Catholic priest, Philip
Berrigan. This Catholic tradition is not only ecumenical but also includes
figures, including British Ploughshares members, who do not identify as
Christian. This is significant because an assumption has remained that
the (Radical) Bible still has some cultural power for political engagement. For instance, one of the Ploughshares Four claimed, 'I'm not a
Christian myself and many other people who've done ploughshares
aren't Christians or any other spiritual or political [background] or any
other sort of background so it's more taking this beautiful vision [of
swords into ploughshares] seriously and taking inspiration from it'.[77] We

75. For summaries see e.g. 'Seeds of Hope – East Timor Ploughshares', *Catholic Social Teaching*, http://www.catholicsocialteaching.org.uk/themes/peace/stories/seeds-hope-east-timor-ploughares/; H. O'Shaughnessy and M. Brace, 'Campaigners face jail for raid on military jet', *Independent* (July 21, 1996).

76. The documentary, from which I have transcribed, 'SEEDS OF HOPE - Women Disarming for Life and Justice', is available at http://tinyurl.com/og2nou9.

77. 'Women Disarming for Life and Justice'. Cf. 'Not all of the women were Christian but because they needed the support of other like-minded people, they joined the Ploughshares Movement, a predominantly Christian movement, whose

might further add that in some ways this could be seen as a leftist equivalent of the 'respect for culture' without 'really believing' argument we saw above in the reception of the King James or Cultural Bible.

5. Same-sex Marriage or Subversive Love? The Case of Peter Tatchell

Another helpful example of seeing how the Radical Bible can differ from the Liberal Bible and how it functions in relation to parliamentary politics is the issue of civil partnerships and parliamentary discussion of same-sex marriage in 2013. We saw in Chapter 8 how on such issues Labour MPs David Lammy and Toby Perkins, like Tony Blair before them, could draw on radical rhetoric about Jesus and bring it in line with the Liberal Bible tradition more ideologically suited to the contemporary Labour Party. Taken alone, their comments on what they perceived to be the inclusive message of Jesus could potentially belong to either the Radical Bible or the Liberal Bible but when analysed in the wider context of their politics, it is clear that both belong firmly in the tradition of the Liberal Bible. By way of contrast we might turn to the gay rights campaigner and atheist Peter Tatchell. Tatchell is perhaps an unlikely torchbearer for the perpetuation of the Bible but as he claimed: 'To paraphrase my Christian upbringing, my own conscience won't allow me to walk by on the other side of the street. I ditched my faith a long time ago, but I think we've all got a duty to be good Samaritans towards other human beings who are suffering.'[78] Throughout his career, Tatchell has been alongside the Radical Bible on the fringes of parliamentary politics, from the notorious homophobic campaign against him in the 1983 Bermondsey by-election to his attempt to become a Green Party MP for Oxford East. Tatchell's position in relation to the centre of political power reveals some notably different emphases on Jesus and same-sex marriage from Lammy, Perkins, and Blair but again it involves looking at the bigger ideological picture.

One notable use of Jesus and the Bible by Tatchell ultimately relates to his ideological position in relation to love, sexuality, and same-sex marriage: his discussion of the (alleged) discovery by Morton Smith of a fragment of manuscript claimed to have been found at the Mar Saba

members do not hesitate to take direct action to create a more peaceful world once all other means have failed' ('Seeds of Hope – East Timor Ploughshares').

78. 'Coming Out as Atheist: Peter Tatchell, Grayson Perry', *National Secular Society* (December 2, 2005), http://www.secularism.org.uk/comingoutasatheist petertatchellg.html.

monastery near Jerusalem in 1958 which was meant to be part of the text of Mark's Gospel (Mark 10, between vv. 34-35). The Secret Gospel of Mark, as it has become known, contained some potentially saucy verses:

> And the youth, looking upon him (Jesus), loved him and beseeched that he might remain with him. And going out of the tomb, they went into the house of the youth, for he was rich. And after six days, Jesus instructed him and, at evening, the youth came to him wearing a linen cloth over his naked body. And he remained with him that night, for Jesus taught him the mystery of the Kingdom of God.[79]

For those unfamiliar with scholarship on Christian origins, there is a fierce debate over whether we are dealing with a genuine discovery of a genuinely ancient text or whether it was a hoax by Morton Smith, thereby making him second only to N.T. Wrong as the greater prankster in modern biblical studies. Tatchell, however, had a different take on the controversy which has received less attention in critical biblical studies:

> The veracity of this manuscript is hotly contested by other Biblical scholars. This comes as no surprise. The revelation of a gay Jesus would undermine some of the most fundamental tenets of orthodox Christianity, including its rampant homophobia.

If genuine, Tatchell wondered what this text might tell us about Jesus and homosexuality. His answer was that it remains difficult to know anything for certain because the 'precise nature of the relationship between Christ and the youth is not spelled out'. As Tatchell argued that the Bible has nothing to say on the matter then that would leave us with no real information. However, he added the following qualification:

> This absence of firm information does not, of course, mean that we can take it for granted that Christ was heterosexual. Far from it! The lack of information about his erotic inclinations begs more questions than it answers.
>
> The truth is that we simply don't know whether Jesus was straight, gay, bisexual or celibate. There is certainly no evidence for the Church's unspoken presumption that he was either heterosexual or devoid of carnal desires. Since nothing in the Bible points to Christ having erotic feelings for women, or relationships with the female sex, the possibility of him being gay cannot be discounted.
>
> In the absence of any evidence – let alone proof – that Jesus was heterosexual, the theological basis of Church homophobia is all the more shaky and indefensible. How can established religion dare denounce homosexuality when the founder of its faith was himself a man of mysterious, unknown sexuality who could, for all we know, have been homosexual?

79. P. Tatchell, 'Was Jesus Gay?', *Peter Tatchell* (March 18, 1996), http://www.petertatchell.net/religion/jesus.htm.

The Bible tells us that Jesus was born a man and therefore presumably had male sexual feelings. It would have been more or less impossible, biologically, for him not to have an element of erotic arousal – even if only having the normal male response of waking with an erection.[80]

While there are undoubtedly provocative elements in Tatchell's suggestion – and more so if they were to be uttered in Parliament – they could still be part of a more provocative Liberal Bible tradition; it is easy enough to find contemporary writers of a liberal persuasion talking about erections and erotic arousal in relation to canonical texts such as the Bible. This is why it is important to contextualise Tatchell ideologically, just as it was Lammy, Perkins, and Blair. We might, for instance, turn to other uses of the Bible by Tatchell. For example, Tatchell received a standing ovation at the Greenbelt Christian festival for attacking church leaders who condone homophobia but praised 'brave, heroic Christians who refuse to go along with the persecution of people who are gay, lesbian or bisexual'. But Tatchell's presence at Greenbelt was condemned by Anglican Mainstream who had even claimed that Greenbelt had put children at risk by including Tatchell on the programme. Tatchell's response was to insist that 'I'm a great believer in free speech; that includes people criticising me' and added that he had been misquoted. He then accused his detractors of bearing false witness: 'I would urge Anglican Mainstream to re-read their ten commandments'.[81] As we saw in Chapter 1, the Ten Commandments recur in the Liberal Bible tradition, regularly deemed integral to western law and democracy, despite their contents. This, of course, means that Tatchell could still be seen within the Liberal Bible tradition but there were hints of a more radical ideological position, particularly in his emphasis on challenging the establishment status quo. In his otherwise popular Greenbelt speech, he more uncomfortably accused Rowan Williams (then Archbishop of Canterbury) of 'colluding' in the persecution of LGBT people: 'The Anglican Church and Archbishop Rowan Williams have a lot to answer for, because they have put church unity before human rights'.[82]

But it is when we turn to Tatchell on same-sex marriage that we see his position on Jesus as being part of the Radical Bible tradition. It is significant that there is no mention of marriage in Tatchell's speculations about Jesus in relation to Secret Mark but there was plenty of speculation about sex and relationships. And in his speculations there was *nothing*

80. Tatchell, 'Was Jesus Gay?'

81. Staff writers, 'Tatchell given standing ovation at Christian festival', *Ekklesia* (August 30, 2010), http://www.ekklesia.co.uk/node/12977.

82. Staff writers, 'Tatchell given standing ovation'.

about whether Jesus may or may not have been married, unlike so much contemporary popular speculation about Jesus. This sentiment of a more anarchic free-love clearly has much more in common with Christopher Hill's radicals of *World Turned Upside Down* than it does with the endorsement of and respect for the institute of marriage we find with Lammy or Perkins. This is consistent with Tatchell's own views on same-sex marriage which is not as positive as might initially be thought for someone known to have campaigned in favour of them. This is because his reasons for campaigning for same-sex marriage, as well as opposite-sex civil partnerships, are about non-discrimination and full equality before the law.[83] Tatchell has even called same-sex marriage a Conservative value and something Tories would deem alongside family as vital for social stability.[84] Tatchell has further claimed that he is not premising his arguments on a 'support for marriage per se' and is 'no great fan of wedlock'. Indeed, he has proposed what he calls a 'radical alternative' to marriage: a 'civil commitment pact' where 'a person can nominate as next-of-kin and beneficiary any "significant other" in their life.'[85] But Tatchell wants to be able to refuse as well as to uphold the 'right of same-sex couples to marry and be just as happy – or miserable – as married heterosexuals.' Perhaps here we have the same sentiment as that found in a reworded form of the old Bill Hicks joke on whether homosexuals should be allowed in the American military: anyone stupid enough to want to get married should be allowed to do so.

However, in an article discussing Tatchell's ideological position, Jin Haritaworn with Tamsila Tauqir and Esra Erdem controversially presented him as a kind of white, liberal imperialist and an Islamophobe in the context of liberal Orientalism in the 'war on terror'.[86] While Haritaworn, Tauqir, and Erdem acknowledged Tatchell's place on the British Left, if their assessment of Tatchell is correct then this could bring Tatchell closer to the Blair agenda we saw in Chapter 8. Of course,

83. See e.g. P. Tatchell, 'Ban on same-sex marriage must be lifted', *Independent* (June 15, 2010); P. Tatchell, 'A marriage of equals', *Guardian* (September 18, 2011); P. Tatchell, 'The same-sex marriage bill does not live up to its aspiration of equality', *Guardian* (May 20, 2013).

84. P. Tatchell, 'Gay marriage is a Conservative value', *Peter Tatchell* (October 13, 2011), http://www.petertatchell.net/lgbt_rights/partnerships/how-the-tories-were-won-to-marriage-equality.htm.

85. Tatchell, 'The same-sex marriage bill'.

86. J. Haritaworn with T. Tauqir and E. Erdem, 'Gay Imperialism: Gender and Sexuality Discourse in the "War on Terror"', in A. Kuntsman and E. Miyake (eds.), *Out of Place: Silencing Voices on Queerness/Raciality* (York: Raw Nerve Books, 2008), pp. 71-95.

matters might be more complex still. Tatchell may be perceived to be part of, or even taken up by, an Orientalising construction of the liberal West; as he has pointed out himself, Tatchell has been accused of being anti-Palestinian, anti-Semitic, Islamophobic, an agent of Mossad, a far-right racist, and an all-round gay imperialist.[87] While wider cultural invocation of gender and sexuality in support for the 'war on terror' is clear enough,[88] this is not obvious in the case of Tatchell. Indeed, Tatchell gained an apology from the publishers for his representation as a gay imperialist, though this provoked further debate over issues of censorship.[89] Moreover, a good case can be made for Tatchell's own words and actions being ideologically understood as something like a democratic radicalism and he is clearly different from liberal figures surrounding the Euston Manifesto and related pro-Iraq War liberals such as David Aaranovitch, Julie Burchill, Christopher Hitchens, and Nick Cohen, or indeed a long tradition of liberal interventionism.[90] If Lammy ticks off a checklist of New Labour concerns, then Tatchell ticks off a checklist of contemporary radical leftist concerns (as the apology to Tatchell made clear): he is a defender of Palestinian rights, a critic of anti-Semitism, an anti-war campaigner (including those on Iraq and Afghanistan), an outspoken anti-fascist, hostile to Islamophobia, advocate and practitioner of direct action (which has brought him in conflict with the parliamentary Labour Party), and has taken a few beatings in his time for holding such views.[91] What unites Tatchell's different interests is his insistence on tying these agendas in with his agenda of combating homophobia. Indeed, he argued as part of his case for being critical of homophobia in African countries that it is not imposing colonial attitudes and that he is not advocating benign imperialism; on the contrary, he claimed, homophobic laws are 'not genuinely African laws. They're laws that were

87.   P. Tatchell, 'Academics smear Peter Tatchell', Peter Tatchell (n.d.) http://www.petertatchell.net/politics/academics-smear-peter-tatchell.htm; staff writers, 'Peter Tatchell accuses academics of smearing him', *Pink News* (November 3, 2009), http://www.pinknews.co.uk/2009/11/03/peter-tatchell-accuses-academics-of-smearing-him/.

88.   See also J. Puar, *Terrorist Assemblages: Homonationalism in Queer Times* (Durham: Duke University Press, 2007).

89.   E.g. U. Erel and C. Klesse, 'Out of Place: Silencing Voices on Queerness/Raciality', *MR Zine* (October 24, 2009), http://mrzine.monthlyreview.org/2009/ek241009.html; Tatchell, 'Academics smear Peter Tatchell'. The apology to Tatchell is available at http://www.rawnervebooks.co.uk/Peter_Tatchell.pdf.

90.   E.g. Seymour, *Liberal Defence of Murder*; Dillon and Reid, *Liberal Way of War*.

91.   See the range of articles at http://www.petertatchell.net/politics/.

inspired by a conquering imperial power.'[92] Of course, we might legitimately dispute the argument about what constitutes 'genuine African'
and 'imperial' in this context, but the evidence is clear on Tatchell's
ideological position: Tatchell's gay activism and, implicitly, his understanding of Jesus and sexuality, are part of radical leftist thinking and
serve as a transmitter of the Radical Bible tradition. Indeed, it might be
said that Tatchell and his Bible have something in common with the
famous comments of Raoul Vaneigem from 1967: 'Anyone who talks
about revolution and class struggle without referring explicitly to
everyday life – without understanding what is subversive about love and
positive in the refusal of constraints – has a corpse in their mouth'.[93]

92. Staff writers, 'Tatchell given standing ovation'.
93. R. Vaneigem, *The Revolution of Everyday Life* (London: Rebel Press, 1983
[orig. 1967]), p. 11.

CONCLUSION:
WHY DO POLITICIANS BOTHER WITH THE BIBLE?

Throughout this book we have seen how the social upheavals of the 1960s generated both radical and reactionary trends which were harnessed in the shift from Keynesianism to neoliberalism, from the post-war consensus to the emergence and consolidation of Thatcherism. Politicised biblical interpretation followed suit and was modified in light of major international political concerns, most notably the Cold War and the War on Terror. One of the other notable features of this period was that the Radical Bible was effectively pushed to the fringes of parliamentary politics or outside parliamentary politics altogether. Thatcher's Bible of individualism, personal responsibility and morality, parliamentary democracy, tolerance, and liberal economics was effectively endorsed by Blair who developed a number of Thatcherite emphases in different directions, including issues of tolerance in the direction of social liberalism. The Blair-modified Thatcher Bible is effectively the Bible of the contemporary Conservative-led government and for the more high-profile users of the Bible among the Labour Party. Whether this Bible survives the longer-term impact of the 2008 recession no doubt depends on the fate of neoliberalism but there is no serious indication as yet of major cultural and ideological shifts; on the contrary, neoliberalism and social liberalism remain dominant (but not the only) ideological positions, seemingly embedded in the current generation.

For all the referencing of Alastair Campbell in the press, politicians do 'do God', or at least cite the Bible. Indeed, Nick Spencer has even suggested that there may even be a gradual rise of the use of the Bible in contemporary English politics.[1] But what is clear from a range of figures covered in this book is that the Bible somewhat conveniently coheres broadly (though in a rhetorically non-partisan way) with a given politician's political persuasions, something hardly uncommon in the history of English politics. This is, of course, a broader cultural phenomenon.

1. Spencer, *Freedom and Order*, Chapter 11.

Building on the ethnographic work of Brian Malley, Deane Galbraith has pointed out that in the evangelical Christian Bible-reading analysed, issues that are not necessarily even mentioned in the Bible are not only still discussed but answers framed in terms of 'what the Bible says on the matter'. Galbraith noted that by 'utilizing the broader concept of "God's word", many evangelical Christians are able to pronounce on what the Bible says about even entirely novel issues, such as global warming or stem-cell research'.[2] This emphasis on the emphases of the reader is crucial for understanding English political discourse.[3] That people make the Bible mean whatever they want it to mean probably will not come as a great surprise to readers. Even so, why would an English politician bother using the Bible at all? There is no European-style Christian Democratic party of any note. It is not as if there is a serious block of Bible-loving voters, or even a significant 'Christian vote', who might potentially swing an election, even if there is evidence, as Martin Steven has presented, that parties know not to ignore denominational and 'religious' votes.[4] Indeed, we might recall Campbell's concerns about the British electorate possibly even hating the idea of politicians using the Bible all the time.[5]

Furthermore, politicians who quite clearly do not claim that God or the Bible agrees with their given political party, are likely to be the subject of ridicule for claiming God does support their party, as we saw (Chapter 9) with the press reaction to Steve Webb and the Liberal Democrats who professed to 'do God'. Why risk press humiliation in navigating too far away from the Safe Bible and towards the Feral Bible? Similarly, it is also clear that there is no danger to a politician to express doubts about faith, before returning to the Bible for support. We have seen this even with the Prime Minster David Cameron. Shirley Williams, one of the most recognisable Christian politicians in the late twentieth century,

2. D. Galbraith, 'The Author of the Bible Revealed! And it's you', *Religion Bulletin* (December 17, 2010), http://www.equinoxpub.com/blog/2010/12/the-author-of-the-bible-revealed/, referring to B. Malley, *How the Bible Works: An Anthropological Study of Evangelical Biblicism* (Walnut Creek: AltaMira, 2004) and B. Malley, 'Understanding the Bible's Influence', in J.S. Bielo (ed.), *The Social Life of Scriptures: Cross-Cultural Perspectives on Biblicism* (New Brunswick, NJ: Rutgers University Press, 2009), pp. 194-204.

3. Spencer, *Freedom and Order*, Introduction, qualifies the idea that the reader is the author of the book but is likewise aware of the complexity of the wide-range of political issues in the Bible and the significance of the cultural context of the political reader.

4. Steven, *Christianity and Party Politics*, pp. 36-64.

5. Campbell, *The Blair Years*, pp. 111-12.

could even reflect that 'I am, however, a person of my times, and therefore in this secular society, beset by doubt. Of all the apostles, the one I find most congenial is St Thomas. They called him "doubting Thomas".'[6] Yet it is notable that Williams, like Cameron, still turned to the Bible to defend principles deemed culturally important. So why have politicians in the UK used the Bible?

One obvious reason which partly explains uses by Blair in particular is that a given politician is a dedicated Christian for whom the Bible has had a central role in their life. But this does not explain plenty of other political figures such as Cameron or arguably even Powell. Another reason might be inherited language. Knowledge of specific biblical passages may indeed not be what it was in the seventeenth century but the Bible is deeply embedded in the history of parliamentary politics and British European history more broadly. It is no surprise that vestiges of this language remain today, even if the 1960s represented a dramatic change in the influence of the Church, a sharp decline in church atten-dance, and the decline of a quasi-Protestant form of biblical literacy. Indeed, the two political parties of the past 40 years have historic tradi-tions of Bible-use and significant Christian influences, whether Tory Anglicanism or Labour Nonconformism, in addition to Liberal Non-conformism. Again, it is no surprise that vestiges of such party traditions remain.

There are more local reasons still. The Bible might be used to gain, or at least not lose, the support of different constituencies, in the way that Thatcher did in attracting strands of morally conservative Christianity in the 1970s. There might not be a significant enough voting constituency which appreciates Bible references but there is presumably no harm in trying to keep them – or indeed Christian lobbyists[7] – happy with vague references and allusions that will not alienate those less impressed. Use of the Bible might also function as a means to keep the peace with church groups or Bishops in the House of Lords, or indeed as a sop to disgruntled elements of a given party. In the case of Blair, we saw that he employed the language of the Radical Bible, or at least biblical language at the heart of the Labour movement's history, to try and convince a sceptical party of the case for the invasion of Iraq. In the case of the Tories and their supporters in the media, there continues to be an element in the party dedicated to issues of 'traditional' morality and Christianity (and with some notably high-profile conversions to Catholicism in

6. S. Williams, *God and Caesar: Personal Reflections on Politics and Religion* (London and New York: Continuum, 2003), p. 21.

7. On which see further, Steven, *Christianity and Party Politics*, pp. 105-20.

protest at the apparent Anglican 'liberalism').[8] Moreover, a well-placed use of the Bible might even gain a potentially positive mention from the often hostile right-wing press. Despite Blair being a Bible-user, the *Daily Mail* reported Gordon Brown's speech at St Paul's Cathedral in 2009 as 'an extraordinary break from his predecessor Tony Blair, whose spin doctor Alastair Campbell famously declared that "we don't do God"' and ran with the headline, 'Brown DOES do God as he calls for new world order in sermon at St Paul's'.[9] Similarly, and despite the more extensive Christian rhetoric and speeches of Thatcher, the *Telegraph* claimed that 'David Cameron adopted the most overtly Christian tone of any prime minister in recent memory with a Christmas address speaking of faith giving hope to "countless millions"'.[10] The *Daily Mail* likewise reported the same story with a similar opening line ('David Cameron offered an olive branch to Christians last night, issuing the most overtly religious Christmas message by a prime minister in recent times') but interpreted it further in the headline in light of a particularly contro-versial issue for contemporary Conservatism: 'PM's Christmas bid to calm Christian anger at gay marriage: David Cameron quotes Gospel of St John in annual message'.[11]

The Bible may also represent some kind of implicit or explicit authority for a politician or political position, which partly explains why the Cultural Bible appears across the political spectrum. Recalling a story and debate from his early career as a biblical scholar at the beginning of his book on the Bible in American politics, Jacques Berlinerblau wrote about 'the most profound insight I have ever absorbed about my subject matter', a lesson learned from a highly respected (and anonymous) European professor: 'Don't you understand, the Bible in and of itself is neither good nor evil. It can be used for both. It says everything. It says nothing. The Bible is just raw power!'[12] This 'raw power' is more-or-less equivalent to what Galbraith, via Malley, picked up on in his analysis of the Bible being utilised to answer issues not in its contents: 'this concept of "God's word" becomes "a placeholder in a community's authoritative discourse" including but not limited to the actual content of the Bible'.[13]

8. Filby, 'God and Mrs Thatcher', pp. 218-33; Spencer, *Freedom and Order*, Chapter 11; Steven, *Christianity and Party Politics*, pp. 121-38.

9. J. Chapman, 'Brown DOES do God as he calls for new world order in sermon at St Paul's', *Daily Mail* (April 1, 2009).

10. Bingham, 'Cameron's olive branch'.

11. Shipman, 'PM's Christmas bid'.

12. Berlinerblau, *Thumpin' It*, p. 2.

13. Galbraith, 'Author of the Bible revealed!'

We can even see reference to this authoritative 'power' in interpreters of political uses of the Bible in the English tradition and representing different political perspectives. From a Marxist perspective, Roland Boer saw the revolutionary power of the Bible and Christianity in his analysis of E.P. Thompson and has framed it in terms of 'myth': 'Any political movement needs its fables, or political myths as I prefer to call them... In drawing upon this stock of images, symbols and stories in order to bring out their radical possibilities, Thompson has managed to recover these stories in the form of political myth.'[14] Connecting ideas such as tolerance with political readings of the Bible, Spencer similarly argued that 'all politics rests on wider myths'.[15] But Spencer's myth appears to be tied in with a preference for liberal parliamentary democracy:

> it is a paradox of the role of the Bible in British political history that so many utterly self-confident and determined pronouncements on the imperative of either political order or political freedom should result in a cumulative tradition that is agonistic and hesitant: freedom *and* order, both necessary and irreconcilable. It is this cumulative, agonistic understanding of human politics that is perhaps the Bible's greatest gift to our national political tradition... [I]t is a message we could do well to recapture.[16]

Despite their differing commitments, Boer and Spencer both share the assumption of the Bible as a powerful political force.[17] But what actual grounding do these myths have? What we may be seeing here, particularly with the appeal to 'myth', is an idea of an unseen authority which underpins, has guided, and might continue to guide, political systems. In many ways this has similarities with the idea of 'spiritual' readings of the Bible, the appeal to something beyond the literal meaning, even an implicit appeal to something transcendent which is unlikely ever to be

---

14. Boer, 'Apocalyptic and Apocalypticism', p. 41. See also Boer, *Political Myth*.

15. Spencer, *Freedom and Order*, Postscript.

16. Spencer, *Freedom and Order*, Introduction. We might add that even when Spencer discusses the 'weight' of biblical language, he is still working with the idea of the Bible-as-raw-power: '...there is a positive argument for deploying the Bible rhetorically in debate, as long as it is done with care and attention. As many politicians instinctively recognise, such usage can lend political speechmaking weight that it often desperately needs' (Spencer, *Freedom and Order*, Postscript).

17. The language of the power of the Bible is found in political discourse occasionally. For instance, Tony Benn: 'Tyndale for his pains was strangled and burned for heresy. Now what was it that was so powerful about the Bible that a man could be strangled and burned for turning it into an intelligible language for the English people? Can anyone really doubt its power?' Benn, 'The Power of the Bible Today', p. 6.

mentioned explicitly in mainstream parliamentary English politics.[18] At this point we are starting to get into broader questions concerning the reception history of the Bible, and assumptions of a guiding third party alongside the reader and the text, which are beyond the scope of a study such as this. But at the very least specific studies such as this one can illuminate ways in which the Bible continues to survive in cultural contexts after the 1960s.

18. I owe this point to a discussion with Deane Galbraith.

POSTSCRIPT (2016):
HARNESSING CHAOS, AGAIN: DAVID CAMERON,
RUSSELL BRAND, AND JEREMY CORBYN

1. The Crystallising of Cameron's Bible

As the Coalition neared its end and the General Election approached, the role of the Bible, religion, and Christianity in political discourse seemed entirely predictable. For Christmas 2014, David Cameron, Ed Miliband, and Nick Clegg maintained the standard view that Christianity and the Bible represent values we are all said to share, or at least should share.[1] Miliband presented a kind of soft-Left Christianity with only distant echoes of the Radical Bible tradition which was once used to justify and provide authority for the trade unions, hostility to the establishment, egalitarianism, nationalisation, collectivism, the founding of the NHS and the welfare state, and so on. He referenced the Labour movement's 'deep roots in the Christian tradition of social activism and solidarity' and vaguely referred to characteristics such as 'generosity, hope and sense of human solidarity'. Clegg's video address was from a primary school in London (presumably school children are one of the few student groups who were then not expected to shout angrily at him in public) and was reminiscent of a textbook primary school Religious Studies/Education class on the sorts of things religions do. He explains that at the 'heart of this festival is the birth of Jesus Christ' and that it is 'a time of joy and celebration for Christians around the world'. Clearly, this is also a visual presentation of a 'festival' that Clegg (and countless other politicians) says is about 'uniting people of all faiths and none', a liberal understanding of Christianity and the Liberal Bible through the classroom. Clegg's classroom is clearly what would be understood as 'multicultural' and notably includes a girl wearing both a head covering

---

1. See A. Chakelian, 'WATCH: Christmas messages from David Cameron, Nick Clegg and Ed Miliband', *New Statesman* (December 24, 2014), http://www. newstatesman.com/politics/2014/12/watch-christmas-messages-david-cameron-nick-clegg-and-ed-miliband.

and a Santa hat and who is prominent in the video as they all make mince pies with Clegg against a backdrop of Christmas decorations. And if the visual message were not clear enough, Clegg explained that 'the core values this story represents—love, charity, hope—are universal'. As with Miliband, Clegg praised emergency services but unlike the leader of the Labour Party—a party still haunted by Iraq—there was a heavy emphasis on praising the armed forces for keeping us 'safe and well' over Christmas. Whereas Cameron would be more comfortable naming foreign interventions and issues surrounding the War on Terror, Miliband and Clegg had perceived audiences less inclined to be so overtly militaristic. Instead, it is perhaps no surprise that both Miliband and Clegg turned their specificity to World War I and the famous truce and, in the case of Miliband, the famous football match. Indeed, for Miliband, this football match was sort of Christian (in the Cameroonian sense): 'In the midst of a tragic conflict the generosity, hope and sense of human solidarity that is characteristic of the Christian faith and culture came to the fore.' What we were not likely to hear were some of the details of the Christmas story and the birth and infancy narratives in Matthew and Luke. It was not likely that we would hear about what Clegg or Cameron or even Miliband thought about angels appearing, the details of Mary's sexual and marital status, John the Baptist's drinking habits, why Elizabeth was a disgrace, leaping in the womb, bringing down the rich and the powerful, Jesus' circumcision, the offering of a sacrifice of turtle doves and pigeons, and so on. Instead, Christmas must be kept liberal!

Cameron, however, was more ideologically explicit. Certainly, Cameron could speak in vague generalities when he spoke of this being an 'important time of year for the Christian faith' and concluded by asking us to spare a thought for those who help others 'as we celebrate the birth of Christ with friends, families and neighbours.'[2] While Cameron did not take the 'Christ' out of 'Christmas', 'celebrating Christmas' was understood in sufficiently broad terms in order to make sure non-Christians are included but associated with 'our' national Christian heritage, a typical move of any mainstream politician, as we have seen: 'thousands of churches – whether in the smallest village or biggest city – will hold open their doors and welcome people of faith and

2. D. Cameron, 'Christmas 2014: Prime Minister's Message' (December 24, 2014), https://www.gov.uk/government/news/christmas-2014-prime-ministers-message.

none to give thanks and celebrate together.'[3] A million miles from the drink-fuelled festive violence of Blackeye Friday it may well be, but these are the usual vague, liberal, and seemingly agreeable issues that almost all politicians publicly agree upon and publicly attribute to the Bible and Christianity.

But, as elsewhere with Cameron, there is a subtle use of Christianity and the Bible to justify more specific political commitments. Certain 'very Christian' values include 'giving, sharing and taking care of others', which may seem vague enough, but this is in line with his emphasis on charity over against state provision of welfare made clearer in other key speeches. This includes a militaristic angle which referenced more specific contemporary interventions than his fellow leaders were prepared to do. This Christmas, he claimed, 'we can be very proud as a country at how we honour these values through helping those in need at home and around the world'. This includes the 'thousands of men and women in our armed forces [who] will be far from home protecting people and entire communities from the threat of terrorism and disease'.[4] This was spelled out in more detail still in more of Cameron's Christmas reflections where the same theme of helping others is likewise dominant:

> …the last of our combat troops left Afghanistan—and they left it a better place. Because of what you have done, life is better for ordinary Afghans. Their daughters are going to school. They are voting in democratic elections for the first time in their history. And life is safer on the streets of Britain.[5]

Thus, 'the Christian values' of 'giving, sharing and taking care of others' is extended to include the war in Afghanistan since 2001 (and all that has

---

3. Cameron, 'Christmas 2014'. Similar comments were made by Cameron the previous Easter: 'Today, 2000 years on, Easter is not just a time for Christians across our country to reflect, but a time for our whole country to reflect on what Christianity brings to Britain.' See D. Cameron, 'Easter 2014: David Cameron's message' (April 16, 2014), https://www.gov.uk/government/news/easter-2014-david-camerons-message. Cameron could also write about how 'being more confident about our status as a Christian country does not somehow involve doing down other faiths or passing judgement on those with no faith at all' and that Britain is apparently not a 'secular country', citing as his example 'the tolerance that Christianity demands of our society [which] provides greater space for other religious faiths'. See D. Cameron, 'My Faith in the Church of England', *Church Times* (April 16, 2014), http://www.churchtimes.co.uk/articles/2014/17-april/comment/opinion/my-faith-in-the-church-of-england.

4. Cameron, 'Christmas 2014'.

5. 'David Cameron praises British troops in Christmas message', https://www.youtube.com/watch?v=n8beSeffkBs.

happened there), a standard liberal justification for the invasion ('the daughters are going to school') and, despite the July 7 bombings and the murder of Lee Rigby, a major explanation for the War on Terror: the non-quantifiable making life 'safer on the streets of Britain'. This use of the Bible and Christianity to provide an implicit defence of, and authority for, foreign policy decisions is not new to Cameron and we will see that it also played a role in his handling of ISIS. It is also broadly equivalent to Tony Blair's biblically based justification of the War on Terror (e.g. bringing democracy to others, gender equality in education) that we saw in Chapter 9.

Cameron's Christmas focused on volunteers who, in addition to those he might think of as the core members of activities of the state (e.g. fire, ambulance, police), are working beyond the state: 'across the country volunteers and workers from charities and other organisations will drop in on the vulnerable and elderly so they are not isolated this Christmas'. Indeed, it is such people who we should think about 'as we celebrate the birth of Christ'. This may seem to reflect standard, popular Christmas sentiments and is similar to the sentiments of Miliband and (less surprisingly) Clegg. But there is something more politically divisive going on. The increase in foodbanks and the handling of the 2014 floods (which he mentioned at Christmas[6]) have been some of the most controversial issues during Cameron's time as Prime Minister. With Cameron we find a reaction along the following lines: people helping others is a good thing…and it is biblical and Christian. What this marks is a notable emphasis in Cameron's Bible to use the Bible and Christianity to justify subcontracting out the state.

As it happens, Cameron had then recently used the Bible and Christianity as a means of justifying foodbanks and the responses to the 2014 floods and was, if anything, intensifying Thatcher's Bible, albeit with more subtle rhetoric. This is clear in his Easter speeches. Implicit in Cameron's Bible is the promotion of his alternative to state-heavy welfare, his controversial flagship policy, the Big Society. The Big Society could, it seems, be traced back to Jesus:

> People sometimes say, you know, 'You talk about the Big Society; don't you realise this is what the Church has been doing for decades?' And I say yes, absolutely. Jesus invented the Big Society 2000 years ago, I just want to see more of it and encourage as much of it as possible. And that is something I think we should all want to see: a bigger role for faith-based organisations in our society… Of course, many of the things that we do are controversial, not least the changes that we're making in

6. 'David Cameron praises British troops'.

welfare, but I hope that even when people will disagree and challenge
with this idea or that idea, there is a genuine attempt to try to lift people
up, rather than count people out.[7]

This emphasis on using the Bible to subcontract the state was more
detailed in another Easter speech where Cameron explained the
outworking of the Bible in Britain today.[8] The 'heart of Christianity' is
'love thy neighbour', which, Cameron claimed, conjures up thoughts
about 'the Alpha courses run in our prisons'. As usual, potentially
illiberal details about the Alpha Course, evangelical and charismatic
Christianity, and conversion are not mentioned explicitly. So, we do not
get Cameron engaging with issues such as speaking in tongues or
whether homosexuality can be cured. Cameron does not talk about the
work of Alpha's controversial figure, Nicky Gumbel. Again, this would
be too alien. What we get instead, however, is Cameron using Alpha to
support the subcontracting of the state. In the hands of Cameron, Alpha
epitomises 'love thy neighbour' for its 'work with offenders to give them
a new life inside and outside prison' just like 'the soup kitchens and
homeless shelters run by churches.' For Cameron, the 'same spirit' was
shown during the storms earlier in 2014: 'From Somerset to Surrey, from
Oxford to Devon, churches became refuges, offering shelter and food,
congregations raised funds and rallied together, parish priests even
canoed through their villages to rescue residents. They proved, yet again,
that people's faith motivates them to do good deeds.'[9]

It is striking that Cameron was more explicit in his use of the Bible
and Christianity from 2014 and some of the reasons for this change seem
to be straightforward. One was the rise of Farage and UKIP who have
been attempting to woo Tory Christians and have used the rhetoric of
Britain as a 'Christian country'. It is also significant that Cameron's
greater emphasis on the Bible and Christianity came after the heavy
criticism for the perception that he was more actively intervening in the
crisis following the storms and flooding only when the Conservative
heartlands were hit, alongside the sustained criticisms (including from
church leaders) over the rise of foodbanks in relation to his government's
austerity measures. The logic of Cameron's Bible is that food banks and
canoeing vicars are something like the Big Society in action. What we
are seeing again is how the Bible functions as an implicit authority for
English political discourse. But, as with Thatcher and Blair before

7. Cameron, 'Easter reception'.
8. Cameron, 'Easter 2014'.
9. Cameron, 'Easter 2014'.

Cameron, the authority that the Bible represents emerges in the light of more controversial policy decisions. Beneath the vagueness, the consensual rhetoric and the praise of church groups, Cameron's Bible and Cameron's Christianity provide the authority for a significant political agenda: the attempt to reduce the role of the state in welfare provision and, by emphasising charity, putting the onus of support on members of society at large rather than on politicians and the state. This, for Cameron, is the true meaning of the Bible, Jesus, and Christianity and, presumably, the audience should agree because these are deemed essential English or British values shared by people of 'every faith and none'.

As the 2015 General Election drew closer, there was one more Easter to allow for additional Bible and religion references in political discourse. It might be thought that the Easter story could be a difficult one for politicians as talk of relentless violence, death on a cross, and resurrection from the dead is not necessarily conducive to issues of job creation, deficit reduction, and changes in welfare. Yet the Easter story does not have to be so bloody and can take some forms not overtly present in the Gospel accounts: see, for instance, the Easter Bunny. But to confuse matters more, we might want to read one less fluffy version of the Easter Bunny story that took place in Glassport, Pennsylvania, discussed by William Arnal.[10] Here Arnal tells us about an event where the Easter Bunny was whipped and Easter eggs broken in order to put the Easter Bunny in its place and to function as a demonstration, of sorts, of Jesus' crucifixion. Arnal ties this whipping in with Mel Gibson's *The Passion of the Christ*, sadism in North American culture, transferable violence, and the War on Terror. This example of whipping for Jesus is, as we will soon see, relevant for understanding what was then the forthcoming General Election in the UK.

Meanwhile, in the *Spectator*, Michael Gove presented himself as a defender of Christianity against its cultured despisers. His defence functions as a checklist of ideas associated with the Cultural Bible, Liberal Bible, and Neoliberal Bible.[11] People who may do strange things like praying are the same people who 'built our civilisation, founded our democracies, developed our modern ideas of rights and justice, ended

10. W. Arnal, *The Symbolic Jesus: Historical Scholarship, Judaism and the Construction of Contemporary Identity* (London and Oakville: Equinox, 2005), pp. 1–7.

11. M. Gove, 'Why I'm proud to be a Christian (and Jeremy Paxman should be ashamed)', *Spectator* (April 4, 2015), http://www.spectator.co.uk/features/9487882/in-defence-of-christianity/.

slavery, established universal education and who are…in the forefront of the fight against poverty, prejudice and ignorance.' This way of thinking about Christianity is, of course, nothing new for Gove, as we saw with interest in promoting the King James Bible (see Chapter 9). Gove's Easter construction of Christianity had more specific relevance for the forthcoming General Election. In his praise of charitable giving, Gove complemented Cameron's emphasis on (Christian) Big Society and promoted a tacit alternative to reliance on state provision of welfare. Churches, he noted, 'provide warmth, food, friendship and support' for those who need. The homeless, alcoholics, drug addicts, mental health sufferers 'are all helped—in innumerable ways—by Christians.' In this respect, we might note the following which implicitly addressed criticisms levelled at the Coalition government and their controversial changes to welfare: 'Churches provide debt counselling, marriage guidance, childcare, English language lessons, after-school clubs, *food banks*, emergency accommodation and, sometimes most importantly of all, someone to listen' (my italics). The mention of foodbanks was presumably significant. As with Cameron, this controversial feature of the Coalition era becomes an attempt to answer critics through the construction of Christianity and Christian authority. The logic is again something like this: yes, it is unfortunate that people cannot eat as well as others, but instead of the state's interfering, churches can do the good work instead!

As ever, we might point out that Gove does not mention all the problematic illiberal things that others might associate with Christianity. We might point out that the end of slavery was a highly complex affair that took, however, many centuries. We might point out that Christian imperialists can be found alongside anti-imperialists. Gove addressed these sorts of issues by using a standard narrative of distortion to establish that such negative deeds are not True Christianity and are distinct from 'genuine Christian faith', which is much more about empathy with the Other. Gove can then make a move that echoes Blair and that Thatcher likewise made in her critique of Communism: this focus on the preciousness of the individual means Christianity celebrates 'our common humanity' and therefore this 'genuine Christian faith' will shield the vulnerable against 'tyrants and dictators' who 'have attempted to set individuals against one another'. Gove's Christianity has 'Bonhoeffer and the Christian-inspired White Rose movement' leading 'the internal opposition to Hitler's rule' with no mention of any other groups leading opposition to Hitler. And presumably discussing (say) any leftist opposition to Hitler would be problematic for Gove's history because the 'moral witness of the Catholic church in Poland... helped erode Communism's authority in the 1980s.' All this, we might add, is grounded in a simplified notion of history (or History): in 'pre-Christian times' moral reasoning was restricted to the elite and built on 'radical inequality'; the earliest Christians ('like Judaism before it') then gave 'every individual the dignity of a soul' and thus 'the capacity to reason, the right to be heard and equality before the law.'

Again, we know that the world is more complex than this. People who historically self-identified as Christians (and non-Christians) have obviously opposed slavery and people who historically self-identified as Christians (and non-Christians) have obviously supported slavery. obviously, to explain history and society in such idealist ways does not explain the chaotic complexity of change. But this is not the function of Gove's rhetoric. As with Cameron, Gove's Christianity, grounded in ancient times, is to give authority to liberal democracy generally, and controversial policies specifically. And given that Gove was defending Christianity against cultural embarrassment, it is striking that he fell back on those things that are emphatically not culturally embarrassing (e.g. anti-slavery, anti-totalitarianism). Why not defend (say) speaking in tongues, speculations about the Whore of Babylon or anything else that is more alien to his preferred discourse? Obviously, this is because Gove is playing the same liberal democratic game as his hypothetical opponents and his Christianity, like their beliefs, can only be acceptable on liberal democratic terms.

Writing in *Premier Christianity*, David Cameron's take on the Bible and Christianity likewise offered no Easter surprises.[12] There was a nod to potential Christian voters who might not swing the election but were worth keeping onside if possible (though this was clearly not working for those in the comments section): 'Just as I've done for the last five years, I'll be making my belief in the importance of Christianity absolutely clear'. We might tentatively suggest that this had an electoral subtext along the following lines: 'I'm a Christian, unlike Miliband and Clegg!' In addition to the Bible, Christianity, and Easter being compatible with his party's agenda, much of the piece was an entirely expected checklist of vague and domesticated values for a well-behaved nation. We are reminded that the nation was built on the Christian faith. We are reminded that the values of Easter are compassion, forgiveness, kindness, hard work, and responsibility, and that Easter is about

12. D. Cameron, 'David Cameron's Easter Message to Christians', *Premier Christianity* (April 2015), http://www.premierchristianity.com/Topics/Society/ Politics/David-Cameron-s-Easter-Message-to-Christians.

'remembering the importance of change, responsibility, and doing the right thing for the good of our children.' We are reminded about the meaning of 'love thy neighbour', which is a 'doctrine' applicable 'at school, at work, at home and with our families'. We are reminded that the values of Easter are for all, the 'views of everyone…something I hope everyone in our country believes'. Cameron's intensification of the Neoliberal Bible continued, particularly in terms of a nation of idealised workers ('hard work and responsibility…hard work…rewarding people for doing the right thing…'). Continuing his development of Thatcher's Bible, we again find support of charity over state provision, including now some of Cameron's own distinctive clichés. The Bible, Christianity, and Easter are effectively Big Society (which, we recall, Jesus invented) in practice, including charities who perform 'minor miracles'. There was even a striking line about the Bible, Christianity, and Easter not being about the state but rather about entrepreneurialism:

> But when I think of the truly great social changes that have helped our nation, they weren't led or started by big governments. They were driven by individuals and activists, great businesses and charities – everyday people working to do the right thing.

In a different popular political memory, major social changes included the founding of the NHS and development of the welfare state by the Atlee government. As we saw in previous chapters, this too was justified in terms of what were deemed to be Christian values and by biblical allusions, particularly due to the influence of the Nonconformist tradition in the Labour Party. In standard retellings of post-war British politics and social change, the founding of the NHS is prominent and was being utilised by Miliband to try and undermine the Conservatives. Cameron, however, presented an alternative to this state-based narrative of True Easter Values with a distinctly anti-state, Thatcherite twist.

But what about the Easter Bunny and its beating? As part of a list of his government's 'fundamental principles and beliefs' to be linked with morality, the Bible, Christianity, and/or Easter, Cameron mentions 'backing those who've fought foreign tyranny'. As we have seen, this reasoning too is not new for Cameron and here, as at Christmas, the Bible again legitimises the monopoly of state violence. Put another way, we are the ones allowed to whip the Easter Bunny. And it is this to which we should turn.

2. True Religion, False Religion, and Terror[13]

Cameron's concern to invoke Christianity and the Bible inevitably provoked a response. In a letter to the *Telegraph*, 50 public figures, including Jim Al-Khalil, Terry Pratchett, Philip Pullman, Tim Minchin, Joan Smith, Polly Toynbee, and A. C. Grayling (but not, curiously, Richard Dawkins), wrote:

> At a social level, Britain has been shaped for the better by many pre-Christian, non-Christian, and post-Christian forces. We are a plural society with citizens with a range of perspectives, and we are a largely non-religious society.
>
> Constantly to claim otherwise fosters alienation and division in our society. Although it is right to recognise the contribution made by many Christians to social action, it is wrong to try to exceptionalise their contribution when it is equalled by British people of different beliefs. This needlessly fuels enervating sectarian debates that are by and large absent from the lives of most British people, who do not want religions or religious identities to be actively prioritised by their elected government.[14]

Use of labels aside, this ideological position is not actually far removed from what Cameron claims Christianity essentially is. For all his talk of evangelising, Cameron only talks about Christianity and the Bible in terms of tolerance and liberal democracy and he is not likely to be demanding mass conversions, women's heads being covered in certain contexts, or to be extolling the virtues of speaking in tongues. Indeed, Cameron's Bible and Christianity conveniently overlap with the views of all other faiths and those with none. Hence, the liberal nationalism of the signatories is not really that different from the liberal nationalism of Cameron: they just want a little more credit for the non-Christian contribution.

What was also significant about the controversy was that it equally inevitably brought Islam into the debate. The former Labour front bencher, Jack Straw, weighed in on BBC Radio 4's *Today* programme (April 21, 2014) in a debate with the former school teacher and speaker for Muslim Council of Britain, Talha Ahmad.[15] Again, despite the

---

13. An expanded version of this section is found in J. G. Crossley, 'God and the State: The Bible and David Cameron's Authority' (forthcoming).

14. J. Al-Khalil et al, 'David Cameron fosters division by calling Britain a "Christian country"', *Telegraph* (April 20, 2014), http://www.telegraph.co.uk/comment/letters/10777417/David-Cameron-fosters-division-by-calling-Britain-a-Christian-country.html.

15. I use my own transcription of the *Today* programme.

rhetoric, there was little sign of any difference in terms of commonly held ideological assumptions. The underpinning assumption was that 'religion', or True Religion, must be essentialised as being liberal, tolerant, and democratic and that False Religion is nothing of the sort. Against the signatories of the *Telegraph* letter, Straw claimed that in Britain 'there are a set of values some of which I would say to the letter writers of the *Daily Telegraph* are indeed Christian based whether they like it or not...there are a set of values which permeate our sense of citizenship'. Clearly, then, the only difference is in the labelling. A similar sort of logic comes through in his comments on what Islam 'really is'. Straw drew 'a real distinction between [Muslim] people who are devout...and those very small minority, who are extremist...verging into militant extremism and to justifying violence.' He added that what is unacceptable is that 'those who proselytise Islam in an exclusive way, who claim that those who are not of the Muslim faith are infidel, or have fewer rights, also argue, for example that women are inferior and ought to have fewer chances in society than should men.' Ahmad's response shared these assumptions. On Straw's response to the fifty signatories, he claimed, 'I don't know of any decent Muslim who would disagree with that'. In response to a question of what it is to be 'in pursuit of your faith', Ahmad suggested that it is 'about respecting the space that everybody has' and that Muslims are, tellingly, 'obedient'. In this discourse, then, differences between Christians, Muslims, non-believers and whoever else or whatever else, mean little as everyone is playing the same liberal democratic and nationalistic game as they defend their own interest groups, constituencies, and ideal citizens.

This understanding of True Religion and True Islam (as well as False Religion and False Islam) is unsurprisingly shared by Cameron and was evident when he was confronted directly by questions of Islam and terror. After the death of Lee Rigby in Woolwich, London, Cameron called the murder 'a betrayal of Islam...There is nothing in Islam that justifies this truly dreadful act.'[16] As we have seen throughout this book, the distinction between 'true' and 'false' Islam is generally code for compatibility (true) or incompatibility (false) with liberal democracy. But this also reveals a focus on 'perverse' ideas ('betrayal of Islam') as the underlying cause of violence which further functions to mask other problematic and highly complex reasons, and even mask any potential state complicity underlying violent acts, irrespective of the motives

16. H. Siddique and S. Jones, 'Attacks on Muslims spike after Woolwich killing', *Guardian* (May 23, 2013), http://www.theguardian.com/uk/2013/may/23/attacks-muslims-spike-woolwich-attack.

professed by the murderers. The comments by the Mayor of London, Boris Johnson, illustrate such mystification: 'it is completely wrong to blame this killing on the religion of Islam and it is also equally wrong to link this murder to the actions of British foreign policy.'[17] In the context of explaining what he deemed a 'perverted, illiberal and hostile interpretation' of Islam, Cameron similarly later claimed on Facebook that 'it is a problem that so many see the West as an oppressor, and buy into the grievances, if not necessarily the violence.'[18]

The not-always-clear assumptions surrounding constructions of True Islam and False Islam in the aftermath of the Woolwich murder also became clear in Cameron reaction to the rise of ISIS. Cameron's speeches contain all the usual clichés about what religion and Islam really 'is' or 'are'. For instance, in one discussion of Islamic State, he claimed:

> They are killing and slaughtering thousands of people—Christians, Muslims, minorities across Iraq and Syria. They boast of their brutality. They claim to do this in the name of Islam. That is nonsense. Islam is a religion of peace. They are not Muslims, they are monsters.[19]

Again, it is obvious what Islam must *not* be for Cameron (and virtually for every major politician). As ISIS is *not* True Religion or True Islam, it instead has to be categorised distinctly as a 'fanatical organisation' and a 'warped ideology'.[20] For Cameron, the emergence of ISIS also represents a battle between Islam ('on the one hand') and 'extremists who want to abuse Islam' ('on the other').[21] In fact, Cameron argues that it is 'vital' that 'we make this distinction between religion [Islam] and political ideology' (which is 'Islamist extremism…often funded by fanatics…who pervert the Islamic faith…').[22] Obvious too is what True Islam should be for Cameron: 'Islam is a religion observed peacefully and devoutly by over a billion people. It is a source of spiritual guidance which daily

17. S. Jones, B. Quinn and C. Urquhart, 'Woolwich attack prompts fears of backlash against British Muslims', *Guardian* (May 23, 2013), http://www.theguardian.com/uk/2013/may/23/woolwich-attack-backlash-british-muslims.

18. https://facebook.com/DavidCameronOfficial/posts/1067675516590099.

19. D. Cameron, 'David Haines: David Cameron statement on killing' *BBC News* (September 14, 2014), http://www.bbc.co.uk/news/uk-29198128.

20. Cameron, 'David Haines'. Later on Facebook (October 19, 2015), 'Islamic extremists' were classified by Cameron as 'perverted, illiberal and hostile' interpreters and he wrote about 'Muslims angry at the hijacking of their faith'. See https://facebook.com/DavidCameronOfficial/posts/1067675516590099.

21. 'MP David Cameron FULL Press Conference: UK Raises Terror Threat Level to "SEVERE"', http://www.youtube.com/watch?v=G4HDt9PUkeI&feature=youtu.be.

22. 'David Cameron FULL Press Conference'.

inspires millions to countless acts of kindness.'[23] This, of course, includes interpretation of Scripture where Cameron makes a Blairite move in claiming that true interpretation must be liberal. 'Globally,' he suggested, 'it is a challenge for all of Islam that a perverted, illiberal and hostile interpretation of this great religion has been allowed to grow' and he praised those 'standing up and challenging the warped interpretation of theology and scripture' who are also 'central to putting forward a liberal, tolerant and inclusive Islam, and demonstrating how it can work in harmony with democracy, freedom and equality.'[24] As all this might already imply, the binary of violent, illiberal, and brutal versus peaceful, liberal, and kind is important for Cameron (and virtually every major politician in Britain) when it comes to how they categorise religion and the state. This is confirmed by what Cameron thinks 'we' (the ideal British subject) are: 'We are peaceful people. We do not seek out confrontation'; 'Britain is an open, tolerant and free nation'; 'adhering to British values is not an option or a choice, it is a duty for those who live in these islands'.[25] More recently still on Facebook (October 19, 2015), he rejected allegiance to 'a religious brotherhood' alone without 'fellow citizens in nation states'.[26]

But what happens when a British national does not behave as an ideal citizen, such as potentially being the murderer of an aid worker? Cameron presented this as a shock, as much a deviation from True Britishness as it is from True Religion: 'People across this country would've been sickened by the fact that there could have been a British citizen, a British citizen who could have carried out this unspeakable act. It is the very opposite of everything our country stands for.'[27] But already Cameron's construction gets complicated. 'We' too are prepared to use violence but do so when provoked and in a 'calm, deliberate way but with an iron determination'.[28] Here the subtle invocation of Christianity (assumed to be about 'peace') becomes important. Cameron mentioned the persecution of 'minorities, including Christians'[29] (he elsewhere claimed that 'It is the case today that our religion is now the most persecuted religion around the world'[30]), and brings in an allusion to the

23. 'David Cameron FULL Press Conference'.
24. https://facebook.com/DavidCameronOfficial/posts/1067675516590099.
25. 'David Cameron FULL Press Conference'; Cameron, 'David Haines'.
26. https://facebook.com/DavidCameronOfficial/posts/1067675516590099.
27. Cameron, 'David Haines'.
28. Cameron, 'David Haines'.
29. Cameron, 'David Haines'.
30. Cameron, 'Easter Reception'.

Good Samaritan: 'but we cannot ignore this threat to our security...there is no option of keeping our heads down...*we cannot just walk on by* if we are to keep this country safe...we have to confront this menace...we will do so in a calm, deliberate way but with an iron determination' (emphasis mine).[31] Cameron here is once again in line with the long established political tradition of the Bible being assumed to be part of 'our' tolerant, democratic heritage. But what Cameron further does is to use Christianity and the Bible to bolster his assumptions about who has the legitimate monopoly on violence. We might compare Obama playing the game of flat contradiction when he claimed that Islamic State is neither Islamic nor a State.[32] This rhetorical move includes assumptions of what is deemed to be True Religion assumptions of what are deemed to be non-rogue states which are also the states which may use violence. The driving narrative is of further importance when the opposition is categorised in metaphysical or fantastical terms. For Cameron, ISIS are *not* Muslims, 'they are monsters' and 'an organisation which is the embodiment of evil'.[33]

There is undoubtedly going to be a sympathetic audience for this rhetoric in light of the (deliberately) shocking cruelty of ISIS. But this simplistic notion of the world of True Religion versus Evil has another function: it covers over the complexity of the situation that gave rise to contexts whereby such actions can occur. There are numerous reasons which might help us understand the rise of ISIS other than the metaphysical 'evil'. These include (among many) the decline of secular nationalism in the Middle East and North Africa, the combination of a rise of slums with sharp population growth, the role of oil in economic growth and crashes, a range of specific issues relating to Saudi Arabia (e.g. Wahhabism, American bases), sanctions on Iraq in the 1990s, the ongoing treatment of Palestinians, drone attacks, and, of course, the invasion of Iraq—its aftermath which, tellingly for someone invoking 'evil' and a 'warped version of Islam' as a seemingly plausible explanation, is denied as a 'source' or 'root cause' for the rise of ISIS.[34] Moreover, George Monbiot pointed out that if we followed the logic of the rhetoric of morality in foreign policy, 'we' might find 'ourselves' bombing quite a lot of people, including 'our' allies, in order to save

31. Cameron, 'David Haines'.

32. 'President Obama: "ISIL is not Islamic"', http://www.youtube.com/watch?v=pwp8qKvE-0g&feature=youtu.be.

33. Cameron, 'David Haines'.

34. 'David Cameron FULL Press Conference'.

lives.[35] So why really choose ISIS here and now and not others? Why not explain why ISIS came to be in a way other than just 'evil' or a 'warped ideology'? Whatever the reasons for choosing the most deserving recipients of state violence, the implicit authority for such simplifications, and ultimately for carrying out violence, is grounded in, and justified by, a given politician's construction of, and assumptions about, the Bible, religion, and Christianity, which again come to the fore when a controversial decision is being made, just as we saw with Thatcher and Blair.

3. The Return of the Radical Bible? 'Milibrand'

And yet, as the May 2015 General Election drew nearer, the Radical Bible came closer to mainstream parliamentary discourse than it had been since Tony Benn through the figure of the comedian and actor, Russell Brand. Close to the election, Miliband appeared at Brand's house to appear on Brand's YouTube show, 'The Trews'. Brand had come to the fore in political discourse after a much-watched and discussed interview with Jeremy Paxman on *Newsnight* (the full interview has had over 11,000,000 hits on YouTube at the time of writing) on 23 October 2013,[36] in light of his guest editing of the *New Statesman*.

Brand's use of the Bible, Jesus, and Christianity to legitimate his political positions has been a constant feature of his time as a public activist. It is all prominent in his stand-up routines, journalism, 'The Trews', his 2014 *New Statesman* editorial,[37] and his popular 2014 book, *Revolution*. We will return to some of these below but a reader might be forgiven for *not* knowing that he had used the Bible, Jesus, and Christianity if they had only read reviews of his book or responses to his *New Statesman* editorial, which, in the UK, were largely negative. Indeed, there were attempts to make Brand an *opponent* of Christianity.[38]

---

35. G. Monbiot, 'Why stop at Isis when we could bomb the whole Muslim world?', *Guardian* (September 30, 2014), http://www.theguardian.com/commentis free/2014/sep/30/isis-bomb-muslim-world-air-strikes-saudi-arabia.

36. BBC Newsnight, 'Paxman vs Brand - full interview', https://www.youtube.com/watch?v=3YR4CseY9pk

37. R. Brand, 'We no longer have the luxury of tradition', *New Statesman* (October 24, 2013), http://www.newstatesman.com/politics/2013/10/russell-brand-on-revolution.

38. Outside the UK, see also the review which is, contrary to Wood, in agreement with Brand's position: C. Wood, 'Russell Brand is wrong about Western religions', *Science on Religion*, (November 2013) http://www.patheos.com/blogs/science onreligion/2013/11/russell-brand-is-wrong-about-western-religions/.

Instead, the (often mocking) focus was on those things that might be labelled 'religious' or 'spiritual' and his interest in Hare Krishna, Hinduism, Buddhism, mysticism, transcendentalism, pantheism, and a host of other –isms a journalist or reviewer may or may not have heard about. Reviewing *Revolution* in the *Telegraph*, Robert Colvile claimed that, rather than 'write about boring stuff like policy and statistics', Brand instead writes about 'the emptiness of being Russell Brand—how he was redeemed from addiction by meditation…how the truth was mystically revealed to him that there is a mysterious karmic, y'know, oneness uniting everything in the universe'.[39] This was typical of reviews in the press. John Crace's spoof of recent books, 'Digested Read', mimicked *Revolution* and intertwines his politics with those ideas which can, in this context, be assumed to be 'new age' or the like:

> what I really want is for everyone to feel the deep inner-connectedness that me and my mate Bob felt when he did this ayahuasca trip and channelled the spiritual transcendence of the planet Gamma before doing this mega Technicolor vom with tons of carrots over the yoga mat I'm not saying I believe the conspiracy theories about the CIA and 9/11 but there's no smoke without fire and what about the third tower that never was you know what I'm saying…what I really think is that none of us is yet fully spiritually aware enough to understand the mystery of the deep mysteries of the universe…it's quite tempting to kill her [the Queen] but my new karma won't allow me to…let's hold hands get this revolution thing done by going on a journey to a oneness with the source of this groovy-woovy electromagnetic realm floating in the cosmos of nothingness and someness and maybe if we just say a couple of prayers and don't vote then everything will be OK…[40]

According to another review in the *Guardian* by David Runciman, Professor in Political Thought at Cambridge no less, was puzzled about how some 'sensible practical suggestions' are helped by the need for a 'belief in a higher power', and how references to David Graeber and Thomas Piketty are supposed to mix with 'talk about yogic meditation'.[41]

---

39. R. Colvile, '*Revolution* by Russell Brand, review: "sub-undergraduate dross"', *Telegraph* (October 23, 2014), http://www.telegraph.co.uk/culture/books/bookreviews/11182073/Revolution-by-Russell-Brand.html.

40. J. Crace, '*Revolution* by Russell Brand – digested read', *Guardian* (October 24, 2014), http://www.theguardian.com/books/2014/oct/26/revolution-russell-brand-digested.

41. D. Runciman, '*Revolution* by Russell Brand review – soft-soap therapy when we need a harder edge', *Guardian* (October 17, 2014), http://www.theguardian.com/books/2014/oct/17/revolution-russell-brand-review-political-manifesto.

Writing of Brand's stand-up show, *Messiah Complex*, Andy Dawson in the *Mirror* reported that Brand 'waxes lyrical about revolutionary figures such as Che Guevara, Malcolm X and Gandhi' before implying a degree of hypocrisy at the money the audience is liable to pay out.[42] Dawson's review is instructive in that he lists three of just four figures discussed in *Messiah Complex*. In fact, we might think that the title—*Messiah Complex*—gives away the identity of the fourth figure: Jesus. In the show itself there were four big posters on stage of the four figures. We might even say that Brand has hardly hidden his Messiah complex or his Christian interests, whether in his Christ-chic, physical self-presentation, his statements, his often visible tattoos (including 'Lord, make me a channel of thy peace' from St Francis), and so on. Indeed, the cover for the DVD would have Brand in a Che-Christ pose. We could go on. On his Twitter account he claimed that his book and the Bible are 'basically the same'.[43] Or, again, the very opening of *Revolution* which uses quotations from St Francis to cast his own religious and political call/conversion in language is also reminiscent of Paul's conversion/call.[44] And yet, Jesus, significantly, gets excluded from Dawson's negative review as do his Christian interests. This is probably for the same reasons why Jesus and Christianity are left untouched in other negative reviews. One reason is that whatever the British Press think Christianity is, it is overwhelmingly a Good Thing and an integral part of our heritage.[45] On the other hand, things deemed 'new age', Hare Krishna, and so on are more likely to receive more critical treatment.

In this respect, we might note some of the other ways in which Brand and religion are dealt with. For instance, whether intentionally or not, Runciman dropped a biblical allusion into his prose:

> He borrows ideas from various radical or progressive thinkers like David Graeber and Thomas Piketty but undercuts them with talk about yogic meditation. He wants us to think seriously about the tax system but also

42. A. Dawson, 'Why Russell Brand IS a 'trivial man' with his apathy-fuelled revolution', *Mirror* (October 24, 2013), http://www.mirror.co.uk/news/uk-news/russell-brand-newsnight-paxman-right-2487661.

43. https://twitter.com/rustyrockets/status/536204789768790016.

44. R. Brand, *Revolution* (London: Century, 2014), pp. 1–5.

45. J. G. Crossley and J. Harrison, 'The Mediation of the Distinction of "Religion" and "Politics" by the UK Press on the Occasion of Pope Benedict XVI's State Visit to the UK', *Political Theology* 14 (2015), pp. 329–45; J. G. Crossley and J. Harrison, 'Atheism, Christianity and the Press: Press coverage of Pope Benedict XVI's 2010 state visit to the UK', *Implicit Religion* 18 (2015), pp. 77–105.

to think in ways that make taxation seem like a speck of dust in the eye of
the universe.[46]

This is, as ever, the Cultural Bible, the Bible of our heritage, and it is
brought into sharp contrast with yogic meditation and Brand's cosmic
thinking. In the reviews of Brand, there is also an unconscious burying
of the Radical Bible as represented by Brand which has been pushed
outside parliamentary and mainstream political discourse since Thatcher
and popular acceptance of Thatcherism. The problem is that Brand might
actually be using the Bible in a long established way and yet Brand is,
from the perspective of certain media commentators, culturally
embarrassing, particularly for the reviewer who wants to be seen as a
serious political thinker. According to this logic, something deemed to
be part of our shared cultural heritage would surely not result in
something as silly as Russell Brand! To further this stream of thought, if
Brand is to be deemed naïve and as someone who uses strange spiritual
and religious stuff, then cannot this logic apply to other religious things
he uses, like Christianity and the Bible, which must likewise be just as
naïve? But this move is not one that would be made other than in a
minority of cases: the Bible and Christianity in the media and in
mainstream political discourse are respected too much for that.

To help us understand this further, let us turn to another negative
review. Continuing the theme of Brand-in-distinction-from-Christianity,
Quentin Letts in the *Daily Mail* claimed that in 'one breath he wants
suicidal fundamentalism' and 'in the next he wants no one to be harmed'.
Letts also explains why he thinks this 'plain deluded twaddle' is also
able to function as 'dangerous rabble-rousing':

> But for the state-backed secularism and the militant egalitarianism of the
> Left, a Russell Brand might struggle to gain a following. A population
> which was better informed by the BBC might realise that this twit has
> little to offer compared with the spiritual wonders of Christianity,
> Judaism and Islam.

So, Letts' construction of Christianity (or True Christianity) has nothing
to do with Brand's views; Brand is, if anything, a grotesque Christ. And
yet, Letts also claimed (and note his construction of the Left):

> The snapshot, which was published in the magazine, was arranged like
> Leonardo's Last Supper, with Brand in the midst, a veritable Christ
> figure. It was hard to know whether to laugh or weep.

---

46. Runciman, '*Revolution* by Russell Brand'.

> For the kids on apprentice schemes, or the young parents trying to save
> for a house, or the volunteers who run Church food banks and give their
> time as school governors: is Russell Brand really such great news for
> them?
>
> This is not simply an argument against the Left. I know Labour MPs who
> recoil from Brand just as I do. The Labour Party has many decent
> members, people attracted by its past Methodist values. Brand is every bit
> as repulsive to them as he is to a pastoral, traditionalist rightie such as me.

This is a telling remark because Brand is effectively constructed as a
pollution of what is assumed to be Pure Christianity and it is not the sort
of thing which should sully a Pure Methodism that thoroughly decent
Labour MPs can even observe. But Letts' political Methodism, to change
the metaphor slightly, is one with its sting conveniently removed.
Methodist values are usually code in the *Daily Mail* for acceptable
Labour MPs behaving in a morally upright manner (e.g. against
gambling, teetotal), even if this ethical Methodism has long been
identified with English or British socialism, or indeed even if it needs to
be made clear that Methodism invented English/British socialism, not
Marx. As we have seen, the Radical Methodist Bible has been
remembered as part of the development of the trade union movement, it
was used polemically against the established (i.e. Anglican) church and
the political establishment, its rhetoric was overtly present in the
founding of the NHS and the welfare state, and Methodists were
prominent in the growth of the Campaign for Nuclear Disarmament. We
might add that the Methodist preacher Donald Soper was still preaching
his socialist pacifism on his soapbox in Hyde Park in the 1970s and Tony
Blair had to use such language about the founding of the NHS to
convince those Labour MPs with those 'past Methodist values' about the
apparent rightness of invading Afghanistan and Iraq (see Chapter 8).

And yet, does not Brand have much in common with Nonconformist
Radical Bible readings too? His language about the church, dogma, and
right-wing interpreters corrupting the original radical Jesus and Bible
could have come from the Congregationalist Tony Benn, as could his
paralleling of this decline and corruption narrative with the fate of
Communism. Just as Jesus and the Bible were betrayed by the church
and interpreters, so Marx was betrayed (in a more overtly bad way) by
Stalin and Soviet Russia. The standard sort of sentiments in the
Nonconformist (including Methodist) Radical Bible are there in Brand's
take on Jesus, the Bible, and Christianity, even if his own language gives
it a certain distinctiveness:

> Any American politician who says they're Christian must have as their uppermost priority the removal of the money-lenders from the temple, the undue, corrupt and disgusting influence of the financial industry on public life. Any British politician, like David Cameron, who claims to be a Christian, which means 'to practice the teachings of Jesus Christ', has to, like Jesus, heal the sick, not, like a cunt, sell off the NHS.[47]

In light of Letts' comments about Methodism, one passage from Brand's *New Statesman* editorial is also worth quoting:

> Now there is an opportunity for the left to return to its vital, virile, vigorous origins. A movement for the people, by the people, in the service of the land. Socialism's historical connection with spiritual principles is deep. Sharing is a spiritual principle, respecting our land is a spiritual principle. May the first, May Day, is a pagan holiday where we acknowledge our essential relationship with our land. I bet the Tolpuddle martyrs, who marched for fair pay for agricultural workers, whose legacy is the right for us to have social solidarity, were a right bunch of herberts if you knew them. 'Thugs, yobs, hooligans,' the *Daily Mail* would've called them.

The Tolpuddle Martyrs—with strong Methodist connections—are one of the most frequently referenced movements in English radical history. Both Brand and Letts (/*Daily Mail* more generally) are effectively fighting over as to who really owns this history, but it is again noticeable that Letts does not reference the politically radical nature of this Methodist influence on the Labour movement. Instead we get the vague and acceptable 'Methodist values'. Like an unwanted, ageing parent that the offspring claims to love but unceremoniously shoves in a care home, so this Bible, this Christianity, must be kept away and wheeled out with a forced smile only when properly medicated.

Nevertheless, Letts has a point: Brand's views, like all other contemporary manifestations of the Radical Bible in political discourse, are not those that will be typically found in parliament today and thus not typical among the Labour MPs and Labour Party members Letts mentions. It is significant that when Brand was effectively told to stand for parliament by a UKIP sympathiser in the Question Time audience, Brand said he could not because he would be afraid he would become 'one of them'.[48] There are other, perhaps clearer, reasons why Brand's Gospel has to be outside parliament and was then alien to the Labour Party. There is, importantly, an emphasis on sex and sexuality that is not

---

47. Brand, *Revolution*, p. 68.
48. 'BBC Question Time 11/12/2014 Russell Brand Nigel Farage', https://www.youtube.com/watch?v=Q2RSKJC-ugk.

typical of conventional Methodism in mainstream political discourse. For instance, Brand preaches a gospel of revolutionary free love (irrespective of sexuality) and worship of the divine feminine, which, as a subversive act, must mean that men should perform oral sex on women and make them orgasm (preferably first) and then the male erotic monopoly on rimming may be opened up for all sexual relations in return, irrespective of sexual orientation. This, he claims, partly ironically, makes him 'a little bit like Jesus'.[49] His free-love message is notable in that it chimes with Peter Tatchell's view, noted in Chapter 8, in that while gay marriage should be supported for reasons that everyone has the right to be miserable, true love and lovemaking should not really involve reactionary constraints like marriage.[50] Does this discourse not owe more to the spirit of 1968 than Methodism?

Letts also has a point in that the emphasis on paganism and the like are not so prominent in politicised versions of Nonconformist traditions like Methodism (Donald Soper was hardly a fan of things deemed pagan), though there has certainly been a degree of ecumenical openness and Tony Benn would certainly embrace figures from various religious traditions. Another more likely allusion, however, would be his fellow comedian, Bill Hicks, whose influence on Brand's comedy is clear enough. The idea for Brand that we are all one consciousness has direct verbal allusions to Hicks, as does the suggestion of redistribution of wealth as a means to alleviate poverty and the vastness of the universe as an absurd point of contrast to pointless views (see Chapter 1). Brand's emphasis on Jesus, Che, Malcolm X, and Gandhi was, as we also saw in Chapter 1, part of Hicks' routine and echoes Hicks' list of those historical figures who are worth singling out. Indeed, both Hicks and Brand made parallels with themselves and such figures, and both even alluded to being shot or martyred. This is part of an established radical and/or liberal (and often atheist or agnostic) tradition which singles Jesus out as one of the great historic moral visionaries (see Chapter 1).

While some reviewers of Brand did not include the Bible and Christianity in the mocking and satire, there were exceptions. And yet in these exceptions we find a very similar game being played. We might, for instance, take Tom Kershaw's subtle distinction to understand this more: 'Being the funny man, Brand is able to poke fun at religion,

---

49. R. Brand, *Messiah Complex* (DVD; 2Entertain, 2013).

50. Brand's list of acknowledgements in *Revolution* is striking in this respect: Tatchell is listed directly alongside Naomi Klein, Noam Chomsky, Thomas Piketty, and David Graeber.

whether it's Christianity or his newly-adopted religion.'[51] Kershaw includes a footnote which links to a sketch where Brand mocks a man who thinks the punishment for adultery should be naked crucifixion in the desert and then further claims that this is in the Bible. But what Brand points out is that this is *not* in the Bible and claims that it goes against what the Bible stands for. This sketch is thus used by Kershaw to claim that Brand pokes fun at Christianity when we might say that Brand used it to *defend* the Bible and thus Christianity. This is typical of Brand (and hardly uncommon in any number of exegetical traditions, including that of the Radical Bible): there is a pure form which gets corrupted by poor interpreters.

An especially curious exception is Nick Cohen's review of *Revolution*. Cohen openly identifies as atheist and is part of a minority voice in the press.[52] First, Cohen frames his argument by illustrating Brand's priorities, claiming that 'The systemic change that means the most to Brand is an embrace of meditation and pantheism.' Second, it is notable who and what Cohen does *not* criticise:

> Anyone who claims that Jesus, Allah, Krishna or the fountainhead of any other religion endorses homophobia instead of the "union of all mankind" is "on a massive blag", he says. Brand has to ignore Leviticus's edict that the punishment for men who sleep with other men is death, St Paul's hysterics about lesbianism and the hadiths that have Muhammad saying that the punishment for sodomy is death by stoning. In other words, he has to ignore several millennia of real and continuing religious repression, so he can make his spiritualism sound emancipatory rather than cranky.

But Cohen does *not* criticise Jesus on homosexuality and he does *not* criticise the Ten Commandments. So what? As it happens, Brand *did* write about both these in direct relation to homosexuality. Brand's discussion of homosexuality in *Revolution*, as well as in his stand-up, *Messiah Complex*, has an extended discussion where he keeps pointing out that Jesus does not talk about homosexuality and does talk about love and he has an extended joke about the Ten Commandments where 'God would prefer you', Brand claims, 'to have gay sex than covet your neighbour's oxen'.[53] But what Brand also did, against Cohen's representation of him, *was* to discuss Leviticus. He is explicit in the very

51. T. Kershaw, 'The Religion and Political Views of Russell Brand', *The Hollowverse* (June 2, 2012), http://hollowverse.com/russell-brand.

52. Crossley and Harrison, 'Mediation'; Crossley and Harrison, 'Atheism, Christianity and the Press'.

53. Brand, *Revolution*, pp. 67–68.

book Cohen is reviewing and sees Leviticus more as an anomaly than as a priority for God because it is not mentioned in the more important Ten Commandments.[54] The idea of prioritising or referencing other parts of the Bible to deflect the problematic 'illiberal' biblical passages is a known move, as we saw in the case of both Blair and Obama in Chapter 8.

In an odd way, are not Cohen and Brand playing a similar game here? This is not, of course, to make any historical judgment on Jesus and the Ten Commandments on homosexuality but rather it is a judgment on the ideological redirection being carried out by Cohen. But what is of potential significance here is that with Cohen (and leaving his personal intentions to one side) there may be ripples of a long tradition of those identifying as atheist and liberal finding some good in Jesus (and, indeed, the Ten Commandments), even if the rest might be illiberal and unpleasant. As we saw in Chapter 1, recent proponents of this tradition might be Douglas Adams, who in his *Hitchhiker's Guide to the Galaxy* writes that Jesus was said to have been killed for saying we should be nice to each other, or Richard Dawkins, who believes that the Sermon on the Mount is hundreds of years ahead of its time.[55] Once again, though implicit in Cohen (and, again, I suspect unconsciously), we have the domesticating of a politically radical Jesus/Bible being replaced with a liberal Jesus, who, ahead of his time, is more typically remembered for being kind to people.

Brand may well be a recognisable user of the Radical Bible. He may indeed be the most high-profile user in recent years. But, if the reviews in the mainstream press are anything to go by, Brand's Bible is also an uncomfortable and embarrassing Bible that has been either kept outside by ignoring it or associating it with more palatable liberal values. While a sustained attack on the acceptable face of the Radical Bible was always unlikely in the press, it is unsurprising that the credibility of Brand's Bible could consistently be attacked through its association with things more easily ridiculed, like meditation, Hare Krishna, and pantheism. These things are just not Methodist. Or, presumably, English. Couple this with Brand's failing to garner enough votes for Miliband, the Radical Bible would have to wait for a more recognisable Messiah to herald its return to parliamentary politics.

54. Brand, *Revolution*, pp. 67–68.
55. R. Dawkins, *The God Delusion* (London: Bantram Press, 2006), p. 250, also referencing R. Dawkins, 'Atheists for Jesus', *Free Inquiry* 25 (2005), pp. 9–10.

4. The Triumphal Re-entry? Corbyn and the Return of the English/British Radical Bible

Milibrand might have been the morning star of the return of the Radical Bible into mainstream party political discourse because after the General Election analysts might be forgiven for predicting the end of the Radical Bible for good. As expected, the Liberal Democrats elected Tim Farron as their new leader, who then faced his own particular but equally predictable problems. As he had previously argued in *Liberal Democrats Do God* (see Chapter 9), Farron tried to make a distinction between his 'personal morality' ('personally, as a Christian' as it was put to him) and his public political liberalism, particularly over the issues of abortion and same-sex marriage and whether he thinks 'homosexual sex is a sin'.[56] Farron's approach has been to try and avoid 'yes or no' answers to questions of whether he personally thinks 'homosexual sex is a sin' by the argument that 'we are all sinners' and citing a favoured 'Bible phrase', Matthew 7.3: 'You don't pick out the speck of sawdust in your brother's eye when there is a plank in your own.' When confronted by Leviticus 18.22 ('You shall not lie with a male as one lies with a female; it is an abomination') he answered that his 'faith is based on my belief who Jesus Christ is who he said he is'. Questioned whether he could therefore be a L/liberal he answered that liberalism was about tolerance of different groups (including religious ones) and the rights of the individual: 'It's a peculiar thing to say that somebody who happens to belong to a religious group, who's a Christian, can't be a liberal – it's exactly the opposite.' Again, the guiding assumptions are liberal; it is now a question of which sort of liberalism is acceptable. Interestingly, citing a more 'liberal' part of the Bible to deflect more 'illiberal' ones is, as we saw in Chapter 8 and in the case of Russell Brand, a tactic used by both Blair and Obama, even if they do not have the same personal conflict over approval of homosexual sex.

Meanwhile, the initial post-Election mood in the Labour Party moved towards how to reclaim Conservative votes as 'aspiration' briefly became a buzzword. But, as we obviously build towards the rise of Corbyn, the summer of 2015 proved to be entirely unpredictable. Labour MPs (and commentators) underestimated how far to the Left much of its wider membership and potential members were. The post-Election shift

56. T. Brooks-Pollock, 'Tim Farron on gay sex: New Lib Dem leader declines to say if he considers it's a sin', *Independent* (July 18, 2015), http://www.independent.co.uk/news/uk/politics/is-gay-sex-a-sin--tim-farron-repeatedly-declines-to-answer-10398546.html.

to the Right among Labour MPs was problematic enough but when the party and three of the four leadership candidates (Liz Kendall, Andy Burnham and Yvette Cooper) voted to abstain on the Conservative's Welfare Bill then an already vocal membership propelled forward the one candidate who only became a leadership candidate through a combination of luck and 'borrowed' votes from otherwise non-supportive MPs: Jeremy Corbyn.

The Bible, religion or Christianity does not seem to have played an overt part in the Labour leadership debates (though a number of locations were churches), at least not in the rhetoric of the candidates. There were occasional moments. Using a standard construction of Christianity, Yvette Cooper said that she came from a 'tradition of solidarity from the coalfield communities' where hard work and looking after your neighbours was stressed and summarised as 'Christian socialism but without the God attached'.[57] Andy Burnham made reference to his Catholic background ('I'm Catholic by upbringing, but I'm not particularly religious now') and his children going to a Catholic school ('so I still believe in the values and the grounding it gives you, I'm a very big believer in that'). He also claimed that 'Catholic social teaching underpins my politics' and that 'we did have to read the catechism at school but it is powerful and strong and right.' But, strikingly for a front bench politician, Burnham was also critical of Catholicism, at least its official channels, though he was reported as saying that his stand on LGBT rights brought him into conflict with Catholic friends and family. On LGBT issues and birth control, he contrasted the official line with the views of 'millions of ordinary British Catholics'. Indeed, he claimed that for 'the church of my youth, and the priests that I knew, the feeling and overriding mood was quite forgiving really, quite humane, humorous, irreverent, even the priests.' But in contrast to the memory of the church in which he grew up, it was the change of Popes which he argued brought about a 'more judgemental mode [which] became much more obsessed with sexuality and issues related to sexual behaviour.' This brought about Burnham's drift away and he particularly criticised Ratzinger for the desire for a '"smaller, purer" church, which I found quite terrifying actually.' He does, however, have 'high hopes' for Pope Francis ('A humble man with great warmth and a fantastic character').[58] Yet while front bench politicians

57. H. Lewis, 'Discipline over dazzle: Helen Lewis interviews Yvette Cooper', *New Statesman* (August 13, 2015), http://www.newstatesman.com/node/200775.
58. P. Waugh, 'Andy Burnham Interview: On Scrapping The "Tampon Tax", Catholicism, Unpaid Internships And Falling Out Of Love With Morrissey',

are not likely to be too critical of religion, this is hardly unprecedented. As we saw in Chapter 9, Tony Blair, who converted to Catholicism, constructed the notion of the socially liberal views of the laity (especially the young) over against the socially conservative views of the church hierarchy. In the case of both Burnham and Blair it is a certain liberal tradition which dictates the understanding of what religion should be.

However, one word of relevance did emerge among opponents of Corbyn to describe his followers: 'cult'. John Woodcock, the Labour and Co-operative MP for Barrow and Furness and chair of Progress, was active in Liz Kendall's campaign team for the leadership of the Labour Party. He wrote an article in *Progress* called 'Cult Logic',[59] which was described by the *Guardian* as a 'blistering intervention' in the leadership race,[60] and it was language that was picked up by other opponents of Corbyn, notably on Twitter where so much of the polemic was to be found.[61] In his *Progress* article, Woodcock made some assumptions about what a cult *is*. In describing 'the flawed logic of the cult', Woodcock included that of 'a growing number think that not only should those who voted Tory in 2015 be ignored, they should be despised'. This also included language that is familiar enough to known popular (and academic) constructions of the meaning of a 'cult' in Woodcock's

Huffington Post (August 10), http://www.huffingtonpost.co.uk/2015/08/10/andy-burnham-interview-catholic-church-tampon-tax_n_7961096.html.

59. J. Woodcock, 'Cult logic', *Progress* (August 14, 2015), http://www.progressonline.org.uk/2015/08/14/we-are-the-true-guardians-of-the-spirit-of-1945/.

60. R. Mason, 'Gordon Brown to speak on Labour leadership as poll gives boost to Corbyn', *Guardian* (August 14, 2015), http://www.theguardian.com/politics/2015/aug/14/gordon-brown-speak-labour-leadership-contest-mps-panic-corbyn.

61. E.g. Alastair Campbell (August 16, 2015), 'CyberCorbs at various points today suggesting that Neil Kinnock and Gordon Brown not really Labour. The zeal of the cult. Cult I said' (https://twitter.com/campbellclaret/status/632944026593968128); Dan Hodges (August 17, 2015), 'Corbyn Cultists: "You're all evil Tories". Me: "OK. You're a bunch of unwashed Trots". Corbyn Cultists: "You can't speak to us like that"' (https://twitter.com/DPJHodges/status/633521968113938432). Other articles and titles on Corbyn followers as a 'cult' include: Archbishop Cramner, 'The cult of comrade Corbyn', *Archbishop Cramner* (August 9, 2015), http://archbishopcranmer.com/the-cult-of-comrade-corbyn/; S. Payne, 'An evening with the cult of Corbyn in Islington', *Spectator* (August 22, 2015), http://blogs.spectator.co.uk/coffeehouse/2015/08/evening-cult-corbyn-islington/; L. Fawcett, 'The cult of Corbyn', *Rife Magazine* (August 25, 2015), http://www.rifemagazine.co.uk/2015/08/the-cult-of-corbyn/; J. Cowley, 'Victory for the Cult of Corbyn? No, the start of a long and brutal civil war', *Daily Mail* (September 15, 2015), http://www.dailymail.co.uk/debate/article-3234590/JASON-COWLEY-Victory-Cult-Corbyn-No-start-long-brutal-civil-war.html.

construction of his opponents: 'anyone asking why the Tories were more popular is not stupid or stuck in the past, he or she is actively *wicked*' and those 'seeking to understand why voters turned to the Conservatives are carrying out a *devilish plan* to steal what is left of the soul of the Labour party' (my italics).

So who are these cult members according to Woodcock's logic? For a start they obviously include those 'growing number [who] think that not only should those who voted Tory in 2015 be ignored, they should be despised'. Rather than establish the sociological usefulness or otherwise of the term 'cult', it is much easier to see what interests and categorisations are at play in such constructions. For instance, Woodcock himself claims (with assumption of True and False) that 'we must be passionately intolerant of the self-indulgence of the new Bennites masquerading as evangelists of a new politics'. Does this self-professed 'intolerance' not fit Woodcock's assumptions and definitions of what a 'cult' is? Indeed, those ideologically close to Woodcock were said to be forming an underground 'resistance' to a future Corbyn-led party and this resistance-in-the-making was reported in the *Telegraph* by Dan Hodges, who likewise used Woodcock's language of 'cult' to describe Corbyn's followers.[62] Might this not be deemed to be the behaviour of a 'cult' according to Woodcock's logic? Did not New Labour (including Alastair Campbell, who likewise used the language of 'cult' to critique Corbyn's followers) and its famous 'on message' approach, mean it too was a 'cult'? What about these comments by Blair on Gordon Brown, his followers and the Labour Party more generally, which make some classic assumptions about what a cult *is* and would include the Labour history Woodcock assumed to be non-cultic?

> We had become separated from 'normal' people. For several decades, even before the eighteen years in the wilderness, Labour was more like a cult than a party. If you were to progress in it, you had to speak the language and press the right buttons...The curse of Gordon was to make these people co-conspirators, not free-range thinkers. He and Ed Balls and others were like I had been back in the 1980s, until slowly the scales fell from my eyes and I realised it was more like a cult than a kirk.[63]

Obviously, the definition of what a 'cult' means depends on the interests and classifications of those doing the defining. Asking questions like this

---

62. D. Hodges, 'Labour MPs are now preparing to go underground to resist the Corbyn regime', *Telegraph* (August 16, 2015), http://www.telegraph.co.uk/news/politics/labour/11805916/Labour-MPs-are-now-preparing-to-go-underground-to-resist-the-Corbyn-regime.html. On Hodges and 'cult', see n. 61.

63. T. Blair, *A Journey* (London: Hutchinson, 2010), pp. 89, 641.

of Woodcock's article makes it easier to appreciate some of the interests at play in the construction of the 'logic of a cult'—it tells us much about the interpreter and their influences rather than any alleged cultic reality.

Unsurprisingly, this sort of argument also constructs what a cult is *not*. And, again, these are familiar constructions using some of the political rhetoric we have seen in this book in that there is the assumption of a source of inspiration and a tradition in which it must be properly interpreted. In this respect, it is the Attlee government of 1945 which was effectively responsible for the creation of the NHS and the welfare state: this is the one government which almost all Labour MPs would aspire to emulate (including, of course, Woodcock's opponents). As Woodcock put it, 'The true guardians of the spirit of 1945 are those who seek to understand how fast the world is changing and change their ideas to meet the new challenges.' It is worth noting too the sub-heading (for which Woodcock may or may not have been responsible): 'We are the true guardians of the spirit of 1945.' On one level we might observe: What Labour politician does *not* think that they are among the true guardians of the spirit of 1945? Presumably, not many. But Woodcock's choice of individuals to highlight this tradition is telling: at least two have long been remembered as being firmly on the Left of the Labour Party, one is its most popular and admired leader across the party, and one was active in the Great Strike of 1926, even if a figure known for being on the Right of the party:

> Messrs Attlee, Bevan, Bevin and Cripps, men who governed through the horror of war and went on to win the peace, would send packing those who espoused the fantasy politics that is seducing many in the aftermath of our latest defeat.

This list of names reveals the interests of the interpreter, in this case to make a pitch for ownership of the constructed heroes of the Labour Left who are reclassified as figures of Woodcock's Labour (himself conventionally placed on the Right of the Labour Party). These are understood as the 'true guardians' of the Party.

Yet even the Left and Right binary is not clear cut, nor is the idea that all would have behaved in the way Woodcock suggests. Is this the Bevan who resigned over dental and spectacle charges? The Bevan who was expelled from the Labour Party? The Bevan who thought Tories were lower than vermin? Or the Bevan who opposed unilateralism and famously pleaded that a foreign secretary should not be sent 'naked into the conference chamber'? Is this the Marxist Cripps with Communist leanings? Cripps the Keynesian? Cripps the founder of *Tribune*? The Cripps who was expelled from the Labour Party? Is this Bevin the anti-

Communist? The Bevin who was said to have responded to the claim that Herbert Morrison was his own worst enemy with 'Not while I'm alive, he ain't'? Would it be any of these figures who were involved in various Labour defeats? What about the less successful 1950 and 1951 elections where the decisions made by the Attlee government were evidently not as popular with Tory voters and marked a period where Labour was out of power until 1964?

Any attempt to hold together complexities of history into a unified tradition will have to deal with all the problematic contradictions. What Woodcock has done (intentionally or not) is to idealise the past and construct a unified tradition. Interestingly, Woodcock (unlike some) acknowledges the complexities of history and very different historical contexts of 1945, 1964 and 1997. Yet by stressing radical difference he is simultaneously creating continuity. For Woodcock, there still needs to be a unifying thread in order to be the 'true guardians' and inevitably that has to be vague (and difficult to falsify?): 'the *spirit* of 1945' [my italics]. There is, of course, no inherently stable or 'true' history. Could not anyone in the Labour Party pick out bits and pieces from Attlee, Cripps, Bevin, and Bevan and make them their own, that is the bits and pieces that the interpreter agrees with? Could another interested party not take from the 1945 government those figures with Marxist tendencies and then claim that the contemporary Labour front bench must do likewise? Or, alternatively, observe that the 1945 front bench included party rebels and so today's Labour front bench should do likewise? And so on. Instead, Woodcock's construction (like any claim to a 'true' party heritage, we might add) has to remove the complexity and select accordingly in order to claim that the spirit of 1945 involves wooing Tory voters and send packing 'those who espoused the fantasy politics that is seducing many in the aftermath of our latest defeat'.

The rhetoric of cult versus orthodoxy was part of a summer of bitter arguments in the Labour Party. Yet despite (or because of?) such fierce polemics Corbyn emerged as the leader of the Labour Party with a landslide 59.5%. The only group within the Labour Party who did not show serious support were his fellow MPs (on the contrary). Corbyn's victory was one of the most unlikely political events in living memory. He was first elected as an MP to Islington North in 1983 where he has held a strong majority ever since. Mentored by his close friend Tony Benn, his politics are recognisably of the minority on the Left of the Labour Party and he has been closely associated and involved with, among others: the Socialist Campaign Group; Rail, Maritime Transport Workers Union; Fire Brigades Union; Defend Council Housing;

Campaign for Nuclear Disarmament; Dalit Solidarity Campaign; Greater London Pensioners Forum; Liberation; Palestine Solidarity Campaign; Refugee Therapy Centre; the Socialist Campaign Group; and Stop the War Coalition.[64] Today, this is not the checklist of a party leader and yet that is precisely where Corbyn found himself.

Corbyn has recalled his religious background in an interview with the Christian magazine, *Third Way*.[65] His mother was described as 'a Bible-reading atheist – no, agnostic, probably' who was raised 'in a religious environment' with a number of clergy in her family, including her brother, as well as some Jewish ancestry. His father is described as a church-attending Christian. Corbyn's school 'was religious' with hymns and prayers every morning and he too attended church. Corbyn no longer identifies as a believer but, typically for parliamentary political discourse, also emphatically claims that he is not 'anti-religious' ('not…at all. Not at all') and added that he probably attends 'more religious services than most people who are very strong believers'. We get echoes of Benn's (and Blair's) 'ecumenical' or 'interfaith' approach: 'I go to churches, I go to mosques, I go to temples, I go to synagogues. I find religion very interesting. I find the power of faith very interesting.' He further ties this in with some of his general political ideals relating to anti-war and communitarianism: 'I think the faith community offers and does a great deal for people. There doesn't have to be wars about religion, there has to be honesty about religion. We have much more in common than separates us.'

Over the summer and autumn of 2015, and in the midst of an overwhelmingly hostile media, there were plenty of ironic comments about Corbyn as Messiah or 'Christ-like'[66] (he shares those most noble initials, JC), as well as his picture juxtaposed next to a Christ portrait under the headline 'Jeremy Corbyn is now bigger than Jesus—on Google' in the *Mirror* ('Sadly for the Son of God, despite making numerous appearances in the Bible, he doesn't feature anywhere in the

64. J. Corbyn, 'About me', http://jeremycorbyn.org.uk/about/.

65. H. Spanner, 'Far Sighted? Interview with Jeremy Corbyn', *Third Way* (June 2015), http://www.thirdwaymagazine.co.uk/editions/july-2015/high-profile/far-sighted.aspx.

66. E.g. P. Toynbee, 'Corbyn's Christ-like position may have nuked his chances of becoming PM', *Guardian* (October 1, 2015), http://www.theguardian.com/commentisfree/2015/oct/01/jeremy-corbyn-nuclear-deterrent-prime-minister-labour.

top four'),[67] allusions to *Life of Brian* (e.g. 'We don't need a messiah; all we needed, it turned out, was one very naughty MP'[68]), and 'revivalist meetings' was a common enough description of Corbyn's talks around the country. Indeed, self-identified atheist, Clive Lewis (MP for Norwich South and Corbyn ally), claimed that there was a 'religious element' to Corbyn's support, which was reported as him detecting 'an almost religious fervour at some of the events'.[69] Here is a more detailed example from one of the minority sympathetic media sources:

> The atmosphere in the hall itself was charged, partly evangelical, a sense of a revivalist meeting. One speaker mentioned a 'revolution'. Hyperbolic, of course. England, as we all know, doesn't 'do' revolutions. But maybe this was the nearest we would get, this sense of a passion reborn, people revitalised, those who had felt in the wilderness, who, despite deep convictions had no-one to vote for, who longed for a more just and fair society but had nowhere to go as almost every automoton of a politician of every shade, every apparatchick mouthed the same platitudes and accepted with barely a blink a doctrine of austerity…I wondered, did the Tories have their own anthem? Jerusalem? Perhaps, except that was penned by a mighty radical, William Blake and thus seemed, despite the cosy bottled jam connections of the WI, slightly ill-fitting…How knackered he must have been after these endless revivalist meetings![70]

This combination of socialism, nostalgia, religion, biblical allusions ('in the wilderness') and reference to Blake and Jerusalem, a specifically English or British tradition, is a common enough theme in discourses associated with the Radical Bible. Similar themes are also picked up in other relatively sympathetic sources. Peter Hitchens, a notable example from the small 'c' conservative Right who have been disillusioned with the current political elites, went to a Corbyn meeting and similarly remarked:

67. D. Bloom, 'Jeremy Corbyn is now bigger than Jesus—on Google', *Mirror* (July 28, 2015), http://www.mirror.co.uk/news/uk-news/jeremy-corbyn-now-bigger-jesus-6150547.

68. Z. Williams, 'Corbynomics must smash this cosy consensus on debt', *Guardian* (August 16, 2015), http://www.theguardian.com/commentisfree/2015/aug/16/jeremy-corbyn-corbynomics-cosy-consensus-debt-radical-fear.

69. P. Wintour and N. Watt, 'The Corbyn earthquake – how Labour was shaken to its foundations', *Guardian* (September 25, 2015), http://www.theguardian.com/politics/2015/sep/25/jeremy-corbyn-earthquake-labour-party.

70. P. Mortimer, 'Jeremy Corbyn has become a symbol of hope for people who had given up on politics', *Evening Chronicle* (August 19, 2015), http://www.chroniclelive.co.uk/news/news-opinion/jeremy-corbyn-become-symbol-hope-9887042.

I walked on creaky knees to Great St Mary's church, to find it ringed by a shuffling queue of Soviet length. These were the people who'd signed up online to attend. Presumably because the thing was being organised by the unions, they were all being subjected to a minute bureaucratic examination, and the line was barely moving. Tangled up with it was another queue, for people like me who hadn't signed up in advance. Having sorted out which was which with some difficulty, I joined this (the Biblically learned will understand why I referred to it as 'the Foolish Virgins') on the basis that you never know.

And so I spent a pleasant hour or so in the lovely, elegiac Cambridge dusk (gosh, September can be the loveliest of all months when it tries), with the sky fading from gold to blue behind the pinnacles of King's College chapel, chatting with the interesting variety of people who'd come along.

By the way, it's interesting to note that Great St Mary's holds 1,400 people, and was totally full, and that there were at least several hundred outside who couldn't get in.

I warmed to Mr Corbyn personally for two things. One was the unaffected, barely conscious way he bent down to scratch the head of a dog belonging to someone in the crowd. The other was when he acknowledged the majesty of the setting, the beautiful heart of one of the loveliest places in England, at sunset.

It is impossible to imagine any other politician living who could draw such a crowd. Tony Benn could have done, and they'd have paid, but that was because he had become a holy relic and because what someone once called his 'lovely, wuffly Children's Hour voice' could create great waves of nostalgia for long ago teatimes in the hearts of a certain generation.[71]

Far less nostalgic, probably the most explicit example of Corbyn's Bible as Radical Bible, was a picture by the satirical artist, Kaya Mar, who had Labour personified as a horrified mother (Mary?) who had given birth to a baby Corbyn with a halo over his head ('St Jeremy…saviour') and the mark of a hammer and sickle on his forehead.[72] Others were less blunt

71. P. Hitchens, 'My evening with Jeremy Corbyn', *Mail on Sunday Blog* (September 7, 2015), http://hitchensblog.mailonsunday.co.uk/2015/09/my-evening-with-jeremy-corbyn/comments/page/3/. Compare also another relatively sympathetic small 'c' conservative piece by Peter Oborne, who locates Corbyn in a tradition of English radicals like Tom Paine. P. Oborne, 'Corbyn will confront a bankrupt foreign policy. That's why he must be backed', *Middle East Eye* (August 27, 2015), http://www.middleeasteye.net/columns/corbyn-troublemaker-1532484034.

72. J. Charlton, 'Just what makes Jeremy Corbyn so popular? We spoke to his volunteers to find out', *Independent* (August 2015 [no precise date given]),

but equally interested in the link between socialism and religion surrounding the Corbyn phenomenon. George Monbiot, a self-identified non-believer, has suggested that in the wake of Corbyn, leftist movements should borrow ideas and survival methods from evangelical Christianity, even though he shares 'none of the core beliefs'.[73] Theo Hobson suggested that Corbyn's lack of belief is a 'defect' because 'these days left-wing idealism is hugely boosted by an alliance with religion'. Hobson predicted that Corbyn is likely to 'start talking about the Christian basis of his socialism, citing Jesus as an early role model' in order to reach beyond his base and even keep himself in a job. As he is 'in the business of selling a vision' he should turn to 'as the very concepts of hope and change have Christian roots'. We might note that Hobson makes reference to a staple of the Radical Bible tradition: 'imagine the British left without its broad imagery of the New Jerusalem.'[74] Hobson might prove to be a true prophet as Corbyn attended a church service organised by Christians on the Left at the 2015 Labour Party conference and supported their campaign for changes to Sunday trading laws.[75] Indeed, on the eve of the 2015 Labour conference, it was striking that when Andrew Marr began explaining who John the Baptist was, Corbyn immediately interjected, claiming he knew perfectly well who he was and that 'I am very familiar with the Bible. I was brought up with the Bible'.[76]

And, finally, in his victory speech, Corbyn managed to give the all-important biblical allusion: 'we don't pass by on the other side.'[77] Irrespective of whether this was intentional or not, some version of 'pass by on the other side' is looking like one of the handful of biblical verses

http://i100.independent.co.uk/article/just-what-makes-jeremy-corbyn-so-popular-we-spoke-to-his-volunteers-to-find-out--ZyghGmGbmNg.

73. G. Monbiot, 'The model for a leftwing resurgence? Evangelical Christianity', *Guardian* (September 15, 2015), http://www.theguardian.com/commentisfree/2015/sep/15/leftwing-evangelical-christianity-corbyn

74. T. Hobson, 'Will Jeremy Corbyn boost his left-wing idealism with a religious message?', *Spectator* (September 16, 2015), http://blogs.spectator.co.uk/coffeehouse/2015/09/will-jeremy-corbyn-boost-his-left-wing-idealism-with-a-religious-message/.

75. S. Beer, 'Jeremy Corbyn declares support for our Sunday campaign', *Christians on the Left* (September 28, 2015), http://www.christiansontheleft.org.uk/jeremy_corbyn_declares_support_for_our_sunday_campaign

76. *Andrew Marr Show,* BBC 1 (September 27, 2015).

77. Labour Party, 'Jeremy Corbyn's first speech as Leader of the Labour Party', *YouTube* (September 12, 2015), https://www.youtube.com/watch?v=xmgvhn13WPk#, at 16:00–16:20.

politicians and journalists tend to quote from the seemingly implicit repository of authority that is the Bible (alongside e.g. 'love thy neigbour' and 'render unto Caesar'). We have seen how Thatcher famously discussed the Good Samaritan and how Cameron has used it to justify a monopoly on violence and any bombing of ISIS. Context is, obviously, key to understanding how the Bible is being constructed. And, in this instance, Corbyn is, unlike Thatcher and Cameron, firmly and recognisably in the tradition of the Radical Bible as the quotation was in the context of a direct attack on the Welfare Reform and Work Bill (in sharp contrast to the party line before him): 'misery and poverty to so many of the poorest in our society…we want to live in a society where we don't pass by on the other side of those people rejected by an unfair welfare system. Instead we reach out to end the scourge of homelessness and desperation that so many people face in our society.' Indeed, it seems a more direct allusion to (and contrast with) Thatcher's famous claim of 'no such thing as society' in his interview with Marr where he suggested that he wants a 'decent democratic society' and a 'society' where 'we don't pass by on the other side while the poor lie in the gutter'.[78] There was also a further qualification when Corbyn delivered his speech to the Labour Party conference in September 2015. In addition to the speech openly containing a number of familiar leftist positions, there was a more immediate qualification: 'Fair play for all. Solidarity and not walking by on the other side of the street when people are in trouble. Respect for other people's point of view. It is this sense of fair play, these shared majority British values that are the fundamental reason why I love this country and its people.'[79] This was delivered shortly after Corbyn had received intense media criticism for not singing the national anthem at a Battle of Britain memorial service and it is telling that, consciously or not, another common aspect of the Radical Bible was invoked and one Corbyn may well have known from his close friend, Tony Benn: the Radical Bible as something home-grown and *British* (or, alternatively, *English*).

We might also note that, in his interview with Marr, Corbyn used another common phrase and construction: the idea that ISIS and ISIL are

---

78. *Andrew Marr Show.*

79. J. Corbyn, 'Speech by Jeremy Corbyn to Labour Party Annual Conference 2015', Labour Press (September 29, 2015), http://press.labour.org.uk/post/130135691169/speech-by-jeremy-corbyn-to-labour-party-annual. Corbyn also ended with reference to probably the dominant figure in the British Christian Socialist tradition, Keir Hardie: 'My work has consisted of trying to stir up a divine discontent with wrong.'

a 'perversion of Islam'. We have seen such common rhetoric and language associated with Cameron, Blair, and Thatcher, and, in the case of Cameron, accompanied by an allusion to the Good Samaritan. Once again, the frame of reference is crucial to understanding the meaning and in sharp contrast to Blair and Cameron, Corbyn, who has always taken a consistently anti-war stance associated with the Labour Left, did not use construction of Islam to justify the use of violence and military intervention (potential or actual). Corbyn's version of the 'perversion' of a pure Islam perhaps inevitably meant that he would have to explain that he would not talk with ISIS and ISIS would not talk with him: this language typically implies beyond the pale. Nevertheless, Corbyn's proposed take on dealing with ISIS was through 'political and cultural' campaign against ISIS and by looking for ways to cut off funding, arms, and oil revenues.

Finally, while Corbyn might have found himself isolated among the Parliamentary Labour Party, he and his Radical Bible were not alone. The 2015 election saw the new MP for Lancaster and Fleetwood, the Corbyn ally and now Junior Shadow Minister for Women and Equalities, Cat Smith. Smith is more explicit than Corbyn in her use of the Radical Bible, or, more specifically, the Radical Jesus. Smith is a particularly significant example as her Nonconformist rhetoric, at least in one interview, is that which seemed to have vanished when Tony Benn retired and associated more with radical politics outside parliament. Smith mentions her Methodist background in her upbringing in Barrow-in-Furness, the claim that the Labour movement owes more to Methodism than Marxism, and that this Methodist background makes her sceptical of 'hero worship' and 'creating false idols'. Instead, she prefers to think in categories of cooperation and internationalism. Most strikingly, she openly claims that 'Jesus was a radical socialist' and that she is 'inspired by someone who was the Son of God, but he was also a socialist'. To highlight the point, Smith refers to Jesus 'turning over the tables in the temple, and healing the sick, and touching lepers' and 'a message of peace and eradicating poverty and disease'. There is also ecumenicalism ('we live in a multicultural society of many faiths and we all rub along and that's exactly as it should be') but, more tellingly, the classic hostility to ecclesiastical and political hierarchy ('it bothers me that we have reserved places in the House of Lords for people of a Christian faith'), an iconoclasm which we might even speculate stretches to the House of Commons itself ('I'm not that attached to the building, I'm not that bothered about the building').[80]

So, is the Radical Bible (/Religion) now back in parliamentary political discourse? Yes, sort of. But it is striking how much of an anomaly Corbyn and his close allies were when they began to lead Labour in parliament and it is clear that the Corbyn movement was pushed forward by popular non- or extra-parliamentary support. Its longevity presumably depends on the fate of Corbyn and the movement which has pushed him to the leadership of the Labour Party. After the 2008 financial crisis, we have seen the most politically volatile period in English and British politics, including the Conservative-Lib Dem coalition, an intensification of Thatcherite economic policies, an apparent increase in support for economic and social liberalism, an SNP-dominated Scotland with a strong anti-austerity agenda, the (sometimes biblically tinged) nostalgia of the so-called Blue Labour and Red Tories, and a socialist Labour leader with a huge mandate from Party members and supporters but with minimal support among MPs. Many of the ideas associated with all these different movements and moments are contradictory and voting patterns are not necessarily reflecting the old binaries of Right and Left. Amidst this chaos is the Bible, still acting as an authority for different ideological positions. It is by no means clear which position will come to dominate party political discourse and perhaps the only reasonable prediction is that the Bible will support whichever one does.

80. O. Bennett, 'Cat Smith talks Jeremy Corbyn, Jesus Christ and why Socialism isn't "radical"', *Huffington Post* (August 25, 2015), http://m.huffpost.com/uk/entry/8030630.

BIBLIOGRAPHY

Abbott, D., 'Cherish J'can dialect, but please, no Patois Bible', *Jamaica Observer* (January 16, 2011).

Achcar, G. *The Clash of Barbarisms: September 11 and the New World Disorder* (2nd edn; London: Saqi, 2006).

Adams, T., 'This much I know: Tony Blair Interview', *Observer* (June 12, 2011).

Adorno, T.W., 'Resignation (1969)', in *Critical Models: Interventions and Catchwords* (New York: Columbia University Press, 2005), pp. 289-93.

Al-Khalil, J., et al, 'David Cameron fosters division by calling Britain a "Christian country"', *Telegraph* (April 20, 2014), http://www.telegraph.co.uk/comment/letters/10777417/David-Cameron-fosters-division-by-calling-Britain-a-Christian-country.html.

Amnesty International, *Amnesty International Report 2009: Egypt*, http://thereport.amnesty.org/en/regions/middle-east-north-africa/egypt.

Anderson, P., *The Origins of Postmodernity* (London: Verso, 1998).

Anonymous, 'Coming Out as Atheist: Peter Tatchell, Grayson Perry', *National Secular Society* (December 2, 2005), http://www.secularism.org.uk/comingoutasatheist petertatchellg.html.

Anonymous, 'Generation Boris', *Economist* (June 1, 2013).

Anonymous, 'Iraq's Weapons of Mass Destruction: The Assessment of the British Government' (September 24, 2002), http://www.number-10.gov.uk/output/Page271.asp.

Anonymous, 'Obituary: Christopher Hill', *Telegraph* (February 27, 2003).

Anonymous, 'Peter Griffiths: an obituary', *Telegraph* (November 27, 2013).

Anonymous, 'Seeds of Hope – East Timor Ploughshares', *Catholic Social Teaching*, http://www.catholicsocialteaching.org.uk/themes/peace/stories/seeds-hope-east-timor-ploughares/.

Anonymous, 'Tony Blair, former Prime Minister, did order Number 10 staff to pray', *Huffington Post* (July 24, 2012), http://www.huffingtonpost.co.uk/2012/07/24/tony-blairm-former-prime-prayer_n_1699362.html.

Anonymous, 'Tony Blair launches Faith and Globalisation programme at Durham University' (10 July 2009), http://www.dur.ac.uk/news/newsitem/?itemno=8243.

Anonymous, 'Yale and Tony Blair Launch Faith and Globalization Initiative' (September 18, 2008), http://news.yale.edu/2008/09/18/yale-and-tony-blair-launch-faith-and-globalization-initiative.

Appleyard, B., 'Jeffrey and Judas', *Thought Experiments* (January 8, 2007), http://bryanappleyard.com/jeffrey-and-judas/.

The Archbishop of Canterbury's Commission on Urban Priority Areas, *Faith in the City: A Call for Action by Church and Nation* (London: Church House Publishing, 1985).

Archer, J., *The Accused* (London: Methuen, 2000).

———. 'The Gospel according to Judas', *Jeffrey Archer's Official Blog* (January 9, 2007), http://jeffreyarchers.blogspot.com/2007/01/gospel-according-to-judas.html.

———. *A Prison Diary. Vol. 1, Belmarsh: Hell* (London: Macmillan, 2002).

———. *A Prison Diary. Vol. 2, Wayland: Purgatory* (London: Macmillan, 2003).

———. *A Prison Diary. Vol. 3, North Sea Camp: Heaven* (London: Macmillan, 2004).

Archer, J., with F.J. Maloney, *The Gospel according to Judas by Benjamin Iscariot* (London: Macmillan, 2007).

Arnal, W., *The Symbolic Jesus: Historical Scholarship, Judaism and the Construction of Contemporary Identity* (London: Equinox, 2005).

Ashman, S., 'Communist Party Historians' Group', in J. Rees (ed.), *Essays on Historical Materialism* (London: Bookmarks, 1998), pp. 145-59.

Atkinson, M., 'Brief encounters: Sleccy's vinyl countdown', *Guardian* (March 13, 2009).

Avalos, H., 'In Praise of Biblical Illiteracy', *Bible and Interpretation* (April 2010), http://www.bibleinterp.com/articles/literate357930.shtml.

Badiou, A., *Saint Paul: The Foundation of Universalism* (Stanford: Stanford University Press, 2003).

Bainbridge, L., 'Ten right-wing rockers', *Guardian* (October 14, 2007).

Baker, L., 'The unsinkable Ian Brown', *Guardian* (February 2, 2002).

Bakunin, M., *Selected Works* (New York: Alfred A. Knopf, 1972).

Baldwin, T., 'Cherie stops Blair being stick in mud', *Times* (December 15, 2001).

Ball, J., and T. Clark, 'Generation Self: what do young people really care about?', *Guardian* (March 11, 2013).

Barber, L., 'Tony Blair: An Exclusive Interview', *Financial Times Magazine* (June 29, 2012).

BBC News, '100 great British heroes', *BBC News* (August 21, 2002), http://news.bbc.co.uk/1/hi/entertainment/2208671.stm.

———. 'Archer jailed for perjury', *BBC News* (July 19, 2001), http://news.bbc.co.uk/1/hi/uk/1424501.stm.

———. 'Blair feared faith "nutter" label', *BBC News* (November 25, 2007), http://news.bbc.co.uk/1/hi/7111620.stm.

———. 'Blair launches faith foundation', *BBC News* (May 30, 2008), http://news.bbc.co.uk/1/hi/uk_politics/7427809.stm.

———. 'I had to top Archer', *BBC News* (November 23, 1999), http://news.bbc.co.uk/1/hi/uk_politics/533362.stm.

———. 'I'm no saint, says Lord Archer', *BBC News* (September 5, 1999), http://news.bbc.co.uk/1/hi/uk_politics/438941.stm.

———. 'In full: Blair on bomb blasts', *BBC News* (July 7, 2005), http://news.bbc.co.uk/1/hi/uk/4659953.stm.

———. 'Judas "Helped Jesus Save Mankind" ', *BBC News* (April 7, 2006). http://news.bbc.co.uk/1/hi/world/americas/4882420.stm.

———. 'Life of Brian named best comedy', *BBC News* (January 1, 2006), http://news.bbc.co.uk/1/hi/entertainment/4573444.stm.

———. 'Looking back at race relations', *BBC News* (October 29, 1999), http://news.bbc.co.uk/1/hi/482565.stm.

———. 'Margaret Thatcher funeral: Cameron speaks of personal debt to former PM', *BBC News* (April 17, 2013), http://www.bbc.co.uk/news/uk-politics-22180610.

———. 'PM attacked on Iraq "God" remarks', *BBC News* (March 4, 2006), http://news.bbc.co.uk/1/hi/4773124.stm.

———. 'Rebekah Brooks reveals "LOL" texts from Cameron', *BBC News* (May 11, 2012), http://www.bbc.co.uk/news/uk-politics-18032027.

———. 'Schools get King James Bible to mark 400th anniversary', *BBC News* (May 15, 2012), http://www.bbc.co.uk/news/education-18073996.

———. 'Tony Blair "godfather to Rupert Murdoch's daughter" ', *BBC News* (September 5, 2011), http://www.bbc.co.uk/news/uk-politics-14785501/.

Beattie, J., and A. Shaw, 'Oh, you are ROFL: Ex-Sun boss reveals PM signed off texts with LOL', *Mirror* (May 11, 2012).

Beckett, F., *Enemy Within: The Rise and Fall of the British Communist Party* (London: John Murray, 1995).

Beckett, F., and D. Hencke, *The Blairs and Their Court* (London: Aurum, 2004).

Beer, S., 'Jeremy Corbyn declares support for our Sunday campaign', *Christians on the Left* (September 28, 2015), http://www.christiansontheleft.org.uk/jeremy_corbyn_declares_support_for_our_sunday_campaign.

Beer, S.H., 'Christopher Hill: Some Reminiscences', in Pennington and Thomas (eds.), *Puritans and Revolutionaries*, pp. 1-4.

Beith, A., 'Should the State Forgive?', in Latham and Mathys (eds.), *Liberal Democrats Do God*, Chapter 5.

Benn, T., *Arguments for Socialism* (London: Jonathan Cape, 1979).

———. *Conflicts Of Interest: Diaries 1977–80* (London: Hutchinson, 1990).

———. *Dare to Be a Daniel: Then and Now* (London: Arrow Books, 2004).

———. *Free at Last! Diaries 1991–2001* (London: Hutchinson, 2002).

———. *Free Radical: New Century Essays* (New York: Continuum, 2003).

———. *The Levellers and the English Democratic Tradition* (Nottingham: Russell Press, 1976).

———. *Office without Power: Diaries 1968–72* (London: Hutchinson, 1988).

———. 'The Power of the Bible Today', in *Sheffield Academic Press Occasional Papers: The Twelfth Annual Sheffield Academic Press Lecture, University of Sheffield, March 17, 1995* (Sheffield: Sheffield Academic Press, 1995), pp. 1-13.

Bennett, O., 'Cat Smith talks Jeremy Corbyn, Jesus Christ and why Socialism isn't "radical"', *Huffington Post* (August 25, 2015), http://m.huffpost.com/uk/entry/8030630.

Berlinerblau, J., *Thumpin' It: The Use and Abuse of the Bible in Today's Presidential Politics* (Louisville: WJK, 2008).

Bermant, A., 'Don't believe the hype: Thatcher's "friendship" with Israel based on pragmatism not love', *Haaretz* (April 17, 2013).

Bez, *Freaky Dancin': Me and the Mondays* (London: Pan Books, 1998).

Bingham, J., 'Cameron's olive branch to the Church in Christian Christmas message', *Telegraph* (December 24, 2012).

Blair, T., 'Blair's statement in full', *BBC News* (September 11, 2001), http://news.bbc.co.uk/1/hi/uk_politics/1538551.stm.

———. 'Faith in Politics', *Speech to the Christian Socialist Movement* (London, 2001), http://www.britishpoliticalspeech.org/speech-archive.htm?speech=280.

———. 'The full text of Tony Blair's letter to Michael Foot written in July 1982', *Telegraph* (June 16, 2006), http://www.telegraph.co.uk/news/uknews/1521418/The-full-text-of-Tony-Blairs-letter-to-Michael-Foot-written-in-July-1982.html.

———. *A Journey* (London: Hutchinson, 2010).

———. 'Preface', in Bryant (ed.), *Reclaiming the Ground*, pp. 9-12.

Blevins, J.L., *The Messianic Secret in Markan Research 1901–1976* (Washington, D.C.: University Press of America, 1981).

Blincoe, N., 'Mark E. Smith: wonderful and frightening', *Telegraph* (26 April, 2008).

Bloom, D., 'Jeremy Corbyn is now bigger than Jesus—on Google', *Mirror* (July 28, 2015), http://www.mirror.co.uk/news/uk-news/jeremy-corbyn-now-bigger-jesus-6150547.

Boer, R., 'Apocalyptic and Apocalypticism in the Poetry of E.P. Thompson', *Spaces of Utopia* 7 (2009), pp. 34-53.

———. *Political Grace: The Revolutionary Theology of John Calvin* (Louisville: WJK, 2009).

———. *Political Myth: On the Use and Abuse of Biblical Themes* (Durham: Duke University Press, 2009).

———. *Rescuing the Bible* (Oxford: Blackwell, 2007).

Boer, R., and A. Andrews, 'Thin Economics; Thick Moralising: Red Toryism and the Politics of Nostalgia', *Bulletin for the Study of Religion* 40 (2011), pp. 16-24.

Bonnett, A., *Radicalism, Anti-racism and Representation* (London: Routledge, 2013).

Booth, A.L., *The Economics of the Trade Union* (Cambridge: Cambridge University Press, 1995).

Borger, J., and S. Bates, 'Judas: this is what really happened', *Guardian* (April 7, 2006).

Bornkamm, G., *Jesus of Nazareth* (London: Hodder & Stoughton, 1960).

Bowcott, O., 'Outcry as historian labelled a Soviet spy', *Guardian* (March 6, 2003).

Bowcott, O., and S. Jones, 'Johnson's "piccaninnies" apology', *Guardian* (January 23, 2008).

Boyarin, D., *A Radical Jew: Paul and the Politics of Identity* (Berkeley: University of California Press, 1994).

Branagh, E., J. Tapsfield, and E. Pickover, 'Lots of love: Rebekah Brooks lifts lid on David Cameron friendship at Leveson', *Independent* (May 11, 2012).

Brand, R., *Messiah Complex* (DVD; 2Entertain, 2013).

———. *Revolution* (London: Century, 2014).

———. 'We no longer have the luxury of tradition', *New Statesman* (October 24, 2013), http://www.newstatesman.com/politics/2013/10/russell-brand-on-revolution.

Brandon, S.G.F., *Jesus and the Zealots: A Study of the Political Factor in Primitive Christianity* (Manchester: Manchester University Press, 1967).

———. *The Trial of Jesus of Nazareth* (London: B.T. Batsford, 1968).

Brinton, B., 'Immigration: "…I was a stranger and you took me in" ', in Latham and Mathys (eds.), *Liberal Democrats Do God*, Chapter 8.

Brooker, C., 'Screen Burn', *Guardian* (February 3, 2007).

Brooks-Pollock, T., 'Tim Farron on gay sex: New Lib Dem leader declines to say if he considers it's a sin', *Independent* (July 18, 2015), http://www.independent.co.uk/news/uk/politics/is-gay-sex-a-sin--tim-farron-repeatedly-declines-to-answer-10398546.html.

Brown, A., 'Gospel according to Powell: Christ was stoned to death', *Independent* (August 16, 1994).

Brown, C.G., *The Death of Christian Britain: Understanding Secularisation* (2nd edn; Abingdon: Routledge, 2009).

———. *Religion and Society in Twentieth-Century Britain* (Harlow: Peason, 2006).

———. 'The Secularisation Decade: What the 1960s Have Done to the Study of Religious History', in H. McLeod and W. Ustorf (eds.), *The Decline of Christendom in Western Europe* (Cambridge: Cambridge University Press, 2003), pp. 29-46.

Brown, D., 'A new language of racism in politics', *Guardian* (27 April, 2001).

Brown, G., 'Speech and Q&A at St Paul's Cathedral: Transcript of speeches by the Prime Minister and Australian Prime Minister Kevin Rudd at St Paul's Cathedral' (March 31, 2009), http://webarchive.nationalarchives.gov.uk/+/number10.gov.uk/news/speeches-and-transcripts/2009/03/pms-speech-at-st-pauls-cathedral-18858.

Brown, R.E., *The Birth of the Messiah: A Commentary on the Infancy Narratives in Matthew and Luke* (rev. edn; London: Chapman, 1993 [1977]).

Brown, W., 'American Nightmare: Neoconservatism, Neoliberalism, and De-democratization', *Political Theory* 34 (2006), pp. 690-714.

———. *Regulating Aversion: Tolerance in the Age of Identity and Empire* (Princeton: Princeton University Press, 2006).

Bryant, C., 'Introduction', in Bryant (ed.), *Reclaiming the Ground*, pp. 13-28.

Bryant, C. (ed.), *Reclaiming the Ground: Christianity and Socialism* (London: Hodder & Stoughton, 1993).

Budowsky, B., 'Tony Blair's messianic justifications for the Iraq war', *The Hill* (February 1, 2010), http://thehill.com/blogs/pundits-blog/international-affairs/79041-tony-blairs-messianic-justifications-for-the-iraq-war#ixzz2R0MXgtxz.

Burton, J., and E. McCabe, *We Don't Do God: Blair's Religious Belief and Its Consequences* (London: Continuum, 2009).

Caesar, B., 'Interview: Linton Kwesi Johnson Talks to Burt Caesar at Sparkside Studios, Brixton, London, 11 June 1996', *Critical Quarterly* 38 (1996), pp. 64-77.

Callinicos, A., *The New Mandarins of American Power* (Cambridge: Polity Press, 2003).

Cameron, D., 'A Christmas message from David Cameron (December 25, 2012)', http://www.conservatives.com/News/News_stories/2012/12/A_Christmas_message_from_David_Cameron.aspx.

———. 'Christmas 2014: Prime Minister's Message' (December 24, 2014), https://www.gov.uk/government/news/christmas-2014-prime-ministers-message.

———. 'David Cameron's Easter Message (April 24, 2011)', https://www.gov.uk/government/news/david-camerons-easter-message.

———. 'David Cameron's Easter Message to Christians', *Premier Christianity* (April 2015), http://www.premierchristianity.com/Topics/Society/Politics/David-Cameron-s-Easter-Message-to-Christians.

———. 'David Haines: David Cameron statement on killing' *BBC News* (September 14, 2014), http://www.bbc.co.uk/news/uk-29198128.

———. 'Easter 2014: David Cameron's message' (April 16, 2014), https://www.gov.uk/government/news/easter-2014-david-camerons-message.

———. 'My Faith in the Church of England', *Church Times* (April 16, 2014), http://www.churchtimes.co.uk/articles/2014/17-april/comment/opinion/my-faith-in-the-church-of-england.

———. 'Prime Minister's King James Bible Speech (December 16, 2010)', Number 10 Downing Street, http://www.number10.gov.uk/news/king-james-bible/.

Campbell, A., 'Baroness Warsi misses point of "we don't do God", writes a pro faith atheist', *Alastair's Blog* (September 16, 2010), http://www.alastaircampbell.org/blog/2010/09/16/baroness-warsi-misses-point-of-we-dont-do-god-writes-a-pro-faith-atheist/.

————. *The Blair Years* (Hutchinson: London, 2007).

————. *Power and the People 1997–1999: The Alastair Campbell Diaries, vol. 2* (London: Arrow, 2011).

Campbell, J., *Margaret Thatcher. Vol. 1, The Grocer's Daughter* (London: Jonathan Cape, 2000)

————. *Margaret Thatcher. Vol. 2, The Iron Lady* (London: Jonathan Cape, 2003).

Campbell, S., *Irish Blood, English Heart: Second Generation Irish Musicians in England* (Cork: Cork University Press, 2011).

Casey, M., 'Some Anti-Semitic Assumptions in *The Theological Dictionary of the New Testament*', *Novum Testamentum* 41 (1999), pp. 280-91.

Chakelian, A., 'WATCH: Christmas messages from David Cameron, Nick Clegg and Ed Miliband', *New Statesman* (December 24, 2014), http://www.newstatesman. com/politics/2014/12/watch-christmas-messages-david-cameron-nick-clegg-and-ed-miliband.

Chapman, J., 'Brown DOES do God as he calls for new world order in sermon at St Paul's', *Daily Mail* (April 1, 2009).

Chapman, J., and V. Allen, 'So that's how close they were! David Cameron signed off texts to Rebekah Brooks with "lots of love" (and they DID discuss phone hacking)', *Daily Mail* (May 18, 2012).

Charlton, J., 'Just what makes Jeremy Corbyn so popular? We spoke to his volunteers to find out', *Independent* (August 2015 [no precise date given]), http://i100.independent.co.uk/article/just-what-makes-jeremy-corbyn-so-popular-we-spoke-to-his-volunteers-to-find-out--ZyghGmGbmNg.

Childs, D., *Britain since 1945: A Political History* (London: Routledge, 2001).

Chomsky, N., *American Power and the New Mandarins* (New York: Pantheon Books, 1969).

————. *Pirates and Emperors, Old and New: International Terrorism in the Real World* (London: Pluto, 2002).

Clapton, E., *Clapton: The Autobiography* (London: Century, 2007).

Clark, H.B., *The Church under Thatcher* (London: SPCK, 1993).

Claussen, D., *Theodor W. Adorno: One Last Genius* (Cambridge, Mass.: Belknap Press of Harvard University Press, 2008).

Cobain, I., 'Was Oxford's most famous Marxist a Soviet mole?', *Times* (March 5, 2003).

Colvile, R. '*Revolution* by Russell Brand, review: "sub-undergraduate dross"', *Telegraph* (October 23, 2014), http://www.telegraph.co.uk/culture/books/bookreviews/ 11182073/Revolution-by-Russell-Brand.html.

Connor, A., 'Top of the class', *BBC News* (October 17, 2005), http://news.bbc.co.uk/ 1/hi/magazine/4349324.stm.

Corbyn, J., 'About me' (no date), http://jeremycorbyn.org.uk/about/.

————. 'Speech by Jeremy Corbyn to Labour Party Annual Conference 2015', Labour Press (September 29, 2015), http://press.labour.org.uk/post/130135691169/speech-by-jeremy-corbyn-to-labour-party-annual.

Corfield, P.J., " 'We are All One in the Eyes of the Lord": Christopher Hill and the Historical Meanings of Radical Religion', *History Workshop Journal* 58 (2004), pp. 111-27.

Cowley, J., 'Victory for the Cult of Corbyn? No, the start of a long and brutal civil war', *Daily Mail* (September 15, 2015), http://www.dailymail.co.uk/debate/

article-3234590/JASON-COWLEY-Victory-Cult-Corbyn-No-start-long-brutal-civil-war.html.

Crace, J., 'The Gospel according to Judas by Benjamin Iscariot and Recounted by Jeffrey Archer and Prof. Francis J Moloney', *Guardian* (March 27, 2007).

———. '*Revolution* by Russell Brand – digested read', *Guardian* (October 24, 2014), http://www.theguardian.com/books/2014/oct/26/revolution-russell-brand-digested.

Cramner, Archbishop, 'The cult of comrade Corbyn', *Archbishop Cramner* (August 9, 2015), http://archbishopcranmer.com/the-cult-of-comrade-corbyn/.

Crampton, C., 'David Cameron's Christmas message', *New Statesman* (December 24, 2012).

Crawford, P., ' "Charles Stuart, That Man of Blood" ', *Journal of British Studies* 14 (1977), pp. 41-61.

Cremin, C., *Capitalism's New Clothes: Enterprise, Ethics and Enjoyment in Times of Crisis* (London: Pluto Press, 2011).

Crick, M., *Jeffrey Archer: Stranger than Fiction* (rev. edn; London: Forth Estate, 2000).

Crines, A. S., and K. Theakston, '"Doing God" in Number 10: British Prime Ministers, Religion, and Political Rhetoric', *Politics and Religion* (2015) 8, pp. 155-77.

Crossan, J.D., *The Historical Jesus: The Life of a Mediterranean Jewish Peasant* (Edinburgh: T. & T. Clark; San Francisco: HarperCollins, 1991).

Crossley, J.G., 'The Damned Rich (Mark 10.17-31)', *Expository Times* 116 (2005), pp. 397-401.

———. 'Defining History', in J.G. Crossley and C. Karner (eds.), *Writing History, Constructing Religion* (Aldershot: Ashgate, 2005), pp. 9-29.

———. 'Enoch Powell and the Gospel Tradition: A Search for a Homeland', in K.W. Whitelam (ed.), *Holy Land as Homeland? Models for Constructing the Historic Landscapes of Jesus* (Sheffield: Sheffield Phoenix Press, 2012), pp. 134-50.

———. 'For EveryManc a Religion: Uses of Biblical and Religious Language in the Manchester Music Scene, 1976–1994', *Biblical Interpretation* 19 (2011), pp. 151-80.

———. 'God and the State: The Bible and David Cameron's Authority', (forthcoming, 2016).

———. *Jesus in an Age of Neoliberalism: Quests, Scholarship, Ideology* (London: Acumen, 2012).

———. *Jesus in an Age of Terror: Scholarly Quests for a New American Century* (London: Equinox, 2008).

———. 'Life of Brian or Life of Jesus? Uses of Critical Biblical Scholarship and Non-orthodox Views of Jesus in Monty Python's *Life of Brian*', *Relegere* (2011), pp. 95-116.

———. 'The Multicultural Christ: Jesus the Jew and the New Perspective on Paul in an Age of Neoliberalism', *Bible and Critical Theory* 7 (2011), pp. 1-9.

———. 'OH-MY-GOD – It's So the Teen Bible!', *SBL Forum* (January 2007), http://sbl-site.org/Article.aspx?ArticleID=615.

———. 'We Don't Do Babylon: Erin Runions in English Political Discourse', *Bible and Critical Theory* 11 (2015), pp. 61-76.

———. *Why Christianity Happened: A Socio-Historical Account of Christian Origins, 26–50 CE* (Louisville: WJK, 2006).

Crossley, J. G., and J. Harrison, 'Atheism, Christianity and the Press: Press coverage of Pope Benedict XVI's 2010 state visit to the UK', *Implicit Religion* 18 (2015), pp. 77–105.

———. 'The Mediation of the Distinction of "Religion" and "Politics" by the UK Press on the Occasion of Pope Benedict XVI's State Visit to the UK', *Political Theology* 14 (2015), pp. 329–45.

Cruddas, J., 'On building the new Jerusalem', *New Statesman* (September 30, 2012).

Crystal, D., *Begat: The King James Bible and the English Language* (Oxford: Oxford University Press, 2010).

Cullmann, O., *Jesus and the Revolutionaries* (New York: Harper Row, 1970).

Cummings, J., 'How British Jews built Thatcherism', *Haaretz* (April 17, 2013).

Curtis, D., *Touching from a Distance: Ian Curtis and Joy Division* (London: Faber, 1995).

Dale, G., *God's Politicians: The Christian Contribution to 100 Years of Labour* (London: HarperCollins, 2000).

Darnton, R., 'Workers Revolt: The Great Cat Massacre of the Rue Saint-Séverin', in *The Great Cat Massacre and Other Episodes in French Cultural History* (London: Allen Lane, 1984), pp. 75-104.

Davie, G., *Religion in Britain since 1945: Believing without Belonging* (Oxford: Blackwell, 1994).

Davies, P.R., '*Life of Brian* Research', in P.R. Davies, *Whose Bible Is It Anyway?* (London: T&T Clark/Continuum, 2004), pp. 142-55, first printed in J.C. Exum and S.D. Moore (eds.), *Biblical Studies/Cultural Studies: The Third Sheffield Colloquium* (Sheffield: Sheffield Academic Press, 1998), pp. 400-414.

———. 'Whose Bible? Anyone's?', *Bible and Interpretation* (July 2009), http://www.bibleinterp.com/opeds/whose.shtml.

Davis, J.C., *Fear, Myth and History: The Ranters and the Historians* (Cambridge: Cambridge University Press, 1986).

Dawkins, R., 'Atheists for Jesus', *Free Inquiry* 25 (2005), pp. 9–10.

———. *The God Delusion* (London: Bantham Press, 2006).

———. 'Why I want all our children to read the King James Bible', *Observer* (May 19, 2012).

Dawson, A., 'Why Russell Brand IS a 'trivial man' with his apathy-fuelled revolution', *Mirror* (October 24, 2013), http://www.mirror.co.uk/news/uk-news/russell-brand-newsnight-paxman-right-2487661.

Derbyshire, J., 'The NS Profile: Ralph Miliband', *New Statesman* (30 August, 2010).

Dillon, M., and J. Reid, *The Liberal Way of War: Killing to Make Life Live* (New York: Routledge, 2009).

Dominiczak, P., Pray consider: would God be a Lib Dem or a Somerset Tory?', *Sunday Telegraph* (August 25, 2013).

Doughty, S., 'Pope faces atheist hate campaign in UK after top German aide says: "When you land at Heathrow you think you're in a Third World country" ', *Daily Mail* (September 16, 2010).

Dowden, R., 'The Thatcher Philosophy', *Catholic Herald* (December 22, 1978).

Dumas, D., ' "I had never been in a supermarket before I came to America": Wendi Murdoch on her childhood, her daughters and being best friends with Nicole Kidman', *Daily Mail* (September 10, 2011).

Dworkin, D., *Cultural Marxism in Postwar Britain: History, the New Left and the Origins of Cultural Studies* (Durham: Duke University Press, 1997).

Dyke, C., 'Learning from *The Life of Brian*: Saviors for Seminars', in G. Aichele and R. Walsh (eds.), *Screening Scripture: Intertextual Connections between Scripture and Film* (Harrisburg: Trinity, 2002), pp. 229-50.

Eagleton, T., *The Illusions of Postmodernism* (Oxford: Blackwell, 1996).

———. 'Occupy London are true followers of Jesus, even if they despise religion', *Guardian* (November 3, 2011).

Edwards, K.B., *Ad Men and Eve: The Bible and Advertising* (Sheffield: Sheffield Phoenix Press, 2012).

———. 'Sporting Messiah: Hypermasculinity and Nationhood in Male-targeted Sports Imagery', *Biblical Reception* 1 (2012), pp. 323-46.

Engels, F., 'On the History of Earliest Christianity (1894)', in K. Marx and F. Engels, *Collected Works Volume 27, Engels: 1890–95* (London: Lawrence & Wishart, 1990), pp. 447-69.

Erel, U., and C. Klesse, 'Out of Place: Silencing Voices on Queerness/Raciality', *MR Zine* (October 24, 2009), http://mrzine.monthlyreview.org/2009/ek241009.html.

Evans, D., 'Spain and the World: Aspects of the Spanish Revolution and Civil War (7)', *Radical History Network* (August 31, 2011), http://radicalhistorynetwork.blogspot.co.uk/2011/08/spain-and-world-aspects-of-spanish.html.

Evans, R.J., 'Michael Gove's history curriculum is a pub quiz not an education', *New Statesman* (March 21, 2013).

———. 'The Wonderfulness of Us (the Tory Interpretation of History)', *London Review of Books* 33 (March 17, 2011), pp. 9-12.

Farron, T., 'What Is Christianity, Do I Need to Take It Seriously, and Can I be a Liberal Democrat and a Christian?', in Latham and Mathys (eds.), *Liberal Democrats Do God*, Chapter 2.

Fawcett, L., 'The cult of Corbyn', *Rife Magazine* (August 25, 2015), http://www.rifemagazine.co.uk/2015/08/the-cult-of-corbyn/.

Field, F., 'Enoch Powell as a Parliamentarian', in Rising (ed.), *Enoch at 100*, pp. 47-53.

———. 'What would Thatcher do today about…the rich', *Times* (April 18, 2013).

Filby, E., 'God and Mrs Thatcher: Religion and Politics in 1980s Britain' (PhD thesis, University of Warwick, 2010).

———. *God and Mrs Thatcher: The Battle for Britain's Soul* (London: Biteback, 2015).

———. 'Margaret Thatcher: her unswerving faith shaped by her father', *Telegraph* (April 14, 2013).

Financial and political staff, 'Archer in DTI Shares Inquiry', *Guardian* (July 8, 1994).

Fisher, M., *Capitalist Realism: Is There No Alternative?* (Winchester: Zero Books, 2009).

Fisk, R., *The Great War for Civilisation: The Conquest of the Middle East* (London: Fourth Estate, 2005).

———. 'Police state is the wrong venue for Obama's speech', *Independent* (June 3, 2009).

Foot, P., *Articles of Resistance* (London: Bookmarks, 2000).

———. 'Those Suits', *London Review of Books* 17 (May 1995).

Footman, T., 'By Request: Thirty Pieces of Archer', *Cultural Snow* (March 26, 2007), http://culturalsnow.blogspot.com/search/label/Jeffrey%20Archer.

———. 'The gospel according to Widdecombe', *Guardian* (October 14, 2008).

Ford, S., *Hip Priest: The Story of Mark E. Smith and The Fall* (London: Quartet, 2003).

Foucault, M., 'Nietzsche, Genealogy, History', in D.F. Bouchard (ed.), *Language, Counter-Memory, Practice: Selected Essays and Interviews* (Ithaca: Cornell University Press, 1977), pp. 139-64.

Fraser, G., 'Occupy London's eviction is a failure for the church, not the camp', *Guardian* (January 31, 2012).

Galbraith, D., 'The Author of the Bible Revealed! And it's you', *Religion Bulletin* (December 17, 2010), http://www.equinoxpub.com/blog/2010/12/the-author-of-the-bible-revealed/.

———. 'Drawing Our Fish in the Sand: Secret Biblical Allusions in the Music of U2', *Biblical Interpretation* 19 (2011), pp. 181-222.

Garner, R., ' "Jingoistic and illegal" – what teachers think of Michael Gove's national curriculum reforms', *Independent* (June 12, 2013).

Geddes, A., *The Politics of Migration and Immigration in Europe* (London: Sage, 2003).

Gledhill, R., 'Jesus was no miracle worker: the Gospel of Jeffrey Archer', *Times* (March 21, 2007).

Godfrey, N., 'Gospel of Judas (Archer/Moloney) fantasy verses', *Vridar* (September 4, 2007), http://vridar.wordpress.com/2007/04/09/gospel-of-judas-archermoloney-fantasy-verses/#more-263.

Goldberg, D.T., *The Threat of Race: Reflections on Racial Neoliberalism* (Oxford: Wiley-Blackwell, 2009).

Goldstein, M., *Jesus in the Jewish Tradition* (New York: Macmillan, 1950).

Goodacre, M., 'Archer and Moloney's Gospel of Judas', *NT Blog* (March 20, 2007), http://ntweblog.blogspot.co.uk/2007/03/archer-and-moloneys-gospel-of-judas.html.

Goodyer, I., *Crisis Music: The Cultural Politics of Rock against Racism* (Manchester: Manchester University Press, 2009).

Gove, M., 'I can't fight my feelings any more: I love Tony', *Times* (February 25, 2003).

———. 'Why I'm proud to be a Christian (and Jeremy Paxman should be ashamed)', *Spectator* (April 4, 2015), http://www.spectator.co.uk/features/9487882/in-defence-of-christianity/.

Graham, E.L., 'Doing God? Public Theology under Blair', P.M. Scott, E.L. Graham, and C.R. Baker (eds.), *Remoralizing Britain? Political, Ethical and Theological Perspectives on New Labour: Social, Ethical and Theological Perspectives on New Labour* (London: Continuum, 2009), pp. 1-18.

Gregory, D., *The Colonial Present: Afghanistan, Palestine, Iraq* (Oxford: Blackwell, 2004).

Groves, J., 'God? He's a Liberal, says (Lib Dem) minister who claims party has support of the Almighty despite languishing in the polls', *Daily Mail* (August 26, 2013).

Gunter, L., 'Tony Blair and wife perform chant ritual to lizards/pyramid in Mexico', *Edmonton Journal* (December 2001–January 2002).

Habermas, G.R., 'Resurrection Research from 1975 to the Present: What Are Critical Scholars Saying?', *Journal for the Study of the Historical Jesus* 3 (2005), pp. 135-53.

Hague, R., 'Confrontation, Incorporation and Exclusion: British Trade Unions in Collectivist and Post-Collectivist Politics', in H. Berrington (ed.), *Change in British Politics* (London: Cass, 1984), pp. 127-59.

Hale, S., *Blair's Community: Communitarian Thought and New Labour* (Manchester: Manchester University Press, 2006).

Hall, S., 'The Great Moving Right Show', *Marxism Today* (January 1979), pp. 14-20.

————. *The Hard Road to Renewal: Thatcherism and the Crisis of the Left* (London: Verso, 1988).

Hall, S., and M. Jaques (eds.), *The Politics of Thatcherism* (London: Lawrence & Wishart, 1983).

Hames, D., 'It's Good to be Green', in Latham and Mathys (eds.), *Liberal Democrats Do God*, Chapter 10.

Hamilton, S., *The Crisis of Theory: E.P. Thompson, the New Left and Postwar British Politics* (Manchester: Manchester University Press, 2011).

Hansard/Parliament, 'Early day motion 678 (2003-4): Anniversary of the Death of Bill Hicks', http://www.parliament.uk/edm/2003-04/678.

————. 'Iraq', Hansard: Commons Debates (March 18, 2003), Columns 767-68, http://www.publications.parliament.uk/pa/cm200203/cmhansrd/vo030318/debtext/30318-07.htm.

————. 'Marriage (Same Sex Couples) Bill', Hansard: Commons Debates (February 5, 2013), Columns 125-230, http://www.publications.parliament.uk/pa/cm201213/cmhansrd/cm130205/debtext/130205-0001.htm.

————. 'Sexual Offences (No. 2)', Hansard Commons Debates (July 5, 1966), Columns 259-67, http://hansard.millbanksystems.com/commons/1966/jul/05/sexual-offences-no-2.

Hari, J., 'A Civil Partnership: Interview with Tony Blair', *Attitude* (April 8, 2009), pp. 50-52.

Harker, J., 'For black Britons, this is not the 80s revisited. It's worse', *Guardian* (August 11, 2011).

Harris, J., 'Generation Y: why young voters are backing the Conservatives', *Guardian* (June 26, 2013).

————. *The Last Party: Britpop, Blair and the Demise of English Rock* (London: HarperPerennial, 2004).

Harris, R., *Not for Turning: The Life of Margaret Thatcher* (London: Bantham Press, 2013).

Harvey, D., *A Brief History of Neoliberalism* (Oxford: Oxford University Press, 2005).

————. *The Condition of Postmodernity* (Oxford: Blackwell, 1989).

————. *The New Imperialism* (Oxford: Oxford University Press, 2003)

Haslam, D., *Manchester, England: The Story of the Pop Cult City* (London: Fourth Estate, 1999).

Hattersley, R., 'The Big Dipper: an interview with Jeffrey Archer', *Sunday Times* (February 19, 2006).

Head, P., 'The Nazi Quest for an Aryan Jesus', *Journal for the Study of the Historical Jesus* 2 (2004), pp. 55-89.

Hebdige, D., *Hiding in the Light: Images and Things* (London: Routledge, 1988).

————. *Subculture: The Meaning of Style* (London: Methuen, 1979).

Heddle, R., and L. Bellingham, 'Anti-Fascism: That Was Then, This Is Now', *Socialist Review* (June 2004), http://www.socialistreview.org.uk/article.php?articlenumber=8931.

Heffer, S., *Like the Roman: The Life of Enoch Powell* (London: Weidenfeld & Nicolson, 1998).

Hengel, M., *Was Jesus a Revolutionist?* (Philadelphia: Fortress, 1971).

Hennessy, P., *Never Again: Britain 1945–51* (London: Jonathan Cape, 1992).

Haritaworn, J., with T. Tauqir and E. Erdem, 'Gay Imperialism: Gender and Sexuality Discourse in the "War on Terror" ', in A. Kuntsman and E. Miyake (eds.), *Out of Place: Silencing Voices on Queerness/Raciality* (York: Raw Nerve Books, 2008), pp. 71-95.

Heschel, S., *The Aryan Jesus: Christian Theologians and the Bible in Nazi Germany* (Princeton: Princeton University Press, 2008).

———. 'Nazifying Christian Theology Walter Grundmann and the Institute for the Study and Eradication of Jewish Influence on German Church Life', *Church History* 63 (1994), pp. 587-605.

Hewison, R., *Monty Python: The Case Against* (New York: Grove, 1981).

Hicks, B., 'Relentless' (Centaur Theatre, Montreal, 1991), http://www.youtube.com/watch?v=JIA5dL7VJxg.

———. 'Revelations' (Dominion Theatre, London, September 14, 1993), http://www.youtube.com/watch?v=w7bcxBf2vK4.

———. 'Shock and Awe' (Oxford Playhouse, November 11, 1992), http://www.youtube.com/watch?v=UTwgooaYC3U.

Higgins, C., 'Philip Pullman creates a darker Christ in new assault on the church', *Guardian* (March 26, 2010).

Hill, C., *Antichrist in Seventeenth-Century England* (London: Oxford University Press, 1971).

———. *The English Bible and the Seventeenth Century Revolution* (London: Penguin Books, 1993).

———. *The English Revolution 1640* (London: Lawrence & Wishart, 1940).

———. *The Experience of Defeat: Milton and Some Contemporaries* (London: Faber & Faber, 1984).

———. 'Historians and the Rise of British Capitalism', *Science and Society* 14 (1950), pp. 307-21.

———. *Lenin and the Russian Revolution* (London: Hodder & Stoughton, 1947).

———. *Liberty against the Law: Some Seventeenth Century Controversies* (London: Penguin Books, 1996).

———. *A Nation of Change and Novelty: Radical Politics, Religion and Literature in Seventeenth-Century England* (London: Routledge, 1990).

———. 'The Norman Yoke', in J. Saville (ed.), *Democracy and the Labour Movement* (London: Lawrence & Wishart, 1954), pp. 11-66.

———. *Religion and Politics in 17th Century England* (Brighton: Harvester Press, 1986).

———. 'Stalin and the Science of History', *Modern Quarterly* 8 (1953), pp. 198-212.

———. *The World Turned Upside Down: Radical Ideas during the English Revolution* (London: Penguin Books, 1972).

Hill, S., 'Would Jesus kick the Occupy London protesters off St Paul's grounds?', *Guardian* (October 20, 2011).

Hilton, R., 'Christopher Hill: Some Reminiscences', in Pennington and Thomas (eds.), *Puritans and Revolutionaries*, pp. 6-10.

Hitchens, P., 'My evening with Jeremy Corbyn', *Mail on Sunday Blog* (September 7, 2015), http://hitchensblog.mailonsunday.co.uk/2015/09/my-evening-with-jeremy-corbyn/comments/page/3/.

Hobsbawm, E.[J.], *The Age of Extremes: The Short Twentieth Century 1914–1991* (London: Abacus, 1994).

————. 'Communist Party Historians' Group 1946–56', in M. Cornforth (ed.), *Rebels and their Causes: Essays in Honour of A. L. Morton* (London: Lawrence & Wishart, 1978), pp. 21-48.

————. *Interesting Times: A Twentieth Century Life* (London: Abacus, 2002).

————. *Revolutionaries* (New York: New Press, 2001).

————. 'The Spanish Background', *New Left Review* 40 (1966), pp. 85-90.

Hobsbawm, E., with A. Polito, *The New Century* (London: Abacus, 2000).

Hobson, T., 'Will Jeremy Corbyn boost his left-wing idealism with a religious message?', *Spectator* (September 16, 2015), http://blogs.spectator.co.uk/coffeehouse/2015/09/will-jeremy-corbyn-boost-his-left-wing-idealism-with-a-religious-message/.

Hodges, D., 'Labour MPs are now preparing to go underground to resist the Corbyn regime', *Telegraph* (August 16, 2015), http://www.telegraph.co.uk/news/politics/labour/11805916/Labour-MPs-are-now-preparing-to-go-underground-to-resist-the-Corbyn-regime.html.

Hooper, J., 'Archer attempts to rehabilitate Judas', *Guardian* (March 21, 2007).

Horsley, R., *Jesus and the Spiral of Violence: Popular Jewish Resistance in Roman Palestine* (San Francisco: Harper & Row, 1987).

Hulse, T., 'James Brown: the latest edition', *Independent on Sunday* (October 5, 1997).

Hunt, T., 'Back when it mattered', *Guardian* (March 5, 2003).

Huntington, S.P., 'The Clash of Civilizations?', *Foreign Affairs* 72 (1993), pp. 22-49.

————. *The Clash of Civilizations and the Remaking of World Order* (New York: Simon & Schuster, 1996).

Hyde, M., 'Jesus may be with Occupy London, but St Paul would have sided with health and safety', *Guardian* (October 28, 2011).

Jäger, L., *Adorno: A Political Biography* (New Haven: Yale University Press, 2004).

Jakobovits, I., *From Doom to Hope: A Jewish View on 'Faith in the City', the Report of the Archbishop of Canterbury's Commission on Urban Priority Areas* (London: Office of the Chief Rabbi, 1986).

Jameson, F., *Postmodernism, or, The Cultural Logic of Late Capitalism* (London: Verso, 1991).

————. *Seeds of Time* (New York: Columbia University Press, 1994).

Jeffries, S., 'The old lefties are back – and so are all the old insults', *Guardian* (April 14, 2013).

Johnson, B., 'If Blair's so good at running the Congo, let him stay there', *Telegraph* (January 10, 2002).

Johnson, C.C., 'Thatcher and the Jews', *Tablet* (December 28, 2001), http://www.tabletmag.com/jewish-news-and-politics/87027/thatcher-and-the-jews.

Johnson, L.K., 'The King James Bible's language lessons', *Guardian* (February 19, 2011).

————. 'Thatcher and the inner city riots', *Huffington Post* (April 16, 2013), http://www.huffingtonpost.co.uk/linton-kwesi-johnson/margaret-thatcher-inner-city-riots_b_3081167.html.

————. 'Trust between the police and the black community is still broken', *Guardian* (March 28, 2012).

Jones Boy, The, 'Top Tips', *Viz* 139 (October 2004).

Jones, S., B. Quinn and C. Urquhart, 'Woolwich attack prompts fears of backlash against British Muslims', *Guardian* (May 23, 2013), http://www.theguardian.com/uk/2013/may/23/woolwich-attack-backlash-british-muslims.

Jury, L., 'The fall of Jeffrey Archer: the media – enemies ensured that the whiff of scandal lingered', *Independent* (July 20, 2001).

Kampfner, J., *Blair's Wars* (London: Free Press, 2004).

Kaye, H.J., *British Marxist Historians* (Cambridge: Polity Press, 1984).

Kazantzakis, N., *The Last Temptation* (London: Faber & Faber, 1975).

Keen, M., 'Christopher Hill: Some Reminiscences', in Pennington and Thomas (eds.), *Puritans and Revolutionaries*, pp. 17-21.

Kelley, S., *Racializing Jesus: Race, Ideology and the Formation of Modern Biblical Scholarship* (London: Routledge, 2002).

Kelso, P., 'Mendacious, ambitious, generous and naïve', *Guardian* (July 20, 2001).

Kelso, P., and N. Hopkins, 'Archer takes refuge on stage from a real life drama', *Guardian* (September 27, 2000).

Kermode, F., *The Genesis of Secrecy: On the Interpretation of Narrative* (Cambridge, Mass.: Harvard University Press, 1979).

Kershaw, T., 'The Religion and Political Views of Russell Brand', *The Hollowverse* (June 2, 2012), http://hollowverse.com/russell-brand.

Kettle, M., 'Obituary: Christopher Hill', *Guardian* (February 26, 2003).

Kirchick, J., 'A friendship without prejudice: Thatcher's kinship with Jews and Israel', *Haaretz* (April 10, 2013).

Kittel, G., and G. Friedrich (eds.), *Theologisches Wörterbuch zum Neuen Testament* (10 vols.; Stuttgart: Kohlhammer, 1933–79).

Klein, N., *The Shock Doctrine: The Rise of Disaster Capitalism* (London: Allen Lane, 2007).

Kovacs, J., and C. Rowland, *Revelation: The Apocalypse of Jesus Christ* (Oxford: Blackwell, 2004).

Labour Party, '1945 Labour Party Election Manifesto: Let Us Face the Future', http://www.labour-party.org.uk/manifestos/1945/1945-labour-manifesto.shtml.

Lacey, H., 'Python with no venom: Michael Palin profile', *Independent* (August 31, 1997).

Lamont, W., 'Review: *The English Bible and the Seventeenth Century Revolution* by Christopher Hill', *English Historical Review* 108 (1993), pp. 979-81.

Lange, E., 'Afro-Caribbean Communities', in P. Childs and M. Storry (eds.), *Encyclopedia of Contemporary British Culture* (London: Routledge, 1999), pp. 13-14.

Langton, D.R., *The Apostle Paul in the Jewish Imagination: A Study in Modern Jewish–Christian Relations* (Cambridge: Cambridge University Press, 2010).

Latham, J., and C. Mathys (eds.), *Liberal Democrats Do God* (Kindle edn; London: LDCF, 2013).

Lawson, D., 'Pope Benedict…an apology', *Independent* (September 21, 2010).

Lawson, N., *The View from No. 11: Memoirs of a Tory Radical* (London: Bantam Books, 1992).

Lazaroff, T., G.F. Cashman, and J. Pau, 'PM: Thatcher a true friend of Jewish People, Israel', *Jerusalem Post* (April 8, 2013).

Lentin, A., and G. Titley, *The Crises of Multiculturalism: Racism in a Neoliberal Age* (London: Zed Books, 2011).

Lewis, B., 'The Roots of Muslim Rage', *The Atlantic* (September 1990), pp. 47-60.

Lewis, H., 'Discipline over dazzle: Helen Lewis interviews Yvette Cooper', *New Statesman* (August 13, 2015), http://www.newstatesman.com/node/200775.

Lezard, N., 'In the beginning God said – Let there be Lib Dems', *Independent* (August 26, 2013).

Licona, M.R., *The Resurrection of Jesus: A New Historiographical Approach* (Downers Grove: InterVarsity Press, 2009).

Licona, M.R., and J.G. van der Watt, 'The Adjudication of Miracles: Rethinking the Criteria of Historicity', *Harvard Theological Review* 65 (2009), pp. 62-68.

Lipman, J., 'Margaret Thatcher: One of Us', *Jewish Chronicle Online* (April 11, 2013), http://www.thejc.com/news/uk-news/105333/margaret-thatcher-one-us.

Littlejohn, R., 'Whatever the BBC say, Britain is still mainly white, Christian and straight', *Daily Mail* (September 30, 2011).

Lüdemann, G., *Virgin Birth? The Real Story of Mary and Her Son Jesus* (London: SCM Press, 1998).

McAuley, P., 'Where cherubim play', http://www.thisisthedaybreak.co.uk/.

McCloughry, R., 'Practising for Power: Tony Blair', *Third Way* (September 14, 1993), http://web.archive.org/web/20070927142102/http://www.thirdway.org.uk/past/showpage.asp?page=43.

McCutcheon, R.T., *Religion and the Domestication of Dissent: or, How to live in a less than perfect nation* (London: Equinox, 2005).

McGee, A., 'Happy Mondays are back. Hallelujah!', *Guardian* (August 27, 2007).

McLeod, H., *The Religious Crisis of the 1960s* (Oxford: Oxford University Press, 2007).

MacCulloch, D., 'All Too Human', *Literary Review* (April 2010), http://www.literaryreview.co.uk/macculloch_04_10.html.

———. *A History of Christianity: The First Three Thousand Years* (London: Allen Lane, 2009).

Malley, B., *How the Bible Works: An Anthropological Study of Evangelical Biblicism* (Walnut Creek: AltaMira, 2004).

———. 'Understanding the Bible's Influence', in J.S. Bielo (ed.), *The Social Life of Scriptures: Cross-Cultural Perspectives on Biblicism* (New Brunswick: Rutgers University Press, 2009), pp. 194-204.

Mansell, W., 'Michael Gove redrafts new history curriculum after outcry', *Guardian* (June 21, 2013).

Martin, C., *Masking Hegemony: A Genealogy of Liberalism, Religion and the Private Sphere* (London: Equinox, 2010).

Mason, R., 'Gordon Brown to speak on Labour leadership as poll gives boost to Corbyn', *Guardian* (August 14, 2015), http://www.theguardian.com/politics/2015/aug/14/gordon-brown-speak-labour-leadership-contest-mps-panic-corbyn.

Middles, M., *From Joy Division to New Order: The True Story of Anthony H. Wilson and Factory Records* (London: Virgin, 1996).

———. *Shaun Ryder: Happy Mondays, Black Grape and Other Traumas* (London: Independent Music Press, 1997).

Mirowski, P., and D. Plehwe (eds.), *The Road from Mont Pelerin: The Making of the Neoliberal Thought Collective* (Cambridge, Mass.: Harvard University Press 2009).

Mitchell, D., 'Michael Gove's biblical zeal is a ruse', *Observer* (May 20, 2012).

Monbiot, G., 'The model for a leftwing resurgence? Evangelical Christianity', *Guardian* (September 15, 2015), http://www.theguardian.com/commentisfree/2015/sep/15/leftwing-evangelical-christianity-corbyn.

————. 'Why stop at Isis when we could bomb the whole Muslim world?', *Guardian* (September 30, 2014), http://www.theguardian.com/commentisfree/2014/sep/30/isis-bomb-muslim-world-air-strikes-saudi-arabia.

Monty Python, *The Life of Brian Screenplay* (London: Methuen, 2001).

————. *The Pythons' Autobiography* (London: Orion, 2003).

Moore, C., *Margaret Thatcher: The Authorized Biography. Vol. 1, Not for Turning* (London: Allen Lane, 2013).

Moore, S.D., and Y. Sherwood, *The Invention of the Biblical Scholar: A Critical Manifesto* (Minneapolis: Fortress Press, 2011).

Morley, P., *Joy Division: Piece by Piece: Writing about Joy Division 1977–2007* (London: Plexus, 2008).

Morrison, S., 'Linton Kwesi Johnson: "Class-ridden? Yes, but this is still home" ', *Independent on Sunday* (December 2, 2012).

Mortimer, P., 'Jeremy Corbyn has become a symbol of hope for people who had given up on politics', *Evening Chronicle* (August 19, 2015), http://www.chroniclelive.co.uk/news/news-opinion/jeremy-corbyn-become-symbol-hope-9887042.

Mount, F., 'Stalin's ghost sits too easily among us', *Sunday Times* (March 9, 2003).

Mountford, M., 'Enoch Powell as a Classicist', in Rising (ed.), *Enoch at 100*, pp. 237-50.

Moxnes, H., *Jesus and the Rise of Nationalism: A New Quest for the Nineteenth Century Historical Jesus* (London: I.B. Tauris, 2012).

Mulholland, G., 'Liberalism, the Liberal Democrats and the Dangerous Drift towards Moral Conformity', in Latham and Mathys (eds.), *Liberal Democrats Do God*, Chapter 3.

Müller-Doohm, S., *Adorno: An Intellectual Biography* (Cambridge: Polity Press, 2005).

North, R.D., *Mr Blair's Messiah Politics: Or What Happened When Bambi Tried to Save the World* (London: Social Affairs Unit, 2006).

Northcott, M., *An Angel Directs the Storm: Apocalyptic Religion and American Empire* (London: I.B. Tauris, 2004).

Nunn, H., *Thatcher, Politics and Fantasy: The Political Culture of Gender and Nation* (London: Lawrence & Wishart, 2002).

O'Carroll, L., 'Rebekah Brooks: David Cameron signed off texts "LOL" ', *Guardian* (May 11, 2012).

O'Connell, M., *Ian Brown: Already in Me: With and Without the Roses* (New Malden: Chrome Dreams, 2006).

O'Neill, B., 'Me and my vote: Anthony H. Wilson', *Spiked Politics* (June 1, 2001), http://www.spiked-online.com/Articles/00000002D0FF.htm.

O'Shaughnessy, H., 'Tony Blair's Faith Foundation inspires ridicule', *Guardian* (May 13, 2009).

O'Shaughnessy, H., and M. Brace, 'Campaigners face jail for raid on military jet', *Independent* (July 21, 1996).

Obama, B., 'Remarks by the President on a New Beginning', The White House: Office of the Press Secretary (2009), http://www.whitehouse.gov/the-press-office/remarks-president-cairo-university-6-04-09.

Oborne, P., 'Corbyn will confront a bankrupt foreign policy. That's why he must be backed', *Middle East Eye* (August 27, 2015), http://www.middleeasteye.net/columns/corbyn-troublemaker-1532484034.

Økland, J., 'The Spectre Revealed and Made Manifest: The Book of Revelation in the Writings of Karl Marx and Friedrich Engels', in J. Økland and W.J.

Lyons (eds.), *The Way the World Ends? The Apocalypse of John in Culture and Ideology* (Sheffield: Sheffield Phoenix Press, 2009), pp. 267-88.

Owen, D., *The Hubris Syndrome: Bush, Blair and the Intoxication of Power* (New York: Methuen & Co., 2012).

Parker, D., 'The Communist Party Historians' Group', *Socialist History* 12 (1997), pp. 33-58.

Parsons, G., 'How the Times they Were a-Changing: Exploring the Context of Religious Transformation in Britain in the 1960s', in J. Wolffe (ed.), *Religion in History: Conflict, Conversion and Coexistence* (Manchester: Manchester University Press, 2004), pp. 161-89.

Payne, S., 'An evening with the cult of Corbyn in Islington', *Spectator* (August 22, 2015), http://blogs.spectator.co.uk/coffeehouse/2015/08/evening-cult-corbyn-islington/.

Pedraza, H., *Winston Churchill, Enoch Powell and the Nation* (London: Cleveland, 1986).

Penner, T., '*Die Judenfrage* and the Construction of Ancient Judaism: Toward a Fore-grounding of the Backgrounds Approach to Early Christianity,', in P. Gray and G. O'Day (eds.), *Scripture and Traditions: Essays on Early Judaism and Christianity* (Leiden: Brill, 2008), pp. 429-55.

Pennington, D., and K. Thomas (eds.), *Puritans and Revolutionaries: Essays in Seven-teenth-Century History Presented to Christopher Hill* (Oxford: Oxford University Press, 1978).

Perry, M., *Marxism and History* (London: Palgrave Macmillan, 2002).

Petre, J., 'Gospel of Judas presents traitor as Jesus's favourite', *Telegraph* (April 7, 2006).

Philipson, A., 'Leading historians back reforms to history curriculum', *Telegraph* (February 15, 2013).

Pierce, A., 'Horror as Cameron brandishes the B-word', *Times* (October 5, 2005).

Plehwe, D., B.J.A. Walpen, and G. Neunhoffer (eds.), *Neoliberal Hegemony: A Global Critique* (London: Routledge, 2007).

Powell, D., *Tony Benn: A Political Life* (New York: Continuum, 2001).

Powell, J.[E.], *The Evolution of the Gospel* (New Haven: Yale University Press, 1994).

———. 'Genesis of the Gospel', *Journal for the Study of the New Testament* 42 (1991), pp. 5-16.

———. *Herodotus: A Translation* (Oxford: Clarendon Press, 1949).

———. *The History of Herodotus* (Cambridge: Cambridge University Press, 1939).

———. *A Lexicon to Herodotus* (Cambridge: Cambridge University Press, 1938).

———. *No Easy Answers* (London: Sheldon Press, 1973).

———. *Reflections: Selected Writings and Speeches of Enoch Powell* (London: Bellew, 1992).

———. *Wrestling with the Angel* (London: Sheldon Press, 1977).

Press Association, 'Tory leader: Archer not welcome', *Guardian* (July 22, 2003).

Pritchett, O., 'What Would Judas Make of Jeffrey?', *Sunday Telegraph* (March 25, 2007).

Prothero, S., *American Jesus: How the Son of God became a National Icon* (New York: Farrar, Straus & Giroux, 2003).

Puar, J., *Terrorist Assemblages: Homonationalism in Queer Times* (Durham: Duke University Press, 2007).

Pugh, J., ' "Doing God" in the Liberal Democrat Party', in Latham and Mathys (eds.), *Liberal Democrats Do God*, Chapter 1.

Pyper, H.S., *An Unsuitable Book: The Bible as Scandalous Text* (Sheffield: Sheffield Phoenix Press, 2006).

Raban, J., *God, Man and Mrs Thatcher: A Critique of Mrs Thatcher's Address to the General Assembly of the Church of Scotland* (London: Chatto & Windus, 1989).

Räisänen, H., *The 'Messianic Secret' in Mark* (Edinburgh: T. & T. Clark, 1990).

Ranelagh, J., *Thatcher's People: An Insider's Account of the Politics, the Power, and the Personalities* (London: Fontana, 1992).

Raphael, A., 'His guilt was writ large', *Observer* (July 22, 2001).

———. *My Learned Friends: An Insider's View of the Jeffrey Archer Case and Other Notorious Libel Actions* (London: W.H. Allen, 1989).

Rawnsley, A., *The End of the Party: The Rise and Fall of New Labour* (London: Penguin Books, 2010).

———. *Servants of the People: The Inside Story of New Labour* (London: Penguin Books, 2000).

Redhead, S., and H. Rietveld, 'Down at the Club', in Savage (ed.), *Haçienda*, pp. 71-77.

Reinhartz, A., 'Jesus in Film: Hollywood Perspectives on the Jewishness of Jesus', *Journal of Religion and Film* 2 (1998), http://www.unomaha.edu/~jrf/JesusinFilm Rein.htm.

Renton, D., 'English Experiences: Was There a Problem of Nationalism in the Work of the British Marxist Historians' Group?', http://dkrenton.co.uk/research/cphg.html.

———. 'Studying Their Own Nation without Insularity? The British Marxist Historians Reconsidered', *Science and Society* 69 (2005), pp. 559-79.

Rentoul, J., 'Intensely relaxed about people getting filthy rich', *Independent Blog* (February 14, 2013), http://blogs.independent.co.uk/2013/02/14/intensely-relaxed-about-people-getting-filthy-rich/.

———. *Tony Blair* (London: Warner, 1996).

Reynolds, S., 'Music to brood by, desolate and stark', *New York Times* (October 7, 2007).

———. *Rip It Up and Start Again: Postpunk 1978–1984* (London: Faber & Faber, 2005).

———. *Totally Wired: Post-Punk Interviews and Overviews* (London: Faber & Faber, 2009).

Riddell, P., *The Thatcher Era and its Legacy* (Oxford: Blackwell, 1991).

Rising, Lord Howard of (ed.), *Enoch at 100: A Re-evaluation of the Life, Politics and Philosophy of Enoch Powell* (London: Biteback Publishing, 2012).

Robb, J., *The North Will Rise Again: Manchester Music City (1976–1996)* (London: Aurum, 2010).

Roberts, A., 'Enoch Powell and the Nation State', in Rising (ed.), *Enoch at 100*, pp. 123-42.

Robertson, M., *Factory Records: The Complete Graphic Album* (London: Thames & Hudson, 2006).

Ross, T., 'Michael Gove aims to be the heir to Tony Blair', *Telegraph* (May 15, 2013).

Rowbotham, S., *Women, Resistance and Revolution* (London: Penguin Books, 1972).

Rowland, C., and J. Roberts, *The Bible for Sinners: Interpretation in the Present Time* (London: SPCK, 2008).

Runciman, D., '*Revolution* by Russell Brand review – soft-soap therapy when we need a harder edge', *Guardian* (October 17, 2014), http://www.theguardian.com/books/2014/oct/17/revolution-russell-brand-review-political-manifesto.

Runions, E., *The Babylon Complex: Theopolitical Fantasies of War, Sex, and Sovereignty* (New York: Fordham University Press, 2014).

Rusbridger, A., 'Canon of St Paul's "unable to reconcile conscience with evicting protest camp" ', *Guardian* (October 27, 2011).

Sabbagh, D., 'How Tony Blair was taken into the Murdoch family fold', *Guardian* (September 5, 2011).

Said, E.W., *Orientalism* (3rd edn; London: Penguin Books, 2003).

Samuel, R., *The Lost World of British Communism* (London: Verso, 2006).

———. 'Tory Party at Prayer', *New Statesman* (January 28, 1983), pp. 8-10.

Sandbrook, D., 'Hubris and a man who thinks he can only be judged by God', *Daily Mail* (September 28, 2012).

———. *White Heat: A History of Britain in the Swinging Sixties* (London: Abacus, 2006).

Sanders, E.P., *Paul and Palestinian Judaism: A Comparison of Patterns of Religion* (Philadelphia: Fortress Press, 1977).

Särlvik, B., and I. Crewe, *Decade of Dealignment: The Conservative Victory of 1979 and Electoral Trends in the 1970s* (Cambridge: Cambridge University Press, 1983).

Savage, J., *England's Dreaming: Sex Pistols and Punk Rock* (London: Faber & Faber, 1991).

Savage, J. (ed.), *The Haçienda Must be Built!* (London: IMP, 1992).

Schaberg, J., *The Illegitimacy of Jesus: A Feminist Theological Interpretation of the Infancy Narratives* (San Francisco: Harper & Row, 1987 [repr. and exp. for Sheffield: Sheffield Phoenix Press, 2006]).

Schama, S., *Landscape and Memory* (London: Vintage, 1996).

Schüssler Fiorenza, E., *Jesus and the Politics of Interpretation* (New York: Continuum, 2000).

Schwarz, B., ' "The People" in History: The Communist Party Historians Group 1946–56', in R. Johnson (ed.), *Making Histories: Studies in History Writing and Politics* (London: Hutchinson, 1982), pp. 44-95.

Seldon, A., *Blair: The Biography* (London: Free Press, 2004).

Sellers, R., *Always Look on the Bright Side of Life: The Inside Story of HandMade Films* (London: John Blake, 2003).

Seymour, R., *The Liberal Defence of Murder* (London: Verso, 2008).

Sheehan, J., *The Enlightenment Bible: Translation, Scholarship, Culture* (Princeton: Princeton University Press, 2007).

Shepherd, J., 'Michael Gove's King James Bible plan rescued by millionaire Tory donors', *Guardian* (May 15, 2012).

Sherwood, Y., 'Bush's Bible as a Liberal Bible (Strange though that Might Seem)', *Postscripts* 2 (2006), pp. 47-58.

———. 'On the Genesis between the Bible and Rights', in M.J.M. Coomber (ed.), *Bible and Justice: Ancient Texts, Modern Challenges* (London: Equinox, 2011), pp. 13-42.

———. 'This Is Not a Bible/Ceçi n'est pas une Bible', unpublished paper delivered to the Biblical Literacy and the Curriculum Conference, University of Sheffield, May 25–28, 2011.

Shindler, C., 'In her fury, I saw values alien to us', *Jewish Chronicle Online* (April 11, 2013), http://www.thejc.com/comment-and-debate/analysis/105329/in-her-fury-i-saw-values-alien-us.

Shipman, T., 'I should never have called myself "the heir to Blair", admits Cameron', *Daily Mail* (May 5, 2010).

———. 'PM's Christmas bid to calm Christian anger at gay marriage: David Cameron quotes Gospel of St John in annual message', *Daily Mail* (December 24, 2012).

Siddique H. and S. Jones, 'Attacks on Muslims spike after Woolwich killing', *Guardian* (May 23, 2013), http://www.theguardian.com/uk/2013/may/23/attacks-muslims-spike-woolwich-attack.

Smith, G., 'Margaret Thatcher's Christian Faith: A Case Study in Political Theology', *Journal of Religious Ethics* 35 (2007), pp. 233-57.

Smith, J., 'Reclaiming the Ground: Freedom and the Value of Society', in Bryant (ed.), *Reclaiming the Ground*, pp. 127-42.

Spanner, H., 'Far Sighted? Interview with Jeremy Corbyn', *Third Way* (June 2015), http://www.thirdwaymagazine.co.uk/editions/july-2015/high-profile/far-sighted.aspx.

Spencer, N., *Freedom and Order: History, Politics and the English Bible* (Kindle edn; London: Hodder & Stoughton, 2011).

———. 'Into the mystic', *Observer* (October 22, 2000).

Staff reporters, 'Thatcher clashed with Church, despite her faith', *Church Times* (April 12, 2013).

Staff writers, 'Peter Tatchell accuses academics of smearing him', *Pink News* (November 3, 2009), http://www.pinknews.co.uk/2009/11/03/peter-tatchell-accuses-academics-of-smearing-him/.

Staff writers, 'Tatchell given standing ovation at Christian festival', *Ekklesia* (August 30, 2010), http://www.ekklesia.co.uk/node/12977.

Stephens, P., *Tony Blair: The Making of a World Leader* (London: Viking, 2004).

Steven, M.H.M., *Christianity and Party Politics: Keeping the Faith* (Abingdon: Routledge, 2011).

Stoppard, M., and M. Thatcher, 'TV Interview for Yorkshire Television *Woman to Woman*', *Margaret Thatcher Foundation* (November 19, 1985), http://www.margaretthatcher.org/document/105830.

Stretton, H., 'Christopher Hill: Some Reminiscences', in Pennington and Thomas (eds.), *Puritans and Revolutionaries*, pp. 10-17.

Stuckler, D., and A. Reeves, 'We are told Generation Y is hard-hearted, but it's a lie', *Guardian* (July 30, 2013).

Stunell, A. 'Three Reasons to Thank God – and Not the Usual Ones', in Latham and Mathys (eds.), *Liberal Democrats Do God*, Chapter 4.

Sugirtharajah, R.S., 'Loitering with Intent: Biblical Texts in Public Places', *Biblical Interpretation* 11 (2003), pp. 567-78.

Tatchell, P., 'Academics smear Peter Tatchell', *Peter Tatchell* (no date), http://www.petertatchell.net/politics/academics-smear-peter-tatchell.htm.

———. 'Ban on same-sex marriage must be lifted', *Independent* (June 15, 2010).

———. 'Gay marriage is a Conservative value', *Peter Tatchell* (October 13, 2011), http://www.petertatchell.net/lgbt_rights/partnerships/how-the-tories-were-won-to-marriage-equality.htm.

———. 'A marriage of equals', *Guardian* (September 18, 2011).

———. 'The same-sex marriage bill does not live up to its aspiration of equality', *Guardian* (May 20, 2013).

———. 'Was Jesus Gay?', Peter Tatchell (March 18, 1996), www.petertatchell.net/religion/jesus.htmTaubes, J., *The Political Theology of Paul* (Stanford: Stanford University Press, 2004).

Taylor, M.L., *Religion, Politics, and the Christian Right: Post-9/11 Powers and American Empire* (Minneapolis: Augsburg Fortress, 2005).

Teather, D., 'Father of lads' mags still loaded with ideas', *Guardian* (August 24, 2007).

Teather, S., 'Liberal Language and the Christian Calling', Latham and Mathys (eds.), *Liberal Democrats Do God*, Chapter 11.

Telford, W.R., *The Theology of the Gospel of Mark* (Cambridge: Cambridge University Press, 1999).

Temko, N., 'No way back for Archer, says Cameron', *Observer* (November 27, 2005).

Tempest, M., 'Archer fraud allegations: the simple truth', *Guardian* (August 16, 2001).

Thatcher, M., 'Britain Awake: Speech at Kensington Town Hall', *Margaret Thatcher Foundation* (January 19, 1976), http://www.margaretthatcher.org/document/102939.

———. 'Dimensions of Conservatism: Iain Macleod Memorial Lecture: Speech to Greater London Young Conservatives', *Margaret Thatcher Foundation* (July 4, 1977), http://www.margaretthatcher.org/document/103411.

———. *The Downing Street Years* (London: Harper Press, 1993).

———. 'I Believe: A Speech on Christianity and Politics (St Lawrence Jewry)', *Margaret Thatcher Foundation* (March 31, 1978), http://www.margaretthatcher.org/document/103522.

———. *The Path to Power* (London: Harper Press, 1995).

———. 'Speech at St Lawrence Jewry', *Margaret Thatcher Foundation* (March 4, 1981), http://www.margaretthatcher.org/document/104587.

———. 'Speech to Conservative Party Conference, Blackpool', *Margaret Thatcher Foundation* (October 10, 1975), http://www.margaretthatcher.org/document/102777.

———. 'Speech to the General Assembly of the Church of Scotland', *Margaret Thatcher Foundation* (May 21, 1988), http://www.margaretthatcher.org/document/107246.

———. *Statecraft: Strategies for a Changing World* (London: HarperCollins, 2003).

Thatcher, M., and B. Walden, 'TV Interview for London Weekend Television *Weekend World* (1980)', *Margaret Thatcher Foundation*, http://www.margaretthatcher.org/speeches/displaydocument.asp?docid=104210.

Thompson, E.P., *Infant and Emperor: Poems for Christmas* (London: Merlin Press, 1983).

———. *William Morris: Romantic to Revolutionary* (2nd edn; London: Merlin Press, 1977).

Todd, R.B., 'Enoch Powell as a Classicist: Two Studies', *Quaderni di Storia* 45 (1997), pp. 81-103.

———. 'Enoch Powell's Classical Scholarship: A Bibliography', *Quaderni di Storia* 42 (1995), pp. 89-96.

Toynbee, P., 'Corbyn's Christ-like position may have nuked his chances of becoming PM', *Guardian* (October 1, 2015), http://www.theguardian.com/commentisfree/2015/oct/01/jeremy-corbyn-nuclear-deterrent-prime-minister-labour.

Trahair, R.C.S. (ed.), *Encyclopedia of Cold War Espionage, Spies, and Secret Operations* (Westport, Ct.: Greenwood Press, 2004).

Trotter, S., 'Archer claimed he fell into trap over pay-off', *Glasgow Herald* (October 27, 1986).

Tuckett, C.M. (ed.), *The Messianic Secret* (London: SPCK, 1983).

Tyler, L., 'Faith, Society and the State', in Latham and Mathys (eds.), *Liberal Democrats Do God*, Chapter 6.

Vallely, P., and A. Buncombe, 'History of Christianity: The Gospel according to Judas', *Independent* (April 7, 2006).

van der Loos, H., *The Miracles of Jesus* (Leiden: Brill, 1965).

Vaneigem, R., *The Revolution of Everyday Life* (London: Rebel Press, 1983).

Vermes, G., *Jesus the Jew: A Historian's Reading of the Gospels* (London: SCM Press, 1973).

———. *Providential Accidents: An Autobiography* (London: SCM Press, 1998).

Vinen, R., *Thatcher's Britain: The Politics and Social Upheaval of the 1980s* (London: Pocket Books, 2009).

Walsh, R., 'The Gospel according to Judas: Myth and Parable', in J.C. Exum (ed.), *The Bible in Film: The Bible and Film* (Leiden: Brill, 2006), pp. 37-53.

———. 'Monty Python's *Life of Brian* (1979)', in A. Reinhartz (ed.), *Bible and Cinema: Fifty Key Films* (London: Routledge, 2013), pp. 187-92.

———. *Reading the Gospels in the Dark: Portrayals of Jesus in Film* (Harrisburg: Trinity Press International, 2003).

———. 'Three Versions of ~~Judas~~ Jesus', in G. Aichele and R. Walsh (eds.), *Those Outside: Noncanonical Readings of the Canonical Gospels* (New York: T&T Clark/Continuum, 2005), pp. 155-81.

Walsh, R.G., *Three Versions of Judas* (London: Equinox, 2010).

Walters, S., 'An identity crisis for Blair: Former PM describes Jerusalem as "home" ', *Daily Mail* (April 12, 2009).

Warburton, J., with Shaun Ryder, *Hallelujah! The Extraordinary Return of Shaun Ryder and Happy Mondays* (London: Virgin, 2000).

Watt, N., 'David Cameron ignores Alastair Campbell's advice as he does God', *Guardian* (April 27, 2011).

Watt, N., and P. Wintour, 'Interview: How David Cameron is trying to reinvent the Tories', *Guardian* (July 16, 2008).

Waugh, P. 'Andy Burnham Interview: On Scrapping The "Tampon Tax", Catholicism, Unpaid Internships And Falling Out Of Love With Morrissey', *Huffington Post* (August 10), http://www.huffingtonpost.co.uk/2015/08/10/andy-burnham-interview-catholic-church-tampon-tax_n_7961096.html.

Webb, S., 'Introduction', in Latham and Mathys (eds.), *Liberal Democrats Do God*.

Widdecombe, A., 'Can a reputation be rescued?', *Guardian* (April 7, 2007).

Wiersma, H., 'Redeeming *Life of Brian*: How Monty Python (Ironically) Proclaims Christ *Sub Contrario*', *Word and World* 32 (2012), pp. 166-77.

Williams, P.H., 'Abbott, Patois Bible and language discrimination', *The Gleaner* (March 27, 2011).

Williams, S., *God and Caesar: Personal Reflections on Politics and Religion* (London: Continuum, 2003).

Williams, Z., 'Corbynomics must smash this cosy consensus on debt', *Guardian* (August 16, 2015), http://www.theguardian.com/commentisfree/2015/aug/16/jeremy-corbyn-corbynomics-cosy-consensus-debt-radical-fear.

Wintour, P., 'Disgraced Archer quits over plot to lie in court', *Observer* (November 21, 1999).

Wintour, P., and N. Watt, 'The Corbyn earthquake – how Labour was shaken to its foundations', *Guardian* (September 25, 2015), http://www.theguardian.com/politics/2015/sep/25/jeremy-corbyn-earthquake-labour-party.

Wood, C., 'Russell Brand is wrong about Western religions', *Science on Religion*, (November 2013), http://www.patheos.com/blogs/scienceonreligion/2013/11/russell-brand-is-wrong-about-western-religions/.

Woodcock, J., 'Cult logic', *Progress* (August 14, 2015), http://www.progressonline.org.uk/2015/08/14/we-are-the-true-guardians-of-the-spirit-of-1945/.

Woodhams, S., *History in the Making: Raymond Williams, Edward Thompson and Radical Intellectuals 1936–1956* (London: Merlin Press, 2001).

Wrede, W., *Das Messiasgeheimnis in den Evangelien* (Göttingen: Vandenhoeck & Ruprecht, 1901); English trans. J.C.G. Greig, *The Messianic Secret* (London: James Clark, 1971).

Wright, N.T., *Jesus and the Victory of God* (London: SPCK, 1996).

Wynne-Jones, J., 'Bible to be turned into patois', *Telegraph* (October 11, 2008).

Young, H., 'Honest John Major landed his party with Lord Archer', *Guardian* (November 23, 1999).

———. *One of Us: A Biography of Margaret Thatcher* (London: Macmillan, 1989).

Žižek, S., *First as Tragedy, Then as Farce* (London: Verso, 2009).

———. *For They Know Not What They Do: Enjoyment as a Political Factor* (2nd edn; London: Verso, 2008).

———. 'Liberal multiculturalism masks an old barbarism with a human face', *Guardian* (October 3, 2010).

———. *Living in the End Times* (rev. edn; London: Verso, 2011).

———. 'Multiculturalism, or, the Cultural Logic of Multinational Capitalism', *New Left Review* (1997), pp. 28-51.

———. *The Puppet and the Dwarf: The Perverse Core of Christianity* (Cambridge, Mass.: MIT Press, 2003).

———. 'Return of the Natives', *New Statesman* (March 4, 2010).

———. *The Sublime Object of Ideology* (London: Verso, 1989).

———. *The Ticklish Subject: The Absent Centre of Political Ontology* (London: Verso, 1999).

———. *Welcome to the Desert of the Real! Five Essays on September 11 and Related Dates* (London: Verso 2002).

INDEX OF AUTHORS